Organization Development

Organization
Development

SECOND EDITION

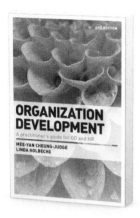

Organization Development

A practitioner's guide for OD and HR

Mee-Yan Cheung-Judge
and Linda Holbeche

KoganPage

LONDON PHILADELPHIA NEW DELHI

First published in Great Britain and the United States in 2011 by Kogan Page Limited
Second edition 2015

2nd Floor, 45 Gee Street	1518 Walnut Street, Suite 1100	4737/23 Ansari Road
London EC1V 3RS	Philadelphia PA 19102	Daryaganj
United Kingdom	USA	New Delhi 110002
www.koganpage.com		India

© Mee-Yan Cheung-Judge and Linda Holbeche, 2011, 2015

The right of Mee-Yan Cheung-Judge and Linda Holbeche to be identified as the authors of this work have been asserted by them in accordance with the Copyright, Designs and Patents Act 1988.

ISBN 978 0 7494 7017 3
E-ISBN 978 0 7494 7018 0

British Library Cataloguing-in-Publication Data

A CIP record for this book is available from the British Library.

Library of Congress Cataloging-in-Publication Data

Cheung-Judge, Mee-Yan.
 Organization development : a practitioner's guide for OD and HR / Mee-Yan Cheung-Judge, Linda Holbeche. – Second edition.
 pages cm
 ISBN 978-0-7494-7017-3 (paperback) – ISBN 978-0-7494-7018-0 (ebk) 1. Organizational change.
2. Personnel management. I. Holbeche, Linda. II. Title.
 HD58.8.C476 2015
 658.4'06–dc23

 2015006670

Typeset by Graphicraft Limited, Hong Kong
Production managed by Jellyfish
Printed and bound in Great Britain by Ashford Colour Press Ltd.

CONTENTS

LIST OF FIGURES

Introduction

We began writing the first edition of this book back in 2010 and by the end of the year, despite the relief of having submitted the manuscript, we immediately felt 'Oh no! There's still so much more we would like to share with the readers'. But the publisher told us not to worry, there is always the second edition – and here we are, presenting our second edition.

Much has changed in the environment and organizations – no organization has been left untouched in the way they are organized, operated, interfaced with clients/customers and their own staff. While short-term solutions continue to thrive, deep in the psyche of the organization leader there is a daunting realization that the current way of running organizations carries with it all sort of vulnerabilities. Those who are in the roles of HR and OD find themselves continuing to search (or scramble) for different approaches to support the organization to navigate through complexity and chaos – with fingers crossed that they will come through on the other side with not only the ability to survive but also having scaled up their ability to thrive by being more agile and with staff more engaged. We recognize this sort of scenario and the challenges organizations, and hence practitioners, face, so we decided to add three new chapters on change, and chapters on how to build agile organizations and a culture of engagement.

We have heard that people have found the original book practical and useful, which we are both pleased about. We believe that what we said in the first edition still stands; therefore it has been hard to weed things out to make room for new material. But we were determined to keep the second edition just as practical, accessible and basic/simple. By that we mean we focus on the essential core, the basic premise, principles and practices of the OD and HR fields. We are eager to encourage the increasing development of both sets of professionals so that the execution of their role will be both impactful and credible.

This second edition, we believe, should retain its usefulness to a wide range of people – from those at the entry level to those who are experienced in both trades. From novices who want to learn the trade to those experienced practitioners who would like to have a book that will facilitate their reflection and review of their practice. We know from readers' feedback from the first edition, that very experienced practitioners found affirmation and revitalization of their passion from the book. Some of the chapters in

this second edition can also be useful for those eager *leaders* who are interested in doing change better as well as eager to learn the craft of building sustainable organization health.

We know from some readers' comments about the first edition that it felt like reading two different books, which is no surprise to us, as we did not aim to do an integrated book; we wanted instead to produce complementary insights. As two very different, committed individuals in both background and practice we chose to come together because of our great shared passion to support both HR and OD practitioners to be better and better at building effective and healthy organizations.

So what is different about this edition compared to the first? This edition has five new chapters.

In **Part One, the OD section** (Chapters 1–11), we added three new chapters – all in the area of change. Chapter 7 takes a short look at two change approaches; Chapter 8 covers the back room and the front room issues; Chapter 9 focuses on an interesting area – can behavioural change be made easy? Mee-Yan has added a new feature in Chapter 8 – the Practice Note, showing how things can be done. Nothing sophisticated or complex – just to encourage readers to turn complexity to simple practice.

Mee-Yan has removed the chapter on the future of OD from the first edition in order to make space for the new chapters, but in its place there is a short postscript to remind the readers that we, the practitioner community, still hold the future of OD in our hands.

Part One has also been reorganized into four sections. **Section 1: OD history and theory overview**, has two chapters – the history and the theory overview. **Section 2: OD cycle of work** has four chapters covering the four key phases of the OD Cycle – entry and contracting, diagnosis, intervention and evaluation. **Section 3: OD and change** has the three new chapters covering the balance of the two change approaches, the back and front room change issues, and can behavioural change made easy? The final section – **Section 4: The Organization Development practitioner** has two chapters – the Organization Development practitioner and Power and politics and Organization Development.

Finally, Mee-Yan has added the Dialogic OD Theory in Chapter 2 – Theories and practices of OD.

In **Part Two, the HR section**, Linda has added two new chapters. First, given the growing recognition of the need for organizational agility and resilience, Linda has provided an overview of what's involved and how HR/OD can help organizations become more sustainably agile. Second, employee engagement has become a major issue for many organizations. Linda's emphasis is less on the transactional mechanics and more on the transformational aspects of engagement – in other words, how to build an organizational culture that is conducive to engagement. To make room for these chapters Linda has combined first edition chapters on transformational and culture change into one. She has also modified other chapters to

highlight recent developments and trends and added new case studies of organizations that have developed sophisticated and agile change capabilities.

So the running order of Part Two is now:

HR in relation to OD; Organization Design; Transformation and culture change; Building organizational agility and resilience; Building the context for employee engagement; Developing effective leadership; Postscript – towards a better tomorrow.

We hope that you will find the book useful as you deal with demands for ongoing transformation, or look to carry out high-impact interventions in complex change situations, or to build the capacity to continually change and adapt throughout the organization.

We recognize that none of this easy but we believe that the possibilities and the benefits may be greater than the challenges. We wish you well on your journey!

PART ONE
A practitioner's guide for Organization Development

PART ONE
A Practitioner's Guide for Organization Development

Section 1

This section gives an overview of the history and the development journey of organization development and the theoretical base of our practice. The field of OD is often not well understood nor is there a consensus on its origin. The field grew out of the **values** of those early founders, their 'sense-making' effort to understand human behaviours in the aftermath of the Second World War, and the cumulative rich research findings of applied behavioural science up to that point. As with other academic fields, the origin was never linear or intentional on the part of those early significant players. There was an emergence of different thinkers from various US academic institutions; based on their values, their academic training, their desire to make an impact in the context of their environment, they headed down a particular path – ie trying to find out how organizations work and how that impacts on individuals within the system, and the dynamic interplay between individuals, groups, inter-groups, and the whole system. Then by both chance and intent, these diverse groups of academics and practitioners began to converge through conferences and network events to exchange their findings. The result was an emergence of a significant field of knowledge, and OD was born. This knowledge field has the characteristics of a movement with diverse groups of individuals and institutions taking their different parts to build a body of knowledge to form the common basis of the field.

While the diverse paths lead to a continuous debate about the boundaries of the field, there is clarity of certain key characteristics that have given the field a loose container throughout its journey. These key characteristics include: a dual concern to use processes derived from applied behavioural science to help an organization to be highly effective in what it sets out to do (optimal performance), while ensuring the health of the organization

continues to improve; that the design of these processes is based on principles of OD from research data, the theoretical orientation that shapes the conceptual and practice framework of the field; and its strong value base; the importance of the 'use of self' for all practitioners. The field is practised within 'a living system' (organizations are made up of human beings), therefore understanding ourselves as a living system and the various dimensions of just being human – psychological, social, emotional, personality preference, life history and relationship orientation, etc. – become a pre-requisite for the ability to be an effective intervener in any social system. These characteristics also point to the trademarks of being an OD practitioner. See Chapter 10 on OD practitioners.

Chapter 2 focuses on the core theories that shape the field and practices. This chapter is based on the sentiment of Kurt Lewin that there is nothing as practical as a theory – theories shape practice and practice builds theory. Given there are around 100 theories that shape our practices, it was a risk to focus on the five key ones only. However, I think they are the foundational ones. In this edition, I have added two more theories – social discourse (Chapter 9), and dialogic OD theory (Chapter 2). Both require a shift of paradigm in the way we work. How big that shift is will depend on what dominant approaches you have been anchoring your work in. A particular strand of economic behaviour studies that shaped the way in which we approach behaviour change will be covered not in this section but in Chapter 9.

These two chapters are foundational in terms of building our understanding of the field of OD. What are its characteristics and what key theories shape our practice?

What is OD?
Its brief history

Organization Development (OD) is not a well-understood field. Often questions like: 'What is it?' will pop up among clients. Even many of the OD practitioners feel that while they intuitively know what the field is about, it is hard to articulate what OD is to others. Through time, a mystery has built up around the term; even the veterans in the field have accepted the state of affairs – the myth surrounding the field. But I believe the time has come to de-mystify the term. Without clarity, it is hard to accumulate knowledge, conduct research, facilitate debates and work towards building a vibrant future for the field.

In this chapter, I would like to give an overview of the following areas:

1 the goals, characteristics, and definition of OD;
2 a brief history of OD;
3 critical founders who shaped the OD field;
4 how the field got its name;
5 values that have informed OD practice;
6 the role of the OD practitioner.

By covering these areas, I hope to help you, the practitioner, to be more confident in articulating clearly to your clients what the field of OD is, what OD intends to bring to the workplace, and how its core characteristics make it an indispensable field of knowledge to those who want to see organizations run effectively and humanely, especially during times of turbulent changes.

The goals, characteristics and definition of Organization Development

Edgar Schein (1965) declared that all organizations, regardless of size and type, face two types of problems:

- continuous external adaptation to a rapidly changing environment;
- corresponding internal integration that will support the success of the external adaptation.

Schein calls the organization's ability to cope with changes and adapt effectively the 'adaptive coping cycle', which is a sign of organization effectiveness. These two dimensions help to lock the relationship between OD practitioners and strategists. While the strategists support the senior leaders to determine how the organization should adapt externally in order to remain viable, OD practitioners support senior leaders to ensure there is adequate internal development to support the delivery of those identified external ambitions. As twin to the strategists, OD is there to help the organization to prepare itself internally to deliver the challenging external ambitions.

The following definitions reveal the heart of the practice of OD, which is to improve the functioning of individuals, teams and the total organization:

- OD is a systematic process for applying behavioural science principles and practices in organizations to increase individual and organization effectiveness (French and Bell, 1999).
- OD is a process (and its associated technology) directed at organization improvement (Margulies, 1978).
- OD is all the planned interventions to increase organization effectiveness and health (Beckhard, 1969).
- OD is about building and maintaining the health of the organization as a total system (Schein, 1988).
- Organization revitalization is achieved through synthesizing individual, group and organizational goals so as to provide effective service to the client and community while furthering quality of product and work life (Lippitt and Lippitt, 1975).
- The goal of OD is to enhance organizational effectiveness by attending to both human and organizational needs (Rainey Tolbert and Hanafin, 2006).
- OD is an organizational process for understanding and improving any and all substantive processes an organization may develop for performing any tasks and pursuing any objectives (Vaill, 1989).

However, the commitment of the OD practitioners is not just to improve a situation where individuals, teams and organizations are not realizing their potential, but to make the improvement sustainable. This then calls for our approaches to ensure development will also take place during the process of change. Therefore any process designed by OD practitioners needs to have the added component to equip the organization members to learn how to sustain that development without external help. It is this point that demarcates the field from other consultancy approaches.

This second prong of the goal of OD was also confirmed by the following two definitions:

- OD is all the activities engaged in by managers, employees and helpers that are directed towards building and maintaining the health of the organization as a total system (Schein, 1988).
- OD is a long-range effort to improve an organization's problem solving and renewal processes... with the assistance of a change agent, or catalyst, and the use of the theory and technology of applied behavioural science, including action research (French and Bell, 1999).

Based on the above definitions, I will now attempt to pull together a set of characteristics of OD and OD practitioners:

- We are 'process' experts to improve any substantive organization processes (eg planning, group meetings and relationships, superior–subordinate communication).
- We focus on the 'total system' even if we are asked to look at a specific organization issue.
- We aim to improve an organization's problem solving and renewal processes.
- The primary practitioners of OD are the organization's managers, not HR/OD professionals.
- OD practitioners are 'helpers and catalysts' to the leaders of the organization (the primary practitioners).
- We use the technology of applied behavioural science to support the organization towards healthy development.
- We are theory based, process focused, value driven.

Taking these definitions, I constructed two grids for easy reference. Figure 1.1 defines Organization Development, while Figure 1.2 summarizes the core characteristics of the field.

FIGURE 1.1 What is Organization Development?

What	A field of knowledge to guide the development of organization effectiveness, especially during change.
How	Using group and human dynamic processes from applied behavioural science methods, research and theories to facilitate movement of groups and organizations.
Outcome	To improve the health and effectiveness of organizations and the people that work within them in a sustainable way.
Values	Respect for human differences, commitment to all forms of social justice. Belief in lifelong learning – emphasis on 'self-renewal ability' of the individual and organization.

FIGURE 1.2 Characteristics of Organization Development

Source of knowledge	Behavioural science disciplines such as psychology, social psychology, sociology, anthropology, systems theory, organization behaviour, management literature, and many more.
Goal	Organization effectiveness and improvement.
Focus	Total system (alignment and interface between parts).
Core knowledge base	Group processes. Human dynamic processes.
Orientation	Planned intervention after diagnosis.
Target	Primarily human system within the social system.
Application	Provide theory and methodology insights for OD practitioners.
Values	Shamelessly humanistic – affirm respect for all and lifelong learning.

A brief history of OD

In the 1950s in the United States, a number of social psychology departments and business schools found that what traditional industrial psychology had to offer was not adequate in helping them understand the complexity of how organizations worked. Insights into individual psychology also did not provide sufficient insight or understanding for those who sought to fix both industrial and production issues faced by organizations. This gap was made more apparent when these academics were approached by industrial leaders for support as many of them in particular wanted to understand better how their organizations worked and what they, as leaders, could do more to improve the functioning/performance of those organizations. These initial consultancies led to an expansion of the practice knowledge of how groups and organizations work, and established the important dual emphasis of OD – linking theory and practice to support the development of an organization. It set the field up to be a 'practice' field. Many of these academics became the founders of OD – it is their seminal work and their practice experience that gave shape to what the field is about.

Those early days of OD were also characterized by parallel developments in both significant social movements and by individuals whose work played a pivotal role in building the field (Gallos, 2006). Critical movements that shaped the development of OD were:

- **The critical work of the National Training Laboratory (NTL) on group dynamics and leadership**: NTL was founded in the United States in 1947 to advance the field of applied behavioural science and to develop change agents for effective leadership of organizations. NTL is credited with conceiving the idea of experiential learning and for 60 years it has served as an incubator for many OD theories.

- **The birth of the T group and other forms of laboratory education**: Pioneered in the United States by Lewin and his graduate students and in the UK by the Tavistock Institute, T group is a small, unstructured group laboratory training in which participants learn from their own actions and the group's evolving dynamics. The lab experience aims to give individuals clear insight into how human dynamics evolved and how groups can play a critical role in one's personal development and increase of self-awareness. The early adoption of T group by corporations led to the systematic training and development of leaders as a critical intervention to build effective work conditions. Carl Rogers labelled the T group the most significant social invention of the century (1968).

- **The larger human relations movement in the 1950s**: This gave force to support the parallel growth of social and developmental psychology. Themes promoted by the movement included: self-expression, individual agency, the release of human potential, the inherent need for human growth and so on. These themes made an impact on the thirst for understanding the role of work and the world of work in individual development, which many early founders picked up and studied.

- **The socio-technical system (STS) thinking from the British Tavistock Institute**: The work done by Trist in 1947 in a British coal mine at Haighmoor and subsequently reinforced by Bamford and Rice asserted that an organization is simultaneously a social and a technical system. When intervention combines important social factors (group relationship) with the technological changes, increased productivity and reduction in damage and costs will be the result. The research into STS showed that effectiveness, efficiency and morale are enhanced if we use STS intervention. The reverse is also true – that if organizations only deal with the technical system during change without paying attention to the human social system, the change will not be sustainable (Rice, 1958; Trist, 1960; Trist and Bamforth, 1951).

- **The development of survey research methods**: Likert and Mann pioneered the first survey feedback with the Detroit Edison Company, using survey results for improvement. The method involves two steps. The first is to collect the data by questionnaire to determine an

employee's perceptions of a variety of factors, mostly focusing on the management of the organization. The second step is to do what Mann called the 'interlocking chain of conferences' to feed back the data to leaders and managers in order to create organization improvement strategies. This survey method helps organization leaders to understand that what they do in the organization will have an impact on the people within the organization, and therefore on the performance of the organization. If leaders pay attention to those causal effects they will have data as to how to 'move' and 'improve' the organization. The work of Likert and Mann has created a clear platform for many of the academics to articulate and practise a new way of working across the social system; individual, group, inter-group, division and total organization (Mann, 1957; Likert, 1967).

Critical founders who shaped the OD field

While the social movements provided an important backdrop for the emergence of the field, there were also a great number of individuals who played a significant role in building up the knowledge base through both their academic work and their consultancy work. It is impossible to name everyone, but the following people and all their graduate students have played a critical role in shaping and pioneering the field of OD:

Kurt Lewin (critical founder of OD): Lewin gave the field some of its most essential theoretical roots – action research theory, group theories and change theories. Schein commented that there is little question that Lewin is the intellectual father of contemporary theories of applied behavioural science, action research and planned change. He was the first to write about group dynamics and the importance of the group in shaping the behaviour of its members. Also, his commitment to extending democratic values in society through his work created a most pervasive impact on Organization Development.

Ron Lippitt: Lippitt was on Lewin's original staff at the Research Center for Group Dynamics at MIT and was also a member of the first group of trainers for T group in 1946. In 1947, he was one of the founders of National Training Laboratory in Group Development, which started holding a three-week session in Bethel, Maine. The summer event evolved into the birth of the NTL Institute for Applied Behavioural Science. Together with Lee Bradford, he invented flip chart paper in 1946 as a convenient way to record, retrieve and display data in OD activities and in training.

Edgar Schein: Schein, a professor at the MIT Sloan School of Management, made a notable mark on the field in many areas

including career development, group process consultation and organizational culture. His career anchoring concepts and tools are forerunners in helping organizations to think of combining unconditional motivation and an organizational way of managing staff career structure. He is generally credited with inventing the term 'corporate culture'. Schein showed us that process consultation is an essential philosophy underlying OD, not just a tool.

Douglas McGregor: McGregor is mostly known for his classic work, *The Human Side of Enterprise*, which has had a great impact on mangers since its publication in 1960. He was one of the first professor-consultants and one of the first behavioural scientists working with corporations to help implement the application of T group skills in complex organizations.

Rensis Likert: Likert showed the importance of holding up a mirror for the organization to reflect how its members think about themselves and how to strengthen their relationships. His early work on this gave rise to the use of organization survey. Later on, his research provided overwhelming data on the superiority of a democratic leadership style in which the leader is group oriented, goal oriented and shares decision making with the work group. This leadership style was contrasted with an authoritarian, one-on-one leadership style (1961, 1967).

Chris Argyris: Argyris was one of the first (following Bob Tannenbaum) to conduct team-building sessions in 1957. He has made extensive contributions to theory and research on laboratory training, OD and organizational learning. One of his several books on OD, *Intervention Theory and Method* (1970), stands as a classic in the field. He asserted that it is important to gather valid information and give clients choice to secure commitment (1957).

Bob Tannenbaum: Tannenbaum received his PhD in Industrial Relations from the School of Business at the University of Chicago. He is known for being the first researcher to conduct the earliest 'team-building' activities in 1952–53 at the US Naval Ordinance Test Station at China Lake, California. Subsequently, he published such team-building work in *Harvard Business Review* in 1955. He and Art Shedline started the first non-degree training programme on OD at UCLA.

Richard Beckhard: Beckhard was a major figure in the emergence and extension of the field of OD. He started from a career in the theatre. He was interested in improving the effectiveness of communications in large meetings, and his first major job after his career change was to stage the 1950 White House conference on children and youth, which involved 6,000 people. He started to pay attention to how

to stage a large convention and enable participative discussion. He developed one of the first major non-degree training programmes in OD – the NTL's Programme for Specialists in Organizational Training and Development (PSOTD).

Herbert Shepard: Shepard completed his doctorate at MIT and then went to join the employee relations department of Esso Standard Oil as a research associate. He was to have a major impact on the emergence of OD through his extensive practice in the corporate world as well as his involvement with the NTL work. In 1960, he founded the first doctoral programme devoted to training OD specialists at the Case Institute of Technology. His continuous experiments in OD at major Esso refineries resulted in significant learning for us; two particular lessons that emerged from his work are: a) the requirement for top management's active involvement in the leadership of the programme; b) the importance of the need for on-the-job application.

Robert Blake: During the Second World War, Blake served in the Psychological Research Unit of the Army Air Force and concluded that looking at the system rather than the individuals within the system on an isolated individual basis is a much more robust approach in identifying how best to help. Later, he spent 16 months in Tavistock and was deeply influenced by family group therapy. Upon returning to the United States, he took up an appointment at Harvard but joined the NTL programmes at Bethel to staff T groups for six years and was significant in shaping the changes in T group.

As I have said, this is not an exhaustive list, but the work and publications of this group of early founders helped to form the core aspect of OD work.

How the field got its name

It is not entirely clear who coined the term Organization Development. What was known is that there were two early pieces of intervention work that gave rise to the name of OD (Beckhard, 1997).

In 1959, Doug McGregor and Richard Beckhard were implementing a company-wide culture change effort in General Mills at Dewey Balch, a project called 'Bottom-Up Management'. When Doug McGregor wanted to write up this work, he knew that if he called the paper 'bottom-up management' it would not receive proper academic recognition. Further, they did not want to call it management development because the effort spanned the whole organization. So they thought a more appropriate label would be 'Organization Development', which means a system-wide change effort.

In the same year, Herbert Shepard and Robert Blake were working at the Esso Refinery at Bayway, New Jersey in a culture change programme. They

developed for this project an educational programme called the 'Managerial Grid' that was attended by hundreds of Esso managers and supervisors. They decided to call their effort 'Organization Development' because the focus was on a total system of culture change with the aim of developing the health of the organization.

It is not accidental that these two major interventions used the name 'Organization Development' because both programmes shared the following common features, which have remained as core characteristics of the field:

- system-wide;
- planned change efforts;
- focused on the total system and not just one aspect of it;
- targeted at the human side of the enterprise;
- aimed at improving organization effectiveness.

These are five core characteristics of the field of OD as we discussed earlier. Finally, there are five other catalytic developments that helped to formalize the birth of OD.

The birth of NTL (National Training Laboratory)

After the sudden death of Kurt Lewin in February 1947, Benne, Bradford and Lippitt held a three-week session during the summer of that year at the Gould Academy in Bethel, Maine. The work of that summer evolved into the birth of the National Training Laboratory, later called the NTL Institute for Applied Behavioural Science. Out of the Bethel experience, NTL grew a significant number of laboratory training centres. Almost every founder of NTL has been involved with staffing in the Bethel laboratory. In Ed Schein's words, anyone who has attended as well as staffed a T group is bound by their experience and has become part of a community of practitioners.

The birth of the OD network

As those early founders who had helped the industrialists successfully wrote about their work, other people became both energized and enthusiastic about the learning and possibilities involved in changing an organization. They began to flock to the field. In 1964, a small group of practitioners began to meet regularly to exchange ideas, experiences and learning; most of these practitioners became NTL alumni or staff. Once they had formed the network, other colleagues also asked to attend. Warner Burke, who was the head of the NTL OD staff, became the first executive director of the new organization sponsored by NTL and called the 'Organization Development Network'. Today the OD Network has about 4,000 members from all over the world.

OD publications

There are four significant publications that began to formally document the field's knowledge:

1 The OD series first published by Addison Wesley in six slim paperbacks, conceived by Warren Bennis, Edgar Schein and Richard Beckhard in1967. They are still the classics of the field.

2 *OD Practitioner*, the first journal in which practitioners shared their practice knowledge as well as exploring new theoretical developments, which was launched in 1968.

3 The first OD textbook, *Organization Development: Behavioural science interventions for organization improvement*, written by French and Bell in 1978.

4 This was followed by a classical second textbook by Warner Burke in 1982.

These publications helped to set the field in the academic context as they gave voice to what the field was all about. They also highlighted what subscribers in the field were doing in practice. The Addison Wesley OD series was more academic than *OD Practitioner*, which focused more on the practice experience. French and Bell's textbook made teaching of the field to undergraduates possible.

Consultancy work in real organizations

The greatest impact on the evolution of OD as a field was the consultancy work undertaken by the early founders. While research was always important to advance the field, the actual experience of those who were working on the ground with real organizations offered rich data to refine OD practices. It is the lessons that emerged from these early consultancy experiences – ie how to deliver and manage change – that helped to build up the knowledge of the field. For example, Shepard working in Esso, McGregor working in Union Carbide, Tannenbaum working in the US Naval Ordnance Test Station at China Lake, and Chris Argyris working with IBM and Exxon with the CEO and the top executive.

The rise of both non-degree and academic accreditation programmes on OD

The birth of the field was supported by the rise of non-degree as well as academic programmes. Tannenbaum, along with Art Shedlin, led one of the first non-degree training programmes in OD – the Learning Community in Organizational Development at UCLA. There were various group development programmes, eg the NTL in Group Development, a three-week

programme organized by Benne, Bradford and Lippitt. When those who subscribed to the field finally got formal and academic accreditation of their training (both in knowledge and in practice competences) the standard governing the practice of OD practitioners began to take off.

Values that have informed OD practice

So far we have been outlining the areas that make OD as a field distinct, but none are more important than these last two areas: a) the values that informed our work and b) the unique role of OD practitioners.

As mentioned, one of the key shapers of the field was a number of strong movements during the 1940s and 1950s: human relations movement, human potential movement, equality and diversity movement, social participation (client rights, citizen rights) movement, etc. These movements were started and supported by those who had an overwhelming commitment to: create conditions that would honour the inherent need for human growth in the workplace; release human potential; enable individuals to have equal rights to develop their own sense of agency and to promote self-expression. This, through time, became the early set of OD core values. As the practice widened, its practitioners and scholars, based on their own value alignment, also imported other core values into our work such as:

- democracy and participation;
- openness to lifelong learning and experimentation;
- equity and fairness – the worth of every individual;
- valid information and informed choice;
- enduring respect for the human side of enterprise.

For those early founders, these values are 'practice values', as they help to signpost what sort of intervention they will need to create in order to facilitate optimal organization performance. They believed that these values, when operating effectively, would engage people collaboratively to address a wide range of organization issues, as well as help organizations to search for lasting solutions to incredible challenges in the changing world. It is these values that help to give them a rudder and bearing.

So the question is, if one does not subscribe to these values, can one still call oneself an OD practitioner? This is a pertinent question as many of the OD values are often not congruent with the focus of today's organizations' values: slim and trim organizations focus on short-term results. At one level the answer is yes, but the potency of the practitioner as an instrument will be weakened, as the person who is using the methods without the personal embodiment of these values will eventually feel hollow. Particularly when clients are doubtful about the viability of the proposed methods, without the subscription of these values, the practitioners will not be able to help the

client system to navigate through doubts into results. One of the challenges for OD practitioners is to adapt our approaches in a changing work context without compromising our core values.

This leads us to the distinction between value and ethics. Values are the roots of the beliefs that matter to us and the field's practitioners, while ethics are the guidelines that should govern how we practice our craft (Tschudy, 2006).

Right now, other than the early work done by Gellermann *et al* (1990) on ethical guidelines in the field, OD as a profession does not have a published, collectively owned set of ethical guidelines. Having said that, practitioners within the OD community are impressively united by a number of practice guidelines that are informally held by many of us. The following ethical guidelines were briefly discussed earlier, but summarized into the following seven points:

1 Collaborative relations between clients and consultants – from jointly deciding the consultant brief and outcomes to deciding how to collect valid data, how to jointly analyse the data and how to choose the best route of intervention, what to evaluate at the end, etc.

2 We are the helper, not the guru and expert to direct the change work. Those who direct the change work are the leaders and managers of the organization.

3 Consultants honour and dedicate time and effort to build high-quality, authentic and trusting relations with clients in order to build the platform to help.

4 We focus on supporting and educating clients to do sustainable change work so that without us they can continue to support the successful implementation of the change programme.

5 While we can advise on content, our primary role is to pay attention to the processes that are needed to get the clients to their destination.

6 While our practice intervention work mainly focuses on working with the basic unit of change within the system, eg groups and people within the group, our primary approach is a total system one.

7 We hold tight to our belief in lifelong learning – hence the practitioner's need to do their own work while delivering work within the client system.

The ethical guidelines that govern our practice are strongly contained by the core OD values that form the heart of the field. It is the application of these values that make the practice of OD so distinctive.

The role of the OD practitioner

The above ethical guidelines mark the practice protocol of OD practitioners. This together with the belief that the systems OD practitioners are invited into are actually capable of sorting out their problems and choosing their own path forward – that is, if they are given the right type of support and facilitation. Therefore, the default style is to move away from the guru-expert style of consultancy to a collaborative helper style. This has major implications on the way OD practitioners approach our work. Mainly we take the role of 'third-party' change agent seriously as we focus on the client and not on us. However, to be able to implement this approach, we need to focus on developing ourselves as the most critical instrument in the helping relationship.

Third-party change agent

Marshak (2006: 15) described the third-party change agent role:

> When working with an organization to help bring about a desired change, the OD practitioner is not the person in charge. Instead the OD practitioner is a third-party change agent aiding the person(s) in charge as well as the system itself to bring about the desired change.

Marshak restated that since the human system is capable of making choices and initiating changes that it desires, the role of the OD practitioner is therefore a supportive and facilitative one, not an expert one – doing the directing as expert consultants do. In practice, this means not collecting data without consulting the clients first, not presenting the data without involving the clients. It also means paying attention to the clients' own perspective, and most of all not recommending a direction which the practitioner wants the client to adopt without working with the client to decide the outcomes jointly with their stakeholder constellations.

If our paradigm is to believe that, in spite of the political complexity, the client system can and should be helped to be fully involved in its own work, then we understand the true gem of OD. When we accept our third-party agency role, we naturally move towards a partnership and collaborative stance – supporting the system to find out what they want, what approach they should take to get there, and what type of internal resources they can deploy to get them there. This is what Marshak calls the 'client's self-directed change effort' (2006: 17).

This approach does not mean that we don't have any content expertise. It simply means whatever we have – our deep knowledge of how organizations and how human dynamics work – we deploy to educate, guide, support and facilitate the client to do their own work. It also does not mean that on occasion, due to the client system capacity and capability issues,

we are unwilling to be a bit more directive. Finally, it also doesn't mean that when clients have blind spots and dysfunctional politics we won't confront them and direct them. But our commitment overall is not to impose our view on them without setting up the platform for them to do their own work. Most of the time, the primary intervention for the third-party agent is to 'suggest and facilitate participative processes for diagnostic data gathering, informed decision making, and building client-system commitment for change' (Marshak, 2006: 18).

While these words seem sensible, those of us in the trade know how hard it is to translate them into practice. It is the combination of our innate need for power, control, approval and esteem and the external expectations where clients want us to be an expert that will move us so easily into the expert and directive mode of working. This is why the concept of 'self as an instrument' is so critical to the development journey of OD practitioners.

Self as the most critical instrument in the helping relationship

Finally, one of the unique trademarks of OD is the concept of 'self as instrument'. In his 1981 article in *OD Practitioner*, Beckhard reminded us that in order to work in this type of 'helping profession', we will need to pay a lot of attention to ourselves and do our own work without counting on others (mainly the client) to meet our own needs. He said, 'If I count on meeting my needs while I work, the clients will be in deep trouble.'

He admonished us to increase our ability to help others by learning more about how to:

- increase our tolerance of ambiguity and individual differences;
- examine our control needs and control roles;
- lower our needs for external approval and feedback;
- become able to work on a higher sense of fun and human need.

If we use ourselves to embody the end game and to move our client towards it by using the deep human dynamics insights we have gained from our own deep inner work to increase our ability to support the human systems we seek to help, we then can and will earn the right to help.

In emphasizing this deep level of self-awareness and deploying our potency and agency of ourselves we demarcate our practice from any other consultancy approach. By embracing that role, we fully recognize the fact that we 'ourselves' are the ultimate instrument that needs to be deployed to shift the client system. It is in that way that our practice is marked by the OD trademark. We do not think this type of training exists among strategic planners or technical experts in organizational design. While we need to respect the type of expertise they bring to our clients, we also know we are fundamentally operating in a different sphere of work.

Summary

Currently there has been ongoing debate from the United States on 'whether or not OD is: dead, viable, new or old'. Such debate can be seen as US practitioners' struggles to reaffirm the importance of the field through its 'midlife crisis'. While such debate has its merit, I think it is more appropriate for the OD community to revisit the following questions which give the field its identity and boundary: 'What are the core characteristics that define the field, set its boundaries, and should therefore be preserved through time and evolution of practice?' 'What set of values will continue to predispose us to do the type of process work that will be client focused?' 'What type of relationship exists between us and the client that we will need to build upon in order to deliver the help required?'

In this chapter, I have reviewed the brief history of OD, how the field got its name, what OD is and its goals, characteristics and definition. I have also covered the two unique pillars of OD – its value and the role of OD practitioners – and by doing that I hope to help practitioner colleagues to take pride in what this field sets out to do.

As the world of work becomes more turbulent, OD practitioners are encouraged to take on board the confidence of what the field has contributed to the world of work. As Schein stated succinctly (2006a: xviii), 'one must recognize how many elements of OD have evolved into organizational routines that are nowadays taken for granted: better communications, team building, management of inter-group competitions and change management, to name just a few'. So as the field moves forward, all practitioners are continuously challenged to adjust and adapt their practice in helping organizations to function effectively without sacrificing our core values and idealism. Indeed, throughout the field's 50-year history, a constant challenge has been for OD practitioners to hold on to our core principles and values while staying environmentally savvy enough to question and evolve our practices so as not to render our practice irrelevant to those organizations, and marketplaces in which they function, we seek to help.

OD has a revolutionary as well as an evolutionary history (Mirvis, 2006). Sometimes new practices and theories emerged to counteract what seemed to be undesirable in the world of work – eg the early work in response to the dominance of the 'machinery approach' to organization and the lack of regard for those who work for the organization. Other times, practitioners experimented with new practices in order to stay 'contextually savvy', such as the whole-system approach to change. The field continues to evolve as different individuals join and try out practices based upon: a) their idealism and values; b) the academic disciplines they've come from; c) the type of organizations and issues they encounter. As a result, the field right now is filled with a rich mix of diverse practices with different premises. After all, this is how any field evolves.

Finally, what developmental journey do we practitioners need to take seriously to improve our effectiveness as sharp instruments through changing times? Such questions are vital for the future development of the field. This is something we will address in later chapters. It is vital for us to affirm what those early founders saw – the link between the conditions in the world of work and the development of individual potential and creativity, and organizational performance. We need to share their belief that if the link was managed well, the success of the organization could be secured. We therefore need to work hard to turn theories and values into practice, and through the experimentation of our practices in turn shape the development of theory. Our commitment is to make organizations healthier and more productive, and their people healthier regardless of how hostile the work environment has become.

Theories and practices of OD: a theory overview

What are our practice building blocks?

A regular question that has been posed to me is, 'What does the OD practitioner need to assemble for his/her practice?' Behind this question lies the quest for clarity as to what constitutes the building blocks of our practice. My attempt to answer this question has often led me to reflect on the development journey of OD practitioners. The following steps are what most of us have followed in our quest for mastery.

First, we started as tool-oriented technicians, mainly interested in what we could 'do' to others and prove our worth. Slowly, we became more interested in the OD consultancy approaches, trying to honour the OD phases of work as we went about doing our job, empowering our clients as much as we could to build sustainability. As we went on, we often discovered, despite the tools and techniques and the consultancy template, our practice was still a bit hollow. It was then we realized that we needed to move towards a firm grounding of theories and actively translating theories into methods. Once we had the grasp of theories, we felt relaxed as we no longer needed to depend on specific tools; we could design any intervention based on theories. Next, we faced the need to ground our practices to something deeper – we questioned what values we held dear and struggled to use them as our rudder to decide our practices. Finally, when all of the above still didn't lift us into the consistent confidence zone, we realized perfecting our use of 'self' in our practice was the only way that would get us there. This realization, and our willingness to engage in deeper inner work, propels us towards the journey to becoming a masterful practitioner.

Of course these phases are rarely linear, and their progression is highly personal. Each phase will pose multiple challenges of growth, but together they are what we need to commit to if we want to refine our practice.

So let's summarize the building blocks of OD practices:

- **Tools and techniques:** Intervention that will execute our intent to enable the system to shift itself. These are our 'theories in action' (Chapter 5).

- **OD consultancy cycle**: Phases of engagement with the system as well as the delineation of major 'units of work' that we will need to pay attention to in the helping process (Chapters 3–6).

- **Theoretical assumptions**: We will look at our organizing 'theoretical frames' which will give us firm grounding of the primary principles that govern our work. Our grasp of theoretical assumptions will help us both to know how to diagnose and what to look for as well as help us to formulate a hypothesis to be tested. They give us the platform for our design so that we will choose the appropriate action to take during diagnostic and intervention design phase (Chapter 2).

- **The value and ethics of OD**: Give us the parameters and moral guidance in our work. This is our practice rudder or 'container' (Chapter 1).

- **The use of self**: We are the engine – the instrument through which we do our work. We need to go 'within' ourselves, in order to be impactful 'without'. (Chapter 7)

Developing ourselves to obtain the five building blocks is a lifelong journey for those of us who have chosen OD as their professional field. This is what this book is about – how to obtain each of the building blocks. For now, in this chapter, I will focus on the theoretical bases of OD.

The theoretical bases of OD

In this chapter I will:

1 review the relationships between theory, research and review work undertaken on OD theories;

2 review five core theoretical bases that shape OD practices;

3 look at the methodological/practical implications of the theoretical perspectives on two specific phases of OD work – diagnosis and intervention.

The relationships between theory and research

As a practice field OD practices are derived mainly from core theories and research from various behavioural science disciplines. From the 1940s to now, academics and practitioners have gone through various guises of relationship. In the early days, the separation between theory and practice did not exist as people like Kurt Lewin were simultaneously undertaking pioneer research and theorizing. He and his colleagues would then experiment with new practices from his many insightful theoretical prepositions. In fact, during the early stage, OD became the action arm of

basic social and organization research. As Lewin said, 'Nothing is so practical as a good theory.' So from the 1940s through to the 1970s, research and practice were relatively closely connected. Then in the 1980s, the changes began when the academic practice of organizational psychology moved its primary location from departments of psychology to business schools, and since then the relationship between research and theories has weakened significantly. In their critique of the widening gap between theory and practice in OD, Bunker *et al* (2005) encouraged practitioners to do more to strengthen the field by increasing two types of activities: a) do more to translate theory-based research into useful knowledge in practice; and b) invent new methods and concepts that can be used as organization interventions which in turn can inform theories. Their concern expressed the sentiment of many of the founders – theories are crucial in shaping practices.

What theories?

OD is an applied behavioural science field – which means we accumulate our knowledge base from a wide range of theories. Each theory offers a certain perspective to guide our work. In reality, very few practitioners are 'pure' subscribers to one theory. Often, our client situation is so unique that we take whatever we need from various theoretical perspectives in order for us to create a composite perspective to work.

In his chapter on OD theories, Burke (2006) said that there is no single theory or conceptual model that is representative or by itself encompasses the conceptual field or the practice of OD. Instead a series of 'mini' theories have made an impact on OD consultative practice. He referred to them as 'mini' not because he thinks these theories are conceptually lightweight, but because each helps to explain only a portion of organizational behaviour and effectiveness. Burke's mini theories include:

- **The Individual Approach to Change** (Maslow and Herzberg – expectancy theorists; Vroom and Lawler – job satisfaction theorists; Hackman, Oldham and Skinner);
- **T Group Approach to Change** (Lewin, Argyris and Bion);
- **The Total System Approach to Change** (Likert, Lawrence and Lorsch and Levinson).

Burke also references others whose impacts on OD practice are significant not so much via their theories as via their descriptive work on specific areas. They are:

- Blake and Mouton's managerial grid (1978), a model of managerial style;
- a practice-oriented contribution such as Beckhard (1969), Schein (1969) or Walton (1969);
- Bennis' work which is broadly explanatory and provocative (1966, 1967, 1969, 1970).

Burke's analysis of these theorists and practitioners is very insightful; hence I highly recommended reading his chapter.

A recent count of 'theories' led to over 100 theories. So where does one start? The focus of this chapter will be on what I call five 'major' core theories that I have identified as having significant impact on OD consultative practices. However, before I review these five core theories, I would like to beg forgiveness from colleagues who have different views about which theories are core, and which are not. I have no intention of declaring exclusivity, except to say these five are where I would advise those who are starting the profession to begin. As I progress in my practice, my theoretical basket gets fuller as many other theories offer unique insights to help me get a better grasp of human nature and system dynamics and offer me psychological insights in supporting people through tough changes. But for now, I will start with these five.

Five core theoretical bases that shape OD practices

Figure 2.1 shows the theoretical roots of OD. There are two layers of theoretical roots: some of them are from earlier times (as signified by the depth of the root) and have exerted a lengthier influence on our thinking; some have emerged more recently (hence their roots are shallower), yet they have all made a significant impact on our practice.

In this section, I will focus mainly on five core theories that impact significantly on the way OD practitioners work. Knowing the gist of these theories forms clear reference points in our practices across all OD consultancy phases.

It is important to clarify that while this is a theory chapter, it is not my aim to give a substantial academic appraisal of the theories. Instead the purpose is to signpost the direction of travel by giving sufficient description of the key points of each theory from a practitioner's perspective in bullet points within a grid. Deeper grounding in theory should be a longer-term goal for every practitioner. The robustness of your practice is dependent on how well you understand the complex intricacies of these diverse theoretical gems.

The five core theories we will cover are:

1 Systems theory;
2 Action Research theory;
3 Change theories: Field theory, Group Dynamics and Three-step Model of Change;
4 Social Constructionism: Appreciative Inquiry;
5 Complexity and chaos theories;
6 Diaological OD theory;
7 Social discourse theory (to be explained in the next chapter).

FIGURE 2.1 Theoretical roots of OD

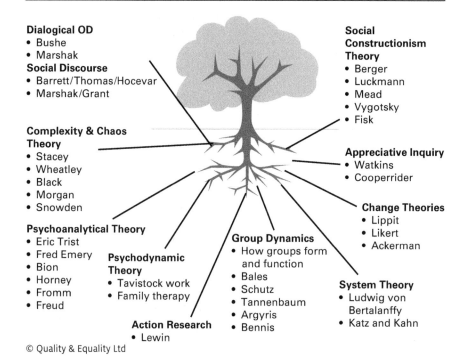

Dialogical OD
• Bushe
• Marshak
Social Discourse
• Barrett/Thomas/Hocevar
• Marshak/Grant

**Complexity & Chaos
Theory**
• Stacey
• Wheatley
• Black
• Morgan
• Snowden

Psychoanalytical Theory
• Eric Trist
• Fred Emery **Psychodynamic**
• Bion **Theory**
• Horney • Tavistock work
• Fromm • Family therapy
• Freud

 Action Research
 • Lewin

Group Dynamics
• How groups form
 and function
• Bales
• Schutz
• Tannenbaum
• Argyris
• Bennis

**Social
Constructionism
Theory**
• Berger
• Luckmann
• Mead
• Vygotsky
• Fisk

Appreciative Inquiry
• Watkins
• Cooperrider

Change Theories
• Lippit
• Likert
• Ackerman

System Theory
• Ludwig von
 Bertalanffy
• Katz and Kahn

© Quality & Equality Ltd

Systems theory

Ludwig Von Bertalanffy first articulated the principles of general Systems theory in 1950, and Katz and Kahn were the first to apply open Systems theory to organizations in 1966. According to French and Bell (1999: 82) Systems theory is one of the most powerful conceptual tools available for understanding the dynamics of organizations and organizational change.

What is a 'system'? In OD terminology, it can be an individual, a team, a sub-unit, a unit, a division or a total organization. However, in order to study and understand how systems operate, we have to see them in relationship to each other. The following definitions of 'system' help to clarify the concept:

● 'A set of objects together with relationships between the objects and between their attributes' (Hall and Fagen, 1956).

● 'System as a set of elements standing in interaction' (Von Bertalanffy, 1956).

FIGURE 2.2 Core concepts from Systems theory

Key subject	Concept summary
Organization	• The organization is an open system, constantly interacting with the environment, influencing it or being influenced by it, which in turn shapes the internal components in order to maintain its ability to produce the required output to stay viable. • No system exists in an environmental vacuum; it extracts resources and fulfils demands from the environment in which it lives (input) and it puts out the appropriate level of service, products and outputs to the different stakeholders in order to justify its position in the market/world (output requirements). • For an organization to stay robust, it must pay attention to external (environmental) inputs, discover the implications of those input factors on the organization and take steps to adjust output requirement to stay relevant in the environment (input causes systemic change). • Organizations are dynamic systems in a continuous state of adaptation and improvement (Senge, 1990). • Systems develop through continuous processes of differentiation and integration (Weisbord, 1987). • Environmental scanning is an important activity – institutions survive if they are externally aware and internally adaptive. This tasks lies in the mandate of the leadership (Katz and Kahn, 1978). • A system is made up of many parts (sub-systems). The quality of the relationships between its parts is important to the functioning of the system. • All of the sub-systems are interconnected and interdependent. Nothing can be nurtured and grown in isolation: not individuals, not groups, not organizations or whole nations (Von Bertalanffy 1952). • Sub-systems contain significant information about the whole. • When one part of a system is affected, all parts are affected (some known and others not). • Every system is both a context for sub-systems and a sub-system of a larger, whole system. • It is not possible to know everything about a system, but watchful attention will give us clues.
Change	• Transformational change will come from the environment (input into the system), which requires the system to rethink its output, all its parts and the relationship of its parts. • Changes in one part of the organization will impact other parts of the organization. Looking out for unintended consequences is important. • Systemic alignment is an essential effort to strive towards restoring sufficient congruence to the systems. • Sustainable change needs to aim for a minimum three levels of systems intervention. • It is not possible to control changes to a system, but it is possible to influence changes to a system and avoid unintended consequences. Paying attention to the complex interdependencies is a critical job of a change agent. • No one sitting at the top will have all the data required for changing the organization. • Robust data need to be drawn from all parts of the system. Tapping into the rich tapestry of the system's wisdom is a must.

- 'An organized, unitary whole composed of two or more interdependent parts, components, or subsystems, and delineated by identifiable boundaries from its environmental suprasystem' (Kast and Rosenzweig, 1985).

- 'A system is an arrangement of interrelated parts. The words "arrangement" and "interrelated" describe interdependent elements forming an entity that is the system. Thus, when taking a systems approach, one begins by identifying the individual parts and then seeks to understand the nature of their collective interaction' (Hanna, 1988).

Action Research theory

Kurt Lewin's planned approach to change comprised four elements: Field theory, Group Dynamics, Action Research and the Three-step Model of Change. Many tend to treat them as separate elements of his work, but Lewin himself saw them as a unified whole, all being necessary to bring about planned change (Allport, 1948; Bargal and Bar, 1992; Burnes, 2004; Kippenberger, 1998a; Smith 2001). While these four theories have suffered much criticism for being considered old-fashioned, they remain the theoretical pillars for OD practice.

Few social scientists can have received the level of praise that has been heaped upon Kurt Lewin. Tolman, in giving his memorial address for Kurt Lewin, stated that:

> Freud the clinician and Lewin the experimentalist – these are the two men whose names will stand out before all others in the history of our psychological era.

Edgar Schein (1980: 239) referred to Lewin as:

> the intellectual father of contemporary theories of applied behavioural science.

At the heart of Lewin's work is his humanitarian commitment to build civil society by resolving conflict – whether religious, racial, marital or industrial. The key to resolving social conflict, according to him, was to facilitate planned change through learning, and so enable individuals to understand and restructure their perceptions of the world around them. Here, I will focus on his first major theory, Action Research.

Action Research is a cornerstone of Organization Development, underlying both the theory and practice of the field. Lewin believed Action Research would address several needs an individual has during change simultaneously (Lewin 1947: 143–53):

FIGURE 2.3 Core concepts from Action Research theory

Key subject	Concept summary
General	• Action Research is a reiterative, cyclical, four-step process: diagnosing, planning, action taking and evaluating action. The process proceeds in a spiral of steps, each of which is composed of a circle of planning, action and fact-finding about the results of the action. It is in this iterative process that research leads to action, and action leads to evaluation and further action. • In practice, the words 'action research' are reversed – research (diagnostic data) is first conducted and then action is taken as a direct result of what the research data are interpreted to indicate. • Action Research attempts to meet the dual goals of making action more effective and building a body of scientific knowledge around the action. • Action in this context refers to programmes and interventions designed to solve problems and improve conditions. • The process is collaborative. Those who are consulting will work with members of the organization or community in a joint democratic inquiry. By creating and executing effective plans together, issues important to leaders, members and their stakeholders in a given context will be dealt with. • The action research method empowers local parties, enabling them to gain the competencies needed to apply action methods independently on their own behalf, thus becoming less dependent upon outside experts, and hence more sustainable. • The action research method generates new knowledge about the subject matter of a change process as well as about the process itself.
Change	• The theoretical foundations of Action Research lie in Gestalt psychology, which stresses that change can only be achieved successfully by helping individuals to reflect on and gain new insights into the totality of their situation. • The best way is to collaborate with members of the system to change it to what is regarded as a desirable direction from their perspective. • To get traction in the implementation stage in change, we need to turn the key people/groups involved into researchers/co-investigators/co-planners as early as possible, as people learn best, and willingly apply what they have learnt, when they do it themselves. • Decisions are best implemented by those who help to make them. • The main role of a change leader is to nurture local leaders to the point where they can take responsibility for carrying out the action research process with their own staff and community. • Action research is based on a firm commitment to democracy that sees the freedom to pursue and test all lines of enquiry as being crucial to achieving the learning in change. (Lewin's group-based, iterative, learning approach to change bears a close resemblance to the concept of self-organization as espoused by complexity theorists.) • Group learning is at the core of the change process and the ability to learn enables groups and organizations to identify the existing 'order-generating rules' that underpin the way the organization works and therefore how to change them to create movement. Once the organization enables the individual group to enter into this 'learning zone', then it can self-organize to change.

* A Research - Act on the findings
* Work collaboratively with org. from the onset.

- the pressing need for greater knowledge about the causes and dynamics of social issues;
- the need to understand the laws of social change;
- the need for greater collaboration and joint inquiry between the practitioners and those who are experiencing the change (system members);
- the need for 'richer' data about real-world issues to increase motivation for change;
- the need to discover workable, practical solutions to problems that are owned by those who are affected;
- the importance of staying in the learning stance throughout the change journey.

Lewin advised, 'no action without research; no research without action'. The significance of this theory is hard to comprehend until you come face to face with its practical utility in intervention. Almost nothing works as well as interventions derived from this theoretical perspective.

Lewin's change theories – Field theory; Group Dynamics; Three-Step Model of Change

Lewin was the first psychologist to write about 'Group Dynamics' and the importance of the group in shaping the behaviour of its members (Allport, 1948; Bargal and Bar, 1992). The word 'dynamics' comes from a Greek word meaning forces. So Group Dynamics refers to the forces operating in groups. It is the studying of these forces – what gives rise to them, what conditions modify them, what consequences they have, etc, that makes up the theory of Group Dynamics. Lewin's pioneering work on Group Dynamics not only laid the foundations for our understanding of groups but also helped us recognize the need to provide a process whereby the members could be engaged in and committed to changing their behaviour.

Field theory is an approach to understand group behaviour by trying to map out the totality and complexity of the field in which the behaviour takes place. Lewin defines the term 'force' from a psychological construct. He believes that individual behaviour is a function of the group environment or 'field'. Consequently, changes in behaviour will stem from changes in the forces within the field. *→ Outdated* *Need for agility?*

Lewin's Three-step Model – unfreezing, movement, refreezing – is highly related to Field theory. Lewin believes that our behaviour is based on a quasi-stationary equilibrium supported by a complex field of driving and restraining forces. The equilibrium needs to be destabilized first (unfreezing) before new behaviour can be adopted. So the concept includes unfreezing (destabilizing the status quo), movement (creating the motivation to learn – aided by Action Research approach), and then refreezing (seeking to stabilize the group at a new quasi-stationary equilibrium in order to ensure that the new behaviours are relatively safe from regression).

FIGURE 2.4 Core concepts from Field theory, Group Dynamics and the Three-step Model of Change

Key subject	Concept summary
Field theory and Group Dynamics	• While human behaviour is a function of a person's personality, discussed primarily in terms of motivation or needs, it is also a function of the group environment or 'field' to which s/he belongs. The group to which an individual belongs is the grounds for his/her perceptions, his/her feelings and his/her actions (Allport, 1948; Lewin, 1948, 1951). • The approach to understand group behaviour is to map out the totality and complexity of the field in which the individual behaviour takes place. • Lewin thinks one should view the present situation – the status quo – as being maintained by an intricate set of symbolic interactions and forces that affect group structures and individual behaviour (Lewin 1943). Individual behaviour, therefore, is a function of the group environment or 'field'. • Lewin stressed that the routines and patterns of behaviour in a group are more than just the outcome of opposing forces. They have a 'value' in themselves and have a positive role in enforcing group norms. • Once we understand a) the type of forces operating in the group; b) what value the individual members put on these forces; c) how they then subject themselves to these forces, we understand why group members behave the way they do.
Three-step Model of Change	• Step 1 – *unfreezing*: For Lewin, human behaviour is based on quasi-stationary equilibrium supported by a complex field of forces. Before old behaviour can be discarded (unlearnt) and new behaviour successfully adopted, the equilibrium needs to be destabilized (unfrozen). This will then create motivation to learn and to change. • Step 2 – *moving*: This is mainly a learning step in which the individual and the group emerge from unlearning the past, understand what is required of them in the new era and begin to take steps to move together the available options or more acceptable set of behaviours that will serve them better. • Step 3 – *refreezing*: This seeks to stabilize the group at a new quasi-stationary equilibrium in order to ensure that the new behaviours are relatively safe from regression. The new behaviour must be to some degree congruent with the rest of the behaviour, personality and environment of the learner or it will simply lead to a new round of disconfirmation (Schein, 1996).

FIGURE 2.4 *Continued*

Key subject	Concept summary
Change from all three theories	• Action research stresses that for change to be effective it must take place at the group level, and must be a participative and collaborative process that involves all of those concerned (Allport, 1948; Bargal and Bar, 1992; French and Bell, 1984; Lewin 1947).
	• Group behaviour, rather than that of individuals, should be the main focus of change (Bernstein, 1968; Dent and Goldberg, 1999). Lewin (1947) maintained that it is fruitless to concentrate on changing the behaviour of individuals because the individual in isolation is constrained by group pressure to conform.
	• The focus of change at the group level should concentrate on the field where individuals function and on factors such as group norms, roles, interactions and socialization processes to create 'disequilibrium' and change (Schein, 1988).
	• Any changes in behaviour stem from changes, small or large, in the forces within the field.
	• In organizational terms, refreezing often requires changes to organizational culture, norms, policies and practices be bedded down.
	• If we attempt to change an attitude or the behaviour of an individual without attempting to change the same behaviour or attitude in the group to which the individual belongs, then the individual will be a deviant and either will come under pressure from the group to get back into line or will be rejected entirely. 'As long as group standards are unchanged the individual will resist change more strongly the farther he is to depart from group standards. If the group standard itself is changed, the resistance which is due to the relationship between individual and group standard is eliminated' (Lewin 1958: 210).
	• Ed Schein (1996) built on Lewin's three-step change theory by identifying three necessary processes to achieve unfreezing: a) disconfirmation of the validity of the status quo; b) induction of guilt or survival anxiety; c) creating psychological safety. However, he was very clear that unless sufficient psychological safety is created, the disconfirming information will be denied or in other ways defended against, no survival anxiety will be felt and consequently no change will occur.
	• Lewin did not see organizations as rigid or fixed but instead believed that 'change and constancy are relative concepts; group life is never without change, merely differences in the amount and type of change exist' (Lewin, 1947).

Social Constructionism – Appreciative Inquiry

A major focus of Social Constructionism is to uncover the ways in which individuals and groups participate in the creation of their perceived reality. It involves looking at the ways social phenomena are created, institutionalized and made into tradition by humans. A socially constructed reality

is one that is seen as evolving mainly through dialectical interaction, and reproduced by people acting on their interpretations and their knowledge of it. This is different from 'realism', which is the doctrine that the external world exists independently of our representations of it, which include perceptions, thoughts, language, beliefs and desires.

FIGURE 2.5 Core concepts from Social Constructionism and Appreciative Inquiry

Key subject	Concept summary
General	• All reality is socially constructed. • The world does not present itself objectively to the observer, but is known through human experience, which is largely influenced by language, history and cultural specificity. • Knowledge is sustained by social processes – how reality is understood at a given moment is determined by the conventions of communication in force at that time. • Discourse and narrative are important processes. Social actors will often take up a preferred narrative to create consequences they desire. • There are multiple realities, and what people focus on becomes their reality. • The language people use helps them to create reality. • Sense-making comes from the interaction people have with each other; hence reality is created/constructed in the moment. • The act of asking questions and the type of questions can influence the group or organization in some major ways. • Human beings respond not to physical objectivity or events themselves, but to the meaning of events. • Meaning is not a property of the objects and events, but a construction between people. • Wholeness precedes parts – interconnectedness in relationships is important in creating collective owned reality. • Human systems can create what they imagine. • A leader or change agent needs to pay attention to how collective action is a vital part of creating a way to enact the values and visions of a group, an organization or a society. • In every society, organizations or groups are sense-making all the time and the meaning they create will affect their actions. **Appreciative Inquiry (AI) (stems from Social Constructionism)** • Human organizations are open books. An organization's story is constantly co-authored by the people within the organization and the topic of study is by choice. • AI believes that in every organization there is something that works. By focusing on what works, the organization will gain energy and confidence to move forward. So instead of focusing on fixing what is broken, AI shifts to creating what is desired. Instead of imposing order, creating systems where all voices are heard and valued and where the responsibility for moving the organization along the path of the future is truly the responsibility of each and every member. • In AI, the leadership's task is to create an alignment of strengths, making our weaknesses irrelevant.

FIGURE 2.5 *Continued*

Key subject	Concept summary
Change	• In change, leaders need to pay attention to the sense-making process of the organization members and the emergent nature of managing change through the process of inquiry and collective sense-making. • Human systems move in the direction of what they study and what they are most frequently being asked about. • Choice point for leaders or change agent is: what topics will help the whole system to create energy to change? • It is the leader's job to create dialogue where people are encouraged to make sense of the situation. • Change using the social constructionism approach tends to be collaborative, highly participative, inclusive, system wide, centred on exploring, seeking and committed to 'distributive leadership'. The methodology focuses on the 'primacy of relationship'. • Inquiry and change are not separate moments but are simultaneous (simultaneity principle). Inquiry is intervention, the seeds of change. The questions we ask set the stage for what we discover. • If AI as a methodology is used, leaders seek to help the system work from accounts of its 'positive change core' and create dialogue around this positive core. They then try to link the energy of this core directly to any change agenda and changes that were never thought possible are suddenly and democratically mobilized. • People have more confidence and comfort to journey to the future when they carry forward parts of the best of the past. • AI involves, in a central way, the art and practice of asking questions that strengthen a system's capacity to apprehend, anticipate and heighten positive potential. • Change technique will focus on using stories, imagery, poetry – methodology that taps into the right brain. • Organizations do not need to be fixed, they need constant reaffirmation. More precisely, organizations' systems need to be appreciated. Every new affirmative projection of the future is a consequence of an appreciative understanding of the past or the present.

The origins of Social Constructionism are in the work of Mead (1934) who found that children learn to interact with others by assimilating a shared system of symbolic representation, which in turn helps them to derive meaning from the social situation. Her work went in parallel with that of Vygotsky in the early 1930s who believed that children internalize dialogue with others and then gradually acquire understanding of the social and cultural meanings of their environment. These meanings mediate the relationship between language and cognition. The fact is, we cannot know the situation on its own terms, but, as most anthropologists remind us, only through the conceptual and linguistic structures of our own culture. The lesson for us is to discover how people make sense of the world, not what the world is.

Constructionism became prominent in the United States with Peter Berger and Thomas Luckmann's 1966 book, *The Social Construction of Reality*. They argued that all knowledge, including the most basic, taken-for-granted common sense about everyday reality, is derived from and maintained by social interaction.

The significance of this theory for practitioners is its belief that if reality is socially constructed, then it can be modified by injecting alternative conversations, stories and narratives into the system. Also, change leaders need to accept that reality is not one-dimensional and hence their job is to work with the diverse meaning of the change from the various stakeholder groups.

Complexity and chaos theories

Increasingly over the last two decades, both academics and practitioners have come to view organizations through the lens of complexity theories and this has a profound impact on our view of how organizations operate naturally and how they should be structured and changed. The work of Pascale *et al* (2000: 1–2) described complexity science this way:

> We are entering another scientific renaissance... also known as 'complexity science', this work grapples with the mysteries of life itself, and is propelled forward by the confluence of three streams of inquiry: 1) breakthrough discoveries in the life sciences, eg biology, medicine, and ecology; 2) insights of the social sciences, eg sociology, psychology, and economics and 3) new developments in the hard science (for example, physics, mathematics, and information technology). The resulting work has revealed exciting insights into life and has opened up new avenues for management.

The work of complexity and chaos theories was derived from different disciplines in natural science which range as far and wide as astronomy, chemistry, evolutionary biology, geology and meteorology where they have shown that disequilibrium is a necessary condition for the growth of dynamic systems (Prigogine and Stengers, 1984).

Black (2000) emphasizes that under the umbrella of Complexity and Chaos theory there are actually a variety of theories, ideas and research programmes that hold diversity of viewpoints about what complexity is and therefore he thinks we must use the term 'complexity and chaos theories' as it is not a singular concept.

The translation of Complexity and Chaos theory on organizations and leadership is championed by people like Stacey *et al* (2002), Stacey (2003), Wheatley (1992), Black (2000) and Morgan (1997). They challenge how the organization should view change and its way of operating. In the words of Richard Pascale, 'Stated simply, when societies, communities and organizations encounter the need for adaptive change (that is, change that departs from the trajectory of "business as usual") social engineering doesn't work. And it never has' (Pascale, 2006).

Under this view, organizations, like complex systems in nature, are seen as dynamic non-linear systems. The outcome of their actions is unpredictable but, like turbulence in gases and liquids, it is governed by a set of simple order-generating rules. Therefore leaders and change agents need to accept they cannot manage change; all they can do is to support the organization to move towards the 'edge of chaos' and self-manage their change journey.

FIGURE 2.6 Core concepts from Complexity and chaos theories

Key subject	Concept summary
General	• All organizations face unknowable specific futures. Ability to learn is critical to navigate through the unknown. • All organizations are paradoxes. They are pulled towards stability by the forces of integration, maintenance controls, human desires for security and certainty and adaptation to the environment on the one hand, but also pulled towards the opposite extreme of unstable equilibrium by the forces of division and decentralization backed up by the human desires for excitement, innovation and the urge to act autonomously. • If the organization gives in to the pull of stability it will ossify and cannot change easily. If it gives in to the pull of instability it disintegrates. • Any organization seeking a stable equilibrium relationship within an environment that is inherently unpredictable is bound to lead to failure. • Systems therefore are constantly changing and the laws of cause and effect appear not to apply. • Emergence of order happens in a dynamic, non-linear and unpredictable fashion; patterns of behaviour emerge in irregular forms through a process of self-organization. • In unpredictable environments, things happen at the micro level where the most powerful processes of change often take place – where relationships, interactions, small experiments and simple rules shape emerging patterns.
Organization	• Organizations are 'complex adaptive systems' which, to survive, need to operate at the edge of chaos and respond continuously to changes in their environments through just such a process of spontaneous self-organizing change. • 'Edge of chaos' is a term coined by Chris Langton, but popularized by Stuart Kauffman (1995). According to them, the success of any organization lies in its ability to sustain itself on the border between stability and instability – the edge of chaos. Organizations live on the edge of chaos most of the time – ie this bounded instability is where organizations need to learn to operate. In this operating position the organization should welcome disorder as a partner and use instability positively. Then new possible futures for the organization will emerge, arising out of members releasing creativity to continuously re-invent the organization. • Feedback in all organizations happens in non-linear webs or loops. Organizations do not only adapt to their environments through feedback, but also help to create them. • All agents within the system cannot be in control of its long-term future. They cannot install specific frameworks to make it successful, nor can they apply step-by-step analytical reasoning or planning or ideological controls to long-term development. Agents within the system can only do these things in relation to the short term. • Political interaction and learning in groups will foster spontaneous self-organization. • In areas of low certainty and low agreement (Stacey's concept) a high level of interaction is needed among organization agents. They need to work together to seek the many alternatives of how to carve out a survival path, each with differing degrees of predictability. • Strong internal culture is generally bad for the organization – the last thing the organization wants is 'group think'. Organizations need to promote divergence and discourage potent pressures for conformity by fostering diversity and agility of thought – prerequisites for the organization's longer-term success. • Organization design needs to be rethought – complexity will require organizations to reconsider the nature of hierarchy and control (rejecting the cause and effect, top-down, command and control approach). The organization must improve its fostering of the self-organizing principles without obsessing over too much order and control.

FIGURE 2.6 *Continued*

Key subject	Concept summary
	• Agility of an organization will come from active encouragement of experimentation and surfacing of divergent views; even allowing rule-breaking. Leaders need to recognize that people need the freedom to own their power, think innovatively and operate in new patterns. • The key to achieving this is a flexible decentralized structure (Jenner 1998). Brown and Eisenhardt (1997) refer to such flexible structures as 'semi-structures' that 'are sufficiently rigid so that change can be organized, but not so rigid that it cannot occur'. • Long-term planning is irrelevant if not a hindrance. Strategy should not be about realization of prior intent, but rather emphasize the importance of openness to accident, coincidence, serendipity and from complex and continuing interactions between people. • Long-term development is a spontaneous self-organizing process from which new strategic directions may emerge. • Organizations should foster learning, especially around how people should view instability. If the future is, in principle, unknowable for systems of any complexity, organization must develop double-loop learning. It is not enough for the managers to adjust their behaviour in response to feedback on the success of their actions – they also need to reflect on the appropriateness, in the light of unfolding events, of the assumptions (the mental model) used to set up those actions.
Change	• The key point emerging from this paradigm is that change simply cannot be managed, and all practitioners can hope for is to work with the chaos and complexity by facilitating the flow of energy within the system. • Changes cannot be driven but must be fostered and supported. • *Dynamic system* – organizations need to think about how to use small changes to create large effects. • Three variables are significant in moving systems to the edge of chaos: *connectivity, diversity* and *information flow*. If agents of stable systems become better connected, if there is more diversity in these connections, and if the amount of information transferred is increased, then the system can move to the edge of chaos. • Stacey (1996) added two other variables: level of contained anxiety and the power differentials in the system. • If the anxiety is too contained, there is no possibility of change or creativity. If there is too much anxiety there will be a tendency for 'headless chicken' type behaviour, or else for the building of spurious and unhelpful defences. If there is too much control in the form of high power differentials between different parts of the organization, creativity and readiness for change are likely to be stifled. Contrariwise, if the control mechanisms are too weak the system can dissolve into chaotic or random behaviour. • In order for organizations to promote change through self-organization, a number of writers have argued that organizations need to operate on democratic principles – that is, their members will have the freedom to self-organize. Authority must be delegated to those who have access to the broadest channels of information that relate to the issue concerned (a balanced distribution of power, strong customer focus, a strategy of continuous learning and an orientation towards community service). • Interventions such as system-wide collaborative inquiry can help to build connectivity and surface diversity. • Introducing a stimulus to the system that is at the edge of chaos may cause change to ripple through, like some kind of domino effect (Bak, 1997). Such movement cannot be directed, but we may be able to influence it.

Dialogic OD

In Spring 2015 a very significant book appeared on the market – *Dialogic Organization Development: The theory and practice of transformational change* (Bushe and Marshak, 2015). The reason this book is significant is because the authors have pulled together the OD journey and evolution of the past 50 years and made both an academic and practice case to build an integrated theory of practice called Dialogic OD. Through their special Winter edition of *Organization Development Practitioner Journal* in 2013 and this 2015 book, they have found the logic behind why dialogic interventions succeed, what informed these approaches, etc. By their work, another body of knowledge has been built and the various publications that tightly or loosely fit into this theoretical orientation have been pulled together with a much greater sense of coherency.

OD is built on a set of democratic and humanistic values – hence it has always put a premium on gathering people together to meet face to face, working through the issues that matter or are of great concern to them so that by being together they will engage with each other in generative dialogue to find ways to move forwards together. This value-in-action has established a solid foundation for the dialogic approach in the practice of OD.

This approach continues to be used even through the dominance of the mechanical period of change, but it has been treated mainly as an intervention, not a dominant coherent framework for change. In the early stages, most OD practitioners were not as equipped as we are now in our methodological competence or our philosophy of scientific understanding. With the surge of dialogic methods (between 27 and 68, depending on who you ask and how they are being counted), the time had come for these two academically distinguished scholars and practitioners to look retrospectively at the 'theory in use' – examine what the philosophical and intellectual bases are for this approach and why, when this approach is used thoughtfully, it always produces better and more sustainable results than most other OD interventions.

For those of us who have participated in a T group (NTL has been offering T groups for over 40 years), we know the dialogic approach to change is deeply embedded in the design of experiential 'laboratory' education. The reason a T group has a transformative impact on those who attend is that through social discourse and dialogue, individual fundamental schema are disrupted and alternative generative images are put before the individual from which they can choose whether they will be bold enough to step out of their own constraints and move towards alternative imagery, text, language and therefore action. The work done on team development in the US military by Tannenbaum in China Lake between 1952 and 1953 and Schein's process consultation work are also built on this foundation. In fact, Schein uses a concept of creating 'cultural islands' where safety as held by the process consultant is to enable members to talk and dialogue about the 'unspeakable' that shares very similar desired outcomes as any 'interpretive' type of intervention. This approach believes that through the power of social discourse

and dialogue, change can happen. The purpose of any OD intervention is not so much to solve people's or teams' problems, as problems will always exist within a human group, but through process intervention we equip system members to learn what they need to do and learn to continuously use those processes for self-renewal and continuous adaptation for the future.

The complexity and chaos of work added another dimension to this approach. Since no one can ever predict what type of change any system will need to deal with at any one time, the role of OD interventions are to increase the system's capability to self-organize, and to unearth the local wisdom so that they can also evolve in their capability to break out from social, cultural, psychological, and paradigm constraints to participate in continuous developmental work.

In such complex situations, the role of OD practitioners will need to evolve also. When change cannot be managed as the agents will act autonomously in reacting to the situation, and network members will interact dynamically with each other in a way that will increase the complexity and chaos, our job is to watch for the emergence, and to nudge the system to identify alternative patterns that will help them to become more agile, adaptive and capable to work with emergence in change. Our job is not to manipulatively shuffle them down a particular change path.

What Bushe and Marshak have done is both brilliant and significant in terms of looking back on our historical journey to put coherence of our practice in this area and then move on to form an important theoretical orientation. I would like to formally salute them, even though I think their differentiation between Diagnostic OD and Dialogic OD is unnecessarily harsh. If I may use an alternative text and narrative to frame their work, I would say something like this:

> In different historical contexts (context is key in our work) the expert and diagnostic OD methods have served our work well, and their relevance still remains in certain consultancy situations. However, such approaches need to update themselves because of the environmental shift. We need to self-adjust work by leaning into our own discomfort to embrace a different paradigm which comes from a mix of experiential learning, group dynamics, social discourse, social construction theory, etc, and learning to go deeper into, and being better equipped in the dialogic way of change.

The way I see this 'old/new' theoretical orientation is not so much about casting off, but adding on, aligning, and shifting into a different way of seeing for some – so that we will be even fitter for the organizations that we work with. I have confidence we can do that, as many OD practitioners are so heavily embedded in the core values of OD, we instinctively know using a dialogic approach to help a system to move on is in our blood already. In fact, both Diagnostic OD and Dialogic OD have different things to offer on our continuous journey in making a rich tapestry of our field of knowledge. As in any such journey, sometimes theories came first and guide our practice, while on other occasions our practices have matured to a point that working theories have emerged and Dialogic OD fits into that category.

FIGURE 2.7 Core concepts from Dialogical OD

Key subject	Concept summary
General	• Dialogic methods have existed in OD for more than 50 years. Dialogic OD change process is based in social constructionism and involves changing narratives that underpin social reality. It has an 'interpretative' origin. • In this orientation of change, very much like social constructionism in that all reality is socially constructed through language, text, narratives and stories, an organization is a sense-making system in which multiple forms of interaction take place every day to shape and reshape meanings through interaction. • Peggy Holman (2013) explained Dialogic OD engages the diverse people of a system to focus in open interactions to catalyse unexpected and lasting shifts in perspective and behaviour. • A basic assumption of Dialogic OD practices is that change occurs through changing the conversations in a system. • While Dialogic OD does not do diagnosis, it does ask questions and engage people in inquiry; the difference, they insist is that they do not carry empirical inquiry and the point is **not** to find 'the truth'. • They believe that only inquiry that is linked to things that address a widely shared challenge has a chance to be transformational. • The conditions that will lead to successful Dialogic OD (Bushe 2013; Holman 2013) include the following: o Have an issue that is important to the community which requires a systemic effort to resolve. o Reframe problem/challenge into possibility centric, future-focused issue that is personally meaningful to community members (ask possibility oriented questions). o Have the right mix of people in the room for the dialogue (invite diversity). o Convene events and design the utilization of generative images to provoke new thinking and catalyse self-generated change proposals from the community (be welcoming, provide loose framework and create safety).
Change	• The generic model of Dialogic OD rests on the assumption that change occurs when the day-to-day thinking of members of any group, organization, and/or community has been altered to the extent that their day-to-day decisions and actions have shifted, which in turn cause disruption and changes to the culture of these social units. • The Dialogic OD writers believe that a Dialogic OD approach to change happens when, through dialogue, the system members' language, stories, and narratives they have been using have been altered which has then led to the profound shift of the thinking and therefore action, behaviour of the members of the system. • Such profound change occurs from a ***generative image*** which Bushe (2007) defines as ideas, phrases, objects, pictures, manifestos, stories, or new words. According to him, a generative image has two properties – a) it allows us to see new alternatives for decisions and actions as such images have the power to disrupt our guiding assumptions and raise fundamental questions regarding current reality which can be taken for granted; b) the image presents new possibilities which become attractors to people and evoke or increase their desire to want to change.

FIGURE 2.7 *Continued*

Key subject	Concept summary
	• By nature, a generative image is an emergence phenomenon and tends to evoke so many different meanings – hence it is inappropriate to try to pin down a tight definition. • In the past, some generative images that have had key impact in how the world deals with ecological matters is 'sustainable development' or in the business world 'trust costs less', 'mistakes present too good an opportunity for us not to leverage to speed up our growth', 'brilliance without collaboration leads to...?'. While these sound like nice quotes, they are not as they are the result of deep inquiry and dialogue among group members, often for a substantial period. • When we use dialogic practices to engage the people of a system in conversations that address their own issues, we not only solve the immediate problem, we leave behind a more evolved system, with a greater sense of direction and hopefully of personal connection, and the energy and will to work across previously unbridgeable boundaries. (Holman, 2013) • Two conditions that will lead to a successful dialogic change process – a) having the right question, worded in the right way, can make all the difference in the success or failure; b) having the right mix of people engaged in those conversations, eg from multiple organizational levels, multiple stakeholders, or people from the outside, etc.
The role of OD practitioners	• The role of the Dialogic OD practitioner is more like a process consultant than a facilitator as we are more a convener of process of inquiry – as Schein has said, we do not go into the work context with a pre-determined agenda as we do not control the outcome. The outcome will emerge. It is important we do not sweat hard to ensure they give us the outcome we think they should achieve. The difference is that dialogic OD practitioners design some genuine open-ended experiences in which those who participate have control over obtaining the outcome they want, not what we want for them. • Our role as a Dialogic OD practitioner is to set up processes to support members of the community to uncover generative images, stimulate new ideas and voluntarily move towards shift in their choices, decisions, and behaviour. • In Dialogic OD, a more critical role OD practitioners have is not to be a facilitator, but to be a 'container' – by first being a designer and planner to set up the conditions for self-generated and self-regulated conversations to take place; and then attending to the interaction of members of the community. Another feature of an effective container is to frame high-quality questions that help members to focus attention and interaction. • The quality of the container is related to the qualities and character of the person that is convening and leading the dialogic change event. The skill of knowing when to hold on to a topic and when to let go, able to read and move with the energy of a group in a non-anxious presence is very important. Bushe (2013) talked about the psychological maturity of the containers and the aim of co-creating the container with the community is very important. • It is important to know that we are part of the reality-making, or meaning-making process; we are not some objective third-party observers, commenting on the work the system is doing. We need to be vigilant about the reality and meaning we bring into the work.

SOURCE: Bushe, G (2013)

The 2013 special *OD Practitioner* Winter issue on Dialogic OD gave full coverage to the subject and the new book (which I had the privilege to preview) offers a rich feast of learning – so I would not attempt in this edition to give a full review of this theoretical orientation, but I hope Figure 2.7 will give readers a grasp of this emerging change theory. I want to acknowledge much of the content of the grid is sourced from the range of articles in the 2013 special issue on Dialogic OD in ODP.

FIGURE 2.8 Dialogic theory of change

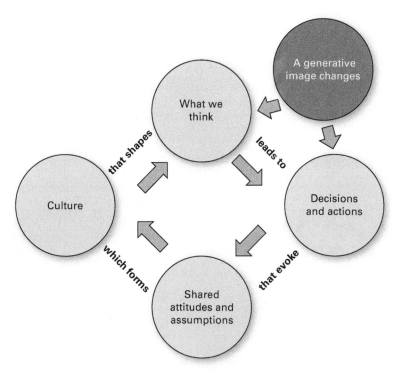

SOURCE: Bushe, G (2013)

Methodological/practical implications of the theoretical perspectives

The demands, nature and scope of a project will always have a major influence on the diagnostic framework and the intervention methods you select. However, in both of these OD phases, you will also need a solid theoretical grounding to guide your decisions. Otherwise your diagnostic process risks being guided mainly by your own perceptual lens or your client's perceptual lens or, worse, by both. In this section I will illustrate how each theory can support our decisions in these OD phases.

Implications on the diagnostic processes

In Figure 2.7 I demonstrate how each of the theories can help to shape the way I/you look at a problem or issue. It is by the combination of these theoretical insights that you and I can reach a better solution. In reality, OD practitioners seldom rely on a single theory to guide their work: it is the rich combination of all these great theories that will make your work brilliantly successful.

Methodological implications on the intervention design phase

The brilliant thing about the theories that I have outlined is that once understood they can help us to do much better design. Their principles are there to guide us to construct activities that will help to move the system. The applications below are just a few ideas to illustrate how theoretical insights can impact on our design thinking.

FIGURE 2.9 Different theoretical perspectives: practical implications for the diagnostic phase

Theory	Practical implications for the OD practitioner
Action Research theory	• Involve the people affected by the change so that they become co-investigators into the reasons for change, and participate in analysing the current reality and discussing the future they need to move towards. • Work to increase the amount and quality of inquiry between people so that they can learn from each other and gather a rich mix of data. • Secure a commitment from senior leaders to give some decision-making power to the people involved in collecting the data so that real change can be achieved. • Set up a temporary diagnostic team by using those key individuals who have to support the implementation of the change.
Lewin's change theories	• Pay attention to the group dynamics and the powerful forces within groups. • Plan the mix of people involved in diagnostic events in order to shift these forces and facilitate change. Diagnostic events then become key learning events which will lead to 'unfreezing'. • Work out what messages the change leaders need to use to engender sufficient survival anxiety while also ensure psychological safety for the people who are being asked to change. • Be clear about the type of 'unfreezing' work that is needed during the diagnostic stage.

FIGURE 2.9 *Continued*

Theory	Practical implications for the OD practitioner
Systems theory	• Use mixed groups to achieve a rich understanding of how the change is seen from different perspectives. This helps to generate a holistic view of what must be done to give the organization a secure future. • Use diagnostic events to enhance people's understanding of important interdependencies and to support them in devising a way forward that will help the different sub-systems to work well together in those interdependent areas. • Use processes that will increase collaboration across units and that will honour the primacy of relationship between different groups. • Whenever possible, bring in outside bodies and data to stimulate the organization to think about the issues. • Expose people to the outside world in which the organization lives to ensure they stay externally sensitive and not insulated in their perspective.
Complexity and chaos theories	• Seek to build the five key variables that the complex theorists mentioned as important to help the organization stay agile – connection, diversity, information, power differentials or level of anxiety. Help the system to move towards 'the edge of chaos' so that they will self-organize. • Maximize the internal staff's freedom to do the self-organizing so that they can identify what the appropriate local actions should be. • Minimize hierarchical power plays and ensure everyone is really able to identify where the system needs to change. • Carry out diagnosis at the micro level: pay as much attention to local data as to corporate data.
Appreciative Inquiry	• Make sure that the subjects/topics/questions of the inquiry are positive. This will enable the organization to focus on the best of the past and figure out what would be best in the future. • Help the organization to identify its 'positive core' – the place from which the change journey can begin and which can be used to maximize progress. • Make sure that the process is holistic, inclusive, highly participatory and collaborative. • Use as many right-brain methodologies as possible to collect data, eg storyboarding, drawing, imagery, poetry, etc. • Use dialogue as the main form of interaction between people rather than focusing on tell and sell.

System theory and Action Research theory: methodological implications

Whenever you can, design processes that will contain some of the following features:

● Send a team (preferably a mixed team) to investigate the outside world and bring outside data into the local system (do their own diagnosis).

- Maximize the interface between all those who work within the system and those who are outside, eg those who provide the service and those who receive the service, the funders and the fund recipients, the policy makers and those who are affected by the policy. They should share their perspectives with one another and help each other to get a more complete view of the issue.

- Give the local members an opportunity to interview each other for the specific purpose of expanding understanding of the interdependencies they have with others in the organization, hence how to think and act more as a whole.

- Equip and allocate clear roles to local leaders so that they can lead the change by involving others to work out the finer details of the solutions by sharing data, information and required outcomes with their staff. Give leaders the right capability up-skilling so that they will be able to conduct 'dialogical' processes with those who are affected by the change to seek their views on options for implementation (best leadership development tactics).

- Use many key people as researchers to investigate the current issues, and design processes to invite them to co-construct with others on how the performance in specific areas can be improved.

- Everyone affected by the change should have an opportunity to voice their opinion about the processes and vote for what they want – practice 'distributed leadership'.

- Use whole-system methodology whenever possible – bring together all those who will need to own and support the implementation of the change and design processes to help them to:
 - share and understand the need for change;
 - jointly analyse current reality and what needs to change;
 - generate ideas on how to change;
 - work together to set out implementation.

Lewin's theories (Group Dynamics, Field theory, Three-step Model): methodological implications

Whenever you can, design processes that will contain some of the following features:

- Always work at a group level or sub-group level. Always maximize group interface because if a group is left alone, they will grow rigid. The job of the intervener is not to shift a group, but to set up processes to enable groups to shift each other through the quality of their interchange.

- Understand that 90 per cent of the group dynamics are around the three issues – inclusion, affection and control. Design processes that will give opportunities for delegates to share laughter and warmth, as well as sharing (equalized) control. Work hard at the inclusion issue, whether you are working at individual, interpersonal, group or total system level.

- Pay attention to the 'membership groups' and 'reference groups' that individuals refer themselves to. Attempt to change the reference group prior to the intervention event, because by changing the reference group of those whom we are targeting, we can fast track the change among those groups.

- Create a 'cultural island' experience so that individuals can experiment with different norms and different ways of doing things. Make sure sufficient numbers of people are involved so that the actual norms will be shifted.

- Never aim for intervening in the whole organization (unless the size is small). Use opinion formers and think of tipping points. Categorize people into different segments. For example: segment 1 – most critical politically; segment 2 – those who are key in the implementation stage; segment 3 – those who are key because of their competences; and so on. Work with each segment to create critical mass.

- Use emergent talents to get to the top leaders, especially if you ask the top leaders to nominate their emerging leaders to support the change intervention.

- Use methodology that will help to build self-induced forces to change by giving people an opportunity to personalize the case of change. Engage them to envision what the change will do for them, their teams and their organization.

- Involve people to become aware of the field in which they function as well as the forces brought about on their behaviour. After the analysis, give them opportunity to ask 'So what?' and 'Now what?'

- Put the whole field together to 'act out' both the restraining and the driving forces – so that the group will gain a better understanding of those forces that influence them and each other. If appropriate, bring in outside 'forces' (eg real clients, partners, supporters, etc) to intercept the strong current field in order to help the group to shift.

- Work hard on creating the three conditions of 'unfreezing' the organization that Schein talked about – disconfirmation of the validity of the status quo, induction of guilt (survival anxiety) and creation of psychological safety.

- Aim to use highly engaged methodology to do data collection as part of 'unfreezing'.

- Involve people to help identify what would be the 'refreezing' mechanism as they pay attention to the field and forces.

Complexity and chaos theories and Social Constructionism theory: methodological implications

Whenever you can, design processes that will contain some of the following features:

- Use dialogical-based methods, eg the art of focused conversation, to help people make sense of the situation and work with others to come up with solutions that would help them to commit to change. Shifting paradigms require a structured way of dialogue and inquiry – not tell and sell.

- Give people a chance to express their reality and the meaning they make of the situation from where they sit. Create the opportunity to get local 'micro' group members to participate, to co-construct.

- Use methodology that focuses on energy. Work through people's passion and value and help them to surface and share what matters to them. Use processes to help them care enough to self-organize to make things happen.

- Use human networks to spread the positive virus. Light as many 'fires' as you can in local areas.

- Pay attention to the social aspect of the work situation and how people see their job in terms of social meaning. Satisfaction is related to whom they work for and whom they work alongside.

- Use creative art medium (theatre, music, and storyboarding methods) to tap into the creative side of people and to facilitate a more fluid expression of what is important to them.

- Use powerful language and symbols to create a vision of the change agenda.

- Use positive psychology and strength-based approaches to build intervention.

Summary

The practice implications for our work from these theoretical insights are huge. First, they help build a platform for us to do robust design work. They have given us insight into how individuals, groups and organizations work. When these theories are brought together, their synergistic insights give us a much broader scope in understanding how organizations and groups operate. It is the mixing of insights from the different theories that gives us rich perspectives as practitioners.

In the diagnostic phase, you can use Systems theory to help you understand where the presenting issues are located in the organization and how

they are reinforced by other parts of the system. The totality of the system perspective will alert us as to what else to pay attention to. Social Constructionism theory will help us understand the meaning-making process of the organization's dominant narrative, and see how you can moderate the type, frequency and quality of the social interaction among the members, so that the dominant narrative can be challenged and an alternative can be put in. Action Research theory can help you to gather local leaders and members to help them get involved in collecting and analysing the data, and to feed back their own data to their community. This will help them to own the decisions and hence motivate them to support the implementation.

During intervention, we can draw on Lewin's various theories for insight into how to moderate the field forces of those groups we need to change. The Three-step Model also helps us to rethink the sequences of work. The complex chaos theories can help us to stir up the micro groups and set up the conditions to facilitate them to self-organize the changes they want to see. The combination of system theories and complexity theories can help us to execute change processes with ease both from planned and emergence approaches.

Further application of these theoretical concepts will come alive in the OD consultancy cycle, Chapters 3 to 6.

Section 2

This section gives an overview of the OD consultancy cycle and its key phases of work. Sometimes I wonder in a fast-changing, complex, emergent world whether such a map is still necessary. In fact, when I mention the OD cycle, it often engenders a look that says 'You don't believe in these old-fashioned steps, do you? Really!?' This frowning has increased as the paradigm of people (including myself) has shifted in the direction of the teaching of Complexity and Chaos theory as well as Dialogic OD. However, it is my position that while I am excited about how the field is evolving, there are also some core or 'older' concepts that still stand us in good stead. To me, the OD cycle and its key phases is still a very much needed anchor in supporting us to work effectively through the complex dynamics of our consultancy work with clients – and in its nature different from change approaches and interventions. We must also remember that this cycle is a non-linear process, and continuous adaptation and various iterations will be necessary as our consultancy relationship and context evolve.

Chapter 3 covers the area of entry and contracting. Regardless of whether we are internal or external, we will all need to gain entry to a client system before we can dispense our enabling role. However, it is important for us to remember and respect that the client system had its own integrity as an entity before we ever existed. Hence we need to be invited in, and when we are in we need to take them as they are without judgement. Without entry

and without a commission (whether it is verbal or written), we have no right to trespass. What we do at this stage will give rise to those conditions that will either make our work with a client easy, successful or not. For example, without clear contracting with the right group of clients, we will have to spend time adjusting our relationship or troubleshooting for the rest of the consultancy journey. Also, if we only agree financial terms without getting the scope of work agreed, then we will be back to negotiating the flow of work continuously. Without sitting down with the client and spelling out the type of partnership they and we want that will support the success of the project, and how we together can align the way we work to deliver that ultimate goal of the consultancy effort, we may set ourselves up for a sub-optimal level of performance. In the context of a complex and chaotic environment, these two phases form the anchor to guide us to adapt, take risks, and support the clients to lean towards their discomfort.

Once we are in, we need to find a way to gauge whether the presenting issues are the real issues, not to mention gaining access to diverse groups for their perspectives (multiple system views) about those issues. The wonderful challenge at this phase is whether we can galvanize the system members to undertake their own diagnostic work so that as joint investigators, they will – through the action research framework and through dialogic processes – investigate their own system, make sense of the data, and in a self-organized way find methods to move themselves and the system forward. Recently, publications on the subject of 'Dialogical vs Diagnostic OD' show us that the 'diagnostic' phase carries some deeply held assumptions, but we in OD also have decades of commitment to use dialogical methods to support the system members to diagnose themselves. However, we can definitely do better if those of us who still hold onto the expert role learn to drop that role and be a container for the system members to have deep inquiry into others' reality by paying a lot more attention to the narratives, stories, text, conversation, linguistic structure. It is through the dialogue we promote a joint inquiry spirit among clients so that people can identify ways to move forward. When well-designed, this phase will transition simultaneously into the intervention phase.

In OD, intervention is actually a 24/7 phenomenon from the moment of entry. This is when the use of self as an agent of change becomes critically relevant. While the methods and technologies of intervention continue to evolve to maintain relevance in this complex world, the core principles of how interventions are designed – the crucial aspects of involving system members to co-construct the design and to co-run some of the more formal interventions – remain the same. OD interventions always aim to increase the self-organized capability of the system. However, there is a shift to a lighter-touch approach to intervention – mainly setting up the conditions for members of the systems to do their own work. Not so much planning but working with emergence, paying attention to patterns, and through the wonderful list of dialogic methods supporting system members to make sense of their situation.

The final chapter is on evaluation. Reminding ourselves of what Einstein once said, everything that can be counted does not necessarily count; everything that counts cannot necessarily be counted. If the evaluation processes create more burdens and generate irrelevant data, then the process will become redundant and obsolete. This is when the work of Michael Quinn Patton (2010) is important here as he introduced the term of 'developmental evaluation'. According to him, this is the type of evaluation that informs and supports innovative and adaptive development in complex dynamic environments. Developmental Evaluation is not the same as improvement, accountability or summative judgement in the process. In Developmental Evaluation, we aim to work collaboratively with the system members, particularly those innovators within the system, to conceptualize, design and test new approaches in an ongoing process of adaptation, intentional change and ultimately longer-term development.

It is true that for organizations which receive external funding, the summative evaluation is still important as both parties need to see whether the funding has gone to the right project and achieved the promised outcome. But summative (final) evaluation happens after all has been done already. If an OD intervention occurs in a highly uncertain, dynamic and emergent environment, a more important agenda for these efforts is to help the project to continuously evolve, become increasingly innovative and adaptive so that there is an ongoing developmental outcome in all evaluative steps. Hence in the field of evaluation of any OD intervention, our role is to elicit and stimulate the innovation and adaptation processes by encouraging the system to use real-time and rapid feedback processes to track the implications and results of any specific intervention so that we can facilitate the ongoing, real-time, data-based decision making in the developmental process. In that way, the evaluation process will become an ongoing powerful developmental intervention both to the outcome as well as to the behavioural changes of the system members. Because of lack of space, I did not add Michael's work into the existing chapter, but do look up his work and that of others who have written about 'developmental evaluation'.

With the pressure on for most internal OD practitioners to prove the worth of any OD interventions, it will be important for OD practitioners to take evaluation seriously, but it is important to treat this phase of OD cycle not as an end state but an evolving developmental phase for the system.

Theories and practices of OD: the OD cycle and the entry and contracting phase

In Chapter 2, I outlined how the OD consultancy cycle is one of five key building blocks in our practice. It is a protocol to guide us through how we should manage the helping processes – from the moment we are called in to help to establish the issues concerned through to intervention and evaluation. The OD cycle reminds us of the key actions we need to undertake in order to keep the process as intact as possible. Based on Action Research theory, the OD cycle is an iterative process in which the cyclical nature of it will mean we revisit the same phase at various times. In a field where it is the practice and process of OD that makes a unique contribution to an organization rather than our content expertise, the process protocol is an important navigation tool or map. Burke, French and Bell and others have written brilliant chapters about the OD cycle. This chapter does not aim to duplicate their work, but to simplify and summarize the core practice and processes of OD and to give practical information and guidance on how to implement them in organizations.

This chapter covers three areas:

1 an overview of the OD consultancy cycle;

2 phase one: entry – initial contact;

3 phase two: contracting

Chapters 4 to 6 will cover the diagnostic, intervention and evaluation phases in greater detail.

Overview of the OD consultancy cycle – six key components

Back in 1993, a number of newcomers to OD at an NTL learning programme asked their trainers to sum up what OD practitioners do, what skills they need, and how everything in OD fits together. The trainers worked overnight to produce the first version of OD – a map of what to know and what to do (see Figure 3.1). Since then, this map has been revised many times and in 2006 it was finally published by Tschudy. The map is critical to understanding what OD practitioners actually do, so I will go through each of the six components before discussing the OD cycle in detail.

Core theories

OD practices are heavily sourced from different disciplines of behavioural science, especially Action Research theory, Systems theory and a range of change theories. In Chapter 2 we covered five core theories. They offer us diverse but rich perspectives on what to look for during the diagnostic phase as well as what type of interventions we can put together to move the human system towards the desired change goal.

Values and ethics

OD practices are guided by the practitioner's values. The range of OD's values and ethics arose out of a number of powerful movements in the 1940s and 1950s including human relations, human potential, equality and diversity and social participation (clients' rights, citizens' rights). OD practitioners use these values to guide them in designing the processes and selecting the approaches they use to support change. The OD values often act as a container to our practices (see Chapter 1).

The 'big I' intervention

This is a central plank of Organization Development. OD practitioners focus heavily on building relationships of trust, authenticity, transparency and mutuality with their clients. It is this use of self, from the moment we meet with the client to the closing of our relationship, that holds the consultancy process together. This requires OD practitioners to look inside themselves and examine what they bring to the helping relationship: to identify what will enhance the relationship and what might derail it. The focus on building the relationship is to 'earn our right to help' – so that we can be facilitative, evocative, or provocative to the clients when the situation requires us to be that (Chapter 7).

FIGURE 3.1 OD: A map of what to know and what to do

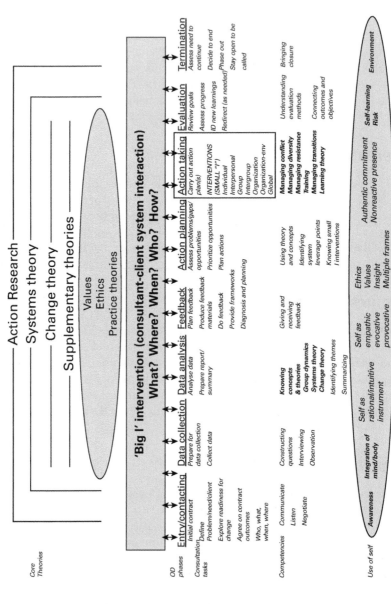

Core
Theories
— Action Research
— Systems theory
— Change theory
— Supplementary theories

Values
Ethics
Practice theories

'Big I' intervention (consultant-client system interaction)
What? Where? When? Who? How?

OD phases	Entry/contacting	Data collection	Data analysis	Feedback	Action planning	Action taking	Evaluation	Termination
Consultation tasks	Initial contract	Prepare for data collection	Analyse data	Plan feedback	Assess problems/gaps/opportunities	Carry out action plans	Review goals	Assess need to continue
	Define	Collect data	Prepare report/summary	Produce feedback materials	Prioritize opportunities	INTERVENTIONS (SMALL "i")	Assess progress	Decide to end
	Problem/need/client			Do feedback	Plan actions	Individual	ID new learnings	Phase out
	Explore readiness for change			Provide frameworks		Interpersonal	Redirect (as needed)	Stay open to be called
	Agree on contract outcomes			Diagnosis and planning		Group		
	Who, what, when, where					Intergroup		
						Organization		
						Organization-env		
						Global		

Competencies	Communicate	Constructing questions	Knowing concepts & theories	Giving and receiving feedback	Using theory and concepts	Managing conflict	Understanding evaluation methods	Bringing closure
	Listen	Interviewing	Group dynamics		Identifying system leverage points	Managing diversity		
	Negotiate	Observation	Systems theory			Managing resistance	Connecting outcomes and objectives	
			Change theory		Knowing small i interventions	Training		
			Identifying themes			Managing transitions		
			Summarizing			Learning theory		

Use of self	Awareness	Integration of mind/body	Self as rational/intuitive instrument	Self as empathic evocative provocative	Ethics Values Insight Multiple frames	Authentic commitment Nonreactive presence	Self-learning Risk	Environment

Tschudy (2006)
NTL Handbook of Organization Development and Change

OD phases

The OD consultancy cycle contains eight phases, which the Gestalt colleagues called 'units of work'. They are based on the cornerstone of Action Research: applying rigorous scientific methods of fact-finding and experimentation to practical problems and issues within organizations:

- entry/initial contact;
- data collection;
- data analysis;
- feedback;
- action planning;
- action taking;
- evaluation;
- termination.

The eight phases of the OD cycle are there to help the practitioner and the client to navigate through the OD consultancy process. Though the OD consultancy cycle may look, on the surface, like any other consultancy cycles in the marketplace, the following things make OD different. They are its commitment to:

- achieving mutual understanding of the issues through data collection;
- collaboration between the consultant and the people in the organization in working together through data analysis and data feedback;
- resolving issues by increasing the knowledge and understanding of members of the system about what is the best way forward in action planning and the design and execution of interventions;
- increasing the insights and capability of the system members throughout the various phases so that the system will not only get engagement and commitment towards the change but also an ability to sustain itself.

Because of the above, OD practitioners always involve leaders and other members within an organization to help to define the issues, collect and analyse data, and feed back the data to the various stakeholders in order to do joint planning of what are the necessary actions. These processes are repeated as many times as necessary until all the issues have been resolved. So what will make an OD practitioner stand out is not just whether they know what the OD consultancy phases are, but also how they navigate through them.

Competencies

In order to carry out the different OD phases and sub-tasks, OD practitioners need to demonstrate a core set of competencies at a high level. They need to take OD education and development seriously and the field needs to enforce more rigorous standards in the training of OD practitioners. You will notice the list of competencies in Figure 3.1 is a mix of technical and process, hard and soft skills.

The use of self

This is the basis of the 'big I' intervention – the use of the OD practitioner's key instrument, the self. During each phase you use your awareness, your rational, intuitive self, your empathic/evocative/provocative self to help the client to shift. You will cultivate your non-reactive presence and commitment to the client in order to create a safe environment that will support the client in examining his/her situation from different angles and through different lenses. It is your ability to take risks in intervening and your skill in straight-talking based on your own values and ethics that will enable you to do the 'big I' intervention. It is the self that provides the reliable engine to drive the OD process (see Chapter 10).

Finally, it is important not to treat the OD consultancy cycle as steps. Instead, they should be seen as phases that are cyclical and organic rather than linear. For example, if it becomes clear during the data collection phase that the organization needs a different outcome – one that neither you nor the client have thought of – you have to go back and revisit the contract with the client. If you have planned and run an intervention and find that it did not go as intended, you have to go back to the drawing board with the client and re-plan. If you carry out a midway evaluation and become aware of new areas that need focus then revisit the scope of the contract, re-examine the data and rework the change processes. In that sense the OD cycle is a dynamic instrument, with feedback from every phase to correct the consulting process in order to help both parties to play their part to support the change processes.

In the following two sections, I will review the first two phases of the cycle – entry and contracting.

Phase one: entry – initial contact

This is an important phase of our work. Put simply, without contact there will not be entry, without entry there will not be a contract, without a contract there will not be commissioned work. Also, how we manage this phase will help us to set the tone of the relationship we aim to build with our client and create a platform for our diagnostic and intervention work.

FIGURE 3.2 Summary of tasks and skills for the entry – initial contact phase

Tasks	OD practitioner skills
• Make initial contact. • Communicate who you are and find out who the client is. • Support the client in defining their issues, problems, needs. • Explore different stakeholders' perspectives on the issues outlined in the original contact – help clients to explore multiple perspectives. • Carry out an initial assessment of who is in the client's constellation (how many others will impact on the process). • Explore the client's readiness to move on the issues stated. • Explore the capabilities of the organization and the level of resources available to support the changes. • Explore the outcomes that the different stakeholders want. • Get a feel for the organization's context and culture and the types of forces operating within its environment.	• Effective communication skills – both inquiry and deep listening skills – to help the client diagnose their own situation. • Ability to remain strategic and analytical – so as to be able to scope out the issues. • Political skills – ability to tune in to the organization's politics – to help the client explore the different stakeholders' perspectives on the issues without them being present. • Ability to remain pragmatic and assess the organization's ability to undertake the change programme – the time that people have to invest in it, financial resources, and readiness. • Ability to remain connected with your own intuitive feelings about the client and the organization. • Ability to plan out the project – size, length, scale – and to clearly play it back to the client. • Ability to make an impact and to win trust. • Ability to call upon a range of theoretical frameworks in order to make a quick assessment of the issues. • Good interpersonal and relationship-building skills and ability to win trust.

Without entry, there will not be work. So how do you go about making first contact? Whether you are internal or external, most probably you would like your clients to come to you directly and ask for your help because they have heard how good you are. Like any normal human being, you want to be wanted, but reality is not like this. Mainly because those you suppose to serve:

• are so busy and occupied that you are not even on their radar screen;

• do not know enough about OD that they would come to seek your help;

- have assumptions of what HR as a function can do or can't do, and if OD sits under HR, that assumption will be automatically transferred to you.

So, in reality, most of you will need to do a lot more to orchestrate the initial contact.

Internal OD practitioners

The first thing you need to do is accept that you are operating in a political environment and therefore you have to build a strong position of influence within a relatively short time. People who are viewed as a 'support function' seldom have power offered to them on a silver platter. But without power (for which you may prefer to substitute impact, credibility or influence) it is hard to play an effective OD role.

Many internal OD practitioners fail to achieve 'entry' to their organization and then, when they lack sponsors or cannot demonstrate what value they can add, they turn around and blame the organization. Remember, gaining entry and making contact is your job. The following five steps may help you to get going, especially if you are a new entry to the organization.

First, work out the critical stakeholders surrounding the OD function. Some people will fall into two or more of these categories:

- the people who hired you;
- the people whom you are supposed to provide a service to and to support – generally the senior line leaders who are leading change;
- potential sponsors – those who will speak on behalf of the OD agenda at board level;
- the people who have the financial resources to fund the OD programme;
- the people whom you report to;
- important colleagues and strategic alliances on the same level as you, especially those who already have direct access to decision makers, eg strategists, senior HR partners in core functions, etc.

Second, find someone within the organization to mentor you and to take you through the complex political terrain in which these various stakeholders sit. You also need to find out, from your mentor or other people, what kinds of people the different stakeholders are, the challenges they face at work, and the expectations they may have of you and of OD. This will help you to align your service to their needs.

Mapping the key political players in the organization will help to make up the first list of people whom you need to contact. It is important that you do not sit in the safety of the HR/LD/OD nest hoping that people will find out what you are offering and come and track you down.

Third, make half-hour appointments to visit all these key political players. Why half an hour? Because offering a short appointment increases the likelihood of them agreeing to meet you. You need to plan each meeting carefully using the knowledge you have gleaned about the person – their role, work priorities and working style. During this appointment, plan to cover the following things (not necessarily in this order):

- **Introduce yourself.** Plan how you will introduce yourself based on what you know about each person. For example, with a leader who is more ISTJ (the Myers-Briggs Type Indicator for personality), the best approach may be to focus on facts, your track record, evaluations and metrics of past projects, etc. With a leader who is more ENFP you may want to talk more about your passions, your experiences, and the things you are excited to be working on. People need to know enough about you to decide whether they can be open with you about their problems. Make sure your introduction only takes a few minutes. Too long would be inappropriate at this stage. It may be a good idea to script your introduction so that you get the balance right.

- **Find out about their work agenda and priorities as well as the crucial issues in their part of the organization.** Ask about their leadership vision, main organizational and business agendas, how they manage the interfaces between their division and other divisions – and if appropriate probe gently about the issues that are of most concern to them (whether there is anything that makes them lose sleep at night!). Show them that you are a good listener and that your insights are sharp by playing back to them the key themes in what they have disclosed.

- **Find out about them.** Go into this meeting with a few questions that will signal to the person that you are interested in who they are. Good personal questions may include: 'How would you describe your career journey?', 'What gives you the biggest buzz in your job?', and 'What is the moment that you are most proud of in your career?' It is important to use strength-based questions so they can experience the affirmative way in which you work.

- **Explore how you can add value to their agenda.** After they have shared their work challenges and priorities, ask them whether there are areas where you can be of help to them. Be prepared to offer some initial ways in which you can support them (something you prepared after gathering intelligence from others) if they don't come up with anything. You may want to mention your previous projects or experience to give them an idea of what you can do for them. Ask if you can come back to them either via e-mail or another appointment so that you can share ideas about how you can be of help to them.

- **Inform them briefly about OD and its value to business.** If the opportunity arises, share with them something you have prepared on OD and the OD approach. It will be good to summarize what the OD function does, what OD is and how OD can be of value to leaders, or a big system framework, etc, on a couple of pages and carry them with you. You can also offer to send them other material depending on what you have discussed.

Of course conversations never flow tidily, so it is important that you go with their flow in order to build initial rapport and create a positive impression. This prepares the ground for you to be invited to work in the person's area later.

Fourth, write to each person after your visit. Type up the key points from your conversation and suggest a number of ideas or contributions that you could make to their situation. Consider offering them a 'taster' so that they can assess the type of support you offer. But it is important to stay specific about what you are proposing. This can open the door for them to call on you later, preferably for a larger job.

Fifth, once you have visited all the stakeholders, spend a good chunk of time mapping out all the needs you have gathered from your visits. Using the information you have gathered from your interview plus the information you have about the organization (its strategic priorities, crucial information you have gathered from external regulators, competitors, etc) you are now ready to formulate your first draft OD plan. You will take this to your boss and other key stakeholders, eg partners and sponsors, to get feedback and hopefully agree an overall contract of who and what you should focus on and what the top OD priorities are for you. While this version is only in draft form and may need major revision, at least you are initiating an official plan of work demonstrating how you can start working your OD magic for the organization. Also, you are starting to build a reputation for yourself of being proactive, client focused and result oriented.

One of the challenges that internal practitioners face is that you cannot play the market. You do not have the luxury of asking yourselves the standard external consultants' questions. For example, 'Do I like the client? Do I think we can work well together?' and 'What do I feel after our meeting – annoyance, frustration or excitement?' However, the good news for the internal practitioner is that the OD commitment to support major players regardless of how you feel often accelerates your development of 'self as instrument'. You have to pay attention to your inner reactions to people as well as challenge yourselves to take value alignment work seriously. By that I mean, live out the values you espouse. The deep learning curve you put yourselves in will then help to sharpen how you manage yourselves and continue to develop and refine yourselves as instruments of change. Also, many of the external practitioners can ask those questions but often they are not in a position to turn away the work especially if the work is impactful and interesting.

External OD practitioners

External consultants almost always gain entry to an organization as a result of a client making the initial contact, often through an invitation to tender or via a referral. Nevertheless, once you have gained entry you still need to go through most of the initial contact steps outlined above. You certainly need to visit the stakeholders that you and your client have identified together, because you need to gain entry to sub-systems and to generate commitment among the different groups. External practitioners often fail to make a proactive plan to contact a wide range of people outside your immediate client group because of the cost issue. But without such contact you cannot obtain robust data to help shape the change agenda and direction – so your tactics will include the contact phase work in the cost proposal.

How many people you need to contact depends on the project budget and on how savvy your own client is at networking. With a well-connected client you can quickly create a political map and move on to contacting key individuals as described above. But if your client has not got good connections within the organization, you need to take time to explain the importance of entry and contact so that s/he can work together with you in getting the data and commitment the project needs. The fact is there is a lot more external practitioners can do to ensure invitation into a client system to help scope out the project before the proposed contract is finalized. A word about budget – if the project budget cannot stretch to contact work, you need to ask the internal client to do the work or suggest a reduced rate to do what you think is important.

The entry and re-entry should be thought of simultaneously. When a project is finished but it is clear that ongoing maintenance work will be needed, external consultants need to find a way to make sure that you can continue to make contact with clients and maintain relationships (this also applies to internal people).

Here are some ways to do this:

- Phone or visit each client about six months after you have completed the project. It is a good idea to build this post-project visit (preferably at no cost to the client) into your formal contract. Such a visit enables you to monitor progress, to encourage the client organization to continue the evaluation process and so assess the longer-term impact of the project, and to find out whether there are new developments that they should pay attention to. Whether you get more work from this contact does not matter as long as you have affirmed the relationship and left the client feeling that talking to you has been useful and has helped them gain clarity.

- Invite your key clients for a breakfast or after-work session in which you talk about a subject that you know they are struggling with. Use the session to stimulate their thinking as well as to help them to

connect with each other. This contact will help you find out the challenges each of them is facing. If, after the session, you can see how you can help any of them, you may want to contact those individuals directly to propose a piece of work.

- When you read an interesting article that you think may be of interest to some of your clients, send them a copy and tell them which bit of the article made you think of them.

- When you really need more work, ask your clients directly for a referral. Many clients, if they like and value the work we have done for them, will have no problem recommending you to others.

It's important not to plan too much on getting more work by these means. The key objective is to maintain these relationships in which you have invested.

Phase two: contracting

OD practitioners need to have answers to three questions in order to construct a good contract:

- Who is my client?
- What is this job about? What are the tasks, the deliverables, the scope, the methods and the metrics that will indicate success (task contract)?
- What type of relationship contract do I want and need to have with my key client(s) (relationship contract)?

Who is my client?

This is a complex question and often there are no obvious answers in the beginning. Do we have one client, or a constellation of clients? If the latter, how do we draw up the contract? Practitioners often regard the person who invited them in as their chief client to whom they are accountable. The reality is usually much more complicated.

To begin with, there are at least four types of clients with whom you may need to engage and whom you need to consider when creating a contract:

- Principal client – the person with whom you have the primary contact.
- Shadow clients – all those people who surround the principal client, to whom s/he must defer for critical decisions, and who also affect the principal client's 'psychological field'. Shadow clients often have more influence on the consultation than the principal client.

- Peripheral clients – any individual or group or sub-group that has an impact on the project and with whom you need to be involved.
- Stakeholder constellations – including people who may be impacted by the project and who may therefore choose to intervene.

(adapted from Massarik and Pei-Carpenter
NTL Institute material)

To create the right contract, it is essential at the very beginning to find out how the principal client perceives the situation, what problems s/he thinks need to be sorted out, his/her personal vision of the project, and who s/he thinks can help the organization. Helping the principal client to understand the complex client constellation is the first piece of system theory input that you may need to do.

FIGURE 3.3 Summary of tasks and skills for the contracting phase

Tasks	OD practitioner skills
Identify and confirm the relevant client constellations for this project.Get clarity from the different parties about the purpose and deliverables of the project.Have an initial discussion on the options for evaluation and metrics.Agree on the types of issues that the client is responsible for dealing with.Agree on the type of issues that the consultant is responsible for dealing with.Agree the scope (dates and budget) of the project.Agree the internal liaison person who will administer the project.Agree on governance: to whom is the consultant accountable? How often does the person or committee overseeing the project want meetings and reports? (The contract often contains an Excel sheet on timeline, phases, milestones, etc).Agree how you and your client will work as partners: agree the relationship.For external practitioners agree the payment schedule and other formal legal matters, eg copyright, before drawing up the formal contract for both parties to sign.	Ability to use a system approach to analyse the client constellations and to get access to different people for information without appearing to be demanding.Understanding of the evaluation method, ability to guide clients in converting their deliverables to metrics (the client needs to be able to set up the evaluation process and metrics with you).Ability to read the 'emotional' data of how different clients feel about the project.Ability to communicate clearly in order to manage the boundaries between practitioner and client and to establish who is responsible for what.Understanding of the importance of governance and accountability processes.Good project management skills – ability to translate the project scope into a project plan with timelines, milestones, etc.Basic financial management skills to help the client formulate the budget and calculate the resources required.Ability to build trust with the different client individuals and groups in the organization.Ability to coach on the spot as needed.

However, it is important to beware agreeing a contract with your principal client that is based on his/her view of the situation, as often this may land the project in trouble. It is important to ask yourself whether you have sufficient understanding of the complex relationships between the different stakeholders as well as their perspectives on the change objectives before you sign a contract. Lacking a clear, systematic grasp of the situation may cause major problems later on. This concept of who the client is and what work you will need to do with them in contracting is described by Argyris (1970) in his definition of intervention and in Burke's (1997) definition of the OD client:

> To intervene is to enter into an ongoing system of relationships, to come between or among persons, groups, or objects for the purpose of helping them.
>
> I believe that our client in OD consultation is never one individual, regardless of position or role, or any particular group, team or subsystem of the organization, or any combination thereof… The truth is that I have come to think of my client as the relationship and/or interface between individuals and units within and related to the system… this in-between-ness is the main subject of my consulting… I am focusing on the perspective of defining the client as relationships and interfaces rather than individuals and units.

What are the practical solutions to a complex client system in terms of creating a contract? There are two ways I would do it. First, work with the principal client on the issues that s/he is charged with sorting out – eg outcome, targeted group, type of methodology s/he is considering, evaluation metrics – and the political terrain in which the different stakeholders sit. Then I will ask the client how the other stakeholders would see what we have discussed. At that point the principal client becomes aware that s/he alone does not have sufficient data to draw up a substantive contract and suggests getting other stakeholders into the discussion or going to them to check out the content of the contract. Second, if time is an issue, I would handle this situation by 'chunking' the contract, contracting one step at a time with the full intention of bringing in the client constellation for the second stage of contracting.

It is important not to make the principal client feel that you are devaluing their perception, but to help him/her understand that your role is to expand their perception about who needs to get involved in order to obtain a wider perspective before agreeing on the final aims of the project. So my initial contract only covers the first phase of diagnostic work and it specifies a review of the contract once we have analysed the diagnostic data together. This ensures that we enter upon the main contract with greater clarity and a surer footing. Some of you may feel this is a risk as you have not signed the full contract. But without doing the first chunk of work well, the full contract will be obsolete.

What is a task-based contract?

This is the formal agreement between client and practitioner that outlines what the job is about: the core tasks, deliverables, scope, methods, timelines and the metrics that will demonstrate that the project has been carried out successfully.

The task-based contract can have two sections: the first is a commercial document outlining all the legal, regulatory and liabilities issues and including the total cost of the OD project and the payment schedule; the second is a working document that the procurement department will see as supplementary but that will in fact be the main document to which you will refer throughout the life of the project.

The working document is likely to contain the following elements:

1 the nature of the consultancy task;
2 the deliverables and the desired outcomes;
3 the methods you will use to collect data (the diagnostic process);
4 the methods you will use to help to achieve the desired outcomes;
5 the resources the organization is committed to putting into the project;
6 your role, the role of the internal change team, etc, and how each party will contribute towards getting the work done;
7 how you will evaluate and monitor the work;
8 how evaluation will be conducted, by whom, when and based on what metrics;
9 the cost of the contract and the invoice/payment schedule.

What is a relationship contract?

A relationship contract is about how we will manage our relationship while doing the work. In OD, it is just as important to be absolutely clear about the relationship aspects of the work as it is on how the tasks are to be done. The relationship contract covers the collaborative aspects of the work: how you and the client will work together to discover, learn and act to bring about the desired changes, and to troubleshoot any problems that arise, and the feedback mechanism you will use together to ensure that things are on track.

Weisbord (1973: 108) summarizes the importance of having two contracts – the 'task-based' contract and the 'relationship' contract – to ensure a successful project.

> What do I mean by contract? I mean an explicit exchange of expectations, part dialogue, part written document, which clarifies for consultant and client three critical areas:

1 what each expects to get from the relationship;
2 how much time each will invest, when, and at what cost;
3 the ground rules under which the parties will operate.

One approach is to use ground rules that spell out the relationship you expect and the important aspects to which both parties need to pay attention in order to make the relationship work effectively. For example, the roles that each party expects the other to play:

- how you will keep each other informed of what goes on during the journey;
- how you will give feedback to each other;
- how you will evaluate interventions;
- what you will do if you get conflicting instructions from shadow clients;
- how you will work together with the change team – so you don't give confusing messages;
- how much time each party expects to put into the project;
- how frequently you should meet or talk on the phone in the first phase of the project to ensure that you jointly give it enough support;
- what type of coaching and capability up-skilling the client would appreciate from you during the change project;
- in a high-risk project, the conditions that would lead either side to end the contract.

Sometimes, during the process of drawing up the ground rules, your gut instincts tell you whether the relationship will work or not and therefore whether the contract is doable or not. It is important to listen to these messages and to be honest with yourself as well as with the client. You may want to share your doubts and explain clearly why you have them. You may want to help the client reconsider the way the change project has been approached and what changes are needed to ensure that it will work.

The contract as an iterative process

Finally, the contract should *not* be a 'once and for all' document – in that when it has been agreed nobody looks at it again until the project has been completed. The best way to think about contracting is as an iterative process. Weisbord (2006) reminds us that 'contracting is like the seasons – repetitive and continually renewable'. In his view, if we have a long-term contract, we should also have a separate contract for each meeting; if we have a contract with the boss to support his/her division, we also need to extend that and create another contract with the teams before we start work. If something comes up from one of the interventions that leads to another

intervention, we should do a temporary contract with the key groups involved. In other words, the contracting process is never ending. We constantly need to ask ourselves, in each encounter with a group, an individual or the whole system, 'Am I clear about what I am doing now? What are my aims? Do I have enough data to proceed?'

Summary

OD exists to build organizational effectiveness through the relationship between practitioner and client. This relationship is based on an Action Research protocol or the OD consultancy cycle: there are eight phases or necessary 'units of work' that will ensure the two-pronged goals of OD can be achieved.

All OD relationships begin with the initial contact between client and practitioner. Whatever form that takes, important dynamics take place instantly, which will lead to early questions from the client such as, 'Can I trust this person? Will s/he be able to help me? Has s/he managed to grasp the issues I presented so far? Does s/he have sufficient experience to handle a job like this?' Because of these dynamics, it is important that the practitioner takes these early encounters seriously, is aware of the tasks and skills required in this initial contact phase and shows up prepared. The next chapter outlines some of the things practitioners can do to ensure they can emerge from the initial contact with further possibility of proper entry.

When contact leads to successful entry, contracting is the natural next stage. One of the most critical phases of OD process work, this is when you and the client jointly agree the scope and the nature of the work as well as how you want the work done. It is important to remember in OD contracting that the client is the central figure but there may be four other 'client types' apart from the principal client with whom you have to engage. You will need to use the contracting process to not only pin down the content issues but also pin down the form of collaborative relationship you need with the client constellation as you clarify what they really want out of the project. If you do this part well, you help the client to pick up the skills to do more to help their organization in the future. This part of the contract negotiation should be a model of your value and helping behaviour.

Contracting is repetitive and continually renewable. As you employ the Action Research framework and gather data that broadens both your client's and your own understanding of the issues, you will need to revisit the contract. It is this learning attitude that keeps the OD contract a dynamic and 'live' document. Remember to do a relationship contract as well as a task contract.

Having begun the contracting phase, you are now ready to move on to establishing what data you need and how to collect them.

Theories and practices of OD: the diagnostic phase

Diagnosis covers four of the phases in the OD consultancy cycle: data collection, data analysis, data feedback and action planning (see Figure 3.1 in Chapter 3). It is a vital phase in any change and development programme for the following reasons:

- Without proper understanding of the nature of the situation and the issues involved, any planned intervention will miss more than it will hit.

- The person or the group that initiates the programme tends to have a view about the issues from their professional, divisional and personal perspective. So the data they offer, while valid from their perspective, is seldom fully representative from the perspective of the total system.

- You, the consultant, will also have a view about the issues from the type of portfolio you have, your consultancy experiences, the sector in which you specialize, your values, and your personal perspective. So you need to build safeguards to prevent all of the above dictating the change process.

- The diagnostic activities set the stage to shift the organization; therefore what you look for and how you look will either set the organization in motion or entrench it deeper in the old ways.

- Diagnostic activities are intervention activities; therefore designing the right process will fast-track the change process.

In this chapter I will cover the following areas:

1 What is diagnosis in OD? What are the wider aims for the diagnostic process?
2 Summary of the tasks and skills required for the diagnostic phase.
3 A political consideration in managing the diagnostic phase.
4 An outline of the different kinds of data you may need.

5 Data collection methods – how to ensure that the data collection process achieves your aims.

6 Data analysis – how to join different data together.

7 Data feedback and action planning phase.

What is diagnosis in OD? What are the wider aims for the diagnostic process?

Julie Nolan offers a comprehensive definition of diagnosis:

> Organization diagnosis is a collaborative process between organization members and the OD practitioner to collect relevant information, organize it, and feed the data back to the client system in such a way as to build commitment, energy, and direction for action planning... organization diagnosis determines 'what is' and 'what could be'; it seeks ways to bridge the gap... it forms the basis for determining subsequent interventions.
>
> (Nolan, 2006: 193)

The **primary aim** of diagnosis is to gather data that will give both you and your client(s) a clear picture of how to proceed with the change journey, and give you a strong base for decisions about what to do in the intervention phase. However, in OD, gathering data is also an intervention in itself. If it is well planned, the diagnostic process will help you move the organization towards achieving the change objectives. So the **wider aim** in the diagnostic stage is to generate sufficient data to become the catalyst for change in the client system (Tschudy, 2006). Therefore, it is important to bear the wider aims in mind as you set up your diagnostic process. They are:

- In all OD diagnostic processes you need to focus on how people react to any diagnostic intervention as well as on the diagnostic process itself. Burke once suggested that diagnosis is like a child throwing a rock into the pond. Our job as OD practitioners is to watch the ripples that the rock has created and not so much where the rock ends up.

- The whole diagnostic process must be designed to gain the engagement and involvement of those key stakeholders (individuals and groups) whose support is essential to the project. They will need the organization to give them relevant data to act upon, to tap into the diversity within the organization in order to surface the common ground, and to be held together to find collective solutions that are implementable. The mark of your success will be that, at the end of the diagnostic process, people will be ready to move towards the next stage and will be more energetic and enthusiastic. They will have greater ownership of the change agenda, and will be more committed to doing things differently.

● The diagnostic process should also aim to foster and increase connectivity between different stakeholders so that diverse views within the organization will be brought to the surface and people will voluntarily re-examine their own mental models. This can be done through a meaningful dialogue process as well as the opportunity to make sense of the change together. Through the mixing of different members, the diagnostic process can also aim to equalize imbalances in power and to help contain people's anxiety about change.

A note about diagnostic models before I go into the summary of the diagnostic tasks. One of the major challenges in the diagnosis phase is to avoid letting your perceptual lens and the clients' perceptual lens contaminate the data. By that I mean all OD practitioners and all leaders have some implicit if not explicit model in their heads when they inquire into the state of the organization. These lenses are often overlooked because they usually operate subconsciously. Like any 'filters', they either give prominence to some data or anonymity to other data, or lead to other distortions without the practitioners or the organizations realizing it. Since these perceptual lenses do occur naturally (based on history, background, paradigm, personal needs, etc) it is hard to avoid them. However, it is possible to limit their impact on data by a) using multiple stakeholders' perspectives, deliberately surfacing diversity in order to hear the 'balanced' view; b) using some kind of diagnostic model to collect data. The diagnostic models are especially useful to minimize both your own and your client's bias, as well as to guide the sense-making process of the data.

There are many diagnostic frameworks around – they all aim to do different things. Many instruments and frameworks exist to look at individual and team functioning; some exist to look at the health of a team or work group. Other frameworks mainly aim to help the organization to map out their existing culture; others will look at the strength of partnership relationships, or customers' attitude towards the services. Whichever area requires assessment, there seems to be a tool available to do the job. For OD, the types of diagnostic frameworks OD practitioners rely on frequently to support their clients during change are mainly the 'big system' frameworks. Among them, the most well-known ones are Weisbord's Six-Box Model (1976); Nadler and Tushman's Congruence Model (1989); Burke and Litwin's Model (1989, 1992, 2002), and Galbraith's Star Model (2002). There are many more and they are each useful to help organization leaders to look at various aspects of the organization.

The focus of this chapter is mainly on the diagnostic processes, hence I will not cover these frameworks in this book. Also, there are too many frameworks to cover across the different levels of system; and each framework deserves to be learnt from its original source if you want to specialize in it.

Summary of the tasks and skills required by the diagnostic process

The diagnostic phase has four sub-phases that supposedly run sequentially. However, decisions for the later sub-phases, eg data feedback, will make an impact on how you will carry out the first sub-phase – data collection. Figure 4.1 will help to identify how all the issues from each sub-phase should be considered together.

FIGURE 4.1 Summary of tasks and skills for the diagnostic process

Tasks	OD practitioner skills
• Work out what type of data will help move the project forward. • Be ready to advise on data collection methods. • Work out timelines, resources required, and logistics. • Work out the 'political' aspects of data collection, including the types of data that will shift the different interest groups. • Who needs to own the data before they are willing to support the change agenda? • Design the most suitable approaches, methods, etc given the culture of the organization. • Decide who to involve in analysing and making sense of the data, and who should help to feed back the data to those people who are crucial to the decisions that need to be made. • Decide who should be present to hear the feedback, and who should be involved in helping to plan appropriate interventions. • Work out the different intervention options (including methods and processes). • Revisit the contract and revise it to meet the overall needs of the project.	• Ability to diagnose the political terrain within the client system. • Ability to design and carry out data collection. • Ability to teach and coach the internal change team on how to carry out the diagnostic work. • Ability to use a structured framework, big system models, and/or specific theoretical approaches to guide the data analysis. • Ability to analyse feedback data and formulate options. • Ability to give clear presentations (and to support others in doing so). • Ability to facilitate joint action-planning meetings: bring diverse views to the surface, help different groups discover common ground, and enable groups to devise a joint approach to moving forwards to the change target. • Ability to support multiple stakeholder groups in working through the data, holding open discussions, and bringing disagreements to the surface in order to achieve common ground. • Ability to support different stakeholder groups in action planning.

A political consideration in managing the diagnostic phase

The first task of the diagnostic phase for the OD practitioner is to collect 'political' data. Without the political data, it will be like conducting the orchestra without the score. All organizations are political in nature and the existence of informal power bases and alliances, covert decision-making processes, back-room trading, etc, often affect the change processes and outcomes more than the formal approach. Therefore, one of the first things you do when planning diagnosis is to think about the 'end game', ie the successful implementation of the change/developmental programme. Ask yourself, 'In order for the change implementation to be successful, who needs to get involved, be informed and become engaged?' So that by the time you get to the implementation stage, the energy and readiness will be there to achieve the goal. By focusing on the 'end game', you will be brought naturally to the questions listed below which deserve attention. It is never too early to map the political forces that may be blocking the system or to attempt to shift them (it will be useful to refer to Lewin's Field theory and group dynamics for further ideas on this).

As with any planning in OD, the answers to the following questions will help you to start shaping the four diagnostic phases.

General questions

- What is the political landscape of the organization and how will it affect the way the diagnosis should be carried out?
- What are the most effective ways to collect the data, given the resources and time the client organization is willing to commit?
- How can you use this diagnostic process to give people more than they expect and thus increase your credibility even at this early stage?

Data questions

- What data do this project need that are both valid and robust enough to support the case for change?
- Given the culture of the organization, what kind of data will support the client in making informed choices and planning actions? Given the organization's current culture, what framework and processes should you use to structure and analyse the data to ensure they are palatable? For example, hard data will be most useful in an engineering firm because engineers are used to basing their decisions on quantifiable hard data. In contrast, people in an arts and media

organization are likely to dismiss a diagnosis that is based only on hard data. They want to know how things feel, and how their supporters will respond emotionally to any changes.

- What kinds of data do people at different levels of the hierarchy need? What data do you need to increase support and engagement among the different groups?
- Given the hierarchy, how can you ensure that all of the key people at all levels in the organization will be given a voice, without upsetting the people at the top?
- What theoretical and conceptual framework will you use to decide which data collection approach and methods to use, as well as for data analysis, so that the key individuals will regard the data valid and robust?
- If you want external data, who, within the crucial stakeholder groups, can help to make these external data collection processes happen?
- What data collection methods will enable you to use internal agents as much as possible? What training do these internal change agents need?

People engagement questions

There are different people who should increase engagement during the diagnostic phase; the minimum numbers are:

- **Decision makers** – who are the decision makers in the system? Who needs to support this change agenda if the project is to fly?
- **Influential people to the decision makers** – who has direct access to the decision makers as well as having impact on their thinking and action?
- **Key implementers** – who are the key people and groups on whom you depend to ensure the successful implementation of the change?
- **Influential people to the implementers** – who has influence on the implementation key groups, eg their boss, their support colleagues and sometimes the trade union?
- **Key political players** – who, from a political standpoint, is powerful so that you should involve them in designing and carrying out the data collection so they will not only own the data but help to disseminate them?
- **Key functional groups** – which functional group or groups will need to carry most of the burden of implementing? How early do we need to involve them in data collection to ensure their professional functional thinking will be present throughout the project?

Once these different types of people are identified, then we can go about thinking how to engage them at every step during the diagnostic phase so that they will support the change.

How do you use this list of questions to collect your 'political data'? First, you can build some of these questions into your first round of interviews. Second, you can ask your client to bring together a cross-section of people from the organization to help both of you to plan the diagnostic process. These diverse groups can provide data about the actual political context as they bring political data from their own different sections of the organization. If this is not possible, encourage your client to spend a couple of hours with you to do some thinking first. The time you spend together will help your client to realize that they will need help from other people in the organization because they do not have all the answers to those questions.

Whatever way you go about obtaining these political data, your aim is to get answers to complete a planning grid as the example in Figure 4.2 shows. Once you and your client can fill in the grid, then you are ready to move on to the proper planning of the diagnostic process.

FIGURE 4.2 The 'who' planning grid for the diagnostic phase

The 'who' questions	Possible names	Who is best to approach this person?
Who should be in the change team?		
Who should be asked to undertake the various data collection work and form the diagnostic team?		
Who needs to own the data in order to approve the next phase? Who do we need to present data to?		
Who should help us to cut the data gathered and form the data analysis team?		
Who should present the data to the different groups?		
Who should play an important role in and/or sponsor public events (so that s/he is seen as a champion of the change agenda and takes on that role)?		
Who – what mix of people – should attend the different diagnostic events so that they can influence each other?		
Who should mentor individual members of the change team?		

At the beginning of your political diagnostic journey you may only have a hypothesis and hunches to guide you but as the data begin to come in, you will soon get clear insights into what else is needed to help the system shift itself. So the likelihood is that you will need to revisit your hypothesis.

Finally, by asking this set of questions I do not want to give an impression that data collection should be seen mainly from a political perspective. The core of the diagnostic phase is still about getting robust and valid data to help the organization and you to make sound intervention decisions. However, on top of that, we need to pay special attention to human dynamics within a power differential domain. So in the tradition of Action Research theory, System theory, Lewin's Three-Step Change theory, and complexity theories, the diagnostic work is to design your diagnostic processes to facilitate the system to self-organize to move towards the change goals. By using dialogical methods in your diagnostic processes, you would achieve connectivity and diversity of perception of the change. It is never too early to pay attention to and attempt to shift the dominant forces that exist in current groups, which may bind the system into an inability to move towards the state of change.

An outline of the different kinds of data you may need

When talking to clients, often in their mind there are only two types of data you can gather for them: hard and soft. As attractive as they are, these are not the only forms of data. There is, in fact, a diverse range that you can tap into, and for a useful analysis you will need several sources. The range of data available includes:

- **Hard data** – for example, trading figures, the ROI (return of investment) eg from the last two rounds of policy change, the turnover rate of staff talent, percentage of returned goods, the change in the rate of grievances following a development programme in diversity and inclusion for middle management, the industrial accident rate, etc.

- **Soft data** – for example, how members of staff feel about the organization, survey findings about their loyalty and commitment to the organization's proposed change of direction, customer feedback on quality, market research data on brand value, etc.

- **Energy data** – people's current feelings of energy and enthusiasm about the proposed change agenda.

- **Readiness and capability data** – whether the people who have to implement the new agenda are both ready to shift and capable of carrying out the change.

- **Political data** – whether the differences between the various power groups will support and facilitate or block the change agenda.
- **Competency data** – whether those groups that have to shift to a new way of working are able to sustain the change.
- **External data** – the feelings and views of external bodies who have a stake in the organization, about the change agenda.
- **Competitor data** – what competitors are doing in this area and how the change agenda will help or hinder the organization in the market.
- **Professional data** – depending on the focus of the change agenda, you may need to obtain additional 'professional' information, eg financial accounting best practices, HR compensation and rewards best practices, etc.

Theoretical insights on what to look for during diagnosis

As we explore what type of data we will need to collect, the various theoretical perspectives will offer some insight as each theory puts a different emphasis on what to look for. Figure 4.3 illustrates which type of data each theory points us towards. Our job is to consider them all in the beginning of the diagnostic phase.

The reality is, while it is your job to guide the client as to what type of data they will need to look for, ultimately it is the client who will make that decision. But whatever data you and your client choose to collect, the decision should be determined by the following factors:

- The data should be sufficiently robust and valid enough for you and your client to feel confident in planning the necessary actions.
- The data should be valued by the major stakeholders identified from your political analysis.
- The data themselves, and the data collection processes, should have the greatest impact on moving the organization and its people from the current state to the future state.
- The data, once people have discovered and owned them, will give them motivation to steer the organization forward.
- The data should give you confidence (from your own intuition and judgement) to design the intervention.

FIGURE 4.3 The influence of different theoretical perspectives on what to look for

Theories	Type of data we may be looking for
System theory	• System theory is interested in an organization acting like an open system (not as closed system), developing relationships between the organization and all the external stakeholders. • System theory is focused on examining the interface and interdependencies between organization variables, often guided by a system model. Relationships, interactions and interfaces matter, as does the congruence, or lack of, between input, output, and throughput. • The nature of the synergistic quality of relationships between parts, the level of cross-boundary collaboration between parts, the quality of partnership work with outside partners and other subtle aspects of organization life, acting as a system, that become the focus areas of our diagnostic work.
Complexity theories	• Complexity theories steer the diagnostic focus onto how the organization deals with environmental changes, how it adapts itself, and how it responds to the randomness of 'happenings' to the organization. The storyline the organization adopts to tell its unfolding history, the impact of different historical moments on the system, the organization's approach to working with feedback, the type of feedback it deliberately seeks or avoids, its ability to relate to the environment, and its change history will be the focus of your data collection process. • The diagnostic focus will also be on the micro data – what is happening at the local level, and how local areas shift to self-organized ways in times of change; on the richness of connectivity, the rate of information flow, the degree and treatment of diversity, the degree of power differential, and finally how leaders contain anxiety during turbulent times. • The data that emerges using this focus will give us a feel about the flow of energy and movement patterns that may impact on the current project.
Social Constructionism and Appreciative Inquiry	• This theory will be interested in looking for the type of narratives that exist in the organization, the dominant stories that have been told and passed on, the cultural template, the frequency and type of dialogue existing between people, especially during change. • In AI, the diagnostic focus will be on what are the best moments, best practices, best decisions, best anything that enables the organization to uncover its own positive core to support the change agenda. • The diagnosticians will be much more like an anthropologist studying the group, the community and the way they go about constructing reality.

Data collection methods and how to ensure that the data collection process achieves your aims

The choice of data collection methods is really dependent on the nature of the task, the timescale available, the capability of the internal agents whom you would like to get involved, and the type of data that will give you the most robust and valid reading of the situation. Most of the data collection methods used in OD aim to elicit two things: the correct kind of data, and data that will increase the commitment of the people in the organization. Because of that, I seldom use only one method, and instead use a combination of methods in order to get a range of data and methods to satisfy the diverse agendas from different stakeholders. Below are three examples to illustrate how diverse the range of methodology depends on the type and scale of the project:

- In a one-to-one coaching project, the diagnostic process may involve interviews with the coachee's manager, colleagues and clients, as well as 360-degree feedback data and the coachee's self-assessment.

- In a team-building project, the diagnostic process may again include a questionnaire, one-to-one interviews with the team's manager, the manager's manager, other teams with whom the target team work, and other people and teams for whom the target team provide a service, as well as the target team's own self-assessment.

- In a project to help build a more collaborative relationship between two divisions, the diagnostic process will be more complicated. Within each division there will be key people whose views are critical. Each sub-group within the two divisions will have a different role and possibly different views on whether to support the move towards greater collaboration. There will also be other divisions in the organization who may depend on the two target divisions to support them to achieve their performance objectives. There are other divisions that may also have a major influence on the two target divisions. You need to think hard about whom you need to collect data from and the type of data that will help to shift the system.

Different types of data collection methods

There are a range of data collection methods. The following listing is not exhaustive:

- **Existing documents** on different aspects of the organization's performance, eg trading figures, consumer feedback, delivery of strategic priorities, annual reports, regulatory compliance reports, peer assessments, divisional directors' reports, etc.

- **One-to-one interviews** with people who have solid data on the areas you have been asked to study, eg head of consumer care, head of the annual organization review.

- **Single-unit focus groups** to discuss the issues and/or carry out self-assessment of the relevant topics.

- **Mixed-unit focus groups** to share perspectives on how best to manage the change agenda and facilitate cross-fertilization between units.

- **Change agenda posted online** to elicit the views of people in different parts of the organization who will be affected by the project. Their views are posted online too.

- **External visits** to gather valuable information. Take a key group to visit one or more external stakeholder organizations.

- **Direct observation**, spending time observing how people behave within the organization, across different departments and activities.

- **Questionnaires** to allow simultaneous data collection from many people in an organization. You could put your questions on the intranet and invite people to respond. Even though you may not get many replies, just seeing these questions may make people think about the issues.

- **'Theatre of inquiry'**, asking a group of actors to act out varying scenarios that portray different relevant features of the organization, for example, the level of energy, the frequency of collaboration, the quality of interactions, etc. Then ask mixed groups to confirm or disagree with what is portrayed and to offer alternative data.

- **Storyboarding**, asking people to draw stories of what generally happens in selected situations.

- **Graffiti**, placing a whiteboard at the entrance to the building where people can add their comments and pictures about the way they see relevant topics or how they feel about the organization.

- **Storytelling**, looking at the range of significant historical moments in the life of the organization and, through the storytelling, collecting the way the organization has reacted to past change in reference to the future change. This can be published as a 'story book' for leaders to consult with their teams.

- **Culture mapping** of the energy, flow of movement of the system, especially facing major challenges.

- **'High-leverage' type of whole-system methodology.** There are over 60 high-leverage methodologies listed in Holman *et al*'s *The Change Handbook* (2007). For example, running a future search conference to look back to the past, looking at the current perception of the system and 'happenings' internationally, nationally, corporately and personally. Any of the methods can be used as a fantastic data collection method.

Remember, behind all these methods lies the core skill of crafting good questions, and the ability to make pure inquiry. Very few questions or lines of inquiry are neutral. The right question can stimulate openness and deep reflection. As David Cooperrider has often said, our questions are 'fateful'. They can focus our client's attention on the right issues or they can divert them to other issues. All questions plant seeds. So it is important to test run your questions with different people before you go live.

Figure 4.4 is a checklist to help us think through the various decisions in the data collection phase.

FIGURE 4.4 Decisions checklist on choice of data collection method

Checklist questions	Answers
1. What type of data will give the organization informed choices about what next?	
2. In light of the cultural context, which blend or mix of data collection methods are realistic and will gather enough data to analyse successfully?	
3. Who are the 'right' people (from your political data) to do data collection with you? Do they have the capability to carry out the task? If not, what development programme can you put together to equip them?	
4. Some methods require more time and money than others. What is the required timescale and budget for data collection? Can the client afford both?	
5. Do you have the mastery to support the client for the types of data collection methods you've chosen?	

Data analysis – how to join different data together

Once the data collection has been completed, you need to help the clients decide:

- Who will be involved in analysing the data?
- How will the data be analysed?
- Who will help to join up the various bits of data and produce a clear presentation to feed back to the different stakeholders?

As the result of your political analysis, you should have up your sleeve the names of those individuals who will be key to the implementation stage. In my work I always try to involve these people in the data collection. They are then automatically on the team for the analysis. But if that was not possible, you should have already obtained permission from senior people to involve them now. In OD practice, practitioners should not do the analysis of the data alone. The more people you involve within the organization in analysing and understanding the data, the better. Whatever you do, your aim is to ensure as early as possible that the clients (rather than you) own the data. Having said that, I often do the first cut of the data on my own so that I will get a feel for the data in order to a) be one of the people to hold the thread of the progression of the project, and b) assess the complexity of the data – which means if they are very complex, I will know how to set up the process of the data-cutting event.

In a situation where lots of people need to be involved, you may set up one group to do the data collection and another group to do the analysis; it is important to have some overlapping membership between these groups to ensure continuity in the process. Alternatively, if there are many different types of data and a large quantity, it may be a good idea to set up different teams to collect and analyse each type of data, eg one team organizing the questionnaires and processing the results, another running all the focus groups and recording the output, another reviewing all the hard data and reporting trends, etc. You then need to set up an event to bring all this data and insight together.

For bigger projects, the joining up of the data begins much earlier on. When you decide on your temporary change structure, for example, you may want to set up the following:

- A backroom team to coordinate the diagnostic process, whose members clearly understand the kind of data you are chasing and why.
- Clear instructions for everyone involved in collecting and analysing data about what to do, how to do it and the deliverables for which they are responsible.
- Adequate training for those who need it. If you are not sure that they will have all the necessary skills even after training, you will need to bring in someone else to help them.
- Clear data analysis processes so that those teams who collected the data will know what to do with the data they collected.
- A team leader for each data collection and analysis team to oversee the process and serve as a link to the backroom team.

The main purpose of the data analysis and later on the data feedback phases is to:

- Help the clients understand all the emerging facts and themes and the perceptions of those who have provided the data.

- Help the clients move from understanding the data to owning them, so that they are motivated to use the information to plan the next phase of work.
- Ensure that the clients are energized about the future and are committed to moving into the planning and implementation phases. Of course if, from the beginning, you have involved all or most of the key people and groups, there will already be some degree of ownership, even though it may be slowly evolving.

FIGURE 4.5 An example of analysing data

Data collection methods	What people need to do with the data
Review of hard data	Summarize trends and figures. Draw conclusions about the selected areas of enquiry.
Visits to external competitors	Pull together answers to questions and other observations to report on what competitors are doing and why, and the implications for 'our' organization and the change agenda.
Internet questionnaire	Use statistical analysis to show patterns, documentation of common themes that emerge, as well as qualitative statements that demonstrate key themes and statistical trends.
Focus groups using storyboarding	Analyse and report on dominant storylines and themes, backed up by votes from participants on which story they prefer when they are thinking about the future. Clusters of energy about the different storylines.
One-to-one interviews	Extract the patterns across the answers to the same questions, looking at the similarities and differences between certain groups in their perspective towards the same thing.

Figure 4.5 is an example of the data collected from one of my projects and how they were analysed.

When all the different groups have finalized their analysis, you will bring together a representative from each group to pull all the different data into one coherent story. This will then be fed back to the other key individuals and groups in the organization in preparation for the action planning phase.

Data feedback and action planning

Your job during the data feedback phase is to energize the clients so that they want to move to the next stage of the change.

How you organize the data feedback will depend on the target group(s), its size, how much time you have been allocated, the number of sessions you

need to do, and the agreement you have made with the steering group about what decisions can be taken by whom at these sessions. For example, presenting the data to the top team alone (maximum 10 people) in an hour will be very different from presenting them to the three top tiers of leaders (up to 50 people) in half a day.

If I can help it, I generally put off the presentation to the top group until last. Why? Because feeding back the data is still part of the diagnostic process. More data will emerge as people work with this first cut of the data. This is especially important if you are still aiming to expand the circle of engagement at this point to those who have so far managed to avoid attending any of the diagnostic sessions. Their reactions to the data and the sense they make of them will give you more information to work with.

I prefer to give the top team the full works only after we have gathered all the data and energy from the other feedback sessions so that sufficient data are available to create the first draft of the action plan. This means that by the time the feedback gets to the board you will be in a position to tell the whole story. If the data are presented to the board too early and the board starts making decisions on the basis of these preliminary data, it will be difficult to approach the other feedback sessions with genuinely open options.

There are many ways to present the data. The most important thing is to keep the purpose of this event in mind: your aim is to transfer the data to the clients and to increase their energy so that they want to commit to doing things differently.

The feedback data should be summarized in as simple a form as possible, but 'without sacrificing the client's ability to grasp the systemic meanings of the information' (Burke, 1982: 209). In other words, you need to avoid data overload but without sacrificing the validity of the data. You could try being creative about the presentation; for example if you used the 'theatre of inquiry' method during diagnosis, you could get the same actors to act out the themes that have emerged.

Pay attention to the psychological aspects in the data feedback session

Nadler (1977) suggested that people often enter into data feedback sessions with some or all of the following feelings:

- anxiety, a degree of uncertainty, not knowing exactly what to expect;
- defensiveness, worry that they may hear something negative and may be attacked;
- fear – people may have all sorts of reasons to be afraid, from undesirable outcomes to fear of retribution;
- hope, that what they hear may improve the situation and be the beginning of a move towards an exciting future.

You need to enable people to bring these feelings to the surface without letting the meeting be derailed.

Your perspective

It is important to make sure that your personal perspective and your own interpretation of the data do not get mixed up with the actual data. The data should be kept as 'pure' as possible. However, you need to have your own interpretation ready so that you can offer it after the initial data have been presented and the different groups have had a chance to discuss them and share what the data mean to them. Figure 4.6 should help you plan your presentation of the data in the feedback session.

FIGURE 4.6 A sample presentation outline

Session	Process
Opening remarks	• Summarize for the group (as a reminder): – the commissioning of the project; – the objectives of this phase; – what you did and why (methodology); – who has been involved (total number of people and type of people where data are collected). • State the aim of this session and give an outline of the meeting.
Presentation of the data	• One group at a time followed by questions and answers. • Note: if there are a lot of sub-groups they should all give their presentations first, followed by all the questions and answers together.
Break the audience into smaller groups to discuss these questions	• What are the key points that stand out for me? Why? • What are the most surprising points? • How do I feel about what I have heard? • What do I think are the most crucial data that we as an organization should pay attention to?
Bring the groups back together	• Ask the groups to report verbally what they have heard or use big pinboards to stick their answers on. • When everyone has reported, facilitate a whole group conversation on the four questions above. Your aim is for the group to come to some agreement on what to do next.
Vote	• People vote on the areas where actions would be required as they emerged from the discussion and how best to tackle them.
Open space forum (optional)	• (If time allows) people decide which action area they want to work on and discuss how they will begin.
Summary of actions (optional)	• Involve the group in finalizing the action planning processes. Be very clear about the decision-making process necessary for the plan to be approved and resourced. Be clear about how people in the organization will hear of the outcomes from today.

I included the action planning in Figure 4.6 as optional, because I think people often need 'brewing' time to process the data and hence are not ready to move into action planning. So while on some occasions people may want to move to action planning, your position as a consultant should be to ensure that people have sufficient time to think over the data and talk to each other before you push them to do the final action planning.

Summary

OD efforts always begin with the understanding of the unique nature and circumstances of the client system – on their terms and context. To have data to show your clients and you how to work with the reality of the whole system is very important. The quality of diagnosis will affect how your clients plan the approach to change. The ways you collect the data and the quality of the data will either support or limit your intervention possibilities and ultimately the overall direction of change. So, if you the practitioner handled this process well, through time you will be passing important skills and know-how to the client organization on how to generate ongoing data for ongoing decisions they need to make.

It is also important to remember that diagnosis is never a pure data-gathering process. As I quoted Lewin before, to study a system is to change it. Once you start the inquiry process, you start the disturbance process – setting up the frame for people to question the status quo. If you link different parts of the system together to discuss the future of the organization, you will be moving the system to a place they have never been. If you ask people to go and study the clients they serve, through those face-to-face encounters they will gain new knowledge about how to serve and delight clients more – hence they will want to commit to do things differently. Therefore, you need to plan the diagnostic process in a systematic way, using an action research approach to increase the involvement of the members of the system; mixing the people up, changing the field of the environment, helping them discover their positive core and watching the whole process with the complexity perspective – watching for opportunities and looking to light little fires everywhere will promote self-organizing so that once the people have caught on to the vision and the logic, they will move the system towards the goals. When that happens, the boundary between diagnosis and intervention becomes very thin. Therefore, in the next chapter you will find many of the criteria for effective intervention will be applicable to this phase also.

Theories and practices of OD: the intervention phase

When the diagnosis is complete and the analysis of the current state has been fed back, the client is now ready to work with the practitioner to identify what steps they should take to reach the ideal future state the system has identified. This phase of work is the action thrust of OD – putting our 'theory into practice'. This is where our theory, models, conceptual frame of reference of organization, group and individual, and our values will be put to use to help the client system to grow, change and adapt.

The type of action can vary from a one-to-one coaching session to a two-day team-building event; from a six-month customer support process transformation project to a two-year global restructuring exercise. The wide range of interventions that practitioners use, coupled with the prolific growth of methods and technology since the inception of OD, makes the documentation of intervention techniques very challenging. But it is this evolution of OD intervention that constitutes one of the most exciting growths of the field.

Intervention must not be associated only with fixing problems. During good and healthy times, it is just as important for organizations, groups, or individuals to consider undertaking various interventions as part of regular maintenance work so that the system will continue to consolidate and build on its strengths in anticipation of future changes. Using Appreciative Inquiry to discover the best of the past to create the best of the future is a great example of that. To intervene is to shift, and you can shift a system from good to great as well as from poor to good.

Behind the deployment of tools and techniques lies the intricate mix of the practitioners' theoretical assumptions, judgement, values, use of self, and their collaborative stance with clients. It is the combination of all these factors that enables practitioners to execute this phase with success.

This is not a chapter on a range of specific interventions; rather, it is a 'how to' chapter on what it takes to design intervention from first principles. By covering these areas, I hope you will have fun and confidence in designing

effective interventions that serve your client system well, and through your experience choose, with clear information, in which level of system intervention you may want to specialize.

In this chapter, I will cover the following areas:

1 definition of intervention, and the key criteria of OD intervention;

2 summary of the tasks and skills required in intervention;

3 cross-dimensional design of intervention – review of the three 'cubes of intervention' frameworks;

4 levels and types of interventions;

5 summary of cross-dimensional checklist based on concepts from the three cubes, levels and types of intervention;

6 building an intervention strategy – construction of criteria for effective intervention design.

Definition of intervention and the key criteria of OD intervention

The term **OD interventions** refers to the range of planned activities that clients and OD practitioners design and execute together during the course of an Organization Development programme for the purpose of improvement. The following definitions from the gurus of OD help to map out the characteristics of intervention:

> The term intervention refers to a set of sequenced planned actions or events intended to help an organization increase its effectiveness. Intervention purposely disrupts the status quo; they are deliberate attempts to change an organization or sub-unit toward a different and more effective state.
> (Cummings and Worley, 2001: 142)

> An intervention is a change effort or a change process. It implies an intentional entry into an ongoing system for the purpose of initiating or introducing change.
> (Rothwell *et al*, 1995: 11)

> OD interventions are sets of structured activities in which selected organizational units engage in a sequence of tasks that will lead to organizational improvement. Interventions are actions taken to produce desired changes.
> (French and Bell 1999: 118)

> To intervene is to enter into an ongoing system of relationships, to come between or among persons, groups, or objects for the purpose of helping them. There is an important implicit assumption in the definition that should be made explicit: the system exists independently of the intervener.
> (Argyris 1970: 15)

Composite definition: If we pull together the various elements from the above definitions to form a composite definition, then to intervene is to:

- enter into an existing system;
- with a structured and planned activity;
- directed at a targeted person, or group, or inter-groups or an entire organization;
- to disturb the status quo and to shift the system towards a different state;
- with the goal of improvement and development.

Summary of the tasks and skills required in intervention

Out of the eight units of work in the OD cycle, this is the most difficult phase to summarize. The list of tasks that need to be done during this phase and the type of skills and knowledge that an OD practitioner needs to have depend on the type of intervention they are doing. For example, if we are asked to support an organization to move from a functional silo to a cross-process bubble in organization structure, what needs to be done will be very different from planning a 700-delegate strategic planning conference, which again will be different from planning a four-day leadership away day to decide the future of the organization. So in the section below, I will attempt to summarize the tasks and the skills required of the intervention phase mainly from a more complex project lens. You will need to scale down or adapt the list according to the type of intervention project you will be doing.

I advise readers to do a tailor-made version of Figure 5.1 for every project they engage in. You can change the second column to the 'change team' competences. By having a document like this (it is best to do this with your client), you will educate the clients on how to think systematically about intervention.

Cross-dimensional design of intervention – review of the three 'cubes of intervention' frameworks

In the design of intervention, there are many variables (dimensions) that the intervener needs to consider before s/he can arrive at the decisions of what tools and methods to use. This cross referencing of various variables of intervention was exactly what some of the early founders attempted to do – by classifying different types of OD intervention in a three-dimensional model. In this section I will present three, three-dimensional cubes which

FIGURE 5.1 Tasks and skills required for the intervention phase

Tasks	OD practitioner skills
• Based on the data feedback and action-planning decision, work with client to identify the range of interventions that may help the organization to achieve its change objectives. • Once the decision is made, take the lead to design the intervention options identified based on clear theoretical and methodological premises. Give advice on the sequencing of intervention. • Seek approval (even if you are working jointly with the internal client group) from key decision makers of the detail design, especially if the intervention carries a degree of risk. • Work out an implementation plan – calculate level of resources needed, on what, with whom. Design a communication plan to enrol participation, set up an event management team, set up central administrative back-up. • Train internal people to carry out the intervention if that is the plan, or brief external providers who are brought in to execute the intervention. • Set up a troubleshooting team (of which you will be a member) to coordinate the execution of the various interventions (if it is a complex set of interventions). • Set up monitoring processes and mechanisms on the impact of the intervention, adjusting the methodology to achieve early success. • Put together a communication resource group and feed them monitoring data so that they are ready to communicate the early visible success to the organization to fuel further momentum. • Stay watchful of the slow adopting groups and see what further support they need in order to be more engaged with the change agenda. • Coordinate the different implementation teams to ensure they are all pulling in the same direction. • Set up a temporary structure and processes to collect evaluative data.	• Provide thought and methodological leadership in the range of interventions the organization considers using (or at least know enough to guide the system in the decision or call in experts in the field to support the design). • Bring sufficient theoretical grasp to the design stage so that the methods designed are guided by theoretical insight. • Have sufficient experience to know how to sequence intervention – advise on which targeted group should go first to gain sufficient momentum for the intervention to spread in an effective way. • Ability to scope out implementation plans – helping client to calculate the practical resources needed to execute the interventions and support the team to work out the logistics. • A commitment to collaborative practice by sharing with clients what and how the intervention will work and involve them in making different decisions at every stage – remember this is the client's work. • A good trainer/developer – design development programme to train internal agents if it is appropriate for them to support the execution of the intervention. • Pay attention to the 'here and now' experience during the intervention event – yours and theirs – and track whether the intended outcomes are being achieved; if not, adjust course if necessary. • Ability to use your presence as a 'safe container' for the clients during the intervention phase as both survival and learning anxiety will be high. • Ability to help clients to treat resistance as something to be understood and worked with as experience, not to be conquered. • Share responsibility rather than build dependency during the intervention phase. • Prepare client to be independent to support and renew itself by the time the intervention phase is done.

will help interveners to start thinking cross-dimensionally when doing design. Though some may think these early authors' intellectual work a bit out of date since there are a growing number of sophisticated intervention techniques as OD jobs have become more complex, I believe the intellectual rigour behind these three cubes will show us how to think about intervention from first principle. Hence I will briefly review three typologies and extract from them the various dimensions for practical application towards building an intervention strategy.

Schmuck and Miles (1976)

They were the first to devise a three-dimensional model, a cube which encouraged practitioners to think about the interaction between three things: a) the *diagnosed problem*; b) the *focus of attention*; c) the *mode of intervention*. See Figure 5.2 to understand how the cube works.

For example, if the diagnosed problem is decision making, and the focus of attention is a team, then the mode of intervention can be either process consultation and coaching or training as well. If the diagnosed problem is culture and climate, and the focus of attention is the total organization, then the model of intervention can be the establishment of an OD task force.

FIGURE 5.2 The OD cube

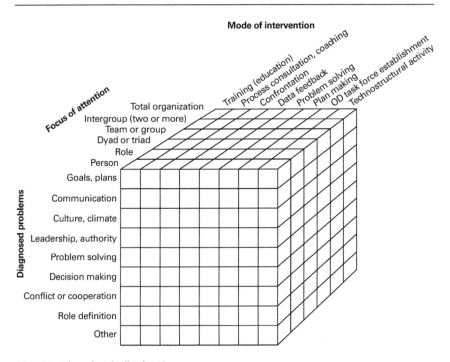

SOURCE: Schmuck and Miles (1976).

By focusing on these three specific types – *problems/issues* – *targeted at whom* – *mode of intervention*, they progressed from the 'single' category typology attempted by Burke and Hornstein earlier (1972), who listed just six categories of intervention: team building, managing conflict, survey feedback, techno-structural, training and miscellaneous, and then clustered different interventions under each of those categories.

Blake and Mouton (1985)

The next major attempt to classify intervention was made by Blake and Mouton (1985) who built the most comprehensive typology of intervention, called the Consulcube, which is also a three-dimension cube but with 100 cells. The three dimensions they outlined are:

First, the *kind of intervention* (what the consultant does) – which includes five basic types:

- **Acceptant** – the consultant gives the client a sense of worth, value, acceptance and support so that they can grow and get on.
- **Catalytic** – the consultant helps the client to generate data and information to restructure the client's perception.
- **Confrontation** – the consultant points out value discrepancies in the client's beliefs and actions.
- **Prescription** – the consultant tells the client what to do to solve the problem.
- **Theories and principles** – the consultant teaches the client relevant behavioural science theory so that the client can learn to diagnose and solve their own problem.

Second, the *focal issues* causing the client's problems; Blake and Mouton have outlined four focal areas: power and authority; morale and cohesion; norms and standards of conduct; goals and objectives.

Third, the *units of change*, which is the target of the consultation. Five units are proposed: individual, group, intergroup, organization and larger social systems such as a community or even a society.

Figure 5.3 shows how this cube works. For example, if you have a group (unit of change) with problems in the areas of goals and objectives (focal issues), and after diagnosis the consultant thinks his/her most suitable role is theory and principle (kinds of intervention) – so uses behavioural principles to help the group to diagnose why they have the confusion over goals and objectives. Behind that choice may lie the consultant's hypothesis, eg there is covert conflict within the team which manifests itself as an objective problem. Or, if the consultant has diagnosed that the problem lies around team morale, then s/he may decide to deliver an acceptant style to give them encouragement so that the team will be able to keep going.

FIGURE 5.3 Blake and Mouton's Consulcube model

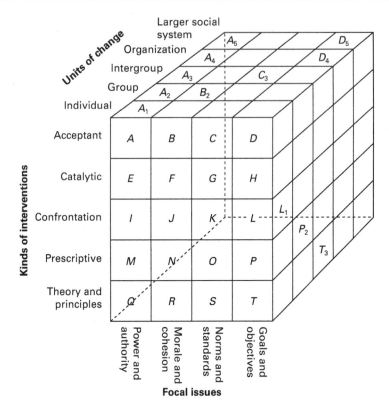

SOURCE: Blake and Mouton (1976). Reproduced by permission of Scientific Methods, Inc.

Reddy's cube (1994)

W. Brendan Reddy devoted an entire book to this intervention cube. The Reddy cube as shown in Figure 5.4 contains:

- **Focus of intervention** – group, interpersonal, individual.
- **Type of intervention:**
 - cognitive: abstract, intellectual or ideas oriented;
 - skill and activity: suggest appropriate skill learning and training;
 - behaviour description: the consultant describes what s/he has observed in terms of behaviour;
 - emotional/reflective: the consultant describes the emotional and feeling component within the group;
 - interpretive: making a hypothesis or understanding of what is occurring at a dynamic level with the intent to prompt members to discuss what they think and feel about what is transpiring.

FIGURE 5.4 Reddy's Intervention Cube

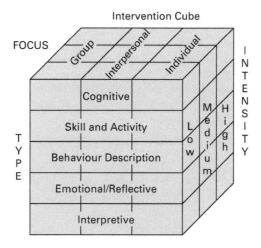

SOURCE: Reddy (1994: 82).

- **Level of intensity** – (low, medium, high) by level of intensity, Reddy means, 'the strength, power or impact of the intervention as the consultant intends it' (Reddy 1994: 83).

While this cube is mainly focused on the work that process consultants do with groups, the concept does have a wider application than process consultation. For example, if the focus of the intervention is at the interpersonal level, and the type of intervention is interpretive (sharing a hunch, a hypothesis to prompt the two individuals to work through the issues), then the level of intensity may have to be high because low-level intensity may not be able to open up the barriers.

What do the three cubes offer?

It is amazing that almost 35 years ago Schmuck and Miles began the first attempt to help practitioners to think three-dimensionally about intervention. What these three cubes have done is given practitioners both the *imagination* and the *framework* to tailor-make their own theoretical cube to guide in robust design. There are three things we can do to reap the benefits of these pioneers' work.

First, I have pulled together each of the three dimensions from each of the cubes to form a six category checklist which can serve as a useful pre-design checklist, as shown in Figure 5.5.

FIGURE 5.5 Pre-design checklist from the three cubes

1. What are the diagnosed problems?
2. What are the focal issues (drill down into specific areas where the issues live)?
3. What is the focus of attention? Or what is the unit of change – or level of system the intervention aims at?
4. What is the necessary level of intensity in order to get the work done?
5. What is the necessary intervention role of the consultant?
6. What is the mode of intervention?

Second, you can keep the conceptual framework of the cube, but replace their categories with those that are important to you theoretically to build your own intervention cube/model. Once you have done that, you will have a tool or map to share with your clients.

Third, you can take the conceptual frameworks that I have gathered from the three cubes and add other types and levels variables to start building a tailor-made intervention strategy plan for your client. Figure 5.8 joins the concepts from the three cubes and the 'types' to make a summary checklist for designing intervention.

Levels and types of interventions

Now that we understand the cross-dimensional way of thinking about intervention design, I want to expand the list of variables (dimensions) that interveners need to consider. This is a complex topic, and in the section below I will cover the following areas:

1 What does 'levels of system' mean in intervention design?
2 What does 'types' of intervention mean?
3 Bringing together types and levels to form the criteria list for effective intervention.
4 Intervention tools and techniques by levels.

What does 'levels of system' mean in intervention design?

In intervention, attention needs to be paid to the level of system at which you are intervening. By level of system, I mean the 'unit of change' you are aiming at, which can range from an individual, to a team, to an organization. Activities aimed at different levels will vary significantly in their intended impact. In OD, according to Phil Mix, Dean of NTL OD programme, there

are at least nine levels of system an intervener has to contend with, and it is an OD belief that unless an intervention can penetrate at least three levels of system, sustainable change will be difficult to obtain. So, the more levels of system an intervention activity can impact the better the outcome will be. But in the midst of a wide cast, there still has to be a primary target or unit of change that your intervention should aim for.

In designing work, you need to ask yourself, 'In order for this change to be effective, in how many levels of system will I need to intervene, and which is the primary level?'

Let's take a look at the nine levels of system:

- **Intra-personal level** – focus is on the individual. Often it involves shifting the mindset, the paradigm, the values and the deep assumptions from which the person operates, or it focuses on unblocking, eg enabling individuals to vent all the pent-up emotion so that they can move on to the next stage of development.

- **Interpersonal level** – the focus is between individuals, where relationships between the two need to be sorted out, eg shifting from competitive to collaborative, or where certain pairs and partners need to be supported to get along better and work together more effectively for the benefit of the organization.

- **Intra-group level** – many sub-groups within the same unit (three-regional group within the sales department) need to learn to communicate more clearly, share knowledge, collaborate more effectively so that they know how to work together better in order to improve the collective performance level of that same unit.

- **Intergroup level** – two units within the same division (eg strategist and OD professional who sit together under the executive support office) need to work more seamlessly in order to serve the client more effectively and not let destructive conflict affect their work output. Or the black and white colleagues in the campaigning department of a third-world charity. To help these groups to work differently will be an intergroup intervention.

- **Intra-unit level** – the various sub-units within the same function, eg the HR partners, the L&D unit, the compensation and benefit function, etc, need to learn how to support each other's work and use procedures and processes so that their functional output will be coherent and acceptable to other divisions.

- **Inter-unit level** – different divisions, eg the marketing and sales divisions or the campaigning and fundraising divisions, need to know each other's core work and learn to dovetail their work in such a way that will give the organization the edge to be successful.

- **Bounded system level** – the environment changes so much that the whole organization needs to adjust itself and adopt a new strategy and mission to ensure survival in the environment.

- **System network level** – a number of organizations, eg organizations dealing with the elderly, get together to co-construct their vision for elderly care for the nation by 2015.

- **Total system in its environment level** – an organization brings together all its suppliers, its customers, its funders, its partners, its staff and its volunteers to search for a viable future that allows them to continue to make significant impact in their core mission.

Having identified what level of system, next the intervener has to identify what type of intervention you can use.

What does 'type' of intervention mean?

There are many ways to talk about the 'types' of intervention. It is the pursuit of the various dimensions of 'type' that will lead practitioners to crucial insights about issues to address when designing intervention.

In the literature, when writers talk about 'types of intervention', they are referring to any of the seven concepts:

- **Level of system** – the individual, interpersonal, group, inter-group, organization, community or society at large towards whom we direct the intervention.

- **The targeted area of change** – as in Reddy's cube (1994). For example, a type of intervention that will help to increase knowledge and understanding of something (cognitive), or to increase ability to do something (skill and activity), or to change current behaviour (behaviour description), or release pent-up emotions and learn how to use emotion to keep us reflective (emotional/reflective), or paradigm shift (interpretive).

- **Task focused or process focused** – for task-focused intervention, people get together to learn how to create a plan, solve a problem, improve a product, or increase efficiency. For process-focused intervention, people get together to work at resolving a conflict, learn how to get the best out of working in a diverse team, learn to see the need of the whole community before working to co-construct the future of the community, etc. Of course you can always do both, eg learn the process that helps a team to work effectively in improving the services so that they can repeat the process again.

- **Structured versus unstructured intervention** – structured are those interventions that are highly planned with every logistical detail sorted; where all delegates will be steered towards activities and there is probably a detailed project plan to 'produce' the event. In the unstructured emergence event there is a general plan, but the event is mainly set up for delegates to self-organize themselves to go wherever their energy will take them. Among unstructured interventions, the human laboratory is one of the most well known. Of course you can

have a highly structured and emergence event like the Appreciative Inquiry Summit.

- **The channel through which the intervention is delivered** – some interventions are delivered through lecture and input, others are delivered mainly as experiential events. Others still are delivered as a joint dialogue and discussion-style event, or through participation in arts, music and theatre, outdoor pursuit, external visit, etc.

- **Size of the group** – in the case of small group or large group, or a medium-sized group, eg with two divisions being joined together, or for a large group – the whole organization.

- **Tools and techniques** that we use to execute our intervention strategy.

It is vital to get clarity as to a) which level of system the intervention is supposed to aim for; and b) how many levels of system the package of intervention needs to intervene in to get sustainability.

Bringing together 'types' and 'levels' to form a criteria list for effective intervention

Why am I interested in the classification of types of intervention? Because by combing through the various 'type' questions, I believe you can get to the heart of the key intervention design issues you will need to address. I will summarize the different dimensions of 'types' to form a design checklist for you to test (Figure 5.6). Let's see whether it makes sense to you.

By working through this list of questions, you will be pointed to increasingly detailed design. These questions are not meant to be used alone; the checklist should be thought of as a whole – with one question cross-referencing to another.

FIGURE 5.6 Criteria list for designing effective intervention based on the 'types' questions

- What **level of system** should our intervention aim for?
- What are the **target areas of change**? What specific areas do we need to address?
- Should the event be more **task focused**? If so, what task do we need to get the participants to undertake and learn? Or should it be **process focused**? If so, what process does the target group need to get better at?
- Given what we know about the group and the culture of the organization, should the event be tightly **structured** or should it be more **emergent**? What would suit this group better? What will give us a better outcome?
- What will be the best **channel** to deliver our intervention? What combination of channels will work best?
- What **size of group** should we deliver this intervention to? The whole system at once, or smaller groups first and then end with a large group?
- What **tools and techniques** come naturally to mind for this intervention?

For example, if the target area of the intervention is to increase under-standing and knowledge (cognition), then the channels through which the intervention is delivered will include input, lecture (which tends to be tightly structured), be task focused, and the event can probably tolerate a larger-sized group. But if the target area is shifting paradigm, then the intervention should be experiential, loosely structured, take place within a small group, and with a clear aim at the intrapersonal level of system.

Intervention tools and techniques by levels

Having gone through the levels and types of intervention, you next move is to help the client to consider a range of tools and techniques, or best still to start designing a tailor-made intervention. Figure 5.7 gives a sample of intervention that you may want to show your client. But it is important to say that in spite of the diversity that can exist, it is not an exhaustive listing of intervention.

Other ranges of large group methodology are not shown here. There are 68 methods that are documented in Holman *et al*'s *The Change Handbook* (2007).

Summary of cross-dimensional checklist based on concepts from the three cubes, levels and types of intervention

Figure 5.8 summarizes the work of the three, three-dimensional cubes, plus the types and levels of intervention have been reviewed. They will be useful as a checklist and later on to help build the intervention strategy.

Figure 5.9 contains a further list of factors that an intervener needs to consider at the design stage which were not covered in the above two lists.

Now that I have these three checklists, I have sufficient material to pull together to build the intervention strategy. But before that, I have three final points about the approach most experienced practitioners will take in designing intervention:

- Always use a design checklist to work with the client to ensure you have all the information you need before doing the design.

- Always adapt or tailor-make whatever methods fit the consulting situation. Never take a 'tool off the shelf' and apply it straight to the client.

- Always have your design template, protocol and theories to refer to when you choose, adapt, and design your intervention. Do not be bounded by tools and techniques you have mastery of.

FIGURE 5.7 A sample of types of intervention by level

Individual intervention	Interpersonal intervention	Group intervention	Intergroup intervention	Total system/ organization intervention
• Coaching • Mentoring • T group • Counselling • Life and career planning support • Education • Behavioural modelling • Individual consultation	• Third-party conflict resolution • Role negotiation • Process consultation • Storytelling from each side • Interdependency exercise • Role swapping • Job shadowing • Partnership work	• Team building • Responsibility charting • Process consultation • Role analysis • Start-up team-building activities • Visioning • Decision-making improvement • Unstructured group training	• Interface discussion • Third-party peacemaking at group level • Survey feedback to each other • Intergroup activities to build interdependence awareness • Restructuring of sub-units	• Organization design • Appreciative inquiry summit • Future search • Organizational mirroring • Real-time strategic change • Partnership and customer conference

FIGURE 5.8 Summary checklists for intervention design – from three cubes and types of intervention

The checklist from reviewing the 'types' of intervention	The checklist from the three OD cubes
• What level of system should our intervention aim for? • What are the target areas of change? • Should the event be more task focused? If so, what task do we need the participants to learn? Should it be process focused? If so, what process does the target group need to get better at? • Given what we know about the group, should the event be tightly structured or should it be more emergent? What would suit this group better? What will give us a better outcome? • What is the best channel to deliver our intervention? What combination of channels will work best? • What size of group should we deliver this intervention to? The whole system at once? Or smaller groups first, ending with a large group?	• What are the diagnosed problems? • What are the focal issues? (Drill down into specific areas where the issues live.) • What is the focus of attention or the unit of change – or level of system the intervention aims to intervene at? And to achieve what? • What is the level of intensity? • What is the necessary intervention role of the consultant? • What is the mode of intervention?

FIGURE 5.9 Further factors to be considered when designing intervention

The intervener also needs to consider the following at design stage
• What stands out from the diagnostic data and intuitive judgement of the practitioners (and the internal change team) as to what the implications are of the data on the type, sequence, and timing of the intervention? • Various design options based on the diverse theoretical perspectives. • Various design options based on resources (time, and monetary budget) issues. • Speed at which the intervention needs to be completed. • Capability and readiness issues of the system when running the intervention. • How deep (level of risk) the intervention should go to achieve the desired outcome. • Level of anxiety the system has about the change, hence the change intervention. • What process would help to increase the autonomy of the system?

Building an intervention strategy – construction of criteria for effective intervention design

The process of deciding what intervention we need to shift the system and how to do the design work is the core work of OD practitioners. So doing intervention well for an OD practitioner is much more than reaching into the 'kit bag' and pulling out an intervention or two to apply to the client. There are many steps you will need to take in order to produce the intervention strategy which French and Bell (1999: 146) called the 'overall game plan' for intervention. According to them, an intervention strategy plan is something that will help the intervener:

> to integrate the problems or opportunity to be addressed, the desired outcomes of the programme, and the sequencing and timing of the various interventions. Intervention strategies are based on diagnosis and the goals desired by the client system.

The intervention strategy is an outcome document which summarizes your intent and then guides you and your clients to execute and monitor those intended intervention(s). But to get there, the intervener needs to proceed through four major steps. In this section, I will discuss each of the four steps and show how they contribute to the construction of an intervention strategy. The four steps are:

1 go through the *pre-design list of questions* (refer to Figure 5.5);

2 work through the list of design questions (refer to Figures 5.6, 5.7);

3 design criteria that OD practitioners need to reference (refer to Figures 5.6, 5.7, 5.8);

4 pull together all the interventions we have planned and do a sequencing of the events.

Before I go through the four steps, some of you may be asking: 'Aren't these steps a bit over the top, especially when I am only doing a one-off small-scale job?' The answer is yes, it can be over the top because intervention strategies are really only needed for large-scale projects. However, the discipline of going through the four steps, at least from my experience, offers a level of confidence to a practitioner that is hard to get from doing anything else. So for me, if I am doing a half-day board meeting or a three-day leadership retreat, I want to go through the thinking process with my client so that when we arrive at the final programme we will both have the confidence that rigorous thinking has been applied. My encouragement to you is to try to go through the four steps to get the hang of the first basic principles in intervention design. After doing it a few times, you will have the confidence to dovetail the four steps into a personalized approach to intervention design.

Go through the pre-design list of questions

- What are the objectives of the intervention? What do we want to achieve?
- What are the diagnosed problems?
- What is the focus of attention? Or what is the unit of change/level of system the intervention aims to intervene at? And to achieve what?
- What are the targeted areas of change (the focal issues) that the intervention needs to deliver?
- What stands out from the diagnostic data and intuitive judgement by the practitioners (and the internal change team) as to the implication of the data on the type, sequence and timing of the intervention?
- What is the level of anxiety within the system which we need to bear in mind when we design the intervention?
- What is the level of readiness and capability of the system?
- How much risk can the system handle given their state of readiness and capability?
- What process would help to improve the autonomy of the system?

How would you use this list? First, it will be important for you to spend a couple of hours looking at the diagnostic data, recall all the conversations you have had with various clients, and think the data through this list of questions. Second, if you are working with an internal change team, it is best for you to call a meeting to take them through the list of questions to secure answers from clients. When is the best time to do this? I have found doing this at the end of a data feedback session is almost impossible, as people are a) overwhelmed by the data they have just heard, and b) need time to think about the data – the brewing time. So I leave it until a few days after the data feedback meeting.

Once you and your client have gone through the above list of questions, you have sufficient information to begin doing the design. Depending upon what you have agreed with your clients, you will either go away to come up with some options so that in the next meeting you and your clients can look at the options and make some preliminary decisions as to what next, or you will bring together an internal team to jointly work on the design.

Whatever your approach, you still need to carve out a couple of hours to hide in a room going through the next set of design questions. At first, some of these questions may seem to be a bit repetitive (because they are), but it is at this stage that you need to come up with much more granular answers than from the first round to these questions.

Review and answer the list of questions on design

Purpose, levels, scope:

- What are we trying to achieve? What metrics would tell us we have been successful?
- What level of system should our intervention aim for? How many levels of system need intervention in order to secure sustainable results?
- What are the target areas of change? Do different targeted areas need different types of intervention?
- Should the event be more task focused? If so, what task do we need the participants to practice and learn? Or should it be process focused, if so, what process does the target group need to get better at?

Channels, groups, size:

- Given what we know about the group, should the event be tightly structured or should it more emergent? What would suit this group better? What will give us a better outcome?
- What is the best channel to deliver our intervention? What combination of channels will work best?
- What size of group should we deliver this intervention to? Should we do the whole system in one go, or smaller groups first then end with a whole-system large group?

Design options based on theory, resources, speed, system capability and psychology:

- What various design options can we come up with based on the diverse theoretical perspectives?
- What design options can we consider based on available resources (time and budget) that the organization has made available?
- What design options can we consider given the nature of the industry, eg is it possible for them to release everyone in that function to come together?
- At what speed does the intervention need to be completed?
- Does the system have the capability and readiness if we decide to run this intervention?
- How deep (level of risk) does the intervention need to go in order to achieve the desired outcome?

Role of consultant, mode of intervention, delivered by whom:

- What is the necessary intervention role of the consultant?
- What is the mode of intervention?
- Who should deliver the intervention?

How do you use this list? First, use it to help yourself to identify the options of intervention. Again, you will need to spend a couple of hours thinking through these design questions. Hopefully at the end, a couple of design options will emerge for you to develop further before taking it to the client for discussion. For each option of intervention you come up with, it would be great if you can write a brief about how the process works, what it aims to achieve, who can run the intervention, and what resources (people, money and venue) it needs. If there are pros and cons, be prepared to share those too. It would be professional for you to bring sufficient details on each option to enable the client(s) to make informed choices and decisions.

Second, in your next client meeting you may consider spending up to 30 minutes taking your client through the list of design questions in order to educate them about the process of design. By doing that, you will help to equip them to work with you as competent partners to make informed choices. You could even set up a specific event to up-skill your client on how to think through design issues so that they will become savvier in the whole area of intervention.

Third, you can combine an up-skilling event with a design event by actually working with the client to do the initial design work. You will find that it is often a pleasure to do that as, despite the fact that the client may not be as savvy as you are, they often come up with fresh ideas that you would not have thought about. After this, you will find that you still have to take their initial ideas to work up to a proper intervention plan.

OD practitioners are encouraged to build a one-page teaching sheet based on these criteria so that they can always, in the moment, take their client through the concepts behind the design process. I remember the joy I experienced often when, after sharing these concepts with a group of clients, they literally took over the design meeting and came up with some of the most creative intervention methods that I had never thought about. Wisdom does lie with the clients; all they need is for us to share with them the conceptual tools we use to facilitate good design work.

When the initial design is done, it is worth double checking it against the next list.

Make reference to a list of design criteria

In this section, I put all the design criteria together to form a summary grid (see Figure 5.10), with further explanatory notes for practitioners to refer to.

Figure 5.10 covers 10 OD criteria for designing effective intervention. Being a pragmatist, I know not all interventions will be able to meet all these criteria. However, the insights from these criteria will increase our chance of delivering effective intervention to the clients.

FIGURE 5.10 OD set of effective intervention design criteria

Criteria of effective intervention	What it means for OD practitioner's design work
Be clear on the purpose of intervention.	OD practitioners need to get this clearly spelt out during contracting phase. It would be even better if the desired outcomes are converted into measurable metrics which will then help in the design stage. It is important that in every meeting, you double check with the client groups whether this has been changed or modified as different data comes in. If, by doing the planning, you realize the purpose is not really realistic, you will need to feed that back to the client and help them to chunk down the objectives in phases.
Be clear about who the targeted group or unit(s) of change the intervention is aimed towards.	Map out the various groups, especially the key group (those groups and individuals that the successful implementation are critically dependent on) that the intervention phase needs to work with. Based on who they are, what role(s) they have in supporting the implementation, their attitude towards the change, their formal and informal power bases – we will have to design an intervention that will engage them. The unit of change concept will also help us to decide whether the whole department, or the whole organization needs to be intervened in order to support the changes we aim to make within the key group.
Be clear about which levels of system and how many of the nine levels the intervention is directed at.	In designing intervention we need to be clear about which of the nine levels outlined earlier we need to aim for. Having clarity about which level can guide us greatly in our design work. What is important for practitioners to bear in mind is that sustainable OD intervention often aims for a minimum of three levels of system even though there is a primary target level.
Be clear about the specific areas you are targeted to change – ie Reddy's cube (task or process).	Once we identify the targeted unit(s) of change, we should be specific about the areas we will need to work on in order to achieve the change. Do we need them to understand something better, to acquire different skills, to shift their paradigm, or to learn about a process? Getting the task and process focus right will help us in our design work.
Be clear that you intervene at the right 'depth' (risk) in accordance with the system's readiness and capability.	By depth, I'm referring to how deep, value-laden, emotionally charged and central to the individual's sense of self or the organization's sense of identity. It is an OD rule that we should intervene at a level no deeper than: a) what is required to produce lasting solutions to the issues at hand; b) that to which the energy and resources of the system can be committed. Too risky (too deep) intervention will bust the system especially when the system is neither ready nor capable of coping with the experience or there are simpler ways to achieve similar results.
Whenever possible, structure the activity to contain both experience-based and concept-based learning.	Most of the changes we aim to bring for people, groups and organizations cannot be achieved through a 'talking shop'. While some interventions can be achieved via that channel (especially if it is to increase their head knowledge), most impactful interventions are experiential, working with minds as well as emotions, creating personal experience of the change scenario so that there will be sufficient self-induced force for them to shift. I would say the most successful interventions should have 2/3 experience-based exercises to 1/3 conceptual 'talk at' stuff.

FIGURE 5.10 *Continued*

Criteria of effective intervention	What it means for OD practitioner's design work
Structure the activity to liberate rather than generate anxiety and defensiveness.	Schein (1996: 27) comments that the key to unfreezing in change was 'to recognize that change, whether at the individual or group level, was a profound psychological dynamic process'. When people face the need to change, three things have to happen to create movement: • disconfirmation of the validity of the status quo; • the induction of guilt or survival anxiety; • creating psychological safety. Schein argued that 'unless sufficient psychological safety is created, the disconfirming information will be denied or in other ways defended against, no survival anxiety therefore will be felt and consequently no change will take place. Those concerned have to feel safe from loss and humiliation before they can accept the new information and reject old behaviours.' Therefore when structuring any intervention activities, we need to pay attention to what we should put in place to induce psychological safety.
Structure the activity to increase the system's autonomy.	The intervention process needs to be designed in such a way that participants will learn not only how to solve an issue/ improve a practice/ invent a new way to do things, but by doing the process, they learn how to learn. In other words, great intervention is while the group works on the task they also learn the process through which the task is done. If it is a team building event, a great intervention is not just having the facilitator do things to them to help them improve their communication, but through participating in the activity, they learn how to do it themselves in the future. This can often be fast-tracked by using the intervention activities that engage the participant as a whole person, drawing participation of not just their role, but their thoughts, beliefs, feelings and strivings.
Structure the activity to help generate valid information, encourage free informed choice and in the process secure the client's internal commitment (Argyris).	If the purpose of any intervention is to secure commitment from the targeted group to the change agenda, then the intervention has to be designed in such a way that will help the targeted group to generate their personalized reason for change. Those processes create the opportunity for them to reflect on the information and decide whether they will support the change or not, eg having a dialogue session with the change leader to debate the pros and cons of the change so that at the end when they decide to shift, they are shifting to the new agenda with clear commitment. This has huge implications on how we design the process.
Use the intervention to help the system to have more congruent communication. Deal with both the covert and overt process of discussion (Marshak).	Marshak (2006) pointed out that much of our communication is covert. In fact during change, five out of the six dimensions of change are covert. Everything does not need to be made overt except when it blocks and trips up the change process. Therefore whenever we can, we should teach the process and skills to members of any system to know how to put things on the table rather than underneath so that the communication will be more congruent and healthy.

How do you use a list like this? First, when you have finished constructing the intervention, you can check it against this list for a comprehensive test. If there are more than a couple of questions you cannot answer, then you should look at the design again. Second, you can turn this grid into a simple diagram as a teaching aid to take to your client so that you can equip them to be savvy in assessing intervention. Third, you can use the list with your client as guidance when s/he wants to explore other types of intervention.

Pull together all the interventions we have planned and do a sequencing of the events

When the design of the intervention is done, even for a small project, you will have more than one thing to implement. For a complex project, there will definitely be a number of events and activities that need coordinating. The way we coordinate or sequence them should be based on some key principles and practical factors.

The practical factors include:

- How soon can we get these interventions set up and ready to roll?

- How long do our internal change teams need training and support before they are ready to go?

- How complicated are the logistical arrangements? How soon can we sort them out for a smooth run?

Key principles for sequencing intervention

I have turned the key principles into question form to help OD practitioners to make sequencing decisions. Some of the points are adapted from the work of Beer (1980):

- **Maximize early success** – which interventions should go first because of ease of execution, and their success will open doors for the riskier ones?

- **Maximize effectiveness** – which interventions will help to develop readiness, motivation, knowledge and skills required by other interventions?

- **Maximize diagnostic data** – which intervention will provide us with the data needed to validate our design of the key event?

- **Maximize speed** – which intervention will be relatively fast to implement in order to get some early wins?

- **Maximize relevance** – which interventions, if successful, will help the key population feel that the change has a high level of appropriateness in their day-to-day work, and therefore motivate them to participate more?

- **Minimize psychological and organizational strain** – which interventions will create the least psychological anxiety and therefore will generate the least amount of defensiveness so that they don't shut down the receptiveness to future intervention?
- **Maximize efficiency** – how should interventions be sequenced to conserve organization resources such as time, energy and money?

Finalize the intervention strategy

By now, you should be ready to finalize your intervention strategy – the overall game plan for this phase. The game plan should have the structure shown in Figure 5.11.

FIGURE 5.11 An outline of an intervention strategy

- A clear direction and purpose for the intervention.
- A clear list of people/groups/units of change for whom you are targeting your intervention.
- A clear list of intervention activities.
- A clear timeline.
- A clear sequence of how they will be staggered.
- A team (other than yourself) who will deliver these interventions (if it is a complex set of interventions).
- A budget.
- A project plan pulling all the above together.
- An accountability reporting structure or forum.
- A critical path – administered by a logistics team.

For a complex project, it is important that you get your client system to sign off on this plan – in fact this should become the detailed (second stage) contract that you agree with your client. In practical terms, this also becomes your blueprint to work from. Once you get to this stage, things should be relatively settled but, as you and I know, things never go exactly as anticipated. Circumstances may change, but having a plan, you will have something to refer back to whenever you are blown off track.

Finally, it is important that throughout the intervention design process, you refer to the various theoretical perspectives as this is where you will get a clear methodological steer. If you keep theories in mind from the beginning of the OD cycle, you will be in a position to design robust intervention as the theories will give you a firm grounding. I have drawn out the various theories and their application in Chapter 2, so I will not repeat them here.

Summary

Intervention begins when we make contact with our clients; from then on, everything you say, signal, hint, suggest, and question begins to have an effect on the client system. The way you contract – both task and relationship contracts, the way you support them in deciding what data the system needs in order to inform their decisions on intervention – all these are your 'theory in action'.

The whole purpose of intervention is to help to shift the client system from where they are to where they want to be; therefore the process you choose, the 'what', 'how' and 'who' should be collaborative. Because the more the client does, the more they will own the outcome and learn how to arrive at those outcomes not just once but again and again. If at the end of the diagnostic feedback, the client has no energy to progress, then it is crucial for you to think about what immediate intervention you will need to put in place to help them get engaged and own the data.

During the period of intervention, it is the OD practitioner who needs to keep an eye on the entire process, helping the client system to go through many decision points to make choices of intervention, execute them, monitor them and adjust the methodology in order to deliver the desired outcome. Burke (1982: 215, 216) points out that OD practitioners need to pay attention to three conditions during the intervention phase. The intervention needs to:

- respond to an actual and felt need for change on the part of the client;
- involve the client in the planning and implementing of the change (intervention);
- lead to change in the organization's culture.

Argyris (1970: 17–19) also lists another three conditions. OD practitioners need to design intervention based on:

- **Valid and useful information** – 'that which describes the factors plus their inter-relationships that create the problem for the client systems'.
- **Free choice** – the 'locus of decision making is in the client system', and the client is provided alternatives. According to Argyris, 'a choice is free to the extent the members can make their selection for a course of action with minimal internal defensiveness... free choice therefore implies that the members are able to explore as many alternatives as they consider significant and select those that are central to their needs'.
- **Internal commitment** – the client owns the choice made and feels responsible for implementing it. So organization members act on their choice because it responds to needs, both individual and on behalf of the organization.

While we have postponed the discussion of the concept of 'self as an instrument' in intervention to Chapter 10, it is important to remind ourselves that we need to own our role throughout this phase, paying attention to what Burke and Argyris taught. An effective intervener is one who knows sufficient applied behavioural science principles, who is clear about the tasks and skills required in this phase, possesses sufficient knowledge of what constitutes effective intervention and knows how to involve clients to turn principles into an intervention strategy. It is the successful execution of intervention to achieve the organization improvement that makes this job so rewarding. This is an area where we OD practitioners must strive further.

Theories and practices of OD: the evaluation phase

In 25 years of lecturing on and teaching OD, some of the questions I am most frequently asked by the audience are about the value of OD to organizations. They are:

'How do you know OD works?'

'What is the return on investment of OD?'

'How do we go about doing evaluation of the effectiveness of our work?'

'How do we and our clients know we actually deliver value?'

Recently, such questions have been asked with greater urgency and eagerness, with a feeling of desperation behind their asking – almost as if the questioner's job future depends on it. This may be because corporations are undergoing a continuous slimming process and every function and activity is scrutinized as to whether it has delivered sufficient value to avoid being made redundant. In reality, many OD units have not survived recent cost-cutting exercises.

This chapter aims to give an overview of the issues surrounding the evaluation of OD, and by doing so I hope you can approach this subject with greater confidence that OD intervention not only works, but consistent and intentional OD interventions (especially in the form of an OD plan that goes with the organization strategic plan) will add tremendous value to organizations' long-term viability.

This chapter will cover the following:

1 What is evaluation and what are metrics?

2 Summary of the tasks and skills required for evaluation.

3 OD perspective on evaluation – evaluation in the OD cycle of work.

4 How to build the culture of evaluation as an integrated part of our OD work.

5 What does one measure and how?

6 The practicalities of estimating return on investment (ROI).

There is a postscript to look at what value an internal OD department offers to an organization.

What is evaluation and what are metrics?

Evaluation is a set of planned, information-gathering and analytical activities undertaken to provide those responsible for the management of change with a satisfactory assessment of the effects and/or progress of the change effort.

(Beckhard and Harris, 1977: 86)

Evaluation is the process of assessment of the extent to which the work undertaken delivered its intended objectives.

Metrics refers to the specific data or measures (hence 'metrics') used to assess the outcome. However, whether a specific metric is a valid indicator of an OD initiative will depend on the initiative's objectives. If an OD programme aims to achieve better customer relations, then improving customer feedback will be a valid metric, as will increased sales, but a change in the number of grievance cases will not. The choice of metrics is also related to what the organization wants to get out of the OD initiative, and whether the methodology chosen based on available resources is robust enough to secure those objectives. Most evaluation will use more than one metric.

Summary of the tasks and skills required for evaluation

Most OD practitioners who have not come through an academic social science degree programme will find the subject difficult, especially when evaluation is not a frequently taught subject in OD education. Hence in reality most OD practitioners have limited knowledge about how evaluation is done, and the result is that most OD practitioners cannot demonstrate the value of their work. The time has come for those who are involved in the education of OD practitioners to introduce this process firmly back into the education curriculum. On top of that, all OD practitioners should be encouraged to develop relevant process protocols that could be used in their contracting stage to the clients so that the evaluative phase will become a clear part of OD work. Figure 6.1 gives a suggested list of the skills required during the tasks of evaluation.

FIGURE 6.1 Tasks and skills required of the practitioner in the evaluation phase

Tasks	OD practitioner skills
• Refer back to purpose and required outcomes of the intervention that were identified during commissioning phase.	• Political sensitivity to ensure the multiple stakeholders all have a say about what they want the OD project to achieve.
• Help clients to determine whether or not what they want can be achieved, within the nature of the intervention and given budget, timescale and level of involvement from people within the organization.	• Understanding of the role of evaluation within the OD cycle and how to raise the subject of evaluation during the contracting phase; knowledgeable enough to decide what can and cannot be achieved based on the nature of the project.
• Help clients to agree the general area of evaluation and the corresponding relevant metrics.	• Know how to build evaluation methods and approaches into the OD programme of work.
• Build the evaluation areas and metrics into the initial contract with a clause 'subject to mid-term review'.	• Working knowledge of how to carry out evaluation measures and the methods to obtain those measures.
• Set up tracking mechanism from the beginning of intervention – so that evaluative data can be collected throughout the project life and used to adjust the intervention approach.	• Know how to set out evaluative tracking processes to obtain data throughout the OD programme. • Ability to coordinate the data collected to give regular reports to clients.
• Involve internal change agents to do evaluative data gathering to increase project ownership. Use evaluative process to reinforce the change process with energy and commitment.	• Understanding and experience in knowing how to calculate ROI and work out monetary figures to metrics chosen.
• Present coherent evaluative data to clients; involve them in analysing data.	• Ability to bring multiple stakeholder groups together to do the above.
• Help clients to determine what actions to take to adjust the outcome of the intervention – reinforce what works, address what does not work, design further interventions, etc.	• Ability to build longer-term strategy to help organization to treat evaluation as an integrated part of their strategic planning work.

OD perspectives on evaluation – evaluation in the OD cycle of work

Evaluation is the final phase of the OD cycle and a key step in the action research framework. The planning of this final phase needs to start at the beginning of the project, at the contracting phase, so that it becomes an integrated part of the ongoing OD cycle of work. In that way, the data collected at every stage will form part of the evaluative data to steer you and your clients in deciding the appropriate next step of intervention. This is especially true for longer-term transformation change projects in which there is really no end point but a resting point at which things are recalibrated and maintained before further changes can proceed.

Let us revisit the action research model and its implications for the role of the phase of evaluation. The action research method is an iterative, cyclical, four-step process: diagnosing, planning, action taking and evaluating action. Its origins derive from John Dewey, who perceived the need to pair research with action in order to solve real-world issues and involve those who need to have emotional investment and commitment to support the action. Once engaged, they are encouraged to become actively involved in diagnosing, planning, taking action and evaluating the effects of action.

FIGURE 6.2 An expanded model of action research

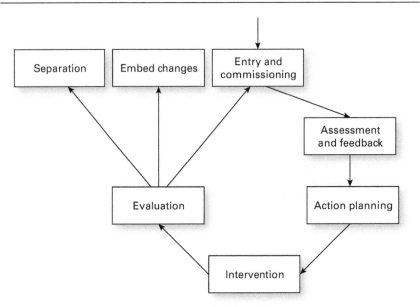

SOURCE: Adapted from Mclean and Sullivan (1989).

FIGURE 6.3 An Organization Development evaluation model

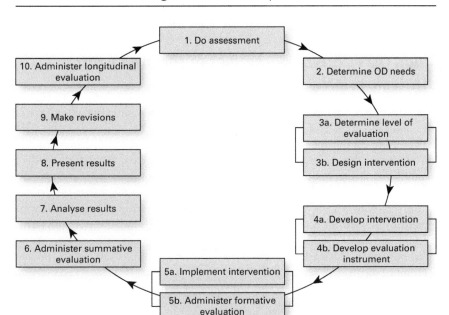

Adapted from: Gary M. McLean, Roland Sullivan, and William J. Rothwell 1995, *Practicing Organization Development*, edited by William J. Rothwell, Roland Sullivan, Gary M. McLean, Chapter 10 – Evaluation.

Figures 6.2 and 6.3 show the action research model with an increasing level of detail about how evaluation fits into the OD cycle of work. Evaluation is an ongoing activity and requires clear agreement with the client from the start about what success looks likes and how the effectiveness of the intervention can be tracked before the work begins. This is a critical starting point for anyone who wants to take evaluation seriously.

How to build the culture of evaluation as an integrated part of our OD work

Before we talk about what to measure and how to measure, I would like to help you to be a lot more strategic by building evaluation into the normal practice in the organization. For OD to survive and thrive in the current tough times, you and I need to be more savvy in measuring and demonstrating the effectiveness of our work. If evaluation becomes an integral part of your organization's operation protocol, you will increase the confidence of purchasers and users of OD services in what the field can offer. The following eight strategic steps will help to make evaluation an integral part of your

OD work. Some of these actions are easier for internal OD practitioners, but external OD practitioners can also gain legitimacy to influence ongoing clients in these directions.

Align OD efforts/programmes to the organization's strategic priority

The most critical step to build evaluation into the organization's culture is to align the OD agenda to the organization's strategic plan. For years, OD has failed to establish its rightful place in organizations mainly because leaders do not know how to view OD and are not sure of its value. Many leaders see OD as an internal consultancy department, or an operation arm of HR, or something to do with project management. Worse still, some see OD as mainly having a coaching or a team-building function. This inability to position OD within a clear organization framework has done major harm to OD because no one knows what value it can offer to the organization. Without this understanding, it is hard for OD to establish its rightful place in the organization's power hierarchy.

If you are an internal OD practitioner, one of the essential moves you will need to make is to align the work priorities of an OD function to the organization's strategic priorities. This will involve working alongside the strategic planning people so that you can play a critical part in the strategic planning process by creating the corresponding OD plan.

Most of the senior leaders live in the 'input' and 'output' world. They are highly aware of the external factors that are impacting on the organization, which they and the top team need to manage. They also know what 'performance output' the organization needs to keep producing in order to justify its place in the market/world. But what they seldom do is to pay attention to the 'throughput' – the alignment of the organizational internal variables in order to support the strategic priorities. So your role is to ensure that leaders understand that if they are to realize their external ambitions, someone needs to lead the adjustment of the organization's culture, Organization Design, system and processes, human capability, climate, skill match, etc, so that the organization is coherently moving towards its goals. Most organizations do not have a brilliant record in delivering their strategic ambitions because while strategic direction can easily be set, achieving the strategic priorities is much harder – because those who have the role to implement the plan have to be brought into the plan itself. Your goal therefore is to help senior leaders to commission an OD plan every time there is a new strategic plan. So the organization will always have one externally oriented plan and one internally oriented plan. By doing this, you will have moved OD into the 'power elite' of the organization, not to mention you would have tied the evaluation of OD to the measurement of the organization's ability to implement its strategic priorities. This is the first condition that aids effective evaluation.

Link OD initiatives to the core business/organization results

Having done the above, it is easier to link OD initiatives and interventions to the core business results that most senior leaders focus on. Things that senior leaders value include: saving money (cost cutting), effective workforce planning (keeping cost to a minimum), keeping talent as the key competitive tool (fantastic human capital), delivery of research and innovation faster than competitors (product launch before competitors), retention of customer loyalty (compete by service excellence) and, ultimately, profit for private sector organizations, better public services for public organizations, and the ability to deliver their mission mandate for third-sector organizations. This is good news as the purpose of any OD intervention is to improve the organization's health. So even if the senior leaders do not make this explicit link, it is the job of the OD practitioner to steer the leaders down this path; if not, the value of what OD projects can offer will generally be missed. You will need to be the ones who are concerned with what any OD project offers to the organization from the leadership lens. If the business case of any OD project is weak, you as the OD practitioner need to be the first one who is prepared to forsake the project and to advise the organization to do so. This is the second condition needed for evaluation.

Build a strategic partnership with other professionals to ensure we improve our evaluative methodology

Many functions within an organization have a shared interest in evaluative methodology. Therefore to widen your perspectives and broaden your resources, you need to build strategic alliances with colleagues from other disciplines, eg strategists, social researchers, project management colleagues, HR colleagues and finance colleagues. Minimally, you need to discover whether there is an evaluative framework that applies to all corporate functions/projects. If there is, then you can work with others to create or revitalize a consistent research framework to demonstrate the value of OD. Once that is done, it is important to share that framework with any external contractors if they are called in to support change work.

Continuous education of clients as to the value of evaluation

Another way is to develop a strategy to educate leadership about the role of evaluation within a continuous learning and improvement culture. Helping leaders to see the process value OD initiatives can offer to the organization in the long run will set the scene for evaluation, which must be defined and worked through from the beginning of every project. See Figure 6.3 for this

concept. Another way to increase the literacy of the leadership is to put evaluation on the leadership development programme, helping leaders to be interested in evaluating not just an OD project but also other strategic projects. In a leadership conference, help the senior leaders run a session that involves others in discussing what different metrics matter to the organization's general wellbeing from different perspectives.

Finally, set up an 'OD friendly' advisory group (make sure some members are from the protégé group of senior leaders) to chart the process value of any OD project. As the backroom support and monitoring group, this group also will have a longer-term educational impact on other key individuals within the organization. Any of the above will help the clients to see that evaluation is part and parcel of the work itself.

Senior leaders commission the OD project and define the metric

The fifth aspect is to facilitate the condition that senior leaders become the true commissioner of any OD project. For example, suppose the organization wants to up the employee engagement score because the last staff survey indicated that the score had dropped to an all-time low. Before the OD practitioner jumps to the conclusion that this is a critical area that deserves an intervention, you will need to create an opportunity for senior leaders to inquire and explore what the data mean to them and whether they think the situation is sufficiently critical to require OD intervention. If the senior leaders agree something needs to be done, then it is with this stakeholder group that the OD practitioner needs to work out the purpose of the OD project, the range of outcomes they want to achieve through this project, and what success would look like for them. You must aim to tap into their personal vision.

Senior leaders take ownership of evaluative data by deciding, who, what and when

Once the project's value has been established during the contracting stage, you need to agree with the senior leaders *who* should get involved in refining the metrics and criteria for evaluation, *when* is the appropriate time for evaluation to take place, and *what* methods should be used. If the leaders are not ready for this discussion then it is the job of the OD practitioner to get back to the senior leaders as soon as practicable to get their approval.

Why is this important? Ownership of evaluative data is a key issue to which the OD practitioner needs to pay attention. Every organization has multiple (and diverse) stakeholders who hold different views about what to evaluate, how to evaluate, and what to do with the evaluative reports. Therefore to manage the diversity of opinion, it is not just the content of

what we evaluate that matters, but whose criteria we need to refer to, and who we need to get involved in any of the evaluative activity.

Asking senior leaders to agree who should get involved will inevitably mean you will have on the evaluation team some of the trusted protégés, and/or credible seconds-in-command of the senior leaders. Having nominated these people, the leaders will be more receptive to the data because they are trusted people – not HR or OD people. This is the fifth condition that supports evaluation.

This is the political aspect of evaluation that OD practitioners often fail to pay attention to and suffer for overlooking. It is also part of the action research philosophy – when you turn the system's people into investigators, they will be more committed to the findings and hence willing to act on them.

Build the habit of having evaluation discussions from the beginning – build evaluation into the contracting process

You need to talk about evaluation as early as you can. It is no good trying to sneak in the discussion of impact and evaluation halfway through the project; evaluation questions need to be built in as part of the diagnostic questions when you first explore the project with the potential client. Questions like those listed below should be included as part of your initial conversation.

Specific project questions:

1 What do you want to get out of doing this project?
2 What would success look like to you?
3 If I were to ask other stakeholders in your organization about the desired outcomes they want from this project, what would they be?
4 What type of metrics will satisfy the key decision makers in this project?

General questions:

1 What does organization effectiveness mean to you and your organization?
2 What type of OD effort do we need to invest in to achieve the above?
3 What issues (organization variables) affect other factors and what are your hunches about their relationships?
4 How can these organization variables be controlled sufficiently for us to determine the cause and effect they have on each other?
5 How would you go about measuring the impact of this intervention on those areas that you suspect to be affected?

6 What do you expect and want to achieve through this change?

7 Who do you think should conduct the research? How will the data be used and by whom?

8 Who needs to own the evaluation data in order for this change to create the type of impact it needs among the leaders, the managers and the staff?

Answers to the above questions will help to set the evaluative framework and guide you on how to evaluate the intervention even before the design stage.

Have a strategy to always involve clients to define evaluation and metrics (as part of a continuous education process)

To set evaluation on a solid platform, you will need help from those who live in the system to become your co-researchers. From day one, you will need to involve the system members to identify the desired state, what intervention methodologies will help to achieve the desired end game, and finally how they will know when you get there. Within this collaborative process, you can do continuous education, and the system members will provide you with ideas about what type of business metrics (impact analysis) are both legitimate and achievable. By involving local leaders (the client system's managers) you transfer the ownership and identification of the metrics/impact to them. This will put evaluation in better hands because those local leaders within the organization not only have the vision about what they want the OD project to achieve, they also instinctively know what variables may be impacted by the interventions. Seeking their partnership is not only prudent but also fits into the ethos of OD. People tend to have a sense of ownership when they have participated in making decisions.

Write up case studies of good evaluative practice to show others how to do it

Finally, this is an area where widespread sharing of knowledge is called for. Conducting a search for articles in this area, I found very little has been published. As practitioners, if you have done a good piece of evaluation work for the change programmes you have introduced, it is important to write it up, publish it, or at least to share it among colleagues.

Now that we have covered the eight areas that you will need to focus on in order to build evaluation into the culture and practice of the organization, let us look at the technical side of evaluation.

What does one measure and how?

Task focus metrics versus process focus metrics

While both OD practitioners and their clients understand the importance of the *task outcome metrics* – as they help to show how OD initiatives are supporting the organization – OD practitioners also value the *process outcome metrics* because you want the client to take on board the process value of the methodology you use to develop long-term renewal capability. So in deciding what to measure, you will need to grasp conceptually what the differences are in what you aim to measure. The work of Golembiewski *et al* (1976) helps to provide some insights to this debate. According to them, there are three types of change results OD practitioners should aim for. They are:

- **An alpha (α) change** is a difference in a measure *before* and *after* an intervention. For example, if the frequency of conflict has lessened after a conflict resolution intervention, then one would say that an alpha change has occurred.

- **A beta (β) change** is a reassessment of the dimension in question. So it is not whether there was an increase or decrease of conflict after the intervention that is measured but whether there was a shift of perception about the definition of conflict. For example, if there is a shift of understanding that conflict is bad or good, then the team need to discern the differences – if the members understand when it is legitimate to have conflict and when it is not, what sort of conditions will lead to the reaping of synergistic results from conflict and so on then a beta change has occurred.

- **A gamma (γ) change** is a complete reframing, redefinition and re-conceptualization of the key domains that affect the team or organization. This type of change result involves a shift from one state to another. Staying with the same example, after the intervention, the members of the system may conclude that in order to achieve more healthy working relationships they need to pay attention to how the system as a whole works – eg clarity of roles and responsibilities, how knowledge is shared, what support structure is needed, how various work processes need to link together. In the long term, it is such general systematic improvements that will help the team to work better together. Shifting from focusing only on conflict management to building more general organizational health is what gamma change is about. The ability to gain understanding of the height and breadth of the issue (from a systemic perspective with a corresponding ability to solve the issue) in a more holistic fashion will constitute a gamma change result.

The tension OD practitioners face is to how to keep to our commitment of offering process value to an organization while bearing in mind that it is the outcome metrics the client aims for – eg profits, turnover, productivity level, costs, etc. This tension will always be there, and ultimately you know you will need to deliver both.

Measuring the impact of specific intervention or the overall impact of an OD project

A frequently asked question is whether one should be measuring the impact of a specific intervention, the composite effects of different interventions, or the overall impact of an OD project. It is important to help the client to be clear about what s/he needs to measure. When s/he asks whether doing this project will work or not, check whether s/he is concerned about the overall impact of the project as a whole or of the various interventions you and s/he have decided to use. My view is, one should be less concerned with the impact of a specific intervention in more complex projects, and instead focus on measuring the overall impact of the package of interventions. This has implications for the timing of evaluation.

However, if you are doing smaller projects, often you will be asked to measure the specific intervention, eg team building. Remember, depending on what the intervention aims to achieve, what you measure will differ significantly. To illustrate this, I have created a grid (Figure 6.4) showing what metrics and evaluative methods can be used for different types of intervention, borrowing some of the concepts from Philips, 2002. In spite of the rigid format in which it is presented, applications are fluid and dynamic as you can apply different levels of evaluation to any intervention and some metrics can be used across all levels and types of intervention.

Figures 6.5 and 6.6 are two examples of the types of intervention results you can measure. Figure 6.5 summarizes the evaluation of a 12-month, cross-agency regional OD capability-building programme in the North East of the UK. Figure 6.6 is an example adapted from the work of Porras and Berg (1978) for use in another transformation project.

Less better than more – but start with a comprehensive list

It is important to clarify that it is not practical for any project to measure all the areas listed in Figures 6.5 and 6.6. However, it is important for you, after initial consultation, to draft an evaluation framework to take to your clients to help them to identify the most important outcome variables they want their OD project to achieve given the stakeholders' perspective.

FIGURE 6.4 Different types of intervention with corresponding evaluation and metrics

Type of intervention	Level of evaluation	Explanation	Example of metrics and methods
• Training programme. • Focus group. • Pilot new communication meeting between management/staff.	• Reaction, satisfaction and planned action. • Short-term and one-off interventions.	• Measure participants' reaction to the programme. • Measure stakeholders' satisfaction with the programme. • Measure the immediate response to the new practices.	• Post-event evaluation form. • Telephone interview of random sample of participants. • Survey six weeks after the event. • Measure the results that the training programme aimed to deliver by checking how many participants have planned and delivered implementation action.
• Development programme. • Job shadowing scheme. • Coaching or mentoring scheme. • Technical learning session.	• Learning. • Short or medium term.	• Measure skills, knowledge, or attitude changes related to the programme. • Measure rate of implementation of new learning.	• Before and after skill/knowledge test. • Two-party joint evaluation, eg of the effectiveness of a mentoring project. • Report from supervisors on impact of the scheme. • Direct observation of performance. • Participants' self-assessment of impact. • Rating of actual performance improvement by users, partners, and peers.
• 360-degree feedback. • Post-appraisal coaching discussion. • Formal education on critical skills. • Joint departmental focus group on how to improve joint working. • Conflict resolution workshop.	• Application and implementation. • Short-, medium and long-term intervention, but tend to be more complex.	• Measures changes in behaviour on the job. • Specific application and implementation of what they have learnt from the programme.	• Multiple party evaluation of the usefulness of the intervention. • Line leaders' direct observation of the rate of improvement. • Self-reporting on new experimental behaviour for joint working. • External partners'/customers'/colleagues' feedback on the effect of better team working. • Fewer conflict situations; shorter time to resolve conflicts. • Greater frequency of meeting deadlines.

FIGURE 6.4 *Continued*

Type of intervention	Level of evaluation	Explanation	Example of metrics and methods
• Involve whole system in strategic planning. • Set up customer relationship improvement task force. • Integrated leadership development programme.	• Business impact. • Medium- and longer-term interventions and almost always complex projects.	• Ownership rate of the strategy plan. • Leadership 360-degree feedback on the leaders. • Measures change programme impact on business.	• Measure how many strategic priorities were delivered and on what timescale compared to previous two years. • Pre/post customer complaint record or satisfaction index. • Cost of repairing customer service mistakes compared to previous two years. • Leadership errors in business decisions. • Leadership implementation rate of corporate people strategy and link to employee satisfaction scale.
• Big transformation project. • Major initiative to improve external reputation and internal delivery capability.	• Return on investment. • Medium- and longer-term interventions are always complex.	• Compares the monetary value of the business impact with the cost of the programme.	• Choose the right metrics, assign monetary value to them, work out the net programme benefit using those metrics and the net programme costs.

FIGURE 6.5 Evaluation framework for a regional, cross-agency OD capability programme

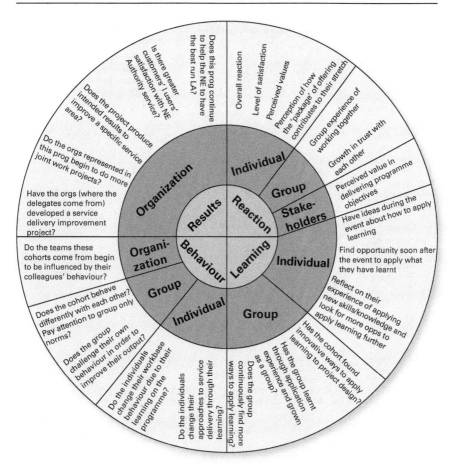

© Compiled by Dr LMY Cheung-Judge, April 2008 for NE Change and Improvement Programme.

The 'how' of evaluation

The 'how' of evaluation is a technical subject that I do not intend to deal with in this chapter, especially when there are specialist books on this subject. For now I just want to raise two issues about the 'how' question for you to consider when doing evaluation. One is about the evaluative methods and the other is about the evaluation process.

There are many evaluation methods available. In OD evaluation is an intervention and therefore can draw from the many intervention techniques. What method to choose depends on the purpose of the evaluation exercise, what you and your clients want to measure, and the resources and capabilities

FIGURE 6.6　Evaluation framework for a transformation project

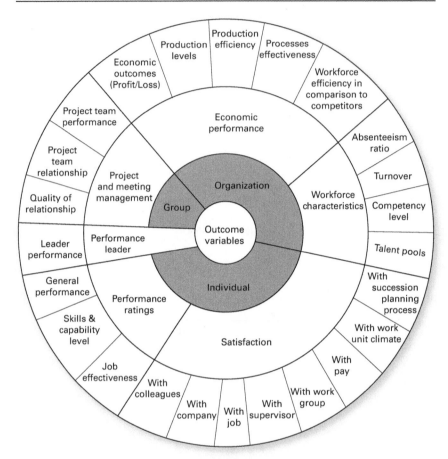

Adapted and revised by LMYCJ from J Porras & P Berg (August, 1978),
The impact of organization development, *Academy of Management Review*, p253.

available (see Chapter 5). Figure 6.7 provides a range of evaluation methods applicable to different system levels.

It is important to set up the evaluation methods from the beginning so that you can monitor the change effort before, during and after the intervention to assess the impact of the change effort.

The evaluation process is the integrated approach you will set up to do the evaluation. Figure 6.8 demonstrates what the evaluation process may look like. Even though this model makes specific reference to return on investment (ROI), it is equally applicable to other processes. It consists of four stages: evaluation planning, data collection, data analysis, and communication of results.

FIGURE 6.7 Sample list of evaluation methods

Any Level	Individuals	Groups	Total organization level
• Interview • Questionnaire • Observation • Focus group • Secondary information • Supplier feedback • Customer feedback	• Individual interview • Standard assessment tools • 180/360-degree review • On-the-job observation to capture actual application • Tests and assessments to measure the extent of learning/knowledge/skills gained or enhanced • Self-rating and assessment • Peer feedback • Supervisor feedback	• Group interviews • Focus group • Cross-group review • Action plans to show progress with implementation of group agreement • Other partners' feedback to a specific group performance • On-the-job observation of the whole group • Follow-up questionnaire • Cross-departmental review	• Survey of questionnaires • Business performance index • Specific performance records and operational data • Funder feedback • Customer and user feedback • Partner and strategic alliance feedback

FIGURE 6.8 Measuring the return on investment methodology model

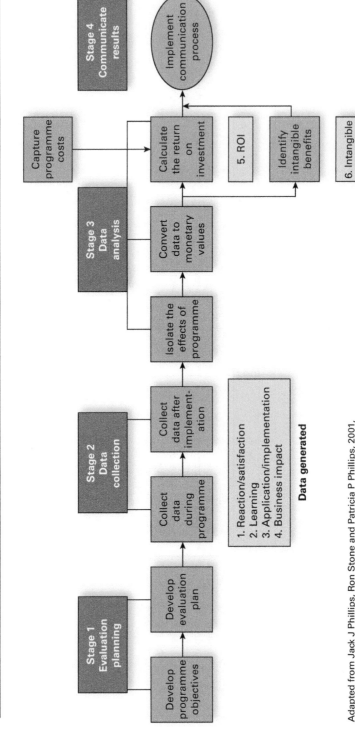

Adapted from Jack J Phillips, Ron Stone and Patricia P Phillips, 2001,
The Human Resources Scorecard: Measuring the return on investment.

Two key points emerge from looking at the framework: evaluation planning really begins at the contracting stage, and collecting evaluative data is a job that needs to be done throughout the consulting period. For further details read this useful framework that Phillips *et al* (2001) have constructed.

The practicalities of estimating return on investment

When organization leaders ask us to demonstrate the 'value of OD', most of them will mean return on investment (ROI). They want to know, in economically straitened times, whether the work of OD can be justified by its financial return. While ROI is mainly about money and its formula is universal, the process of calculation is more an art than a science. In order to calculate ROI you need a set of metrics, and you need to assign a monetary value to each of those metrics. The latter process is highly individualized, depending on the nature of the OD activities, the metrics chosen, and the decision makers' perspective on those metrics.

Another reason why ROI is more art than science is that there are harder metrics that are more visible, more tangible, and easier to measure, and softer metrics that are less visible, less tangible and more difficult to measure. The word intangible may be a bit misleading because sometimes such data can have more significant impact on the organization than the harder data, and yet they are tough to translate into monetary value.

Figure 6.9 gives examples of a range of metrics I have used in my work. From the list you can see there are many types of metrics and no one formula can be used to assign monetary value to them all. Each metric would have to be considered and studied by those who know that type of activity well before someone could step forward to put a pounds or dollars sign on it.

How do we go about setting up evaluative metrics? What should you do? There are two things that you can consider.

First, you can draw on the expertise of other colleagues. Inevitably, within any organization, there is always someone with the right type of skill set to help you to place value on the metrics identified – you just may need some time to locate them. For example, someone from finance, project management and/or research departments will know how to estimate ROI, especially in an organization that is task- and result-focused. If you can find them, you will discover they are more knowledgeable than most OD practitioners in placing monetary value on the metrics in a professional way. So by soliciting their help you not only get their support in getting the ROI right, you also help them to have a vested interest in the success of the programme.

Second, depending on what metric you are using, there are bound to be some local line leaders who are responsible for the area you want to measure and know how to do this. From my experience, those who are closer to

FIGURE 6.9 Sample list of monetary metrics based on clients' chosen indicators

Example of metrics	Example of metrics
• Staff retention rate rises • Job performance errors down • Increased sales figures • Customer complaints decrease • Employee time to do a job reduced from four hours to two hours • Unscheduled absences down • Sexual or racial harassment complaints down • Increased customer satisfaction index • Take-up of new technology rises from 60% in projected six months' time to 80% in 4.5 months • Innovation time from ideas to market shortened • Lost time accident rate (preventative measures lead to drop in rate) • Core work process reduction in steps and time • Roll out of development programme hitting 100% target rate	• Delegates' reaction to an intervention event • Degree of learning and application of new methods in work • Better public image • Customers recognize the brand • Policy adoption rate by departments • Employee satisfaction rate linked to employee turnover rate • Work group conflict frequency – time to resolve issues • Work group collaboration – reduction of process steps as a result of collaboration • Team performance – longitudinal mapping of improvement • Supervisors' time spent in resolving conflict between individuals • Rating of managers and leaders and how that links to individual performance • Reduction of stress level • Increased sense of wellbeing • Improved psychological contract from survey results

the operational area or functional area to be measured, given time and good facilitation, will always be able to work out the monetary value on the metrics from that area.

I believe most metrics OD practitioners deal with can have a monetary value assigned because you can be methodical and rational, especially when you involve those who know the work best. The message I want you to take away is that if some of the less tangible metrics are critical to the project, do not shy away from them: find someone to help you to convert them into monetary value.

In this section we will look at three issues:

1 What is ROI and how does one calculate it?

2 The 'how' of ROI – practical tips.

3 Example of evaluation template.

What is ROI and how does one calculate it?

While the specific strategy will vary from programme to programme because of the objectives and the metrics used, the basis formula for ROI remain the same.

Formula of ROI (Return on Investment):

$$ROI(\%) = \frac{\text{Net programme benefits}}{\text{Programme costs}} \times 100$$

Before we can calculate the return on investment, we will need to know a) the total cost of the intervention; b) the net benefit of the intervention. The latter will involve turning organizational impact data into monetary values. This will require you and your client to place a value on each metric they have chosen as 'dependent variables'.

For example, suppose the change programme is a major customer relations campaign. You have done a number of interventions, and decided the following areas (dependent variables) will result from the intervention:

- improved customer response time through trimming the processes;
- drop in customer complaint rate;
- increased customer satisfaction rate;
- increase in sales;
- improved rate of retention of customers.

You will need to involve those who know these areas as well as your finance colleagues to help you to put a financial value on each of the metrics. Figure 6.10 is an example of the sort of value the organization may put on these five impact variables.

Add up all the values in those five areas to obtain a total value; deduct how much the customer relations campaign cost, and divide by the programme cost to calculate the ROI of this OD intervention. This is conventionally presented as a percentage.

For example, if the estimated net programme benefits are £800,000 and the customer relations programme cost £250,000 then the ROI will be

$$= \frac{800,000 - 250,000}{250,000} \times 100$$

$$ROI = \frac{550,000}{250,000} \times 100$$

$$= 220\%$$

Which means each £1 invested in the programme returns approximately £2.20 in net benefit after costs are covered.

FIGURE 6.10 Example of financial value assigned to impact variables

Impact variables	Financial value put on each of the variables
Improved customer response time through trimming line processes	Calculate the value of going from an average response time of, say, six hours to four hours as a result of trimming the processes. This is two hours of employee wages and benefits (x number of employees doing this job) + the value that the customer relations manager puts on the increased number of customer inquiries processed within a week + the value put on goodwill feeling from customers = the monetary value.
Drop in customer complaint rate	Calculate the cost of each hour spent in handling each of the complaints + the financial compensation given out to customers per quarter. Then factor in the specific percentage drop in hours handling complaints and the drop in compensation to calculate the value.
Increased customer satisfaction rate	Calculate the value of the 'goodwill' factor from satisfied customers and do a conservative estimation of whether a) that will generate more sales or b) there will be more referrals – hence new customers.
Increased sales	Calculate the profit contribution of additional sales.
Improved customer retention rate	Calculate the value of each retained customer and their average spend versus customer loss and their average non-spend.

Let's look at another example. If we undertake a staff engagement exercise, and based on the value assigned to the set of metrics, our net programme benefit (cumulative value from a set of metrics) is £581,000 and the cost of running the programme is £229,000 then the ROI of the programme is:

$$= \frac{581,000 - 229,000}{229,000} \times 100$$

$$\mathrm{ROI} = \frac{352,000}{229,000} \times 100$$

$$= 154\%$$

This means each £1 invested in the programme returns approximately £1.50 in net benefit after costs are covered.

When calculating ROI, it will be wise to stick to the 10 guiding principles (Phillips, 2002) to ensure your approach is conservative (accurate without exaggeration) and that the impact study can be replicated, making it a crucial part of the organization evaluation practice (Figure 6.11).

FIGURE 6.11 Ten principles of implementing ROI measurement

1. Report the complete story	When conducting a higher level of evaluation, data must be collected at lower levels. ROI is a critical measure, but it is only one of five measures necessary to explain the full impact of the programme. So, lower levels of data must be included in the analysis as they provide important information.
2. Conserve important resources	When an evaluation is planned for a higher level, the previous level of evaluation does not have to be comprehensive. Lower-level measures are critical in telling the complete story, and cannot be omitted. However, short-cuts can be taken to conserve resources.
3. Enhance credibility	When collecting and analysing data, use only the most credible source. Credibility is the most important factor in the measurement and evaluation process. Without it, the results are meaningless. Using the most credible source will enhance the perception of the quality and accuracy of data analysis and results.
4. Be conservative	When analysing data, select the most conservative alternative for calculations. This principle is at the heart of the evaluation process. A conservative approach lowers the ROI and helps build the needed credibility with the target audience.
5. Account for other factors	At least one method must be used to isolate the effects of the programme. This step is imperative. Without some method to isolate the effects of the programme, the evaluation results are considered highly inaccurate and overstated.
6. Account for missing data	If no improvement data are available from certain quarters, assume that little or no improvement occurred. It damages the credibility of the evaluation to make assumptions about improvements you cannot be sure of.
7. Adjust estimates for error	Adjust estimates of improvement for the potential error of the estimate. Using estimates is very common in reporting financial and cost-benefit information. To enhance the credibility of estimated data used in ROI evaluation of improvement programmes, estimates are weighted with a level of confidence, adjusting the estimate for potential error.
8. Omit the extremes	Extreme data items and unsupported claims should not be used in ROI calculation. Steps should be taken to be conservative in the analysis when we have extreme data. For example, if you have a list of numbers all ranging from 30 to 70 and one 100, that 100 would be considered an outlier or extreme data item. Extreme data items can skew results – omit them from analysis.
9. Capture annual benefits for short-term programmes	Only the first year of benefits (annual) should be used in the ROI analysis of short-term programmes. If benefits are not quickly realized for most improvement programmes, they are probably not worth the cost. For more extensive programmes, where implementation spans a year or more, then multiple year benefits are captured.
10. Isolate all programme costs	Programme costs should be fully loaded for ROI analysis. All costs of the programme are tabulated, beginning with the cost of the needs analysis and ending with the cost of the evaluation. As part of the conservative approach, the costs are loaded to reduce the ROI.

SOURCE: Adapted from Phillips (2002).

To help you get started with the evaluative process I have put together a checklist (see Figure 6.12).

FIGURE 6.12 Questions for starting up the evaluation process

Crucial questions	Further detail
What is my intention in collecting these data?	• How will I/we use the data?
How do we revisit the essentials?	• What are our project objectives? • What do we want to achieve? • How do we know we have achieved what we set out to do? • Does what we want really matter?
What do we want to measure and at which level?	• Participant reaction • Participant learning • Participant applying learning to job • Change in behavioural measures • System improvement • Relationship improvement • Change in culture • ROI • Others
Do we have the right balance of measures?	The need for balanced measures: • Need a good debate as to what should or should not be measured and which results provide the most valid evidence of the impact of the intervention • Soft measures – attitude, climate, reaction • Hard measures – output, quality, cost, time
How will we continue to follow through the evaluation journey?	• Develop an evaluation plan (evaluative processes) • Plan data collection • Data analysis process • Communicate results • Who will pick up the action points to adjust the change programme after the feedback of the evaluation data?

Postscript: the value an internal OD department can offer an organization

I would like to end this chapter by making a case for the value of an in-house OD unit. I am a firm believer that having skilled internal OD support is essential for organizations if they are to survive and thrive in this environment. All organizations, regardless of size, face two key challenges in order

to stay vibrant in a turbulent environment: they need to adapt to a constantly changing environment – by adjusting strategy, mission, approach to market, competitive stance, and product innovation; and to accomplish this they need to make corresponding internal changes (Schein, 1965). Strategic ambition will not in itself get the organization into top form – ensuring the internal integration to support the strategic ambition is equally important. This is the core aspect of what an OD unit can offer to the organization.

The two questions each organization needs to face are:

- Who within the organization is currently carrying that task?
- Who within the organization has the capability and competence to help the leaders to coordinate the internal integration?

I feel strongly that all organizations need OD support because OD practitioners are dedicated to helping the growth and development of organizations and we are the left hand to senior leaders, as strategists are their right hand. Projects go more smoothly and have a higher chance of success when the organization has been exposed to OD thinking.

Recently, two global organizations came and asked whether I could help them in justifying the setting up of an OD function. Underlying both situations lay an interest in what value an OD function can give to an organization, especially in times of economic downturn. However, the rationale for an OD function goes beyond an economic one. When considering whether to have an OD unit or not, there are three perspectives to consider:

- economic;
- capability;
- culture.

Let's go through each of these perspectives.

The economic perspective

In this case, the justification for setting up an OD function will be the estimated return on investment of having an OD function. This is actually not difficult to determine because most likely the ROI question has been asked of other corporate functions, such as finance, IT, PR, and marketing. If the organization is task- and result-driven, it will be likely that there is someone whom you can consult for support to calculate the ROI of the OD group. This way, you will not fall foul of not doing ROI the corporate way.

Before I discuss the benefit of having an in-house OD unit, I need to introduce the concept of 'negative cost ratio' (NCR) – the cost incurred for not having any form of OD support. The negative cost ratio turns the benefit question of, 'What value and benefit will we gain from having an OD function?' to 'What is the cost of not having an OD unit?' I would ask what would happen to the organization's strategic ambitions and what would happen to the people capability? Or what are the consequences if the

organization's systems, culture, processes are out of alignment with the organization's strategic priorities? That is how I get the discussion going.

As mentioned before, the big question facing leaders when it comes to strategy implementation is, who is currently supporting them to adjust the way the organization works internally when they shift the (external) strategy? I would guess that either they will name some of their direct report or say it is the divisional head's responsibility. But most likely they would also say that they are using quite a lot of external support for different initiatives.

Using external consultants is not the main issue because given the strategic priorities of the organization, there will always be areas of growth or transformation that the organization needs external support for. However, the questions the organization's leaders need to ask themselves are:

- How much are we spending on external consultants because we do not have internal resources?
- What do we get from this level of external support? What value do they add to the business?
- Is the type of support from external consultants crucial for our organization's wellbeing, and if so, should we have ongoing internal support?
- Is this a normal (annual) expenditure? Can we afford to keep paying out this amount?
- Is it easy to find the suitable and competent consultants that understand our industry/sector/organization and are palatable to our senior leaders? If not, should we recruit and grow our own?

Depending on the answers to these questions, you can decide whether to go on to do the economic calculation of having an internal OD function or not. But if you do, here is how I would do it.

The economic calculation

Let's simulate some figures to do the calculation. For example, if the organization has seven divisions and each, in the past year, has used an average 50 days in engaging external consultants, then the total would be about 350 days (this may be a very conservative calculation). Given the average consultant daily fees are roughly £1,500–£2,500 ($2,000–$3,000), the sum will average between £525,000–£875,000 ($700,000–$1,050,000) before adding expenses to the total cost.

In addition to that, there is also: the amount of time the organization's members have to spend in setting up the tendering process; briefing the consultants prior to the bidding process; vetting the tender and selecting and assessing suppliers; their time and the consultants' time (which needs to be paid for) to familiarize the consultants with the organization and the issues before they start work. Depending on whether the external consultants read the organization culture right or not, their interventions and support may or

may not be as on target as required. So, a monetary figure should be assigned to these processes.

For now, assume the organization needs to take the annual sum spent in external consultants and compare it with what it would cost to hire a team of, for example, three OD consultants who would work full time for the organization.

If three OD consultants are hired who have the spread of skill set that the organization needs and they each deliver an average of 180 days a year for the organization (they need relationship-building time, design time, refuelling time), this will average 540 days a year – 190 days more than the 350 days at similar or lower cost.

If you are part of an internal OD team, I would encourage you to add up all the intervention activities you have carried out in the past, calculating the financial value of these activities for the year. This will include the metrics data as well as adding how much it would have cost the organization if they were to have paid external consultants to do the jobs. Then subtract the employment cost of your team. This calculation will, in most circumstances, show that the cost benefit of having internal consultants outweighs the cost of relying on external consultants. However, being realistic, there will always be some senior leaders who would prefer to use external providers, particularly if the rank of the internal team is not at their level. Therefore, in your calculation, you should have a separate budget heading for hiring external consultants for that senior population. By acknowledging this, you will become the broker for the senior leaders, and hence have some control over who the organization brings in.

Capability perspective

What else would the internal OD team contribute to the organization? I believe that while most organizations will have a team of strategists and market intelligence people to help the leaders to do the *external adaptation*, there are very few organizations that have people who are in charge of supporting the leaders to do the *internal integration* job – at least in a systematic way. If there are no specific individuals who are capable of managing the interface between these two issues of external adaptation and internal integration, there will be a long-term impact on the organization.

Ultimately all leaders, regardless of rank, will need to have the capability to carry out these two aspects of organizational life – strategic formation and internal Organization Development. But where does one begin to build that capability? Building OD understanding into mainstream leadership educational programmes is one way. Having a team of internal OD consultants to support delivery of successful results, build high-performing teams, resolve conflicts between departments, and manage change well is another way to help leaders to think systemically. There is a marked difference between those leaders who come out from an organization that have over 20 years' experience in OD support and those who do not. The awareness

of organization health, systemic alignment, the importance of a people-centric approach to change and the adjustment work needed to support change is much higher if leaders have the experience of working with OD teams.

The culture perspective

Another benefit of having a capable internal team of OD consultants is that through time they will inject the OD thinking and OD approach into the leaders' behaviour, and hence into the organization's culture. Many leaders, like those in Johnson and Johnson, have become some of the most OD-savvy leaders through their regular work with OD practitioners in change projects. Many of them have benefited from having regular dialogue (informal coaching) with OD practitioners on top of receiving formal leadership development programmes on OD. Through the exposure, they develop sufficient understanding of systematic Organization Development and approaches to change that whenever there is strategic change, they automatically ask for OD practitioners to help them align the rest of the system to support the external ambition. This aspect of having your own OD function gives much longer-term benefit to the organization.

I know that leaders should ultimately have the capability to manage this type of interface, but that takes time, and the system needs to experience how these interfaces are handled before they are motivated to learn and own that role. So while that is happening, the baton falls into the hands of either senior HR managers who have been trained in OD and/or OD consultants or staff (whose role is to help line leaders to deliver the synchronization of strategy and internal alignment).

Start proving your worth now

The Organization Development team needs to start taking what you have been doing for the organization seriously in terms of proving your worth. If the team starts writing up some of their bigger interventions, asking clients to evaluate the outcome, and providing the evaluative data to the senior leaders, then the organization will become aware of the ROI of OD activities, and hence of the value of an internal OD team.

On top of that, OD practitioners must actively find opportunities to deliver short educational pieces to as many senior leaders as possible so that they will understand what OD is about, the role of OD, the purpose of OD and be aware of specific examples of what OD interventions have achieved for the organization. During this session, you can also give examples of good practice in what an OD unit has achieved for competitors compared with those who do not have an internal OD unit. This way, you are helping the leadership team to understand that OD is a legitimate area of work that supports the organization. Help them to see that OD is a twin to strategy – and therefore is necessary for the organization to achieve its strategic ambition. Without this sense of OD being a legitimate corporate

unit, it will be hard to help the organization to embed OD approaches as part of the culture.

To conclude, no matter what perspective you use to answer the question about the value of an internal OD team, I believe that by investing in an internal OD consultancy function, support will be made available to all the leaders when they go about implementing any strategic change initiatives. In that way, the organization will benefit from having leaders who know how to consistently develop and maintain the system. No matter what the future throws at such organizations, they will have the adaptability to see them through.

Summary

The field of OD exists to ensure organizations achieve effectiveness for those who work for them and for those who benefit from them. OD practitioners put theory in use to design interventions to help organizations to achieve that. In doing so, you and I intend to do good rather than harm. Sometimes, your clients and you can both testify that indeed is the case. Sometimes, you feel you did not achieve the process objectives, but your clients are satisfied. Sometimes, you feel you did well, but the outcome is not clear to the client. Behind this dichotomy lies a complex set of issues, eg issues about power, the sharing (or not sharing) of understanding and paradigms between you and those you serve, the tension between a scientific versus organic assessment paradigm and methodology, and your own lagging behind in your diligence in ranking evaluation as part of your core work with clients.

In this chapter I have covered the OD approach to evaluation – conceptually, methodologically and practically. By placing evaluation at the heart of your processes of intervention (the OD cycle), by building evaluation into the fabric of the organization and by educating organization leaders on evaluating OD interventions you equip yourselves as practitioners and your clients to prove the worth of OD.

On a tactical level, you will need to take heed of the following five points:

- collaborate with your clients in the evaluation effort (the action research model);
- develop a research (evaluation) strategy and make that clear to clients from the point of entry and contracting;
- develop a research (evaluative) design that is tied to the diagnostic model – and use it consistently at every phase of the OD consultancy cycle;
- study business metrics in other disciplines to stay on top of the discussion;
- aim to lead/teach/provide effective methods for data collection and analysis in evaluation.

(Burke, 1982)

This chapter reminds the OD community to take evaluation and business metrics seriously. If this happens, I hope you will enjoy expanding the positive value of OD and hence help to build a firm future for OD. The time has come for us to take up the baton from the front-runners of our fields who took evaluation seriously, but whose practice has not been sustained – as demonstrated by the lack of significant research in the field of OD on evaluation in the past 20 years.

The mandate has now shifted to this generation of practitioners to re-surrect the value-added brand of the OD field. OD is not dead, OD is not in demise (Bradford and Burke, 2005) – OD is alive and kicking (Gallos, 2006) particularly in the UK and Europe. The time has come for the latecomers to the field to do something to rescue the reputation of the front-runners (American colleagues) by dedicating ourselves to evaluation with enthusi-asm and professionalism. When you and I do that, not only will the field benefit, but you and I will also benefit as we prove our worth to those whom we work for – after all, that is why we are in this profession.

Section 3

The other day, someone told me we should turn SST to SSS or BDD in change. 'What are SST and BDD?' I asked, and he said SST is Structure, System and Technical system and BDD (or SSS) is Behaviour, Dialogue, and Development, backed up by Stories, Styles and Skills. This person was not a change-savvy or experienced manager, yet he expressed a profound summation of how change needs to embrace the elegant and sophisticated way dialogic OD and complexity/chaos writers portray.

The current reality is that change is changing – it becomes the new and then the old normal, happening more frequently, radically and complexly. Yet failure rates remain high mainly because:

- Structure, system and technical system are still the key focus in change, instead of people engagement, behavioural change and upping the change capability of system members. The style is still tell and sell, advocacy versus inquiry, getting buy-in versus gaining commitment through meaningful engagement.

- People are often not sufficiently engaged and hence have low commitment to the new ways of work. Over time, people become cynical as they accumulate experience of being continuously under attended.

- Change competency of the system members (all line leaders) has been low. There is an underinvestment in their training and development when they take on the role of a change agent. Many of them have not been shown how to work with different dimensions of change. When the ability to support change mainly resides outside of the organization, there is no strong internal change capability to continue to develop and embed change within the organization. This in turn compromises the system's ability to evolve into an 'ever-changing' organization.
- All the above plus having a power elite that still holds the traditional change paradigm in the driver's seat of the change.

Given this context, and with a word count restriction, I faced the difficult choice as to whether I should devote a chapter to a deeper drill into Complexity and Chaos theory, a chapter on Dialogic OD and Change, and a chapter on all the other new academic research on other approaches. But I finally chose three relatively narrow areas that I think may offer readers less confusion and greater confidence, which are practical enough to apply. There are two reasons for my choice: one is because there is a wide range of excellent publications on those topics that readers can access directly, and it would not make sense for me to summarize their work. Second, I think the time has come for OD practitioners to do more integrating of the existing thinking and practice in change – especially when there are abundant topics of change to which we have all have been exposed. There is always a season for everything. This is the season for us to do more of our own synthesis and integration of what we know and what we do. Without that, it is hard to know what to do when more and more new exciting findings and ideas come our way. I have seen many practitioners suffer from unnecessarily low esteem about their skill and knowledge, as they always feel they do not know enough. Given the proliferation of change publications, each tries to differentiate their work from other previously published work, and it is confusing and almost impossible for most us to know what to think. This is especially true when mentally we cannot learn every piece of writing nor every single tool and method in change. I would like to encourage colleagues that what you know is good enough for now, especially if you are an experienced practitioner. At this stage in your career, it is more important for you to take stock of what you already know and do some integration work as informed by practice experience. That way, you will be in a position to develop a steering map for yourself. Part of the journey going from technician to professional to being masterful is developing an increasingly fine-tuned sense of well-developed intuitive insights to steer us.

The reason I called Chapter 7 'Living at the edge of chaos of change' is because that is where most practitioners live. We exist between the dominant world of traditional change culture and the exciting, ever-evolving world of OD and complexity science change paradigm. This chapter aims to

explore the merits of both different approaches to change, the distinctive characteristics of each, and the implications of our practice by being in the 'in-between zone'. The blending of approaches may give those practitioners who work in a predominantly traditional change culture more confidence to navigate through the old and new to operate on the edge of chaos.

Chapter 8 focuses on how to balance the need and the role of the back room matters with the front room matters – again a strategy to be operating on the edge of the chaos zone. The key point I am trying to make is that any change needs the balance of a strong back room set up to serve as a financial, resource, man and women power, governance, temporary change structure, etc, as a container to support the dedicated front room work with people engagement which will continue to emerge in the complex changing context. I have put in a few practice notes to give readers tips on how to blend these two worlds. You may find this chapter more practical than inspiring, but hopefully useful.

But here comes a clear warning – it is disastrous if we allow the back room work, the project plan, the infrastructure to dominate or lead the change – which is still the dominant change approach for many organizations. While certain infrastructures, eg budget, resources, scale, scope, reasonable outcome expectation, and temporary change structure, etc, are needed to be in place, the back room work must serve under the front room agenda. Working in tandem they are there to support the change that needs to cross the borders of functions, divisions, locations etc.

In Chapter 9 I attempt to write a practical and simple (dumbed-down) version of how to shift patterns, especially behavioural change. Culture change has become a mega phrase for decades and we all know that if a business is to attain its higher performance goals, then there will need to be a genuine need to change the way its people behave across the board, and ultimately change its culture fundamentally. Yet after all this time, 'how to change culture?' is still the most frequently asked question posed to me and those change agents I know well are still feeling wobbly about how they can start working at culture and behaviour change from the beginning of the change initiative.

There is no substantial research as to what type of culture will be most **fit** for organizations to operate in a turbulent world. However, through time, there have been some cumulative hints, especially from various complexity and chaos writers. Based on those writings, I have pulled together the following 'cultural patterns' grid. The premise is that if these cultural features exist, there will be more conducive conditions to build 'ever-changing' capability. None of the contents of the grid are from me, but in retrospect they gel very nicely with my consultancy experiences. Finally, remember that **context** is everything. There is no good or bad culture, only 'fit' or 'misfit' in light of the strategic ambitions operating within their context.

People at all levels are environmentally savvy and willing to share knowledge with whoever needs the information to act and make more robust decisions.	Someone is taking responsibility to monitor how the inner org workings match outer environmental demands, and to track whether the speed of inner change matches the speed of outer changes.	All leadership are trained system thinkers – and decisions are taken with a whole-system perspective.	Leaders, staff, partners take building effective relationships as their top priority work. They know it is through relationships that things get done in a speedy way. They refuse to let structural constraints become an impediment.
People tend to be more proactive rather than reactive – they think ahead and they are ready for different scenarios to happen. They thrive on living at the edge of chaos.	Leaders and staff are more collegial than hierarchical. Whoever can do their best is being helped to achieve that. Rank and wisdom have no correlation. All system members operate from a dialogical and inquiry mode.	There is an intentional effort on the part of leaders to encourage an ever-increasing capacity for people, units to self-organize in ways that will enable everyone in the organization to function at the optimal level.	People welcome diversity as it gives the organization an edge. People have sufficient skills to surface diversity, tensions and differences for the sake of reaping a more innovative way to work.
People in the organization do not have any difficulties living with ambiguity, polarities, and dilemmas. They are comfortable working through things in a complex manner without prematurely closing down the debate/thinking.	The organization recruits, trains and develops people to grow an agile mental model and agile adaptive behaviour – so things can be shifted with no time lag. Such behaviour is being rewarded.	People are supported to engage in transformational learning – through achievement, failures, and missed opportunities, etc. Every situation offers an occasion for individuals and the organization to learn how to be better in the long run.	Transformational learning requires leaders and staff to minimize ego and be willing to share mistakes, vulnerabilities, lessons learnt, resources, knowledge, information – and thinking of the collective good.

All the above at this time have limited research back-up, yet intuitively and experientially they feel right for some practitioners. I have definitely seen organizations that are in possession of some of these characteristics operating well at their output level while their internal climate is much more positive and motivating. Try to reflect and integrate your experiences and insights – and see whether this grid makes sense to you. This is what I mean when I say that the season has come for more of us to reflect and integrate, so that our working theories can emerge.

I hope all three chapters offer some ideas about how we can stay on the 'edge of chaos' of change – the intersection of stability and instability, old and new, big data planning, striving for emergence. For now, I would like to encourage practitioners to stay pragmatic and utilize all the most helpful bits from the traditional approaches, the OD approaches and the complexity lens that are necessary for any change journey to ensure we are versatile and agile enough to capture the prize of transformational change.

Finally, in working with change we will need to pay attention to our own instrumentality – how we consult, how we behave, how we embody the 'end game' that the system transformation needs to get to. We have to be as clean as we can be in working through all our relationships, especially with those who press any of the buttons that will send us to an 'off-guard and off-awareness zone'. Our job is first to become an expert of our own behaviour change before we can support others (individuals and systems) in using the content of Chapter 9 to achieve deep change. Embrace the OD and complexity and chaos principles **plus** stay politically savvy and pragmatic as a sensible means to gain more power to influence the transition work that needs to be done within the organization to work with change in a more humane way.

Note

Before we move on, I would like to clarify two concepts that are used frequently in this section. One is 'complex adaptive system' and the other is 'edge of chaos'.

Complex adaptive systems have been defined with variation by writers in the complexity and chaos field. For this section I chose to define it according to Glenda Eoyang from HSD (2010) through her teaching programme – 'a collection of individual agents who have the freedom to act in unpredictable ways, and whose actions are interconnected such that one agent's actions changes the context for other agents.' Examples of complex adaptive systems include the stock market, groups of people, ant colonies, bee colonies, the internet, any networks, gardens and human beings. They are all diverse living elements made up of multiple interconnected agents that have the capacity to change and learn from experience.

So in reality, all organizations are complex adaptive systems, ie inherently adaptive, which is where we OD practitioners should start from in our assumptions. All living systems are naturally adaptable, but the fact that they do not behave in that way is because there are multiple factors that restrict them from exercising their nature. Osborne and Hinson, in their consultancy work, (Change Fusion, 2014) identify six factors that affect the ability to adapt. They are: drive for fitness, safety, diversity of views, degree of stability, connectivity, and control. They use the concept of dialling up or down of any of these factors in order to unleash the adaptive part of any of the system. For example, if the control and stability is *high* and drive for fitness, connectivity, diversity and safety are *low*; the natural capacity to

adapt will be restricted. So when we talk about the complex adaptive change approach, we are talking about what the change processes need to do in order to unleash the system's ability to adapt.

The second concept is 'edge of chaos' which has two aspects to its definition. One is how I treat this term in this section – the *state* or *condition* of living at the edge of both stability and instability. While this can be a confusing state, it also offers some of the unthinkable opportunities to experiment and be agile – a bit like Bridges' neutral zone in his transition work (2004).

The second use of 'edge of chaos' refers to the characteristics of living in this zone. For example, if an organization chooses to build patterns in living on the edge of chaos, some of the patterns one can see may include: just enough procedure, not too little, and not too much. Having just enough clear parameters, but not too many rules and not being too rigid so that everyone can act within parameters, having well-connected relationships etc. These characteristics can be seen in the grid below which I use sometimes to do my diagnostic and educative work with clients.

Chaos	Edge of Chaos	Order
Too little procedure	Just enough procedure	Too much procedure
Anarchy	Clear parameter and key	Too many rules
Confusion	The what is clearer than the how	Rigidity
Risk taking	Risk taking base on data and past learning	Low/ no risk
Too many connections	Everyone can act within parameters	Only purposeful connections
Free for all, everyone can act	Good discerning mix	Command and control
Informal rather than formal contacts	Well connected on relationships	Formal rather than informal contacts
Gossip	Info for all	Isolation
Polarity		
Purposeless		

LMYCJ , Q&E adaptation of Stacey (1992)

I provided these two explanations in this overview with the purpose of helping readers to see and understand the context in which we write about change.

Living at the edge of chaos of change

It is very common that in the opening of any publication on change there is a statement of contrast of what the author has to offer in change management against the change approach sourced from the Newtonian science.

While 'traditional change practice' has its value in the back room (see Chapter 8), its continued dominance in shaping the current approach to change alarms most of us whose current reality is firmly rooted in our actual experience working with change in a complex, turbulent, emerging, and sometimes chaotic context. However there are encouraging signs that things are shifting:

- There is a slow, daunting realization among those from all persuasions who lead change that there are now too many unpredictable and unexpected dynamics in change, and the experience of the rise of 'autocatalytic processes' (which means change takes place spontaneously) is leading the assumption of how systems transform down towards the dissolution stage.

- Many traditional change managers (there are still a lot of them out there) know that the current approaches are ill-equipped to help organizations move fast enough to become more self-organized, with an accompanied greater agility and autonomy as a necessary survival strategy.

- Organizations that always run their change from the centre have seen that a centrally led change approach fails to equip them to be opportunists on the lookout for the continuous emergent patterns from simple actions that are taken at local levels. From experience, they know centralized change programmes lead to a lack of ability to instantly 'sweat' the various small efforts which potentially can create great impact.

- Leaders who are wise and thoughtful know in their hearts that the current deeply held cultural assumptions and established behaviour patterns are impeding the growth of the 'distributed leadership'

necessary in complex change, which requires those who do not have legitimate power in the hierarchy to be able to act, spread, disrupt, push, and create alternative patterns which are 'fitter' to stay agile.

Many OD practitioners know that within this context (where conditions, people, and events are shifting continuously), the traditional change approaches of orderly planning and control are becoming increasingly limited in their utility – in fact they render any change effort vulnerable. The dilemma OD practitioners face is that while they know about the fitter and more appropriate change methodologies, their organization and the powerful elite they work for or with are still deeply rooted to the mechanical way of working with change – so the question becomes how to be evocative/provocative/ educational in a highly political, anxiety-ridden context whose leadership is there to defend their own and organization belief system.

CASE EXAMPLE

Let's take some of my recent experiences as case examples of the dominance of the traditional way of doing change:

1 One transnational pharmaceutical company was spending millions of pounds to secure strong external project management expertise to tell the top how to restructure their global organization by involving only the top 100 leaders.

2 Another transnational energy company exhorted a 4-step approach to roll out their global diversity and inclusion talent management approach – without due regard for the diverse cultural context in which their organization operates.

3 A UK public sector organization carried out its organization-wide public service transformation by edict from the top leaders as to what each department needed to do by when – all with great haste with almost no people engagement effort.

4 Another pharmaceutical organization bought in an expensive external consultancy firm to help them to deal with a regulatory verdict about the lack of compliance in their quality standard, without involving the shop floor and other parts of the system to figure out the quality issues and solicit their support to solve the issues.

These few recent cases exemplify some of the major challenges faced by many internal and external OD practitioners. Let's name three:

1 Most of the power elite and the dominant decision makers in organizations are still basically dedicated Newtonian followers – even though experientially they are in touch with the major shifts happening in the external environment.

2 Many OD practitioners have found it hard and unsafe to do otherwise as they know deviating too much from the traditional change approach may risk rejection, loss of credibility and impact.

3 There are not many internal partners who have the synchronized understanding of the OD and complexity approach to change, hence in that context exhortations like 'please be courageous', 'exercise your voice' 'step out and step up' only increase the sense of guilt, as they are often not in positions powerful enough to deviate from the dominant culture in approaching change.

These dilemmas – stay true to the OD change approaches, yet stay pragmatic to gain credibility – face all OD practitioners. This new section on change is my effort to help boost the practitioners' sense of safety to be more impactful and willing to lead the way to do change differently with confidence (not with guilt) all within the core theories and principles of OD.

In this chapter, I will touch on four areas:

● What is the Newtonian change approach?

● What are the differences between the traditional and OD change approaches?

● What are the differences between the traditional and the complex adaptive change approaches?

● What are the implications of living on the edge of change?

What is The Newtonian Change Paradigm?

This approach has been called by many names – traditional change approach, classical approach, expert-led change approach, the 'old' change approach. For consistency's sake I will refer to it as the 'traditional change approach.' I decided to put together a composite list of characteristics which comes from many sources but especially from Eoyang and Olson (2002) and Marshak (1993) who succinctly captured many of the key assumptions behind this paradigm. I have turned the characteristics into a checklist so that you can take it to your leadership team to start the conversation as to what are your current organization change approaches.

When one puts this list down on paper, it seems that this way of running organization and change is so old-fashioned it is hard to imagine any organization still uses it to tackle their change situation. Surprisingly, there are

FIGURE 7.1 Characteristics of the traditional change approach (in no specific order)

Instruction: Tick those descriptions that fit into your organization change approach.

Tick box	Dominant Approaches	Notes
	Change is often planned/managed by those who are at the top or by outsiders (eg consultancy firms) and not by those who really know the change situation – can be seen as an elite-led process.	
	Change occurs in a more linear fashion and there is a belief that prediction is possible and hence it can be run by project management processes. A dominant project management approach overtakes a people-centric approach.	
	The dominant focus of our change is economics, efficiency and effectiveness and not organization and people development; great emphasis on fixing structure/system; deficiency is often the starting point.	
	Wisdom lies at the top – senior managers are the ones that will provide the vision of the change programme and the top need to have a greater managerial control – control means we will need to provide the rules and regulations.	
	The mode of change leadership is 'engineering and directing' – with the message that destiny has already been shaped and hence any communication is about cascading down the right way of doing change, with a tight time scale for delivery.	
	We can describe our change approach as more formula led, with strong a heritage from a rational, bureaucratic framework – assume machine dominated.	
	By deduction, our change approach assumes humans are passive – and if we say they should go that way, they will all go; the human dimension of change is low priority in any change effort.	
	We are concerned with metrics/measurement, linear pathways, and evidence-based decision criteria versus energy, imagination, and unleashing the capability of the people through this change effort.	

more organizations that operate from this change philosophy than one would think, and therefore it is normal for OD practitioners who operate within such organizations to feel unsafe if they need to break away from this approach to do change in a complex, adaptive way. However, I believe there are some useful approaches and insights to be learned from the view

FIGURE 7.2 Traditional change approach versus OD change approach

Change approach	More emphasis	Methods	Dominant values	Management of change as:
Traditional change management	Outcomes	Elite processes – expert led	Economic focus	Engineering and directing – destiny-shaped and cascade down
OD	Dual emphasis – processes and outcomes	Participatory processes – people-led with clear parameters set by senior leaders	Humanistic – people focus as a key way to achieve economic gain	Facilitating and engaging – giving people a voice, inviting people to co-construct and re-shape/revise the destiny

Adapted from Robert Marshak's teaching slide in a UK NTL OD Certificate Programme

that any change does need to pay attention to. By embracing the positive bits in our approach, we resolve the dilemmas posed by the two worlds and get ourselves to be more acceptable to the power elite, and hence earn the platform to influence the organization to shift their perspective in change.

In Figure 7.2, I have adapted Bob Marshak's work to contrast the traditional and OD change approaches. This figure gives us the 'range' to spread to from the traditional approach – especially in terms of our design work in intervention. By 'range' I mean we keep as much as we can from traditional change management and 'blend' that with OD methods to form an approach that will satisfy the top whose paradigm still focuses on tasks, project management, linear and mechanical approaches to change, yet allows us to either covertly or overtly build the OD approach into the change processes. This, to me, is what living at the edge of chaos mean as a practitioner.

Let's use a practice example to illustrate this way of balancing.

If you find yourself living in that edge, may I advise you to do the following in the contracting state: set up an event gathering together all the top group members to ensure there is a collective view on the required outcomes, level of gains, and the spelling-out of the non-negotiated parameters (value, resources, delivery, etc) within which the change processes have to operate.

In the same meeting, ask them who they think should chair the change team, and what should be the governance structure. Once they have agreed these matters, in a tentative way, inform them of the possibility that you will try a 'number of things' or 'this and that' in order to get some data from certain target groups with internal people whom they recommend. Also ask when they would like to hear a report from the next phase of work.

It is important during the contracting with them that you repeat what you have heard as their non-negotiable parameters and check whether you have got those right. If you feel comfortable, then give them your guarantee that you will stay within those parameters. After those agreements have been made, in a 'light touch' way use a variety of methods to ensure you will set out the change project to be successful. The number of things you may propose includes the various ways the change team will involve and engage people within the parameters they have set. It is important for us to know that if we aim to do what we can to direct the change path towards its eventual success, the **how** does not matter as long as:

a) we operate within their agreed parameter;

b) we are successful in delivering what they asked.

But the discernment and judgement in these situations requires us to be politically savvy and building alliance across all level of systems.

There are too many OD principles of change to list, but the following are those that may have most practical implications for OD practitioners in working with change. In fact, after scanning the book, it will be fun for you to attempt to build your own OD principles of change. Here are a few examples:

- Start from the end game up – involve those who the successful implementation is critically dependent on as early as possible to gain their commitment.

- The more complex the change, the greater the necessity to bring the whole system together in the room to collectively make personal meaning of the change.

- People need to have their voices heard and be able to work through their divergence before they will converge to set up the platform for successful implementation.

- People do not resist change; they will support what they help to create, especially when they can make their choices in a voluntary way.

- Unleashing the self-activated energizing commitment to issues which people care deeply about is the key to sustainable change.

- At the end of the change journey, simultaneous personal and system development will guarantee that the change will be sustainable. In other words, change needs to be synonymous with development.

- Systemic thinking and systemic alignment are key to give coherence before and after the change process.

- Change is NOT an event but a series of interventions, both planned and emergence, directed at specific level of system.

FIGURE 7.3 Traditional and CAS models of organization change

Traditional approach to change	Complexity approach to change
Well planned with prediction; tight specification	Semi-plan focus on emergence; loose specification
Hierarchical and directive	Distributed leadership and influence
Parts, disjointed silo, low in connection	Whole, see interdependence, high in connection
Focus on centrally led plan and watch for compliance to plan	Focus on the role of local leaders and watch how it spreads randomly
Focus on system, structure, process	Focus on patterns and behaviour
Prone to standardise approaches, variation is not welcome	Discovery, explore, experiment, and welcome diversity
Known solutions	Solutions unknown (unknowable in advance)
Big plans show direction	Small is beautiful, sweat them to discover (take advantage of chance and serendipity)
Plan, reflect, learn and re-plan	Act, experiment, reflect and see, then learn, and plan
Programme led	Movement spread

Adapted from work by Stacey, Euyong, Quade, Osborne etc for this book

What are the differences between the traditional and complex adaptive models of change?

In Figure 7.3 I contrast the traditional and the complex adaptive models of change which I put here with the intention to further expand the 'range' of our change approach. By 'range', I mean you can now blend Figures 7.1, 7.2 and 7.3 together to identify how to take the best from the traditional change management, use the OD key principles as your methodological backbone and use the Complex Adaptive Model of change to focus on the context in which change takes place and how best to work with emergence in an opportunistic way, not to mention challenging us to make relationships our top work to empower the client system to get things done in this complex environment.

What are the implications for our change practice when operating at the edge of chaos?

What are the implications for OD practitioners who are savvy and committed to apply the OD approach and the complexity lens to change within a traditional change management culture? It is important that all OD practitioners know how to navigate through this type of dilemma in the following ways:

1 **Actively promote OD and a complexity change approach AND stay as acceptable as you need to be to the organization you work for.** We need to stay on the upsides of exposing and educating clients to the OD and complexity lens and start to challenge them to change the way they do change, while remaining 'acceptable' within the Newtonian culture by being strong in the project management approach and using some of the strong aspects of the traditional change management approach to gain influence.

2 **Stay safe by working OD principles covertly into the change methodology AND use OD and complexity methodology overtly to help clients learn how to do change differently.** We need to be sensible not to exceed the 'weird' factor within organizations to avoid rejection, especially before we have built up sufficient street credibility. But that should not stop us from covertly instilling or blending the OD and complexity approaches into the Newtonian way of doing change. Look for every opportunity, especially in working with an appointed change team or eager local leaders, to overtly teach the OD and complexity lens into the 'new' approach to change – we need to constantly think of new strategies to influence and educate the traditional client in this different paradigm.

3 **Build the OD/complexity change approach into the formal leadership development programme AND use the change process to educate leaders in 'real time'.** OD practitioners need to be far more intentional to start working at the leadership level in whatever client system we work in, using a powerful leadership development programme to introduce the OD systemic and complexity lens to them, using their local case of change to teach on this approach and then synchronize the two approaches. We also must forever try to find innovative ways to build this aspect of leadership development into the various change teams and change agents we work with. In that way, we will help to build a cadet of leadership, sharing the same approaches to change in every project.

4 **Increase our ability to operate in polarities.** In supporting change in this complex context, we will need to know how to work with a set

FIGURE 7.4 Types of polarities OD practitioners need to work with in change

Back room versus front room approaches	Analytical/rational versus intuitive	Science versus arts, hard science versus soft science
Facts, figures and data versus emotional and feeling	Content creating versus people engagement	Profit and cost conscious versus customer centric
Reality focused versus dream inspired	Fast work versus slow work	Head, analytic, task focus versus conversational/ dialogical focus
Task-centric versus people-centric	Top trend direction versus abundance in grass roots innovation	Detailed planning, grab opportunity, work with emergence

of two opposites that are interdependent and not mutually exclusive. These opposite poles always produce ongoing tensions which can create a lot of discomfort for us and others. Our way is to try to problem-solve them, but in fact they are polarities to manage and not problems to be solved. This ability to stay in lots of ambiguity and tension is a key competence for us as change agent in the complex world. Hence knowing how to work with polarities is an asset. See **www.polaritymanagement.com.**

Whatever polarities that we will need to work through, most of all we need to function well both professionally as OD practitioners and in our relationship traction to build an impactful presence within the system and earn the right to break the established model of change work. We need to get the best 'upside' of both poles and not fall under the 'downside'. Figure 7.4 outlines other types of polarities that we need to work with to improve our savviness in supporting change in this context.

Conclusion

In conclusion, given that the majority of organizations are still operating in the prevailing Newtonian paradigm, it would be prudent to encourage the readers to stay savvy by being **both/and** – do not throw out all the Newtonian approaches, but glean the useful methods and techniques from that traditional way of doing change, and then blend them with the OD systemic and complexity lens – which should remain as our dominant professional base. By staying pragmatic and in the spirit of the contingency theory, practitioners need to be emergent in our means of delivering support given the context in which we operate. That is the gist of what I intend to do through the chapters in this new section.

FIGURE 7.5 OD Map to Change

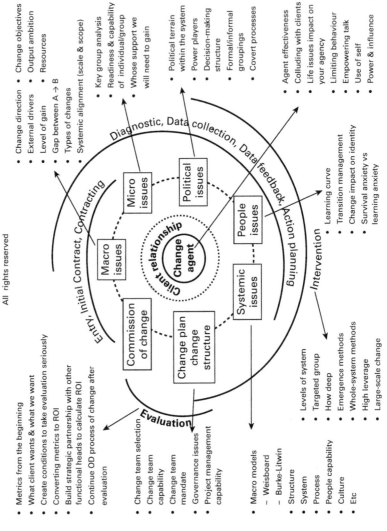

OD Map to Change

By LMYCY @ Q&E Consultancy and Training Services

- Change direction
- External drivers
- Level of gain
- Gap between A → B
- Types of changes
- Systemic alignment (scale & scope)

- Change objectives
- Output ambition
- Resources

- Key group analysis
- Readiness & capability of individual/group
- Whose support we will need to gain

- Political terrain within the system
- Power players
- Decision-making structure
- Formal/informal groupings
- Covert processes

- Agent effectiveness
- Colluding with clients
- Life issues impact on your agency
- Limiting behaviour
- Empowering talk
- Use of self
- Power & influence

Diagnostic, Data collection, Data feedback, Action planning

Entry, Initial Contract, Contracting

Micro issues

Political issues

Macro issues

People issues

Client relationship

Change agent

Systemic issues

Commission of change

Change plan change structure

Intervention

- Learning curve
- Transition management
- Change impact on identity
- Survival anxiety vs learning anxiety

Evaluation

- Metrics from the beginning
- What client wants & what we want
- Create conditions to take evaluation seriously
- Converting metrics to ROI
- Build strategic partnership with other functional heads to calculate ROI
- Continue OD process of change after evaluation

- Change team selection
- Change team capability
- Change team mandate
- Governance issues
- Project management capability

- Macro models
 - Weisboard
 - Burke-Litwin
- Structure
- System
- Process
- People capability
- Culture
- Etc

- Levels of system
- Targeted group
- How deep
- Emergence methods
- Whole-system methods
- High leverage
- Large-scale change

Theoretical Platform

It is OK to continue to salvage anything from anywhere that proves useful to support our clients' change work in their diverse context while ensuring we are both 'acceptable' and 'effective' agents of change without compromising our values, field discipline, principles, and intent. I believe that the field of OD has always been a bigger and more inclusive container to host diverse perspectives and practices, all in the service of those whom we are called to support.

Figure 7.5 is my effort to sum up the OD map to change by combining the OD cycle as a base process with all the key areas of change to which practitioners need to pay attention. It is descriptive, not summative, normative or exhaustive. I constructed this for teaching in the NTL programme, but always encourage others that it is important for them to build a personal map like this one to guide their own change work. This is what I mean about focusing on more integrative work.

I hope in the end, these three chapters will help to:

a) lessen your confusion and guilt about what paradigm you are using, and what methods you should stick to without your colleagues thinking you are out of date;

b) help internal practitioners to survive pragmatically in a world where the Newtonian approach is still held by the power elite as the only way to do change;

c) cross-check your own paradigm and practices to make you fit enough to support those who trust you to come alongside them to do change;

d) update and equip you to be even more dynamic and effective in your change work, as there are many exciting complexity writers and practitioners to learn from and update our practice;

e) show you how to blend the three perspectives of change together in order to support the change work of your client.

A word about change vocabulary

I have been making a concerted effort to stop using words and phrases like:

'managing change';

'dealing with resistance';

'allowing them to…';

'giving them the opportunity to…';

'how to gain buy-in, change project or programme'.

Instead, I have been using phrases like:

'invitation to participate and mould the change initiatives';

'what to expect from the change journey experiences';

'journey co-ordinator';

'those who are asked to support the members of the system to do their own navigating through changes…';

'asking them to join us in setting up processes that will help to make sense to themselves'.

You can tell some of the phrases are not easy to use, but I hope that the intent is clear to you. To subtly move away from the Newtonian way of 'doing' change to people, we will need to be conscious to use language that reflects the OD approaches – 'walking alongside people to support them to help themselves in a more and more self-organized way.'

Back room and front room change matters

Overview

This chapter aims to convey the synergistic value of blending the Newtonian, OD and Complexity and chaos theories and practice to help practitioners to gain power and influence in a traditional world of work and yet remain effective in supporting change using the core of OD value and methods.

There are many 'change matters' to which any change agent/team needs to attend to during the process of change. I have chosen to focus on two key areas:

1 Back room matters (logistics, plan, infrastructure matters that support the change);

2 Front room matters (the people dimension and the engagement issue).

I will end the chapter on the importance of blending the two matters together.

Back room matters – macro level of change work

OD cycle and change:

First, before reading this chapter, do revisit Chapter 3 on entry, contracting, diagnosis, intervention, and evaluation. The OD cycle is our 'non-linear' navigation map whenever we are asked to support any change initiative, as it will guide us through the essential phases in our consultancy work with clients.

Second, it is important for us to identify the change commissioners, build relationships with them and obtain a clear brief, confirm what they want to

achieve through this change, and agree with them as to who we can access to undertake the diagnostic work before we can scope the scale of the work – in other words, undertake all the work before we can formulate a proposal for final approval. The proposal we make will need to have a clear scope and methodological outline, with timescale and resource implications before the contract can be formalized and we move on to the next phase of work.

Finally, we must decide how we can map the output from the change initiative as part of evaluation, even in that initial contracting stage.

List of macro Issues

Against this context, let's look at the first set of 'back-room change matters', also known as the **macro** matters because these are the essential macro organization issues that require clarity before we can support the clients in planning, re-planning, and constantly re-adjusting as the change journey evolves.

The following macro list is by no means exhaustive, but it does capture some key areas that most leaders (who grew up with the traditional change culture) care about but may not find a way to articulate clearly. I designed Figure 8.1 as a grid so that the change team can work through the list to gain clarity on what the change is about, and then they can involve others to work through the questions as part of the collective sense-making processes in the data collection phase.

Getting these macro issues spelt out at the beginning of the change, especially by multiple parties besides the commissioners, is a prudent thing to do. For example the groups that can give data include: the commissioners of change, the temporary change team, cross-functional members who have a view, staff and especially the group(s) the change will impact, and those whom the organization will rely on for implementation. The methods on how you may go about doing that can be found in Practice Note 1. As mentioned earlier, the list can be adapted as part of the engagement exercise. In that way, sense-making of the change initiatives will be done individually within the collective consciousness context.

Let's take a brief look at each of these questions.

a) What is the change about?

Starting out, it would be helpful to ask the system leaders a simple question which often has significant consequences, such as 'What is this change about?' When the question is asked, you may get a frown and a curt response – 'What do you mean? This is a re-structuring change project.' To which the reply is, 'Yes, I know this is a restructuring project, but what is the change really about? When we get to the new structure, what would you and the organization like to see happen? What would you like the change to achieve for the organization and for what reason?'

FIGURE 8.1 List of back room macro questions

List of macro questions	Who have data to give?	What are the most appropriate data collection methods?
A) What is the change about? Change to what – what is the arrival point? What would it look like? How far is it between where the organization is now and where they need or want to arrive?		
B) What is the business case – why change? What is the benefit case – what benefit will we gain if we achieve the change purpose?		
C) What is the minimum gain (level of gain) that will make this change worthwhile? What value will the change create for the organization to justify the effort?		
D) What type of change is this? What is the nature or focus of this change? What scope and scale will this change be?		
E) What type of resources would the change need? Do we need to have a back room office set up to stimulate and co-ordinate the change?		
F) What type of temporary change structure will we need to support the change journey?		
G) What systemic issues would the change create? How extensive would the systemic alignment work be?		

The real challenge of such questions is to see whether the change commissioners can summarize the essence of the change in one sentence or even in one paragraph (the answer you will get will be useful for future communication). If they stumble in answering the question, this may mean a number of things:

- there is a lack of clarity on what the change is about;
- those who think the change is a good idea have not yet thought through what the change is really aiming to do;

PRACTICE NOTE 1 There are many ways to get answers to the macro list

You can use the macro questions to design a 2–3 hour event where you can ask those who commission the change and their highly valued stakeholders to get together to jointly get the change issues right. You can use this event to share relevant information to engage those who are asked to attend.

If you cannot get a whole group together, then do separate events for separate groups, but still aim to get the whole group together to look at the data gathered from this type of event.

Train local leaders to help run this type of focus group as part of engaging them to take a 'distributed leadership' role.

In this way, we can also use the training and briefing sessions to help them to make personal sense of the change, so that they will be able to work through their personal doubts and questions.

In this way, when they go out to run focus groups, they can be confident that they find the change not only doable but important to the organization's survival.

Design a short online questionnaire in which everyone in the relevant parts of the organization is asked to share their views about the change from their perspective – data for system alignment issues.

Ask another group of people to learn how to 'cut' the data. Also ask them to report the data from the online questionnaire to the governance body and/or executive team.

Use the data from the initial batch of focus groups to construct an educational multiple-choice tool for people to get involved in guessing the answers to some of these questions.

Show the group how to use imagery to run this type of diagnostic but 'meaning-making' type of group eg car race, climbing a mountain, etc.

Train supervisors/other local leaders to run information briefing sessions. Prepare the information pack for local leaders – so to grow and reinforce them for their role in supporting the change. Consider using the multiple choice tool to start each information session. Have prizes for those who score highly in the questionnaire.

Set up 'action research' sessions where people can join different teams to investigate how the other divisions think about these macro issues. Have talented and shop floor people work together to interview key leaders about these macro issues. Again, involve them to 'cut' the data. At every opportunity, mix up the systems and turn them into joint investigators so they can be helped to make personal meaning of the change.

- they have not been clear what level of change the organization is aiming for;
- whether there are any real benefits even if the organization can get to the end point.

Given the emergent nature of change, a pristine sentence cannot be expected. But often there are real differences between those leaders who can hold their line and articulate what the change is about and what it is aiming to achieve and those who cannot.

b) Business case and benefit case

What is the difference between a business case and a benefit case? The business case focuses more on the reasons why the organization needs or chooses to respond because of the challenges presented from within the organization or pressure coming from environmental factors. The business case is often (but not necessarily) based on a deficiency lens – something does not work, or could work better, or needs to do better, hence those who propose the change express sound logic as to why the business/organization needs to go down that particular change path.

Conversely, the benefit case may often come from the organization eager to scale a higher summit, achieve greater market share, be known for giving greater and higher quality of service to their customers, etc. Of course there are times an organization has to undertake change because the business case is so strong, although they may get dismal benefit from the change. Or sometimes the benefit case is so strong it does not need a business case to support the need to change. It is important to remember the context in which change has to take place and the narrative organization leaders use to mobilize the troops for action.

c) What level of gain will make the change worthwhile?

Having worked out the business case, the benefit case, or both, the next question for commissioners is whether it is worthwhile to go down this particular change track by identifying what different levels of gain they intend to achieve given the potential risk involved – especially given the scale and scope of the change versus the organization's current capacity and capability.

No one can be a real prophet, but helping the client group to use their best analytical and intuitive functions to project possible levels of gain against possible risks can help the organization to sort out one of the most critical decisions, ie 'In light of our current capacity and capability, and other risk factors, would we be able to achieve a minimum level of gain – and what would that look like? Given this level of gain, is it worth our

FIGURE 8.2 Levels of gains

Levels	What that means	Which levels we should or must aim for
Level 1	minimum gain	
Level 2	acceptable gain	
Level 3	more than acceptable gain	
Level 4	excellent gain	
Level 5	best scenario gain	

while to undertake this change or would we be better off staying in this current form? Do we need to rethink the whole situation?'.

The aim of this type of dialogue is not so much to help the organization members to change the decision to either do the change or not, but to help them think in a much more expansive way about the nature of the change, and how best to handle the change journey in order to reach the minimum 'acceptable level'. This is a backhanded way to do visioning.

d) Type of change (nature and focus of change)

With the ongoing and increasing complexity in which human systems operate, is there any value for us to delineate the different types of change other than complex change? I believe so. Even though the complexity lens is a given, having a feel for what type of change can aid our intentionality about what processes will be most relevant to support the level of system alignment and the people involved.

There are many types of change, but Figure 8.3 captures the main ones.

FIGURE 8.3 Types of Change

Type of change	vs	Another type of change
Transactional		Transformational
Incremental and continuous		Radical and discontinuous
Evolutionary		Revolution
Local		Total system
Continuing flow		Episodic
Planned		Emergence

From Burke (2002) and Nadler's (1998) definitions, we know all organizations are engaged in transactional-incremental-continuous change as they try to eliminate problems and increase efficiency. They are not necessarily small, but they are part of the orderly flow, hence continuous.

Transformational-radical-discontinuous change is drawn from the Latin *transformare*, which means changing shape. This is the complex, wide-ranging change brought on by fundamental shifts in the external environment. The responses require **radical** departure from the status quo in structure, culture, and key production processes. **Discontinuity** suggests there is substantial disruption to the normal way of functioning and the organization will need to unlearn years of habits.

This latter category is deemed **profound** change as it requires a 'matching' **inner** shift of people's values, aspirations, and behaviours to go with the outer **shifts** in processes, strategies, practices, and systems. In profound change, the organization does not just do something new, it builds its capacity for doing things in a new way. In other words, it builds capacity for ongoing change. Agility is often the outcome of an organization learning how to work with profound change.

Evolutionary versus revolutionary change or continuous versus episodic change are all similar in nature to transactional and transformational change.

Among the literature of the complexity and chaos scientists, eg Stacey (Figure 8.4) and Snowden (Figure 8.5), there are four categories of change: simple, complicated, complex, and chaos, which hold different meanings from the above categories listed in Figure 8.3.

FIGURE 8.4 Stacey Matrix

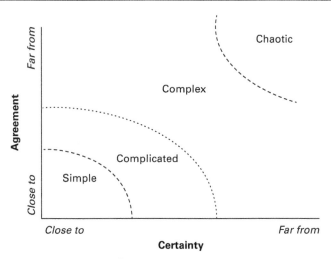

Adapted from work by Stacey. No published source could be traced.

FIGURE 8.5 Cynefin Framework

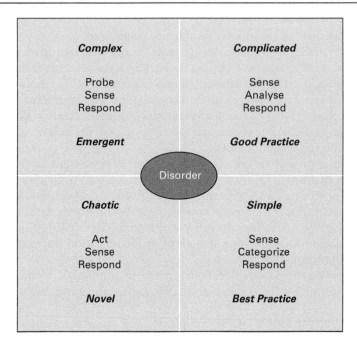

SOURCE: Snowden, D (2002)

- **Simple change** is like making a cake; there are reliable recipes that you can follow, and as long as one does that, a cake will be baked.
- **Complicated change** is not simple but still doable. It is like building an aircraft: very complicated, but as long as one has top-notch engineers and a reliable engineering manual, the plane will be built as there are certain degrees of predictability.
- **Complex change** is often discussed as a **type** of change, but in fact it is more like the conditions we live in and hence the nature of change is complex. Change becomes complex when the future is not knowable even if you have **big** data; when understanding parts does not reveal the whole complex web of facts, networks, and relationships; when cause and effect are difficult to trace, especially when prediction and control of the future is impossible nor is control over nature to improve our life doable.
- **Chaotic change** – when there is inherent variety and uncertainty in a dynamic environment, that requires continuous interpreting and sensing, together with having a collection of individual agents who have the freedom to act in unpredictable ways, and whose actions are interconnected such that one agent's actions can and will change the context for other agents. These multiple interconnected agents make the change hard to predict and can easily fall into the state of disorder and chaos.

When dealing with complex change, shifting one's mental model/paradigm is a critical turnkey – while we can still go on planning, the outcome is not predictable, and one has to be much more eager to spot patterns and opportunities to glean a clue about the next steps. A light touch approach, focusing on sweating the small stuff, disrupting local patterns, and working with emergence are all part of working effectively in complex environments.

OD practitioners need to be interested in what type of change we are supporting because there will be implications for approaches, resource allocation, speed and our change practice, etc. The following list outlines the implications arising from discerning the type of changes:

1 The scale of the back room infrastructure support; the extent of the set-up, the role and governance of the 'change programme office'.

2 The intensity and effort spent in working with those who are affected by the change, and how early the processes need to target behavioural change at which level? Do we know how to achieve that?

3 The type and scale of distributive change leadership the organization needs to build and equip, especially among local leaders and the middle management level, and by when?

4 The type of change support needed from seasoned change leaders to front the change.

5 The level of systemic alignment (structure, processes, policies, competencies, operational protocol, brand, behaviour, partnership relationship, etc) that the change needs to accomplish.

6 The level and type of communication to different stakeholders to achieve what at different phases?

7 How many different levels of organization change we will need to work at, eg the *individual*, the *group or work unit*, the *inter-group level* or the *relationship between different work units*, and the *total system* in order to achieve sustainable results.

Figure 8.6 is designed to help us to think about the dynamics between type of change, practice implications, and task delineation scale/scope, and what type and the extent of resources required. In this grid, I will not define 'simple' and 'complicated/complex' change, as different organizations will have their own definitions of these.

e) What type of resources would the change need?

What type of resources any change initiative needs will depend on the following factors:

- the scale and scope of the change initiative;
- the geographical spread of the organization;
- the speed that is required to achieve major milestones;
- the extent of complexity in the change areas;

- how critical and strategic this change is and whether there is any margin of error allowed in the change initiatives;
- intensity (amount of effort, time, resources speed required, etc.) and complexity (level of interdependence, scope and levels of interventions that need to be done) of the change initiatives;
- risk level it can afford or not.

FIGURE 8.6 Type of change, practice implications and task delineation

Areas that have practice implication	Tasks/resource issues for 'simpler' change	Tasks/resource issues for complicated and complex change
The scale of the back room infrastructure support; the extent of the set-up; the role and governance of the 'change co-ordinating office'.	Do we need a back room set up at all? Is a small team sufficient to co-ordinate the work? All within their current work roles?	A well-set-up back room will be needed to assist the change processes with the right level of staffing and type of personnel, eg OD, communication, financial, HR, events management, project management, strategic planning, etc.
The intensity and effort spent in working with those who are affected by the change, and how early the processes need to start targeting behavioural change.	People who will be affected by the change should be rolled up during the early stage to involve them in designing how to go about the change and implementation. The behavioural piece should be up front as early as possible.	Not just the people who will be affected by the change, in fact the whole system needs to be involved to design, give their views on how the change should be thought of from where they sit and how the change may impact on them. The identification of behavioural shift needs to be done as early as possible with as many groups across the system as possible.
The type and scale of distributive change leadership needs to be built and equipped, especially among local leaders and the middle management level.	It is important to identify who will be leading, supporting, reinforcing, rewarding, correcting and embedding the change, and to pull them out as early as possible to help them make sense of the change and allocate a role for them to opt in or opt out as a supporter of the change in their local area.	The requirement is similar, except the scale and the depth of this piece of work will need to be system wide. We will need to run a large group intervention for the middle management population and build in the type of change capability into the leadership development programme, assigning clear roles to local leaders as early as possible.

FIGURE 8.6 *Continued*

Areas that have practice implication	Tasks/resource issues for 'simpler' change	Tasks/resource issues for complicated and complex change
The type of change support – especially how great is the need for seasoned change leaders to front the change.	Putting together a cross-professional team who know the content of the change matters with some support from local HR/OD professionals may be sufficient.	This scale of change may need more than a 'change journey office' with all sorts of professionals set up to support the change processes. It may also be beneficial to put some experienced internal leaders into the governance and change structure. If the change scale is huge, then different OD support at different stages for different groups – especially in the setting-up stage – will be both necessary and useful.
The level of systemic alignment.	Ongoing systemic alignment should be done as or soon after major milestones are reached.	This will require an ongoing systemic alignment effort – this should be mapped out at the beginning of the change by multiple parties so that alignment work can be ongoing from day one.
The level and type of communication to different stakeholders.	The communication can be incorporated into the 'normal' 'ongoing' communication channels.	The communication needs to be both externally/internally focused. It will be useful to have 'change-specific' brands and channels for communication, supported by a communication professional.
How many different levels of organization change intervention will we need to aim for?	All sustainable change requires a minimum three levels of system intervention – eg any of the following based on the type of change it is: intrapersonal, interpersonal, group, inter-group, divisional, inter-divisional, whole system, inter-system.	For this scale of change, the targeted interventions will almost certainly need to hit as many levels listed in the previous box as possible, as well as with greater intensity and frequency. Internal and external OD practitioners will be needed to support this scale of change.

Based on Figure 8.6, questions need to be asked about whether the change work should be done through normal management processes. Can it be done by delegating a number of local leaders to undertake it in tandem with their day job? Can the change work be done by integrating the change agenda into the normal executive project portfolio? Can the change work be done only through a back room office with full-time change agents running the office and ensuring all streams of work will be integrated to achieve the change within a given time period without losing its people-centric framework?

A note on the impact of insufficient change capacity on change outcome

Insufficient change capacity has more negative impact on the change work than one can imagine. In my experience, many change offices suffer the following problems. They:

- take too long to give a strong start;
- fail to capture unforeseen opportunities to propel the change forward;
- fail to keep the change momentum of the change up; or
- simply do not get to achieve impressive and good-quality change work because members of the change team often have to carry their change duties on top of meeting the relentless demands of their day job.

Instead of seeing the cost of a failed change initiative, many organizations see deploying talents to run the change processes as an unnecessary burden for the organization. Somehow there is a form of madness organization leaders engage in – 'no extra resources need to be deployed – once we declare the need for the change, it will just happen.' By not taking the long view to invest in gathering sufficient people with change capacity, many change projects are set up to fail. This inevitably will lead to those being asked to support the change becoming overwhelmed – subsequently, the stress levels will then undermine morale and change progress. Worst of all, their own leadership credibility will be questioned. This scenario is expounded by Miller's (2013) change article which cited that a major reason change fails in organizations is that people feel overwhelmed by the sheer volume and speed of change initiatives impacting them, hence are unable to take meticulous care of the change work.

One way to increase the willingness of the executive to put realistic full-time resources towards support of the change is to align talent management with change resources. I often challenge the organization and its leaders (with facts and figures) to see that the whole-system change situation is the most fertile ground to:

- Stretch the talent in terms of putting them through a 'real-time strategic' leadership development experience, as the work will give them a whole systemic view of the organization. This would be crucial as by working in a whole-system change initiative, they would shed their myopic view of the organization from only their functional/region/business unit perspectives.

- Gather data on those talents as to whether their strengths and areas for development are the same or different when they are working in a different context – outside of their technical job role. Their involvement in the change office will provide data about whether their talents are more suited to stay on their specialist track or to switch to general management. Those who may be more suitable for the general management route have more rounded competences – the ability to be strategic, to be detail conscious, able to work with different types of people, more people savvy, result driven and can

think more broadly about issues. They tend to be better in systemic thinking. Those who belong on the specialist track are more valuable to continue to grow their depth in their specialist area, free from the demands of a generalist portfolio.

● By putting together a cross-functional talent pool to support the change work, the organization is building a future community of leaders who – by working together in the change journey – find themselves being changed in the process and relying on the group to support themselves in the continuous self-development journey. This will, at the right time, create a leadership cadre to assist the major shift to the organization culture.

This approach has worked very well for organizations that decide to do just that, (Tanser and Lee, 2012 outlines the case I helped them set up). By using the change situation as an opportunity to develop and stretch the talents, they help to ensure change is synonymous with development.

f) The temporary change structure

The temporary change structure can appear to be such a bureaucratic topic, yet when used effectively it can be a very useful engagement tool to gain commitment from relevant stakeholders.

There are at least four types of group any change initiatives can consider establishing:

1 *Change programme office* (tends to be called the change team);

2 *Steering group* – which can also be the governance group;

3 *Reference group* – which can be subject or content expert groups which can give expert advice/insight to the change team on matters for which they need guidance (there can be more than one reference group);

4 *Champion groups* or individual sponsors.

How many of these temporary structures any change initiative wants to set up will depend on the political landscape of the organization (ie how many types of groups or individuals would need a formal role to be enrolled into the change initiative), the complexity of the change, the logistical factors (how widespread people are), and the cultural context of the organization. For some smaller organizations dealing with a deep transformation, up to 40 or 50 per cent of people can be involved in different roles, which in turn will speed up the implementation of the change impressively – because by using these temporary structures, we fast track the personal meaning-making journey through their involvement. As a result of that high level of involvement, the speed of successful implementation is hard to imagine. This phenomenon has happened in some change initiatives I have been involved in.

The role, terms of reference, key activities, and membership of the four temporary change structures are described in Practice Note 2.

PRACTICE NOTE 2 Four temporary change structures: their terms of reference, tasks and membership

Type of group	Terms of reference	Key activities (sample)	Membership
Change co-ordinating office	**Terms of reference:** their job is to co-ordinate and sometimes lead the overall delivery of the various work streams and to ensure there are joined-up efforts in delivering successful implementation. The frequency of their meeting would be as often as it is necessary in the beginning of the change initiative, at least once a week – to give the change a strong start. This will include team launch and other initial training programmes.	Involve/engage as many stakeholders to • Map out key groups and how to engage them • Co-ordinate the design of the change processes • Scope out specific change areas (carry out necessary diagnostic work, test the viability of various options) • Calculate the resources needed and solicit them • Deliver some of the change intervention • Manage a multi-functional team • Oversee and co-ordinate the execution of the change steps • Serve as local centre of communication • Set up the evaluative process • Report regularly to the steering group	This will include an internally named change leader and the leaders of all the different streams of work and support resources, eg strategic project planning, financial, HR/ OD practitioners, administrative support, communication professionals. Person specification – members should have strong... • Performance record • Interpersonal skills • Result driven • Proactive approach • Learning attitude • Team player • Innovative/creative • Good reputation • Content expertise
Steering group	It is the group that the change team/office will be accountable to and will regularly report to. It is the group that will hold the overall 'steer' of the change initiatives. It is also the governance group where the overall direction of travel, key decisions are made and approved.	• They will attend the initial workshop with the team members to work out the list of macro questions, and possibly do the initial navigation map. • They will put themselves in a learning stance with the team to learn about possible methodology and how best to work with this change initiative.	Members should be appointed by the top leadership group. Preferably they will: • Be interested and believe in the change initiatives • Have strong commitment to the future of the organization • Have strategic insights into the business

PRACTICE NOTE 2 *Continued*

Steering group	Frequency of meeting: once a month after the various set-up retreats	• They will show their visibility by helping the team to give briefing sessions to the staff and managers about the change. • They will make a case for the change to the top decision makers. • Offer personal support to the group of change agents.	• Be well respected w/strong reputation • Have strong core business competence • Be well connected to the power elite.
Reference group	These are subject expert groups where the co-ordinating team can consult whenever they need to. One can have more than one reference group depending on the core skills/professional knowledge people need. Frequency of meeting: as often as the team request after initial set-up meeting.	These groups will have an important function at the beginning of the change initiative as they should be the group to help the team to identify the key content areas to focus on, the data the team would need, and also what up-to-date information the team should have in order to make robust decisions. The members of the reference group will be asked to volunteer to join the team to get initial training on how to work with complex change (this is to covertly educate some senior people who would not attend such training otherwise).	Any content and subject experts who can give diverse perspectives about the change. They need to be interested in supporting the change from a secondary role as most are probably either too senior or too busy to be part of the team. Eventually we would like this group to have so much fun working with the teams and doing things that stretch their leadership skills, they will also become key agents for the change.
Champions and sponsors	The role of any champion or sponsor is to demonstrate personal support of the change by taking personal interest in both the team and the individual team members.	Their key role is to be visible supporters of the change by personally leading and explaining to others their own personal reason for supporting the change. Meet regularly with individual change agents and respond to requests from the journey office.	• Someone senior in position • Who believes in the change direction • Who is willing to champion the change to others • Who is interested in developing people • Who wants to learn and be a role model for the change

The practice note lays out an ideal set-up of the various temporary change structures – ideal in the sense that if the culture of the organization supports involvement and is willing to establish some of these temporary structures as a means to expand the engagement process of the change – which is called 'engagement by formal role' – then these structures will work well to involve, enrol, increase participation, and help many to make sense of the change through a role within the change structure. The temporary change structure can become a dynamic engagement platform, maximizing the chance for real-time behaviour change opportunities. Finally, in order to ensure the core change team is successful, the organization also needs to invest in giving them the right type of support.

g) What systemic issues would the change need to align?

Please refer to Chapter 2 to refresh your memory about system theory. The gist of the system theory in change is twofold:

- The open system concept – with input and feedback from the external environment, many organizations will need to adjust their output (in products and services) in order to survive in the turbulent context. Once the output has been adjusted, then the organization needs to align their 'through put' eg internal capability, structure, system, policies, other infrastructure, etc in order to support the strategic goals of the organization. Ultimately, all organizations are trying to match their internal working to the changing external demands, hopefully at the same speed as the change happening externally.

- Since systems have many parts which are 'nested' (interconnected) and are interdependent on each other – when one part changes, it will inevitably impact on other parts. In the past, many change programmes (especially restructuring) acted as if that change only focused on **one** specific target area without attention to the alignment of other parts. It is no wonder so many restructuring processes failed. It is very important to focus on what impact and hence what level and type of systemic alignment we would need in order to ensure change initiatives will be sustainable. As to how extensive the systemic alignment work would be, that depends on the scope and scale of the change.

It is important that very early on a dialogue should take place between the commissioners, the governance group and the change team, identifying the various systemic issues surrounding this change initiative that would need attention – that is if sustainable implementation is to be a reality.

For example – if the primary focus of the change initiative is on restructuring and organization design, then the key alignment question is what else needs to be adjusted in order to achieve the purpose of the change in structure. Would certain key processes need to be adapted? Would certain

relationships and collaboration between different functions need to be more integrated? Would the new structure demand any changes to the required competences and characters of top leaders and middle management? Do any of the HR policies need to be adjusted? Does the leadership role need to be scaled up?

At the end, there should be a list of the 'primary' and 'secondary' focuses of change alignment. The terms of primary versus secondary can be defined by your organization – primary can refer to the 'critical', or the 'key gate opener factors' that will help to set up the natural alignment of other factors. Finally, the most critical alignment question we will need to ask is, 'What type of mindset, paradigm or thinking will support this change initiative and what is the most sensible way for us to shift these inner models from the beginning?'.

Systemic alignment work can often be aided by using one of the system models listed in the diagnostic chapter. Practice Note 3 gives a systemic questionnaire based on the Burke-Litwin Model as an example of how to go about discussing the systemic alignment issues from change.

At the end of working through the list of macro issues, a more robust change plan will be in draft form. However, they form only half of the plan as the other half will come from working through the front room issues.

Front room matters (the people dimension and the engagement issue)

Front room matters are what I call the **heart** and **soul** of change. Change is not successful until the people voluntarily shift their behaviours. So this is the **heart** of all change matters.

Basically, front room matters concern:

- engaging people as much as possible so they will embrace the intended change through rightful participation, meaningful dialogue, having a voice, being heard, and being able to make informed choices through shared data;

- encouraging people to be increasingly self-organized in the process of change – supporting them to make things happen within certain parameters and helping them to leverage the impact they want to have in order to build the future they desire during the change processes;

- working with people to create the conditions where behavioural shift can be made as easy as possible.

PRACTICE NOTE 3 Systemic alignment questions:
(based on the work of Burke and Litwin)

1 What are the external factors that steer us to change?

Is the leadership group responsible for taking an active role in:
- Scanning the environment/competitors?
- Setting strategy?
- Aligning culture and leadership behaviour to deliver strategy?

2 How will delivering the objectives of the change help us to achieve our mission and vision? What else we will need to do to stay responsive to the world we live in? Will the change help us to remain competitive and relevant in this market?

3 Would our current strategies still remain relevant or do we need to revisit the strategic planning process and content so that we will achieve congruence? How well does our culture support our mission and strategy? What areas of alignment will we need to focus on to ensure the inter-connectedness will work?

4 How effective are our leaders and does their behaviour live out our values and steer us in the strategic direction? To support the change, what type of leadership behaviour should we grow and nurture in order that they can lead the organization to a new destination?

5 How efficient is our management population (the spinal core) at managing the input and output loop? How well do they manage the work unit climate? To support this change, what intervention and development will we need to support them?

6 How well does our structure help us to organize tasks to deliver our strategy? Do we need to consider a different organization design as a result of our change?

7 How do our systems and processes support our culture? Are they 'fit for purpose' or are they bureaucratic? What type of new patterns do we need to grow to support the change objectives?

8 How do the individuals know what is expected of them, know their contribution and feel motivated? Do our performance management system and the reward and compensation policy and practices need to be adjusted?

9 How well do our performance levels help us to stay competitive in the market? What new outputs will we need to consider to support our change objectives?

Micro List of Issues

There are a great number of 'front room matters' which change agents need to pay attention to, but I will focus mainly on the following areas:

a) figure out the **key** groups and individuals in reference to the change;

b) assess the attitude of the key groups towards the change, their state of support to the change and their relevant level of ability to influence others to support the change;

c) how to use group dynamics to engage and support key groups in their personal change;

d) what level of capability we will need to offer to the key groups so that they can support themselves in the change processes;

e) supporting people and groups to work through their sense of resistance – both at individual and group level. Support change agents to learn how to use the energy created by resistance to adapt and evolve the change journey.

It is important to note that front room matters are the heart of OD practice, and OD practitioners should be at our best when applying behavioural science research data and practice tips to ensure change and system and people development are synonymous. If at the end of the journey neither people or system have been developed, then change has not happened at all.

Let's look at each of the five questions.

a) Who are the key groups – definition?

Groups and individuals are defined as 'key' when successful implementation of the change is critically dependent on them, relying on their skills, knowledge and competence to achieve great results. Whether they accept the change or not will be crucial because they hold the roles of guardian angels of the new way of doing things.

For example, if a new safety procedure in an off-shore oil and gas platform is being implemented, the key group would not only include professional safety officers, but also the operation and shift supervisors and all those operators who day by day are supposed to handle the operation within the safety frameworks.

Or if the organization wants to establish a new online sales system with a 'WOW!' customer ethos, one key group will be those sales personnel who daily handle the online sales system from processing the order through to dispatching the product on time and seeing it arrives in top condition. However, another key group will be call centre personnel who handle all the customer inquiries and complaints and, through their interface with the customer are the ones who are responsible for creating the 'WOW!' brand.

Of course, supporting such behaviour among the key groups are those who are in charge of the reinforcing systems and procedures, eg those who hire the workforce; those who train and induct them to deliver the 'WOW!' brand; those who decide reward and compensation; line managers and

those who support the managers to implement the quality standard and 'WOW!' customer behaviour in the performance management system. But mainly the key groups are still the ones who directly hold the successful implementation of the intended change in their hands.

b) Assess the attitude of the key groups towards the change, their state of support to the change and their relevant level of ability to influence others to support the change

At the beginning of any change initiative, it is important to gather a cross-hierarchical, cross-functional team to help identify the key groups and individuals whom the change implementation will be dependent on. Also, it is important to try to understand the context, ie the various micro systems in which these key agents/groups function and how the context may impact both their behaviour and perception of the change.

Once we map out the key groups and individuals, further diagnostic questions need to be asked about them – for example:

- What is their current attitude towards the change? How ready are they to move in the direction of change? Psychologically, how deep a shift will be required of them?

- What type of engagement and transition processes will support them best to voluntarily take up the change as part of their own agenda?

- What conditions will we need to create to facilitate their self-organizing ability to do their own action research and to co-construct the different routes the change journey can take to get to the desired destination?

- What capability upskilling will they need and what type of resources will enable them to make the change happen?

To give further data as how we can best work and support the various key groups and individuals, we should also look at them from two dimensions: – power and influence to support the change and their state of commitment to the change.

Figures 8.7 and 8.8 show two ways to map the key groups along those two dimensions. Both diagrams plus Figure 8.9 have been adapted from practitioner colleagues' work whose origins I cannot trace.

The ideal situation is for the majority of the key groups to be high in commitment and readiness for the change and to have significant enough power and influence to help make things happen (eg people rated in boxes 6, 8 and 9), but life seldom works out that way. We will find people displaying low commitment and readiness for change and high power and influence, or those who are medium in readiness or even high in readiness but low in power and influence. The important thing is that if we do not map the key group readiness and capability, we will never be able to gauge how easy or difficult the change will be. Also, we will not have any idea as to how best to support them in the change journey.

FIGURE 8.7 Commitment to change and capability and power to support the change

Key people/groups	Commitment to change			Ability to make it happen		
	High	Medium	Low	High	Medium	Low

FIGURE 8.8 Mapping key groups on readiness and capability

Readiness for change

	Low	Moderate	High
High	7	8	9
Moderate	4	5	6
Low	1	2	3

Power and influence to support or derail the change

NOTES:

1. Put the name of your key groups into the grid.
2. Anyone who appears in the 'High in readiness' column (boxes 3, 6, 9) should be supported.
3. People in boxes 8 and 5 need to be helped to make personal sense of the change.

c) How to use group dynamics to engage and support key groups in their personal change

Next, in order to gain clarity as to how we can support key groups and individuals through this journey, we should look at the mapping of where they sit from a group dynamics standpoint. Questions like the following are useful to ask: Who can influence whom? Who has street credibility that can leverage a lot of respect from whom? How much influence can who yield from which group? If we increase the visibility of some of them during the change process, would they be able to champion the change within their local areas and for what effect? Who are the potential early adopters of the change and will putting them in the same task force or design group with other credible champions of the change help them to get greater engagement of the change?

Understanding the group dynamics will make change agents more informed about how to design processes that will help the key groups to navigate their own change journey. The design process can be used as an engagement opportunity – pulling together some members from some of the boxes in Figure 8.8 to co-design a process to work through the list of macro issues has been proven to be very effective. One of the important tactics is to ensure the various key groups get to interface with other groups in a 'maximum' way – a methodology called 'Max-Mix'.

Max-Mix believes that when people work on the various macro questions with members from other parts of the organization and whom they do not know, it will help them to:

- gather diverse perspectives from other groups about this change;
- make personal sense of the what, the why, and the how aspects of the change;
- feel positive about having a voice and a role to self-organize themselves within that diversity to find a meaningful path forward;
- have a whole-system perspective about the change.

If such a design is set up, it gives individuals opportunity to share their voices, exercise influence and support to one another; to debate and argue through their own perspectives of why change or why not? What to focus on in change? What are the systemic issues that worry them? They can give feedback as well as having an opportunity to co-construct the change planning process. OD practitioners need to attend to the group process so that the process of working together will help the group to a) learn from other people's perspectives; b) take steps to become a community (community in action).

At the end of such group processes analysis, there should be clear data as to whether these key groups and individuals think it is worth their investment to support the change; or, if it is a non-negotiable change, how they can undertake the change with the least damage to the morale and motivation of themselves and the group. Also, after using the various groups to work through the macro issues, the change team should have sufficient data to know the ease or difficulties of implementing this change.

FIGURE 8.9 Where are we?

Where are we? Do we need to chunk the change?

Strategic fit

		Low	Moderate	High
Difficulty of Implementation	**High**	Not worth doing	Rethink or chunk the change	Risk it if it is a must
	Moderate	Not worth doing	Depends on level of gain	Good enough to risk
	Low	Not worth doing	Possible state	Excellent state

Strategic fit

d) What level of capability we will need to offer to the key groups so that they can support themselves in the change processes?

To ensure the change momentum is maintained and there are sufficient change agents (sometimes called the guardian angels) to maintain the new changes, we would need to ask what type of competence, know-how, expertise and mastery we will need to help build among our target change leaders.

The basic question all change commissioners and governing bodies need to ask is 'what capability equipping will the change project need to give to which group to ensure change will be supported and sustained through time?'

This is such a common-sense approach and yet a majority of change teams receive little or no capability development and support. This will often lead to ineffective leadership in change, and with those in charge of the change failing to know what to do and how to lead.

An example of a change capability programme for change agents I have used is listed below:

An example of a capability-building programme for a change team

- An introduction to working with complex change
- The people dimension in change and intervention methods
- How to deal with the psychological aspect in change
- How to be an effective facilitator
- How to evaluate the change processes
- Self-awareness and the use of self in leading change

It is important to work with leadership development colleagues to plan such programmes and to ensure not only the centre, but also local change leaders get such development opportunities. Recently in a public sector organization, the centre and the local leaders (the biggest gathering was around 500) went through five workshops together – from learning how to run large group interventions, to using HSD (Human System Dynamics) methodology to work with diverse conflicting groups, to facilitation skills, to learning how to use system thinking in leading transformational change, and finally learning how to design interventions. The leaders discovered that through the capability-building initiative the existing cultural and behavioural patterns had been disrupted, which later on opened the pathway for further behavioural interventions.

When this type of capability development programme is made available, its inevitable results (often unknown to the leaders) are that we are not only enabling people to lead change, but equipping them to disrupt the current patterns by using more people-focused methodologies to involve people in a new high involvement pattern.

e) Shifting our perspective of resistance and learning how to tap into the resistance energy

There are a wide range of reactions to change – from 'Finally, we are doing this' to 'How would this change help to address the core issues?, 'We are dealing with the wrong issue', 'This is definitely not the way to go about this change' and 'What will happen to the integrity of me, my team, or the organization if the change flops?'

Edwin Nevis, a well-known Gestalt psychologist (1987) advised leaders to see this wide range of reactions as a map of the terrain of the consciousness (awareness) of the group that the change agent needs to explore and surface as part of the critical change data so that we get clarity on how to engage the different groups. We need to do what we can to help leaders adopt this 'healthy' and 'effective' perspective in working with resistance by taking the lead and role-modelling the way.

Some helpful perspectives on resistance that we can use to help leaders to work with resistors in a different way are:

- Approach resistance from the inherent multiple realities people carry with them in the system which will affect how they see the change – every perspective will yield different data for the change office.
- While resistance is mostly rationally based, it is often emotionally expressed – we need to know how to work with both the rational and affective dimensions.
- Resistance must be respected as a statement of who people are and what they stand for – we can do so much once people have expressed this.
- Resistance gives us an opportunity to broaden and deepen our understanding of the environment in which the change must take

place – this will help us to express our own bias about what needs to happen in what specific way.

- Resistance is not an 'all or nothing' phenomenon. It is best seen as ambivalence, or agreeing with some aspects but not the whole package – there are indeed many doors we can work on.

- Most people are sincere about their resistance, as it stems from a different but honest perspective – if we honour their sincerity, they will respect the change process.

- When resistance has no legitimate form of expression, it often turns into the 'underdog' fighting the 'top dog' – which is definitely not where any change team wants to find themselves.

It is important for leaders to make sense of resistance, develop a stance of curiosity about the origin of resistance and commit to help themselves to accept that there will always be different ways of seeing things, and resistance is absolutely normal. After, all as David Whyte (1994) pointed out, 'I do not think you can really deal with change without a person asking real questions about who they are and how they belong to the world.'

Adopting a different attitude, one can then work with rather than against the energy field that comes from resistance. Our job as practitioners is to ensure we use processes to extract the rich data from resistance in order to tap into it and the energy to do the engagement work with different groups. To state the obvious, it is important never to take sides as all positions and views about the change are real and legitimate. See Practice Note 4 for possible ways to work with resistance.

PRACTICE NOTE 4 How to work with the resistance energy

Design an intervention where all resistors have a chance to voice their reasons for resistance. After they share their reasons, ask what needs to happen in order for the organization to help them to be less doubtful. Gather their ideas and then start implementing them in a visible way to show the resistors we respect their logic. Some of the resistors would become champion for the change after that.

Put champions and resistors together to have a lively exchange about the pros and cons of the change (to enable both sides to listen to each other as well as influence each other as new perspectives are shared). After the dialogical session, ask resistors and champions to pair up to undertake some action research in those areas where the resistors have doubts – and to deliver feedback together after joint data analysis.

PRACTICE NOTE 4 *Continued*

Use a continuum to ask people to line up according to how much support they have for the change – eg from 0 – 10. Ask people on the continuum to explain to each other why they put themselves on which point of the continuum. This will help to give voice to the resistors.

Once they have shared their views, write on a flip chart all the main points of complaint resistors have raised about the change – and then put each of these points on an individual chart around the room – and encourage people (especially those who are low and high on the continuum) to go to each flip chart station to have discussion with others gathered there. This way we give legitimacy to the dissenting voices while encouraging mutual dialogue among colleagues to iron out differences.

At the end, it is best to give resistors a job to do to help the organization to decide how best to undertake the changes. For example, put them in a short-term task force to address one of the doubts they have, etc.

Run a two-hour (lunchtime) workshop for up to 30 people where there are four flip charts in the corners of the room, each with a question. The questions are:

- What objections do I have about this change?
- Why do I support this change?
- What worries me about this change? (list all the worries I have about this change)
- What requests do I have for the senior leaders if I am to come with this change?

Agenda:

- Opening by senior leader about the change and what s/he wants from these sessions.
- Give instruction – grab some lunch and walk around to all flip charts and a) have a discussion with those standing around the flip chart; b) express your views and write them down.
- Give 30 minutes for people to go around every flip chart expressing their views.
- Then ask those who started each flip chart to report key points from the postings to the big group.
- After all the reporting, ask people to share what stands out for them. After some time in debriefing, announce that all the data will be compiled and when all the sessions are completed they will be gathered together to look at the data and together decide how to proceed.
- Make sure the resistors are given a chance to join some task force to address the issues they raised.

Conclusion

All the front room work is to ensure people have space and room to be part of the change process – bringing in data from local areas that others may not have, supporting them to make personal sense of the change, giving them a sense of agency to have some control of their own future, especially because all changes impact on people's sense of psychological identity and autonomy. The focus of this work is both **engagement** and to gather robust data from people in every part of the organization.

All the back room work is to ensure the change is approached and set up in as 'rational' and logical a manner as possible – especially since all complex changes require an effectively run back office.

There are no short cuts and easy ways to help an organization navigate through complex changes – we will need to use every channel, approach and varieties of methodologies to support the organization. If we only take care of the back room matters without due respect for the front room matters, then we are bound to fail as not only is the organization a living system, but it also connects with other living systems – and that interaction will give rise to different forms of emergence that the change agents need to work with.

If we only work with the front room matters without paying attention to the cost, the risk, the compliance requirement, the level of gain, the proper infrastructure required to support the change, the change timeline, and the change outputs, then we are also vulnerable as we stir up the passion and commitment from people, yet there is no capacity to carry out the change implementation.

So while the OD and complexity and chaos change approaches should be the dominant lens for us to see and work with complex change, we practitioners need to be just as savvy as those consultants in the big four consultancy firms – know how to cost the change, how to set up metrics, how to measure change, and how to support the change using fit project management tools. It is a 'both-and' **not** an 'either-or' approach. Our job is to excel in our ability to integrate the front and back room matters to form a robust change plan.

Let me end this chapter with Figure 8.10, which shows what types of issues should appear in an integrated plan, and how we can plan intervention to go across each side to deal with both sets of issues. For example, we can run an event for the **key** groups and individuals that will involve them to identify most of the questions listed on the back room side. By involving them to do the scoping, we can also expand their engagement and identify whom we can recruit to visibly lead the change.

Working out the issues both from the back room and front rooms will help us to set up the changes for success.

FIGURE 8.10 Integration of back and front room matters

Front room matters	Back room matters

Front room matters

1. For each area of work, who are our 'Key' groups? Successful implementation is dependent on them.

2. What is the 'readiness' and 'capability' of the key groups?

3. What are their 'transition' issues that we will need to manage?

 • ending
 • neutral zone
 • new beginning

4. How do we ensure the **capability** of the key groups is maintained and upgraded to support the change implementation?

5. How do we expand our **engagement** of the key groups so that they will support the change?

6. Who should be **visibly leading** the implementation of this stream of work? How do we prepare them to take on the role?

7. Who are the other **stakeholders** we will need to keep informed?

8. What are the **HR issues** we will need to manage? How best to handle them?

9. Who should be in the **temporary change structure** to offer sustainable momentum?

10. What do we need to do to 'encourage the heart' and who should be given that accountability?

Back room matters

1.

Where we are **Where we want to go**

Distance

What is the change about? What is the arrival point? How far is the distance between where we are and where we want to go?

2. What type of change is this? How many 'Big' areas do we aim to change? What is the focus of change: structure, culture system/process, leadership, people, operational protocol etc...?

3. What's the business and benefit case for change? What level of gains must we aim for?

4. How do we set up clear deliverables in each area – what are we measuring for success?

5. What are the sequences of change? – what area will we need to deal with first? – what should go first to stabilize the heart?

6. Within what type of time frame, finance, policy and value parameters?

7. How do we 'safeguard' our production capability during change? Who should have that accountability?

8. What systemic alignment will we need to make in order to achieve sustainability of the change?

9. What will the change plan look like? Who is holding it together?

Can behavioural change be made easy?

Overview

Change is a verb meaning to a) alter or make different; b) make to pass from one state to another; c) exchange one for another. It is all about movement, but whose movement? That is the key question.

> The core of the matter is always about changing the behaviour of people.
> In highly successful change efforts the central challenge is not strategy, not
> systems… but the need for significant shifts in what people do.
>
> John P Kotter and Dan S Cohen (2002)

How many times have we heard this – 'Once we finish the process of restructuring, we will then think about the people and behavioural components.' Those who utter this sort of statement have a distorted view of what organization change is about. In a lecture Margaret Wheatley and Kellner-Rogers gave in 1998 they put it succinctly,

> Failures at organization change are the result of some very deep
> misunderstandings of who people are and what's going on inside organizations.
> Such misunderstandings must be corrected before effectiveness and hope can
> return to our experience.

Research shows approximately 70 per cent of change initiatives fail because:

- the results of the initiative land significantly below expectations;
- the organization reverts back to its original starting point;
- the initiative never garners support and fails to launch.

However, among those 30 per cent of change initiatives that succeed, the common characteristic is the ability to change individual employee behaviour. The reality is that every change initiative, whether it is large or small, **does** require employees to work differently, and sometimes in an extensive, fundamental way. Being able to help employees to shift their behaviour voluntarily in change is often the linchpin that defines success or failure.

Who has the power in any organization to actively demand a shift in both the way employees think and the way they behave? Who has the right to ask people to exchange one state of existence for another; move from a position of comfortable mastery to a psychologically disoriented state; change their behaviour from one form to another?

The simple answer, of course, would be 'those who pay the wages of the staff'. But do they? What changes can organizations legitimately ask from their people? The full deployment of their specialist knowledge, skills, competency, and an acceptable standard of performance within the job role, yes, but does the organization have the right to demand an employee become a different type of person and shift their approaches and personality preference as they execute their job? This is both a philosophical question and a civil liberty issue. It is one question that is seldom debated properly, but it needs to be because I believe that if organization leaders have a niggling doubt about whether they have the right to insist on behavioural change, they may end up being more humble, tentative and take a more compassionate and conciliatory approach – instead of focusing on forcing, demanding, or shaming as tactics to get the behaviour changed. In the arena of behaviour change, leaders need to learn how, with OD support, to create conditions that facilitate voluntary enrolment for behavioural change.

In this chapter I will cover:

1 Can behavioural change be made easier?
 a) Three different perspectives for looking at culture and behavioural change
 b) Concept of patterns
2 A look at four ways that offer alternative insights on how to do behavioural change
 a) Shifting language and narratives
 b) System I and System II thinking
 c) Using group dynamics
 d) Using CDE – a method from Human System Dynamics (HSD)
3 Conclusion – the practice implications for practitioners

Can behavioural change be made easy? Culture, patterns, behaviours

In Chapter 8, we talked extensively about 'key group analysis', referring to the group upon which the successful implementation of any change initiatives is critically dependent. However, that is only half of the picture of successful implementation. The other half is what the organization does in facilitating cultural and behavioural change among these groups, because sustaining change results is not possible without that.

There are over 300 definitions of culture, but the gist can be summarised as the *commonly held and relatively stable beliefs and attitudes that*

exist within an organization. This view holds that the culture of any organization stems from belief systems and basic assumptions (often becoming subconscious once the patterns are formed) through formal induction and informal observation of what constitutes successful behaviour. These are then translated into reportable attitudes and values which manifest into observable behaviours.

Basically, culture means the way people **think** and **do things** around here. In its latin root, the word culture means the act of cultivating, eg a ground. Whatever yields results will be kept and become the patterns which people will repeat again and again until it no longer serves them. Even then, it is hard for a group to escape that well-set pattern, as by then it has become the norm sustained by individual and collective behaviour.

In that way, a pattern is formed by what leaders believe is 'successful' action they take, which is often drawn from core values as to what's important, then transmitted into norms and behaviours of the system members. The collective behaviours in turn reinforce the core values. This process is supported by a wide range of signs, logos/symbols, policies, stories, ethical codes, explicit and implicit beliefs, etc, which include who have been designated as the organization heroes, specific use of language, values and principles, sometimes organization architecture and metaphors the organization uses. The constellation of the range of reinforcers is what makes the act of changing culture and behaviour patterns such a daunting task.

Once culture is formed, there is a powerful evaluative connotation attached to it as the organization clearly uses it to delineate what is 'acceptable' and 'unacceptable' behaviour which the organization will reward or covertly punish.

Figure 9.1 spells out the shapers of culture, and there are many shapers one has to work with when it comes to a culture change initiative.

a) Three different perspectives in looking at culture and behavioural change

In my many years of experience in supportive culture change initiatives, somehow, I have never been satisfied with the 4-step, 6-step or 5-phase types of approach, as those methods are too mechanistic for me and take too long. Instead, I mainly apply three methods of looking at behavioural change within any culture change initiative, as they make culture change a more liberating task for all.

1 **Pragmatic approach:** As shown in Figure 9.1, if we work backward, focusing on the desired results of the organization (often, the change goals) and then focusing on the type of behaviour that will be 'fit' enough to support the delivery of the change goal and hence what areas of decision we can start looking at – type of decision, how those decisions are currently made – this approach is more matter of fact and practical without provoking a heavy heart to seek behavioural repentance and that helps clients become more relaxed

FIGURE 9.1 Shapers of Culture

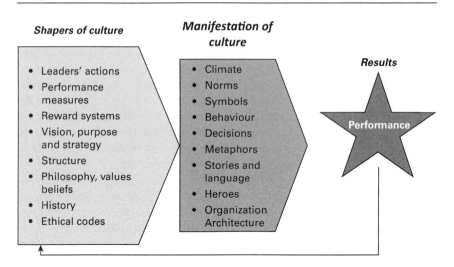

and less defensive. In any culture change project, what OD practitioners want is to set up processes for people within the system to pick up and work with the issues themselves, asking if that is our goal, what would **fit** behaviour look like? In different situations, what would people we interact with say about us if they experience that type of behaviour, etc? This approach does not focus on 'culture change' it focuses on how to align decision-making behaviour to what we desire.

2 **Anthropological approach:** The second view about culture change comes from an anthropological perspective.

In the study of culture, there are two views:

- The first focuses more on the mechanical and scientific view of culture, which defines culture as what an organization **has**; culture is conceived as one of the objects or components of an organization. Therefore, changing culture tends to be seen as a modular design and hence the culture the organization needs will have to be shaped, manipulated and engineered. While this perspective is firmly grounded in system thinking, its utility is limited in culture change, especially in comparison to the next perspective.

- The second view on culture is an anthropological one. This view believes that an organization does not have culture – the organization *is* culture. Culture therefore is not only a component, but a pervasive paradigm for interpreting the external world and the organizational

life processes within. The **key** point that emerges from this anthropological view is that culture exists not so much **inside** or **outside** but '**in between**' people. The concept of cultural change effort is aimed at altering the quality of this '**in between-ness**' of individuals, groups and organizations. Cultural adjustment and alignment is therefore a day by day affair, especially during the change between individuals and groups. This approach always aims to support people to shift their own pattern of 'in between-ness.' In other words, we are encouraged to 'think culturally' (ie for everything we do in change, we think in cultural terms) instead of 'think about culture' (ie how to do culture change). This view of culture breathed life into my soul as I instinctively knew that was the right approach to look at behaviour change – focusing in every transaction and always looking out for opportunities to improve the quality of interface and exchange between individuals, groups, and systems.

3 **Pattern vs Culture Change Approach:** The final approach is to stop using the term 'culture change', instead re-labelling it as a less complicated concept, ie 'shifting patterns' – a term made popular mainly by the complexity and chaos theorists.

What is a pattern?

b) Concept of patterns

The Merriam-Webster dictionary defines a pattern as the regular and repeated way in which something happens or is done; once it is formed it becomes a model proposed for imitation and used as a model for repeating; this configuration becomes a reliable sample of traits, acts, tendencies or other observation characteristics of a person, group or institution.

The concept of pattern originated from the biological world in which all living matter has patterns in the way it functions. For highly functioning plants, animals and people, there is a tendency to adapt their pattern as the environment changes in order to survive and thrive.

In OD, Schein (2004) defines patterns in his exposition of culture:

> Culture is a pattern of shared basic assumptions – that was learned by a group as it solved its problems of external adaptation and internal integration – that has worked well enough to be considered valid and, therefore to be taught to new members as the correct way to perceive, think, and feel in relation to those problems.

Glenda Eoyang, a well-known thinker and practitioner in the school of Human System Dynamics (HSD) has defined patterns as 'recognizable similarities, differences, and relationships that have meaning across space and time.' In other words, patterns are much more recognizable and identifiable than 'culture', something that members of any system can be helped to understand and use. This is the reason why focusing on **pattern shifting**

rather than **culture change** makes the work in behavioural change easier and more accessible for members within the organization.

Patterns of groups, like patterns of individuals, are highly observable, and not only can members within any group identify them, they can also deduct what simple rules sustain such patterns. Hence, instead of working with heavy-duty concepts like values, belief systems, core principles, ethical code, paradigm, mental models, moral action (which are still very important for forming the backdrop of simple rules), and focusing on behaviour that gives rise to patterns and how those patterns are supported or not by the simple rules, the whole culture change journey becomes a more achievable process.

Sustainable culture change requires a high degree of voluntarism and all genuine behavioural change requires:

a) the process of meaning making – ie those whose behaviour the organization wants to shift must make sense of 'why such change is required';

b) generating motivation for the people to become more literate about the concept of behavioural patterns;

c) the know-how to assess the fits/misfits of patterns of behaviour to what they want for the organization; and

d) people learning how to take small steps to support themselves to do the shift.

Hence, it is crucial for OD practitioners to use a more accessible method of supporting members of the system to choose the path they want to undertake; in that way the chance of success will be increased significantly.

In our OD practice framework, it is always important that we create the change process to support members of the system to do their own action research, analyse the pattern data they have collected, and by looking at the implications of such patterns on their new desired state, they will then be willing to move themselves into action. By using the concept of adaptive action ('WHAT? SO WHAT? NOW WHAT?'), the system and its members are empowered to have both the language and the concept to do its own work supported by some processes which they should be able to play a part in designing.

Armed with these three key perspectives in looking at culture change, I have started to work with simpler concepts, focusing on patterns and behaviour from day one of any change initiative – mostly in a covert way – by using some of the methods shared in the next sections. When things start shifting, I lead a retrospective discussion, asking people what they have observed, and what might have happened, which in turn creates an opportunity to show the system how to use these concepts and theories to continue to adapt behaviour as part and parcel of the change process. Maybe in that way we are acting more from an anthropological perspective – helping system members to be 'thinking and acting culturally' rather than 'thinking about culture' as a big set of interventions we will need to instigate.

Four ways that offer alternative insights on how to do behavioural change

I will focus on four ways that can aid in the pattern-shifting work that needs to start from day one. I will briefly introduce what they are conceptually and then share some practice examples to aid your application:

a) Changing behaviour by changing language – Social Discourse theory;

b) System 1 and System 2 thinking – the work of Daniel Kahneman;

c) leveraging group dynamics to shift behaviour;

d) CDE – the HSD methodology that help inter-groups to shift their behaviour.

a) Changing behaviour by changing language – Social Discourse theory

Social discourse thinking is very much based on the key premises of social constructionism which core concepts and application in the area of change are in Chapter 2, so I will not repeat them here. Instead, I will highlight some key insights and how they can apply in our practice.

Berger and Luckmann (1966) expounded that all knowledge, including the most taken-for-granted common sense of everyday reality, is derived from and maintained by social interaction. The sense-making process in any situation comes from our interaction with people during which the reality of the situation is interpreted, debated, created or constructed in that moment. Dialogue either gives rise to new or reinforces the old narrative and – through language – will continue to be passed on, often unchallenged, and shape the members' perspective of the situation which they hold in their head.

In 1995, a publication called *The Central Role of Discourse in Large-Scale Change: A social construction perspective* by Barrett, Thomas, and Hocevar reinforced the concept that change occurs when one way of talking replaces another way of talking. The authors believe effective change requires that organization members alter their cognitive schemas for understanding and responding to organizational events as language frames and creates how and what we think about things. As new language begins to generate new actions, it will in turn trigger different action possibilities; basic assumptions and beliefs are altered.

This is echoed by Marshak and Grant (2011) who believe that 'talk reflects how the person sees reality; and talk informs and shapes action.' Marshak's diagram on the relationship between talk and action and how language shapes meaning and action is presented in Figure 9.2

Figure 9.3 is a grid that I have constructed to illustrate and give examples of how talk may lead to different action – something readers can use as their teaching points.

FIGURE 9.2 Language shapes meaning and action

Adapted from Marshak (2002)

FIGURE 9.3 How different talk will lead to different action

Narrative 1	Possible action	Alternative narrative	Possible action
The environment trend is always changing and is so hostile, we are exhausted.	We just cannot afford to do any more. Let's wait and see how these trends develop.	The challenges present in the environment are tough, but we have been there before and we know we can identify new ways of operating that will get us up a notch or two.	We'll carve out some time now to work through the key issues so we will be ready to deal with them in case those challenges become real in the future.
People are so stuck in their own silos, it's hard to continue down this one-way street.	I think we should give up our effort to support them when we get no reciprocation – time for them to learn.	People are so over capacitated, what can we do to make collaboration easier for them?	I wonder if we put ourselves in their shoes, what type of help they would appreciate from us so that they will be willing to collaborate more with us?
We tried for three years to get an organization strategy done, but we have never made it. Do we need to do it again?	The process is both obsolete and unnecessarily painful. I think we should just give up and continue to do our own thing.	We have done our best to share our strategic priorities but we did not know how to integrate them, so this time we will need help to integrate all our objectives.	We must not give up, as our staff needs us to have an aligned strategy so let's find some external help who can support us to do better in this process. Let's ask the OD team what they think.

I am sure that all of us have experienced or witnessed how different narratives often produce different types of energy that lead to different ways of seeing their own situation or lead to possible action they have not thought through, or both.

Surprisingly, this simple intervention has not been used extensively by practitioners, even though many of us believe in the power of changing the language. I wonder whether in the Newtonian world, where clients value the show of expertise (as that is what they think they are paying for), some practitioners think this type of simple intervention would not be impressive enough. Indeed, one of my senior clients complained to me about her OD team – 'what rubbish they are telling me – change happens one conversation at a time'. If you work for a boss like her, then you may lose heart to apply this theory in your change methods.

If you belong to this group, then I have two tips for you. First, integrate this into your day-to-day methodology without raising a big banner about it – in other words, use it covertly, along the line of the anthological sense of culture; use it to impact the day-to-day interface or the 'in between-ness'. Second, get together a small group of keen clients who are eager to learn and show them how to do this. Once they are excited about this methodology, send them out to act as covert agents, subtly shifting the pattern by introducing new ways of speaking. Gather them after a period to review the results their personal tactics have managed to produce and then reinforce their further application.

CASE EXAMPLE

Organization X was undergoing a very complex change initiative. Its culture placed a high premium on intellectual rigour, expertise, and being perfect – standard phrases like 'we need to structure for success and there is no margin of error' were used in almost every situation. This complex change required a radical shift in the set of behaviours that came from that cultural context, as the organization saw innovation and experimentation as high-risk activities. The organization readiness to change was low and the change team I had were all from the elite talent pool. So I knew very early on that I needed to start a covert change process by introducing a number of new words and phrases that offered alternatives to the perfectionist, expertise and task-focused culture.

Figure 9.4 shows examples of my alternative text changes.

FIGURE 9.4 Alternative text

From	To
That is such a bad and unnecessary mistake.	Every mistake is too good an opportunity not to learn something to achieve even greater growth.
What a nightmare response we got from this senior management event.	What a normal blip we are getting when we work with 120 very clever, headstrong leaders and their response shows that their caring energy is still there for us to tap into.
This move is career suicide.	This is a courageous move that requires us to think a bit more about the power and politics behind it. Well done on this idea.
Why does that department always block us?	Do they block us, or do they block themselves because of their anxieties about their future, let's see what we can do to promote a win-win situation from our joint working.
We as middle management never have power to act on our dream.	Where would the organization be without the middle managers in operation? Let's talk about the key contribution middle managers have made to this change effort. Shall we have a middle management conference to showcase your achievement?

I also started to highlight those forgotten stories of past organization heroes and heroines who survived mistakes and still managed to do great work and be respected. Of course, changing words, language, narratives is more than just that – we were directly (though subtly) disturbing their cognitive schema, their normal thought patterns and assumptions by substituting them with workable alternatives which then helped the shift to take place in baby steps, often even without them knowing it. When these baby steps led to different, positive results, I got my change team together to make sense of what was happening and encouraged them to list the rest of the standard culture talk that was impinging the organization's move forward with the changes and find alternative words and narratives to change the talks.

An alternative way to introduce this set of principles is to build in 'subtle teaching' through your diagnostic work. Ask those with whom you work, eg the change office, some of the following questions:

- What discourses (narrative, stories, metaphor, etc) are holding things the way they are in our organization?

- How can we use conversation as opportunities to construct new premises and possibilities?

- How are prevailing narratives reinforced in day-to-day conversations throughout the organization and how might we change those conversations?

- What alternative narratives and language can we introduce to raise different perspectives of what can be done or what cannot be done in regard to this change?

- What existing social discourses are supportive of this change? How can we multiply these social discourses?

- How may we seek to change the discourse at multiple levels to support this change effort?

- What form of organization power and political processes can we use to deal with the counter discourses in order to shift perspectives and grow new behaviour?

- How many levels (intrapersonal, interpersonal, group, inter-group, total system, etc) of system shall we target in our attempt to shift social discourses that will give us maximum impact and speed in shaping this change effort?

As Marshak often encourages us to pay more attention to the power of transforming talk and text, hence we should do more to support clients to transform meaning and action, which in turn will transform talk and text, which in turn will transform meaning and action, which in turn, etc.

From these theoretical insights, we practitioners should be on the lookout for the current story/narrative from different members of different parts of the organization that may support or derail the initiative when supporting the organization in behavioural change. Basically, always be interested in gauging the impact of the current narrative on people and the organization. Then we can move to what future or alternative story and narrative the organization could have that would positively support the change. Use a simple intervention like getting people in pairs to share the current narrative/ story they hold that impacts on their view of the change, and then move them on to discuss what alternative story and narratives they are willing to

explore that will help them to deliver a 'different future'. Combining this intervention with the 'preferred vs probable future' methodology or the solution focus methodology will enable us to witness quite magical shifts in behaviour among people.

Finally, I must warn that there is a grave danger we need to watch for and manage, which is our own discourse and narratives we hold of the client system as a change agent. Often, we fail to reflect on the words we use, the stories we hold in our head about the clients, our emotional reaction to the way they use power, how we see their level of resistance, whether we respect their values and our hopes about the probability of the change initiatives. If we do not check our orientations, our self-talk and possible biases we hold regarding the client system, people and the change will leak out and we will be visibly incongruent in what we teach and share. The lack of ownership of our self-talk about clients will leave both us and our clients very vulnerable. This is one of the ultimate tests of our use of self.

b) System 1 and System 2 – the work of Daniel Kahneman

When Daniel Kahneman's book *Thinking, Fast and Slow* reached the market in 2011, it created a storm as it revealed a different way of thinking about decision making and economic behaviour. Investment bankers, governmental policy makers and other decision makers from all realms embraced his work in a significant way. He demonstrated that there are two ways to change behaviour (from economic transactions, health-related habits, paying tax, to making major corporate decisions, etc).

The first way to change behaviour is based on influencing how people consciously think. This is often called the 'rational' or 'cognitive' model. Most traditional behavioural interventions follow this model and the assumption is that the individual will analyse various pieces of information from others, eg government, regulators, senior leaders, consumers, market analysts, etc, and then make a decision to change their behaviour or not. This approach is demonstrated by the various incentives offered by the change instigators who, by offering that, assume they are actually helping people to act in their best interest. The track record of this approach has not been impressive at all.

The second way to change behaviour is more about moving away from facts and information alone, to a contrasting model which focuses on the more automatic processes of judgment and influence by altering the context within which people act. In other words, the aim is to shift from rational, persuasive argument alone to influencing the automatic way of acting.

This is often called the 'context' model of behaviour change, which recognizes that sometimes when people seemingly act irrationally and inconsistently in their choices, it is because they are influenced by surrounding factors which have power to trigger automatic levers within individuals and are often not conscious.

This way of 'changing behaviour without changing minds first' comes through the concepts and principles of automatic and context-based drivers

of behaviour which emerged from the discipline of 'behavioural economics' – which seeks to combine the lessons of psychology with those of economics. Not only are they closely related but they also share similar roots with the neuroscience insights on change reaction.

The first way of changing behaviour is called System 2 and the second is System 1. The work was made even more accessible and popular by one of Kahneman's mentees and colleagues, Professor Paul Dolan of the London School of Economics.

This body of work has shown us that the rational model of changing behaviour is limited because there is a real limit in information giving even though it has been a prominent part of those who are heading up changes. Sharing information is a crucial intervention, but what it will not achieve is to help people choose to behave differently. The assumption behind System 2 thinking is that the more information people are given, the more they will rationally choose to behave in the new way. For example, knowing the harm in smoking should lead to a drop in smokers, and the introduction of calorie labelling should create discernible change in the consumption of fatty food. But in both cases, it has not. In fact, most health research and subsequent education programmes aiming to prevent teenage pregnancy, obesity, smoking, etc, have not led to automatic behaviour changes.

Figure 9.5 sums up System 1 and System 2 thinking.

FIGURE 9.5 System 1 and System 2 Thinking

System 1 thinking	System 2 thinking
Automatic	Deliberate
Effortless	Effortful
Faster to act	Slower to act
Habitual	Intellectual
Reactive	Proactive
Specific purpose	General purpose

Adapted from Stanovich (2000)

The published work in this area, from my experience, is more accessible and offers more practical ideas in shifting behaviour than the work of the neuroscience group. In the following sections, we will focus on the work of Professor Dolan, who has been helping the UK Cabinet Office think about how to shift citizen behaviour. I would recommend practitioners learn more from his model, which is called MINDSPACE. I will briefly outline the model here and give some practical examples of how it works.

There are nine elements in the MINDSPACE model, which, according to Dolan, are those that the researchers consider to be the most robust elements that operate largely, but not exclusively, on automatic effects. They illustrate some of the main ways that individuals, communities and policy makers can influence behaviour. The nine areas exerting robust influences on human behaviour and change are underpinned by considerable research from the fields of social psychology and behavioural economics.

The following grid of the MINDSPACE model and its explanation are adapted from Dolan's report for the Institute for Government, MINDSPACE: Influencing behaviour through public policy, 2 March 2010. For a more complete explanation, please refer to the full report.

FIGURE 9.6 The MINDSPACE Model

MINDSPACE

Messenger	We are heavily influenced by who communicates information
Incentives	Our responses to incentives are shaped by predictable mental shortcuts, such as strongly avoiding losses
Norms	We are strongly influenced by what others do
Defaults	We 'go with the flow' of pre-set options
Salience	Our attention is drawn to what is novel and seems relevant to us
Priming	Our acts are often influenced by sub-conscious cues
Affect	Our emotional associations can powerfully shape our actions
Commitments	We seek to be consistent with our public promises, and reciprocate acts
Ego	We act in ways that make us feel better about ourselves

SOURCE: Dolan, P (2010)

I will endeavour to adapt Dolan's definition of each of the MINDSPACE variables and briefly explain what they mean and give short examples of the practice implications in how we go about shifting behavioural patterns.

Messenger: we are heavily influenced by who communicates information:

- our response to a message depends greatly on the reactions we have to the source of that information;

- we are affected by the perceived authority of the messenger (whether formal or informal);
- we are more likely to act on information if experts deliver it, but also if the messenger has demographic and behavioural similarities to ourselves;
- we are also affected by the feelings we have towards the messenger.

Practical implications:

- We will need to think about whom we should ask to lead and speak about the change at every level of the organization as change champions at the top will provoke no reaction from the people on the shop floor.
- Identify those leaders from all levels who are respected and 'loved' by the people, and work with them from the beginning of the change. If the change makes sense to them, they will then be the right messengers to speak to people about the why of this change.
- Use the same group to lead on the behavioural change by role modelling it.

Incentives: our responses to incentives are shaped by predictable mental shortcuts such as strongly avoiding losses. The impact of incentives clearly depends on factors such as the magnitude and timing of the incentive:

- we dislike losses more than we like gains;
- we value positive feelings others have for us;
- we tend to avoid public shame;
- we tend to keep what's working for us;
- if someone shows us a new way of working that will produce even greater payoff, we tend to repeat that new behaviour;
- we overestimate the likelihood of small probabilities;
- we usually prefer smaller, more immediate payoffs to larger, more distant ones.

Practical implications:

- Involve people to experiment with the change and aim to ensure the experiment will yield the early encouragement that people need – if they see the change is going to bring greater payoff, they will tend to shift their behaviour to support the change.
- Since people dislike losses more than they like gains, creating an appropriate amount of 'psychological anxiety' while giving some safety measure will help people to shift to a different way of behaving, especially if they do not want to experience public shame – shame for themselves, their units, the organizations.

- Give real-time rewards (praise, affirmation, chance to do bigger project, a bit of financial reward, etc) as often as possible when someone demonstrates new behavioural patterns. This will help to reinforce the practice of new behaviour.

Norms: we tend to do what those around us are already doing:

- social and cultural norms are the behavioural expectations, or rules, within a society or group;
- norms can be explicitly stated ('No Smoking' signs in public places) or implicit in observed behaviour (women speak less in meetings);
- people often take their understanding of social norms from the behaviour of others, which means that they can develop and spread rapidly through social networks or environmental clues about what others have done (eg litter on the ground);
- some social norms have a powerful automatic effect on behaviour (eg being quiet in a library);
- behavioural interventions using social norms have been successful in a number of areas, and most are based on telling people what other people do in a similar situation.

Practical implications:

- Intentionally use group dynamics to reset new norms. Use one of the more prominent business units, or a high-performing team to test-run the change and ask them to identify the type of 'fit' patterns that the group needs to grow and nurture in order to keep them high performing. When they begin to get some traction, spread their story around to stimulate more behavioural change.
- Showcase other groups that have tried and done well by using different patterns and approaches to achieve impressive results.
- Use key OD methods to support voluntary changes in behaviour.

Defaults: we go with the flow of pre-set options:

- many decisions we take every day have a default option, whether we recognise it or not;
- defaults are the options that are pre-selected if an individual does not make an active choice;
- defaults exert influence because individuals have an in-built bias to accept the default setting, even if it has significant consequences;
- restructuring the default option can influence behaviour without restricting individual choice.

Practical implications:

- Encourage multiple and simultaneous experimentation, or **pilot** to reset the existing default position. Once decisions are made during this period that work successfully, they will soon migrate to become the default pattern.

- Use systemic alignment as a needed process to reset what would become the default behavioural pattern, especially by using HR policies and processes to support the spreading of 'default' behaviour – eg capture by statement – 'we in this company always put customers first by being politic, firm and courteous.'

Salience: our attention is drawn to what is novel and seems relevant to us:

- Our behaviour is greatly influenced by what our attention is drawn to. In our everyday lives, we are bombarded with stimuli. As a result, we tend to unconsciously filter out much information as a coping strategy. People are more likely to register stimuli that are novel, accessible and simple.

- Simplicity is important here because our attention is much more likely to be drawn to things that we can understand – those things that we can easily encode.

Practical implications:

- Use innovative and novel processes as part of the change methodology (one organization adapted an old warehouse into an innovation centre and bussed leaders into the building to experience how innovation can be done using a mixture of technology – visual experiences – joined-up behaviour – high level of collaboration – delivering real results where the senior people will come to hear (like *Dragon's Den*).

- Work on the 'WOW' factor of leadership behaviour, eg showing up in a call centre to take calls for two hours and then personally asking the operators to teach him or her (and their team) how to provide superlative customer services.

Priming: our acts are often influence by subconscious cues:

- Priming is about how people's behaviour is altered if they are exposed to certain sights, words or sensations. In other words, people behave differently if they have been 'primed' by certain cues beforehand.

- Priming seems to act outside of conscious awareness, which means it is different from simply remembering things.

- The discovery of priming effects has led to considerable controversy – the ability to manipulate us into buying or doing things that we didn't really want.

- Subsequent work has shown that primes do not have to be literally subliminal to work.
- The effect of priming is real and robust; what is less understood is which of the thousands of primes we encounter each day have a significant effect on the way we act.

Practical implications:

- Ask marketing and sales staff and an external specialist on priming to run training for the change team so that those who lead on change will become savvier about how to prime people's behavioural changes.
- Use music, true inspirational stories from previous employees and imagery to prime a great emotional involvement with those whom the change requires to shift their behavioural patterns.

Affect: emotional associations can powerfully shape our actions:

- affect (the act of experiencing emotion) is a powerful force in decision making;
- emotional responses to words, images and events can be rapid and automatic, so people can experience a behavioural reaction before they realise what they are reacting to;
- moods and emotional reactions can precede and override more 'rational' or cognitive decision making, resulting in decisions that appear contrary to logic or self-interest;
- for example, people in good moods make unrealistically optimistic judgements; those in bad moods make unrealistically pessimistic ones.

Practical implications:

- Whenever you can, use a strength-based methodology, eg Appreciative Inquiry, to evoke positive emotion and sense of pride that comes from people's real experience.
- Always build hope in an organization during change – affirming what they did in the past, and what confidence they have in shifting their patterns for the greater good of the organization. Involve them to build behavioural patterns that they are confident they can repeat.
- Ensure the change team members are energetic people who have a sense of humour. When the change team is of high energy, they can build the affective environment for people to undertake behavioural change with a sense of lightness.

Commitment: we seek to be consistent with our public promises and reciprocate acts:

- we tend to procrastinate and delay taking decisions, especially long-term interests;
- many people are aware of their willpower weaknesses and use commitment devices to help them make decisions;
- research has shown that commitments usually become more effective as the costs for failure increase: for example, making commitments public, so breaking the commitment leads to reputational damage;
- even the very act of writing a commitment can increase the likelihood of it being fulfilled;
- we have a strong instinct for reciprocity, which means that, for example, accepting a favour acts as a powerful commitment to return the favour at some point.

Practical implications:

- Ask leaders to make public commitment to what behavioural change they are willing to make and lead. Also ask leaders from all levels to make small promises regarding what they will do differently once a week, so that they will carry out the role modelling of new behaviour.
- At the end of any event, ask people to stand up and share with the group one baby step they would undertake to make things different, but surprise them by recording what they say, and after 2–3 weeks, ask them whether they have done that.

Ego: we act in ways that make us feel better about ourselves:

- We tend to behave in a way that supports the impression of a positive and consistent self-image.
- When things go well in our lives, we attribute it to ourselves; when they go badly, it's the fault of other people, or the situation we were put in – an effect known as the 'fundamental attribution error'.
- We think the same way for groups that we identify with, to the extent that it changes how we see the world.
- We also like to think of ourselves as self-consistent.
- So what happens when our behaviour and our self-beliefs are in conflict? Often it is our beliefs that get adjusted, rather than our behaviour. It has been shown that once people make initial small changes to their behaviour, the powerful desire to act consistently emerges.
- The initial action changes their self-image and gives them reasons for agreeing to subsequent requests.

- This challenges the common belief that we should first seek to change attitudes in order to change behaviour.

Practical implications:

- Use as much common sense as possible to work with, not against, human nature and human needs – the need to be loved, affirmed, recognized, to have a sense of significance and ability to contribute, a chance to live larger than oneself. If we do that we will appeal to the need for ego (without any negative connotations attached to that word) and be able to support people to move forward in self-initiated behavioural change.
- Ask someone to support the change team to think about how to shift the behaviour of their team and when they give a great idea, ask them to lead the movement and publicly recognize their contribution.

c) Leveraging group dynamics to shift behaviour

We have mentioned the importance of group dynamics in Chapter 8. This third way that helps to support behavioural change can be an uncomfortable area for many applied behavioural scientists. We know the power of group, of which history has also brutally reminded us. Group dynamics can breed so much evil and yet also so much virtue. For example, the fact that leaders like Hitler could close down the values of the Gestapo population and make them willingly massacre so many Jews; the fact that Reverend Jones could order hundreds of professional members of his cult to commit group suicide by asking them to make their children to drink cyanide before they did; the fact that gangs can spread within a local area and assume dominance over so much youth behaviour shows the power of group pressure to breed unsocial and uncivil behaviour. Contrast the above with the fact that many who had nothing to gain decided to march with Gandhi and support Nelson Mandela, not only because of their religious beliefs or the commitment to the course of civil rights but because the group they belonged to had powerful norms that inspired certain group behaviour. All the above cases demonstrate that the group not only has an immense amount of power but exercises it to yield conformity by defining what is acceptable and unacceptable behaviour, and connotations of what type of behaviour will lead to inclusion or exclusion of individuals within their own community.

For good or evil, the reality is that once a group is formed, the leadership's norms, group decisions and group behaviour can exert huge pressure on groups. Hence, many of us are uncomfortable to mention using group dynamics to change behaviour.

From the Hawthorne study through to the many writers (Berstein, 1968; Dent and Goldberg, 1999) who study group dynamics, the belief is that the group is the main focus when it comes to changing behaviour. Lewin (1947b) maintained that it is fruitless to concentrate on changing the behaviour

of individuals because the individual in isolation is constrained by group pressures to confirm. Consequently, many OD practitioners – including myself – believe that the focus of change in behaviour must be at the group level and intervention should be planned around factors like creating new group norms, group roles, changing the quality of interactions between group members, reshaping the socialization processes to create 'disequilibrium and change (Schein, 1988).

So how does this work in shifting behaviour?

Practitioners need to consider how groups come together to form patterns. Through understanding that process, we can then change some of the processes to create shifts in the patterns of groups and individuals. In simplistic form, when people get together on any occasion, eg at work, at a club, at a community issue-based group, they start sharing their basic assumptions about how they think the world is, the work is, whether there are certain ways to undertake the task they are interested in, etc. Through stable membership and the settling of power differentials between people, the group begins to establish norms through which they recruit and socialize new members. Through years of continuous sharing of experiences, successes, and learning, the group begins to be bound by shared history and – depending on how stable and successful the group is – strong patterns will be formed. Figure 9.7 shows this process in more detail.

FIGURE 9.7 How group patterns are formed

Once the group is formed, group and individuals will experience quite a strong container for their behaviour. Within that container, some behaviours will be branded as great, helpful, supportive, and acceptable, while others will be branded as 'out of line' and unacceptable; 'people who are in the know do not behave like this'. This delineation will become clear through the evaluative narrative people hold in their head, while passing them to newcomers.

Because a group or system does not live in an environmental vacuum, sooner or later the container will be challenged. Its rigidity will render it closed to any system feedback and sooner rather than later the patterns will become a 'derailer' to interaction with the world outside. This is when the group needs to revisit and update its patterns. However, this process will be painful as it is within an affiliated group that we receive most of our social and psychological needs. So, one of the tasks of any change catalyst would be to support the group to do its own pattern updating.

By using Figure 9.7 we can purposely do a number of the following to enable a group to do self-facilitated change to its own behavioural patterns:

- Invite members from other systems to share ideas and give feedback on how the group is doing in reference to execution of its mandate.
- Invite people to highlight the group's patterns that are helpful and vice versa.
- Ask members to share part of the history that was valid but failed to get into the storybook of the system heritage.
- Invite reverse feedback from new members after an initial period of working with the system.
- Ask for volunteers from within the system to discover the powerful 'hidden' or 'unwritten rules' that shape current behaviour patterns and then return to the system to run a workshop and discuss the what, the so what, the now what of these patterns.
- Run a workshop to ask people to identify the external shifting conditions and how that impacts on the group. Afterwards, discuss the case for change and whether the change makes sense to the group before asking them to identify the current patterns that are driving the system behaviour, which behavioural patterns should remain as the cultural DNA and which need to be shifted – and how they can support each other.

May I encourage readers to be creative to design processes to strengthen group norms that will in turn influence those individual and group behaviours that will support the change goal.

d) CDE – the HSD methodology that helps inter-groups to shift their behaviour

Human System Dynamics is an institution set up by Glenda Eoyang which offers a collection of concepts and tools that help make sense of the patterns

that emerge from chaos when people work and play together in groups, families, organizations, and communities. HSD uses metaphors from the physical, mathematical, and computer sciences to help practitioners understand what is happening in the everyday dynamical interactions in organizations and groups. The concepts are grounded in science, but they continue to emerge as we explore the complex behaviours of human systems.

As mentioned in Chapter 7, in their significant 2001 book, *Facilitating Organization Change: Lessons from complexity science*, Eoyang and Olson demonstrated how to take lessons from complexity science to facilitate organization change. For Glenda, all behavioural change points towards the ability to act in a self-organized way. 'Self-organizing is the fundamental thing we need to understand and to learn to work with' (Olsen and Eoyang, 2001). According to them, complexity science reveals a world that is both patterned and surprising, both ordered and random.

As I shared earlier, Eoyang's definition of patterns is 'similarities and differences and connections with meaning in space and time.' The complexity writers believe that once the pattern is formed it will constrain us – hence the job of any change agent is to be trained to **see, understand**, and **influence** patterns.

As do all OD practitioners, she believes that our key work is to help the system to reveal itself to itself. Hence, at any single point in time, system members should be curious about how they hold their similarities and differences within their context and what is the current quality of their connection. In this time and space, which differences are holding us or draining us? Which of our similarities are strong enough to hold us together and which ones are weak? How do we connect with each other in ways that will facilitate our work and vice versa?

Figure 9.8 shows in graphic form the definition of patterns which also defines the CDE method by Glenda Eoyang (1997). The C stands for 'similarities/container' – too much, too little, too tight, too loose? The D stands for 'differences and tensions' – too much unresolved difference, or too little. The E stands for 'quality of exchange' – what is the current way the system members interact with each other?

FIGURE 9.8 CDE concepts

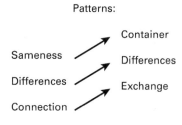

Patterns:

Sameness → Container
Differences → Differences
Connection → Exchange

Shifting patterns can start with
shifting any of the three

Adapted from HSD Institute (2013)

When groups of individuals or different work units are not functioning well, we can use this simple and accessible method to help shift individual and group behaviour. The process I will be describing is a very much 'dumbed down' version of the CDE process, so please refer to the publication and website of HSD to get more details.

CASE EXAMPLE

In a technological service organization, those working on the client site and those running the centre did not get on. The current communication was very tense and there was extensive blaming from both sides. People knew they needed to collaborate, but their behaviour demonstrated otherwise. So I carried out the CDE process steps to help the two groups to self-diagnose themselves and learn to behave differently to increase the quality of exchange they have with each other in order to service their clients as **one** unit.

The description is a way to capture the gist of what needed to be done. For a fuller description of the method and how to use it, contact the HSD website.

Step 1

We arranged to run an event that representatives from both groups attended. The event was part of their annual gathering and our session was preceded by a strategic priorities planning session. We were given three hours in the middle of the day.

Step 2

As we had about 100 people attending from both sides, we set up eight stations with roughly the same number of representatives from each side (corporate centre staff and off-site staff) in each station.

At each station, there was a big sheet of butcher's paper (the size of four flip charts put together) with a T written across the top half of the paper, and their own in-house facilitator whom I had equipped and briefed about the CDE methods.

Step 3

For the next 120 minutes, the group worked through a few simple rules designed to help them obtain the best dialogue from the session and came up with statements like: talk straight, stay factual, listen empathetically, inquire rather than advocate,

before they were asked to work through three questions. The initial instruction was given up front by me, and then eight local facilitators took over. The three questions we took the group through were:

1 What are the similarities between the two groups?

2 What are the differences between the two groups?

3 Describe the current characteristics of how we interact and connect with each other.

For these first three questions, the facilitator encouraged people from each side to use the simple rules that they had agreed to ensure the exchange was of an honest nature.

Step 4

The group then progressed into the next four questions – one at a time, again being drilled from the front by me (to ensure consistency of understanding):

1 What similarities can we leverage to give us a strong container to work with?

2 Out of all the differences we listed, which ones will make a real difference in the way the two groups work – ie if we are willing to sit down and resolve them? 'What are the real differences that will make a real difference in the way we work?'

3 What is the current quality of exchange they have with each other?

4 What are the possible action steps we can take to improve the way we connect with each other and raise the quality of our exchange?

The process encouraged a real dialogue between the two parties working through tough issues, especially focusing on the behaviour that led to a very dispirited level of exchange day by day.

Step 5

Before joining the whole system together, the facilitators asked the two groups to look at and discuss the four questions that come from Adaptive Action. The facilitators referred to some of the sub-questions in Figure 9.9 to encourage even more honest dialogue:

1 WHAT have they just done?

2 SO WHAT – the implications of the patterns they uncovered, and how FIT is the current pattern to support their common goals and mandate?

FIGURE 9.9 The adaptive action questions

Adaptive action questions

- **What?**
 - What are the current patterns?
 - Are they facilitating or constraining our goals?
 - What bits of the history stand in the way? What aspects we need to update and move on?
 - And...?
- **So what?**
 - What are the implications of the patterns you see?
 - So what is the state of fitness our patterns have in reference to our goals and our mandate?
 - Are there options for action?
 - And...?
- **Now what?**
 - What do we need to make happen now to shift to alternative patterns? What are our practical first steps?
 - Who will should? Who we get involve to do something?
 - And...?
- **What simple rules will help us to get there?**

Adapted from HSD Institute (2013)

3 NOW WHAT?

4 What SIMPLE RULES will get them there?

Step 6

The last 60 minutes were spent bringing the whole system back together with each station being asked to share the outcome from their discussions, their 'NOW WHAT?' action points and the simple rules they had set up to support their new CDE.

After every station had shared, we asked them to return to their station to indicate what doable actions they personally were willing to start implementing, and what requests they wanted to make to leaders and management for support.

Outcome

What had been accomplished at the end of this three-hour session was a rapid cycle of diagnosis establishing the 'WHAT?', a discussion of 'SO WHAT?' for both themselves and the clients, then an ending of 'NOW WHAT?' and a set of simple rules that would support them to build new behavioural patterns.

The process that day was the beginning of a) helping the two sub-systems to reveal their behavioural data to themselves and each other; b) instead of going deeply into why they were behaving in that way, they looked at what

alternative behaviour they could contemplate along those three key dimensions that form patterns; c) in doing this, they began to disrupt their own pattern that had not served their client or themselves well, and realized what they had contributed to turn the workplace into a very unhappy one for themselves and others.

Some simple behavioural supportive follow-up work was carried out after the event, and other reinforcers adjusted, eg how they ran communication, task allocation, who can commission work, how the delivery timeline can be negotiated, etc. Nine months after the CDE event, behaviour between the two groups has continued to shift in the direction the group themselves desire. Behaviour change in this case was made possible because of HSD's CDE methodology.

This process description is a very simplified version of CDE; it can be used much more extensively than what has been described. I highly recommend that you explore the HSD website and get onto to their online programme.

Final note on CDE

In this theory of change, agents interact in real time (the anthropological view of culture – the 'in between-ness' of agents). As they interact, patterns emerge from the system as a whole (interaction produces patterns; some work and some do not in terms of helping to achieve what the system needs). Eventually those patterns that agents within the system agree on will stay.

These system agents begin to interact with counterparts from other systems, and suddenly their interaction helps them to experience the similarities and differences they have with each other. If they have a strong container, a set of joint goals, they will want to work on identifying their similarities so that they can leverage them to create a strong bonding (container) as well as wanting to resolve some of their differences – a possible source of conflict. As there are far too many differences, they can only choose to work on those that are significant and by resolving them, they can work more effectively to deliver the joint goals.

What will play a significant role in this process of creating new patterns is the quality of their interaction; whether the quality is affirmative and collaborative or adversarial and competitive. If the quality of that 'in between-ness' is high, new patterns will emerge and the part will begin to move towards acting in the context of the **whole**. By interacting within the complex adaptive system, the agents have played a role in creating an emergent pattern through self-organization.

Conclusion – the practice implication for practitioners

Behavioural change is a complex matter. Ethologists, cognitive psychologists, psychologists, psychoanalysts, anthropologists, social psychologists, sociologists, economists, etc, have all invested time and resources in the past decades to try to help us understand human behaviour – ours and others. The debate about the internal versus external determinants of behaviour which has surrounded us for many decades (the work of John Watson) still remains. Hence theories like the needs theory, the expectancy and operant conditions, the equity theory, the goals theory, the role basic human needs play in shaping our behaviour, etc, are still offering applied behavioural scientists a lot of food for thought.

What I have covered in this chapter is really only a drop in the ocean in terms of how we can improve our ability to work with behaviour during change. I am, however, eager to whet your appetite to learn more about human behaviour. By stating this at the end of this chapter, I want to share the following practice points for practitioners:

- For incoming OD/HR practitioners, do try to study some more about human behaviour, as any knowledge in this area will serve you well in your practice.

- For leadership development colleagues, try to build the need to understand human behaviour better into your organization leadership development programmes. It is never too late to learn about the nature of who we are and how we work.

- For practitioners, do make sure you never get jaded or cynical about human behaviour. Instead of being judgmental, stay curious and inquiring as just when you want to say 'I have seen it all', I can guarantee that you have **not** seen it all when it comes to human behaviour. Also, continue to pursue your own understanding of your own behaviour, as we cannot take people to places we have not gone to.

What is so special about being in the field of Organization Development is that, despite our own human fragility, we are asked to work with human behaviour every day, hoping that we are well informed by applied behavioural science research to give us that sense of competency to set up processes and conditions that can support others to shift their behavioural patterns. We should never take this task lightly because we are in the same position as those whom we are supposed to influence – daily struggling with shifting our own behaviour. Let us do this work with greater humility, greater commitment to increase our own competency in the field, and with greater compassion in all that we do.

Section 4

THE ORGANIZATION DEVELOPMENT PRACTITIONER

Chapter 10: The Organization Development practitioner

Chapter 11: Power and politics and Organization Development

In the four years since the publication of the first edition, I have been keenly aware of the differences between those practitioners who have done deep work in themselves and those who have not. Most practitioners I have met say they have taken 'self as an instrument' seriously in their development journey but, judging by the low level of awareness of their own impact on others and by their reactions to messy situations, eg being criticized, they have not. Do those differences matter? They absolutely do and they have a critical impact on the credibility of the field – especially when we operate in such dynamic work situations where power and politics are being played out in a high-frequency and high-velocity manner.

Greiner and Schein (1988b) remind us that in the political context, we need to take the high road of power use by combining OD values and principles and power in an effective way. By taking the high road of power use, we will need to be intentional in our behaviour, the way we work, and our presence – through teaching, consulting, role modelling and encouraging people to deploy power strategies that are open and above board, eg use collaboration in decision making, uphold the concerns and interests of those with less power, support the power elite to voluntarily confront and transform itself. All these require us to be grounded no matter how we are affected by day-to-day power dynamics in our client system, knowing we are not there to work out our needs through our client work.

This high road of power requires us to know how our values and our identity play out in the work context – going beyond just 'knowing ourselves' to 'knowing how our patterns impact in group, in one-to-one exchange, and in our relationships with clients, partners and stakeholders' and how we work with feedback from those with whom we work.

Another prerequisite for us to take the high road of power use is for us to be in touch with our anxiety and worry as we go about this tough work. So often I have witnessed that OD practitioners are unaware of how their anxieties drive them to take actions that are not for the greater good of the client system, but to help themselves to look good, feel OK, or to manage and diminish those anxieties. If we have not done sufficient work to enable us to truly know the gap between our

constructed reality of ourselves and the reality others hold of us, then we will always be a fragile member in the power-playing processes in the consulting arena.

Recently I found Joseph Campbell's work on the hero journey (2008) has offered me another way to think about the OD practitioners' own development journey to be an effective instrument. Rebecca Chan Allen's writing (2002) has been especially helpful to steer me in this perspective. In order to sharpen our own sense of instrumentality, OD practitioners need to undergo that first heroic journey where we are willing to leave the comfort of our familiar territory, take courage to enter into an unknown journey which will eventually take us to the dragon's lair to overcome that dragon in order to capture the precious jewels which we will proudly carry back to our community to share. In our lives, our first piece of tricky and tough consultancy work can be thought of as the original journey. Some of us failed in that journey and some of us made it – but often wonder how we did it. Eventually we managed to capture the precious jewels of seeing people and systems change, and we took our precious learning back to our action learning set or our peer support group to share.

The test of that first journey got us going and ushered us into multiple 'heroic journeys' ahead of us. 'Hero' in this sense for an OD practitioner is often a private experience as none of us like to brag, nor should we, about 'how great I am'. But we cherish the joy, fulfilment and satisfaction that come from having done something great in service of others on our professional journey.

As we continue to allow the interface with our clients, partners and colleagues to impact on our development, we soon find that we have to pay attention, especially to two other types of dragon in our hero journey – the 'relational dragon' and the 'power dragon'. The relational dragon is our aim to be acceptable to others through being attractive and appealing to them. However, in order to be acceptable and enable others to trust us, we have to go beyond the personally acceptable concept to being known as someone who takes relationship-building work seriously in an authentic way. The essence of that relational energy is a sense of belonging or being part of something bigger than oneself which translates into a concern to create a legacy, to leave something of oneself behind. Healthy relational energy exhibits in partnership, collaboration and community. Such energy can be distorted by two types of fear: fear of rejection and fear of abandonment. It is these fears that we will need to 'slaughter' in order to become friends with the relational dragon.

In our professional life, we need to develop a strong partnership between the relational dragon and the power dragon, whose energy comes from the need for a sense of efficacy. Power energy is about the will to create and having the confidence and resources to get things done. When this energy is functioning properly, the hero will feel competent and impactful, being skilful and resourceful to support the client system to take their own hero journey.

When you have the relational and power dragons living in harmony, OD practitioners will experience resourcefulness, competence, authenticity, community and confidence to do what we set out to do.

This is what this final section is about – how we get to a place where we know who we are, and from that place, build exceptional relationships and partnerships in order to maximize our influence and power to help the system to get their work done in boosting the journey outcome as well as showing the system that the only way to work is to share power and build strong and effective relationships to get things done. When the use of self is at that level of potency, our work with any organization will have that magical touch to it. As you read these two chapters, reflect on your own hero journey and what you have done well and what further work you can do to sharpen that instrumentality of self.

The Organization Development practitioner

In Chapter 1, I stated that one of the unique characteristics of the field of OD is the role and practice of OD practitioners in the organization improvement process. In this chapter I would like to explore more fully this unique characteristic by covering the following:

1 roles and tasks of OD practitioners;
2 concept of 'self as instrument' which is critical in this field of practice; what the 'use of self' means in theory and in practice;
3 competence profile of the OD practitioner;
4 development journey OD practitioners should engage in;
5 practice trademarks of OD.

The roles and tasks of OD practitioners

The OD practitioner community is a versatile group and they come in many forms and often carry multiple roles. Some act as sounding board, partner, guide, coach; some are designer and methodology leaders; some are facilitators, process custodians, group process consultation specialists, group dynamic monitors, trainers. The list can go on. Some OD practitioners work as internal change agents, others as external consultants. Other practitioners mainly focus on intrapersonal work, some focus at the group level, some work at the inter-group level, and others at the organization, inter-organizational or community levels. Some have a mixed-level portfolio. So the challenge is how to distil what they do and summarize their work. Figure 10.1 illustrates the diverse approach authors in the field use to describe the roles of OD practitioners.

FIGURE 10.1 Roles of OD consultants

Authors	Roles of OD consultants
Burke, 1982	One who provides help, counsel, advice and support.
Schroeder, 1974	One who serves as a sounding board, an adviser, a confidant for the consultant who is working directly with the client (shadow consultant with other consultants as clients).
Lippitt & Lippitt, 1978	OD consultants can hold any of the eight roles along a continuum with directive and non-directive at either end of the continuum. The eight roles are advocate, technical specialist, trainer or educator, collaborator in problem solving, alternative identifier, fact finder, process specialist, reflector. These roles are not mutually exclusive. The OD consultant may play different roles simultaneously depending on the tasks/assignments.
Schein, 1988	Key role defined as process consultation, ie a set of activities that help the client to perceive, understand and act upon process events in the client's environment in order to improve the situation as identified by the client.
Tichy, 1974	Outlines four change agent key roles: • OP (outside pressure) – advocating certain changes, planning strategies for advocacy; • AFT (analysis for the top) – conducting a study for a client organization and providing a report for top management; • PCT (people change technology) – providing a service for individuals within the organization; • OD (organization development) – serving as external consultant to develop systems.
Beer, 1980	Lists two key roles that he considers important: 1. Generalist and specialist – 'the OD consultant is generalist in his organizational administrative perspective and a specialist in the process of organizational diagnosis and intervention'. 2. Integrator – OD consultant's job is to make linkage between client and needed resources, between various sub-systems, between top management and staff.
Ferguson, 1968	Lists 18 roles of OD consultants ranging from capturing data to promoting a proper psychological climate to assisting in the management of conflict, serving as plumber or obstetrician in-between, etc.
Nevis, 1987	Outlines five basic roles/activities of a Gestalt-oriented consultant: 1. Attend to the client system, observe, and selectively share observations of what you see, hear, etc. 2. Attend to your own experience (feelings, sensations, thoughts) and selectively share these, establishing your presence in doing so. 3. Focus on energy in the client system and the emergence of or lack of issues (common figures) for which there is energy: to act to support mobilization of energy (joining) so that something happens. 4. Facilitate clear, meaningful, heightened contacts between members of the client system (including contact with you). 5. Help the group achieve heightened awareness of its process in completing units of work, and to learn how to complete units of work so as to achieve closure around problem areas and unfinished business.

SOURCE: Cheung-Judge (2001).

From the figure, it is clear that some authors define OD practitioners by their roles, others define them by the processes in which OD practitioners engage, and still others define them by the types of activities in which they engage. However, in spite of the differences, some common characteristics of OD practitioners do emerge:

- OD practitioners play a variety of roles;
- OD practitioners are there to help clients to improve their work situation;
- practitioners focus on the use of processes to support the client within an organizational context;
- OD practitioners are relational focused;
- practitioners use themselves to effect change and development.

Given these common threads, what does anyone need to be or do to wear the label of 'OD practitioner'? I believe that the definition of an OD practitioner is not so much about what they do and the role they have, but how they go about doing their job. I believe that it is the approach they take to support their clients that gives hints to the practice trademark of OD practitioners. I will address this more deeply at the end of this chapter. For now, building on what has been reviewed in Chapter 1, I have put a statement together to describe who is an OD practitioner:

> OD practitioners are behavioural scientists who, through effective relationship-building skills, deliver help and support to a client system with the goal of improving the health of the system. While they can be expert in specific areas of organization as well as being technically competent, they are primarily process-oriented practitioners with an aim to pass on the process skills to the client system, so that the client can pursue continuous development independently. The practice design skills of OD practitioners are heavily influenced by their value set.

The concept of 'self as instrument'

In this section, I will review the critical concept of 'self as instrument', discuss what 'self' means, and what the 'use of self' means in practice.

Background to 'use of self'

From the historical perspective, there has long been a debate about the 'use of self'. Those from the positivist epistemology perspective (which dominated the world view of natural science for a long time) assert the importance of maintaining the most detached and objective stance when working with others, eg patients and service users. Those who subscribe to this belief think that if not sufficiently controlled, the personal experience of

the therapist/helper will negatively influence the work of the client. Freud belonged to this school and there are stories that he would sit behind his clients in therapy sessions so that he remained detached from them.

The non-positivist perspective offers an alternative paradigm. It underscores the value of subjective information and believes that the social world is relative and thereby best understood from the vantage point of the individuals involved in a given activity. They believe that the ultimate success of any intervention rests with the practitioner and what s/he brings to the process. It is in this context that self is the most important tool of the practitioner.

To understand this philosophical position, one has to bear in mind the backdrop against which OD entered into Western society, where racism, the aftermath of Nazi Germany, the massacre of Jews, the break-up of community, the rise of capitalism, etc, all played a major role in organization and community. Riding the waves of the human relations movement and sensitivity training in the 1960s, OD prides itself as being a value-driven profession with a unique set of assumptions about people and work. One of those assumptions is that the practitioner is very important to any change process and therefore it is legitimate that s/he taps into and acts upon personal data and observation in an effort to influence the client, whether the client is an individual, a group, or an organization. Use of self, as believed by OD founders, creates a more powerful and compelling engagement between us the helpers and those who are being helped.

This idea is legitimized through the pioneering work of Fritz Perls (1969) who believed that it is important to bring both those who help and those who receive help onto the centre stage together 'to illuminate their actual relationship as clearly as possible' (Perls, 1969).

The following list of quotes shows how founders see the primacy of the concept of 'self as instrument':

- 'The primary instrument in OD work is the consultant practitioners' (Burke, 1982: 358).

- 'The bias of this book is that the OD consultant should be a finely tuned instrument' (Burke, 1982: 350–51).

- 'The use of self as a concept is central to the current practice of OD' (L. Porter, in a paper presented at the 1997 Academy of Management Annual Meeting).

- 'Perhaps the most powerful instrument we have in helping our clients navigate change is ourselves' (Curran, Seashore and Welp, in their presentation to 1995 ODN National Conference in Seattle, Washington).

- 'The principal instrument that we have to use in this field is ourselves. We do have the toolkit, but the effective use of that toolkit depends upon us... very much depends upon us and who we are' (Tannenbaum, 1979: 5–6).

What does 'self' mean?

There have been complex philosophical discussions on this topic since the beginning of time and my job here is not to participate in that discussion. Instead, I want to give a simplistic description of 'self' mainly to prepare us for the exposition of the next topic – the use of self.

Self is defined as the emotional, perceptual and cognitive processes that make up a person, and using the self as an instrument means becoming aware of and using these emotional, perceptual and cognitive processes (McCormick and White, 2000: 2). Within this self, the total personality, there is a known and unknown (persona and shadow) aspect (Jung, 1921). The known is the public self that Jung called persona, which Goffman (1959) speaks of as a presentation of self in everyday society. The persona makes life manageable and pleasant; it is the compromise between self and society. The shadow is the private self – often associated as that inferior self that may cause shame, but in reality does not need to. Everyone has both persona and shadow – they are a collective phenomenon. But for anyone who wants to use self to engage clients and to effect change, they need to pay deliberate attention to assessing and assimilating the shadow into a healthy persona. The more the practitioner learns about this self, whether it is persona or shadow, the more effective the self as an instrument of change can be.

What does the 'use of self' mean?

Different fields use the term 'self as an instrument' – and each has a distinctive definition that caters to their field requirement. The concept when used in OD refers to the focus on the practitioner bringing their whole selves to the work they do, using their own intellectual, emotional, cognitive resources in any consulting situation in order to create the impact that is needed in the system. This requires the practitioner to be constantly aware of self and others and to intentionally, selectively use that awareness to advance the work with the client. Over time, intent becomes second nature. By constantly paying attention to one's inner world as well as others' reactions, the OD practitioner becomes more and more conscious to use their intent to impact on the situation. This is called the 'Big I' intervention (Tschudy, 2006).

The 'Big I' approach refers to OD practitioners' ability and commitment to build trusting relationships with those whom they work with. Trusting relationships require us to stay authentic, congruent, open and transparent. Our possession of these qualities is not so much from the use of techniques and toolkits, but the result of our deep inner work. This central focus on effective relationship building and maintenance remains the same regardless of the consultancy assignment. McLagan (1989: 7) stated this succinctly:

Organization development's primary emphasis is on relationships and processes between and among individuals and groups. Its primary intervention is influence on the relationship of individuals and groups to reflect the impact on the organization as a system.

The 'Big I' approach requires us to have a sense of efficacy and agency (both concepts draw heavily on the work of Albert Bandura, 1997). Self-efficacy refers to our belief in our capacity to successfully achieve desired ends. Agency refers to our ability and capacity to act as our own agents in carrying out and implementing our courses of action.

From the first client contact, to the last contact, the practitioner needs to stay constantly aware of what s/he can do to shift the system. This can range from paying attention to building a trusting and effective relationship with members of the client system, to using one's self to demonstrate (embody) the goal of intervention, using one's emotional reaction to help explore working hypotheses, to give a presence that is otherwise missing in the client system.

In more specific description, Burke (1982) pointed out the importance of one's instrumentality in conducting both diagnosis and intervention, using one's heightened self-awareness to carry out the various aspects of organization consulting. McCormick and White (2000) went further to point out five methods for using one's self to do diagnosis: emotional reactions, initial perceptions, understanding bias, postponing judgement and the use of images and fantasies. They pointed out that self is an important instrument in the collection and analysis of data. So this brings us full circle back to the 'Big I' concept.

Presence

The field also encourages OD practitioners to focus on a continuous process of learning about one's conscious and unconscious reactions in different settings with different people (Berg, 1990). In doing this, you will slowly expand your presence. So what is 'presence'? Simply put, presence is an elevated level of the use of self. When you continue to use yourself to make a difference by giving, risking and providing a force that can be experienced by the client, you are cultivating presence. It is this directing our action and our best intentions to move the system that is so critical in the role of OD practitioners.

Presence, therefore, is the practitioner's DNA. By working on the ability to help the client examine situations, gain perspective, generate ideas and explore implications, and by understanding people and their feelings you are cultivating a presence that can effect change in the client system. Ultimately your presence will be felt and seen by your style, wise insight, value embodiment, incisive perspective and the way you go about handling challenging situations while building trusting relationships.

This practical use of self and presence is summarized by Nevis (1987: 54):

> the practitioner is not only to stand for and express certain values, attitudes, and skills, but to use these in a way to stimulate, and perhaps evoke from the client, action necessary for movement on its problems. This means that the practitioner is generally more open and revealing about thoughts and feelings than might be true in other forms of process consultation. The aim is to take advantage of the issue of difference, marginality, and attraction by the client so as to use oneself in the most powerful way possible. Thus the Gestalt-oriented organization practitioner primarily focuses on interaction with the client as a means through which movement toward improved organizational functioning will occur. Specifically, the practitioner models a way of approaching problems and through interest in the attractiveness of this way of being, hopes to mobilize the energy of the clients.

Gifts practitioners can offer

This aspect of the use of self was portrayed by Funches (1989) as an offering of three gifts a practitioner can give to the client system: discernment, presence and heart. She believes that the exercise of these three gifts will be driven by: a) our motivation to serve others; b) our desire to see real impact on the client system; c) our willingness to put ourselves on the line to shift the system. When that happens, the three gifts will be working potently and our work will not be hollow; instead, the potential of our impact will be infinite. The three gifts are:

- **Gift of discernment** – The gift of discernment involves using one's cognitive powers to sift through vast amounts of data to frame issues and gain understanding of the situation at hand. It is our ability to frame and focus the nature of clients' current situation in ways that enable clients to understand the impact of their behaviour and therefore see the choices they can make to change the situation to achieve their personal goals.

- **Gift of presence** – This gift is twofold. First is the ability to be present fully in the 'here and now'. From this 'here and now' perspective, one assists the client to take stock of where they are and where they want to go, examining the different levels of reality: what is actual, what is desired or potential, what is possible, what is probable given current situations through the consultant's use of his/her integrated 'self' – our approach, our words, our values.

- **Gift of heart** – The gift of heart is the ability to attune and connect oneself to the system in which one is working. In Funches' words, 'This gift includes qualities of compassion, humanitarianism, grace for others, passion for one's craft, and the will to extend oneself in the service of the work of learning and growth. This gift involves the inherent struggle of giving versus withholding of the self, recognizing

people's infinite capacity for love and the finite capacity of our physical selves. This is not a gift given lightly, for in expressing it we make impact on others' lives and draw ourselves more and more into relationships with others' (Funches, 1989: 149–67).

Funches emphasized the importance of joining up the three gifts so that they will flow together as they represent a higher order of doing, being, and knowing:

> into which we can integrate the theoretical and technological frames we use in our work... Together they are similar to the brain, heart, and courage that were so essential for Dorothy to find her home in 'The Wizard of Oz', 'home' really does rest in effective use of self... Together, I think the three gifts provide significant symbols for facilitating and creating change at deeper levels. Indeed the gifts are essential if we are to help create new ways of seeing and knowing in organizations that are necessary to move forward into the next century.
>
> (Funches, 1989: 161)

If you take this whole aspect of use of self seriously, then the implication is enormous. You know that you cannot attempt to teach emotional intelligence or guide others to develop it if you are deficient in it. You cannot teach self-awareness, self-management and social awareness if you are not actively and consistently engaging in personal growth and development – a practice of lifelong learning. If you choose to engage leaders and their organization in this kind of personal, group and organization development, then you will need to seek to deepen your self-awareness, understanding how your emotions and your experience have an impact on your behaviour. It is obvious that this type of work cannot be done in a vacuum or simply by reading. It requires a practice of mindfulness, being awake, aware, attentive to self and others and the environment (Boyatzis and McKee, 2005). In so many words, we need to do our own work first.

In concluding this section, I believe that many of us are in the trade because we share the ethos and core beliefs of OD and believe that in some small way we can make a difference about things that really matter to us in this life by using the principal instrument that we have – ourselves. In turn, by using ourselves intentionally, we also become a more complete person. This way and manner of using ourselves is a core belief articulated consistently and eloquently by OD founders.

The competence profile of the OD practitioner

What competences should OD practitioners have? This question has been the subject of great interest among the field's founders. From the beginning,

the subject occupied a lot of debate, research, and discussion and as a result, the field is not short of profiles of what makes an OD practitioner effective. Sullivan and Sullivan (1995) involved over 2,000 OD practitioners in defining essential competences and listed 187 required competences. The OD Network listed 141 competences in 2004, the OD Institute defined 139 competences, and recently CIPD in the UK (the HR professional organization) also listed 12 behaviours essential for OD practitioners.

Figure 10.2 summarizes briefly a few key authors' definitions of competences required for effective OD consultation, as gleaned from a review of the literature. Since there are so many listings of competence, I want to bring coherence to the diverse ways of describing a competent OD practitioner

FIGURE 10.2 OD consulting competences

Authors	Required competences for OD practitioners
Burke (1982)	The ability to: 1. Tolerate ambiguity. 2. Influence. 3. Confront difficult issues. 4. Support and nurture others. 5. Listen well and empathize. 6. Recognize one's own feelings and intuitions quickly. 7. Conceptualize. 8. Discover and mobilize human energy. 9. Teach or create learning opportunities. 10. Maintain a sense of humour. 11. A sense of mission.
Argyris (1962)	1. Self-confident. 2. Interpersonally confident.
Beer (1980)	1. Be credible. 2. Be neutral. 3. Ability to stay marginal.
Sullivan and Sullivan (1995) McLean and Sullivan (1990)	Based on McLean and Sullivan's earlier study, they involved over 2,000 OD practitioners in defining essential competences of internal and external consultants and listed the required 187 competences under 10 categories of OD activities. 1. Marketing phase (3 competences). 2. Initial contactivity phase (20 competences). 3. Start-up phase (10 competences). 4. Assessment and feedback phase (45 competences). 5. Action planning phase (16 competences). 6. Intervention phase (12 competences). 7. Evaluation phase (15 competences). 8. Adoption phase (13 competences). 9. Separation phase (13 competences). 10. General competences (40 competences).

FIGURE 10.2 *Continued*

Authors	Required competences for OD practitioners
Nevis (1987)	Outlined the skills required to be effective in using a Gestalt approach based on the Cycle of Experience as an orientation for both client and self. He organizes skills in terms of the consultant's major tasks: 1. Ability to stay in the present and focus on the ongoing process, with faith in natural developmental sequence. 2. Considerable sensitivity to sensory, physical functioning of self and others. 3. Frequent tuning into your emotions. 4. Ability to separate data from interpretation and to emphasize non-judgemental observations. 5. Awareness of your intentions, of what you want to do or say, together with the ability to be clear in letting others know what you want from them. 6. Ability to see where the client is at any time, and to respect that in working with the system. 7. Ability to face and accept emotional situations with a minimum of personal defensiveness. 8. Ability to make good contact with others. 9. Ability to present self as a highly attractive yet non-charismatic presence. 10. Capacity to be both tough and supportive during the same work session. 11. Ability to help the client system draw meaning or understanding from its experience with the consultant. 12. Appreciation of the significant contextual issues involved in system intervention. 13. Awareness of the aesthetic, transcendent and creative aspects of working as a consultant.

SOURCE: Cheung-Judge (2001).

by first defining the key categories for the various competences to be clustered under them.

In Figure 10.3 I have created six categories that I think are critical for an effective OD practitioner. In Figure 10.4 I have put the different competences under the six categories in diagram form. This framework was first created eight years ago for a post-graduate programme in a UK university whose dean asked me to design a framework that would help them to formulate a suitable curriculum to train OD practitioners. At that time, I based the design on two decades of working with and supporting OD practitioners and reviewing literature. Amazingly, eight years on, I feel the framework is still relevant except I have added one more circle – the ability to lead change.

I want Figure 10.4 to show that self-awareness and self-confidence are the two lynchpins holding the rest of the competences together. One needs

FIGURE 10.3 Cheung-Judge's six categories of OD competences

Conceptual competence	Intellectual capability to see the big picture, understand the context in which organizations function and specialized knowledge on how organizations function.
Ethics and values	Subscription to OD values, ability to role model those values in behaviour, and use the value to shape own consultancy practice.
Technical expertise	Have in-depth knowledge of specific intervention methodologies.
Strong individual and group processes and skills	Deep expertise in group dynamics and human dynamics. Able to understand how to facilitate both interpersonal work and group work, fluent in process consultation skills.
Self-awareness	Committed to lifelong work in knowing oneself, interested to develop awareness as to how one impacts others; able to make choices and not easily get hooked by others' issues.
Self-confidence	Having a grounded sense of self, ability to centre oneself and not be dominated by the need for approval and the need to be needed in client's relationship.

strategic oversight about the world of work and to have knowledge on how the organization works as a system. It is important for the practitioner to have some expertise in specific intervention skills and strong group dynamic skills, and practice needs to be backed up by clear ethics. But what will make a practitioner amazing is his/her level of self-awareness and self-confidence. Whether you agree with this framework or not, one thing for sure is that this type of competence profile will require a different development journey.

Whatever competence framework you choose, OD practitioners need most if not all of the following:

- training in behavioural science;
- knowledge of how organizations work;
- specific areas of expertise in conducting different types of interventions;
- strong group processes skills and a working knowledge of group dynamics;
- a working knowledge of complex change and know-how to support clients to navigate through the change;
- understanding and curiosity about how to work with diverse human dynamics;

FIGURE 10.4 Cheung-Judge's OD competence profile

© Cheung-Judge (2010)

- a clear sense of their own values and ethics and how to translate them into practice;
- a clear sense about who they are and how they work;
- willingness to work on our unresolved issues.

Where should we start this journey?

The development journey that OD practitioners should engage in

Lynn (1997), in a timeless article, outlined four levels of practitioner development which offer insight into the stages of the development journey:

- level one – beginner;
- level two – technologist;
- level three – professional;
- level four – master practitioner.

Many of us, as a *beginner*, started by having curiosity about how organizations work and how applied behavioural science operates within the world of work; so we began to study different aspects of organization science.

Next, we became intrigued by the various methodologies made available to organizations, and we began to perfect the methodologies we pursued. For example, some of you will begin to invest everything in learning to become a 'team' specialist – getting qualified in the team instruments and attending training to perfect your team facilitation skills, while others may want to invest in becoming a professional coach. Still others may choose to learn how to use specific culture mapping assessments so that they can become a culture change specialist. Often it is at this stage we become aware of the level of system work that we are either good at or feel motivated by. By that I mean you become clearer as to whether you like one-to-one, group, or complex system change work. The important thing is to stay in tune with your motivation as you move into the next stage.

While this type of specialist development is exciting and can often bring in a steady work portfolio, the critical thing in your development (that is, if you aspire to be an authentic OD practitioner) is not to allow yourself to get stuck at the *technologist* stage. In fact your ability to shift beyond just being a technologist is an important milestone in your development journey. Being an effective technologist is a very tempting place to remain as it gives you the reward of short-termism and the instant world of solutions, not to mention the seduction of the expert role. Having said that, there is nothing wrong if that is where you want to stay – many technologists make great impact in the world of work.

What I am saying is only applicable if you want to be wearing the OD label with integrity. If so, the longer you stay at the technologist stage, the greater the lure of techniques and methods. This is a critical warning I'd like to give to aspiring practitioners – do not let yourself get stuck in this stage, move on to the next phase of development.

The *professional* stage of development is to focus on developing yourself as an instrument – the trademark of an OD professional, which is the gateway to becoming a master practitioner. There is no shortcut to get there as good OD work requires you to delve deep within your own self in order to ensure the resources are there to be used in any consulting situation. This is when you shift your development focus from tools and techniques to experiential learning that drills deep – personally and interpersonally – so that the self as instrument is refined over and over again. The time will come when one day you wake up and realize you can walk into any situation and any type of project and use yourself for results. When that realization comes, it is a sure sign of arrival at the *masterful* stage.

Practically speaking, how does one start to become an OD practitioner? It will vary for different individuals; there are multiple entry points but only one destination. Relying on Lynn's four levels, a sample journey may go as follows.

As a beginner, you will probably start in a job learning how to do HR, LD or project management. During this stage, you will become more and more curious as to how organizations work and how people and groups within organizations work. This can be done by observation and by volunteering to take part in projects that have a people dimension.

For the next level, you will start taking courses on specific methodologies – eg basic facilitation skills or how to do team development work. You may want to get a few psychometric testing licences under your belt, and to expand your toolbox in the type of interventions you are most interested in. If you are an internal OD practitioner, you will start looking for opportunities to volunteer your services, eg supporting a project change team by offering an extra pair of hands, or by facilitating the induction of a longer-term project team, or undertaking a research project for the internal communications department.

The transition to OD professional requires you to get some formal development in the field of OD, learning the current theories and practice of OD, and starting to attend some experiential laboratory education (in the tradition of NTL and Tavistock) to get to know who you are and how you work. Some business schools also have great post-graduate programmes that you can explore.

When is a good time to start the development of 'self'?

While all these different stages are happening, the question is, when is a good time to start the development of self? The answer is – from the beginning and with great intention.

The following 10 steps are general guidelines suggested by Curran *et al* (1995) and Cheung-Judge (2001:14) to grow one's use of self.

- **Begin with owning our instrumentality** – devote time and energy to learn about who you are and how issues of family history, gender, race and sexuality affect self-perception. It means you are committed to develop your self-knowledge and expertise to ensure you are effective consultants in the field. Finally, it also means you regularly identify and explore the values by which you live your lives, as well as developing your intellectual, emotional, physical and spiritual capacities.

- **Take steps to regularly refine our instrumentality** – refining your instrumentality implies regular maintenance work on self. In practice, it means dedicating time to the ongoing maintenance of both self-knowledge and technical expertise. Employ a shadow consultant, a mentor or even enter into a therapeutic relationship to continually

heighten your self-awareness. Silent retreat once a month to regroup and reflect is also a good step.

- **Develop life-long learning habits** – continually develop and enhance competences in order to move flexibly among the various roles required of the OD consultant. Develop relationships with peers and professionals with whom you can check perspectives, talk through challenges and strategies, and align values and practices. Take responsible risks that stretch your professional comfort zone and proficiency.

- **Expand our 'positive core'** – identify the 'positive core' within yourselves and deploy it to achieve the impact you want. Find out what is your gift and your motivation. Be ruthless in sticking to what matters to you; be it level of system work, or type of work that motivates you. It is important to be able to wake up and 'skip' to work with a thankful heart.

- **'Putting first things first'** (Covey, 1995) – try to achieve a balance between work and life and ensure you are running by the compass and not the clock. Work will never go well for long if the rest of life is a shambles. The integrity of your work will demand that you have clarity about what is also most important to you value-wise. Some of us feel strongly about doing pro bono work for a charity serving the Global South or two-thirds world, for example.

- **Build a habit to reframe, giving/receiving feedback** – reframing allows the emergence of new perspectives and feedback helps to promote a continual effort to change and adapt. Using others to help you to be the best you can in moving towards the direction of choice is an important habit.

- **Build up a strong support system** – a support system can be used to provide support, identify expert resources, and develop and maintain a sense of self-efficacy and agency. This can also be useful to help us deal with issues of transference, high anxiety, etc. Having access to a consultant action learning set, or building a team of virtual mentors who can give different types of advice on methodology and on ways of consulting will be a good move.

- **Work to reclaim our own shadow** – Bates (1991) talked about the importance of claiming the unknown part of ourselves so that we can claim our shadow. This can come about by engaging in deep intrapersonal work, eg attending T group sessions or other advance laboratory work that both Tavistock and NTL are famous for. Other suppliers run intensive personal growth workshops, or weekend renewal programmes, etc.

- **Work through issues of power** – develop strategies to manage your own and others' power dynamics. This area of work is more about shifting mental models and accumulating political skills,

not to mention about being comfortable to use personal power for results.

- **Build a self-care package** – use self-knowledge to build a package of self-care based on the many suggestions listed above in order to ensure that instrumentality is sustainable and lasting.

To conclude, doing OD work is doing life work. By that I mean a) we use our lives to impact in areas that are important to us; and b) we push to know ourselves better and better. This level of development is justified because the field requires us to bring not just our intelligence, but intuition, observational skills, energy, commitment, theoretical knowledge, process skills, personal integrity and value orientation to do this work; practitioners need to develop the corresponding growth of self-knowledge as a significant aspect of becoming that sharp instrument.

My question for you before leaving this section is, how has your development journey been in the last couple of years? Are you like one of my colleagues who has done no development work for the last 20 years or are you like the most serious OD practitioners who accept that it is an ethical obligation for us to pursue continuous development if we aim to have the right to walk into organizations to 'do' OD?

The practice trademarks of OD

I'd like to end this chapter by looking at the eight practice trademarks that distinguish OD practitioners from other forms of consultancy. Having spent nine chapters sketching out the definition of OD and its practices, I am now ready to answer the difficult questions: 'What is OD and what is not?' and 'Who is doing OD and who is not?' These are controversial questions and my intent is not to be 'right' but to put the debate back on the table because if the field of OD is to move on, accumulate knowledge, develop its practices and increase its impact, grow its scholars, expand its pool of researchers and practitioners, there needs to be a common understanding (no matter how rough it is) of what makes the field distinctive from other fields. Also, if the field of OD is to thrive, we need to identify the parameters so that it is neither too tight (elitist) nor too loose (anything that improves an organization can be called OD). We have come upon a critical time when organizations really need this field to stand out and support them through tough terrain. To do that, we need to have a clear articulation of the definition of OD, our core values, core purpose and practice trademarks of OD practitioners.

So while I fear the disapproval of colleagues, I will venture to delineate the key characteristics of OD practice and lay a bold claim that if practitioners do not demonstrate these practice trademarks, they are not doing OD – despite the fact that they can be very competent, very impactful

and effective in what they do. I hope this will yield subsequent debate from other esteemed colleagues so that the field parameters will become more distinct.

What are the trademarks that make the OD field distinctive?

To understand the practice trademarks of OD practitioners, it is important to revisit the nature of OD work. Burke (1982: 354) reported an occasion when a human relations consultant was speaking to a group of aspiring OD consultants and said, 'You can learn the technology of OD in 15 minutes.' But, he went on to ask the group, 'How can you learn a technique, design, methods, tactic – that is, a technology – for dealing with dependency?' The point Burke was making is that while it is relatively easy to learn a lot of 'how to' techniques in OD, understanding the nature of such human processes as trust, dependency and conflict will take a lifetime.

It is in this context the following eight practice trademarks are presented as key anchors in our practice of OD. All these eight trademarks have been discussed throughout the book, but here I will summarize them as a coherent set of characteristics:

1 the two-pronged goal of OD;
2 the focus on human enterprise;
3 the collaborative and developmental approach in our work;
4 the importance of relationship building in our work;
5 focus on process just as much as task;
6 process-facilitative-educator role rather than the expert-advice-giver role;
7 the use of 'Big I' intervention – self as instrument;
8 the total system approach.

The two-pronged goal of OD

There are many forms of consultancy that work hard to improve the function of an organization but their work is often marked by the lack of two things that define real OD work: (1) sustainability and (2) intentionality to increase the client system's ability to engage in self-renewal in an independent effort.

The goal of OD is not just to improve the health of the organization but also to ensure change is synonymous with development. In the process of doing the work, the client system is being supported to develop their own capability to sustain the change. This firm commitment of OD to develop the client's self-renewal ability is based on our belief that when given the

right type of support, most clients can solve their problems. Also, if they have solved their problems once, they are more likely to solve problems again and again. Our job, therefore, is to expand the system's understanding of human dynamics in such a way that it will impact on the cultural fabric of the organization. This is a critical feature of what makes OD unique.

So we pride ourselves not just on our ability to adjust system policies, do Organization Design, or support effective change but we put a lot more methodological focus into designing processes that will help the members within an organization to create the change they want and learn how to do it again and again. It is these two prongs of deep expertise backed up by knowing how to get people engaged in processes that can change their future which makes OD work stand out clearly among the jungle of consultancy approaches.

Reflective question: Have you been achieving these two goals simultaneously in your change work? Do your clients believe that every time you finish a project, they have learnt a lot more about how to do things themselves?

The focus on human enterprise

What has made the OD field so dynamic and controversial – even from its earliest days – is that it overturned the dominance of classic theory of organization and fundamentally questioned the whole machinery image of organization (Burke, 1997). From the very beginning the assertion was that if any organization is to remain healthy it has to take its people seriously and by that it means all the people; those whom the organization serves, those whom the organization employs, and those with whom the organization partners. Unlike the machinery focus, OD practitioners take the human dimension within each of the jobs assigned to us seriously. We build our expertise in human dynamics, group dynamics and system dynamics and it is this knowledge base that gives us the know-how to build the capability of those who live within the system to fix and improve it.

Our targeted group is the leaders of the organization. The early founders insisted that those who run an organization need to be supported to take this human dimension seriously. The OD practitioner's job is to help the leaders to understand that their organization is made up of soul-alive, spirit-kicking individuals. Any areas that will support the people who work for the organization, eg effective processes, fluent communication, effective teams and collaborative inter-group relationships, should receive leadership attention.

This belief that organization is a 'living system' is what shapes our approach to work. While our commission may be technically focused, eg doing Organization Design or aligning processes, we will always simultaneously focus on the impact of these changes on the people within the system. If someone is great in designing organizational structures but doesn't pay

close attention to the psychological impact of the redesign on people and fails to build change processes to support people through the changes, then they are not doing OD work.

Tichy (1974: 169) clearly sums up the nature of this focus:

I work on the human side of the enterprise. That is I help people, mostly top executives, work out their problems of interpersonal relationships and communications, and conflicts of interest. I get involved in planning and implementing procedures of goal setting, decision making, conflict resolution, and the delegation of authority. In this way, I help an organization develop and modify its governance and problem-solving mechanisms.

Reflective question: Have you been putting the people element at the heart of your change work? Have you managed to put the people issues squarely in front of leaders when you support them?

Collaborative and developmental approach

Since the aim of OD is not to do the work of the client but to facilitate processes to enable the client not only to do their own work, but learn how to sustain the momentum of such work, our approach inherently is a collaborative one. We seize every opportunity to turn our clients into collaborators, co-investigators, diagnosticians, joint planners, helpers in executing the interventions and co-evaluators. We do this because we want to engage the client system in understanding their own issues, and become better able to carry on with the OD phases on their own, and eventually own the change processes. This way, we know we are building momentum for implementation – which is what sustainability is all about. This approach is informed by the action research theory of Lewin, who believed that the best way to study the system is to collaborate with members of the system so that as people get involved as researchers, they will become a lot more willing to apply what they have learnt when they do it themselves. Moreover, decisions are best implemented by those who help to make them.

The collaborative approach requires practitioners to work harder to build a mutually trusting relationship that we, at the beginning of our contact, have to aim for intentionally.

Reflective question: If you were to ask your client for feedback on whether your approach in working with them is developmental and marked by collaboration, what would they say?

Importance of relationship building in our work

In order to provide support to the clients in the way I have just described, we need to turn our attention to building a trusting relationship with our clients from the beginning. We know that without establishing effective, helping

relationships with and among individuals and groups within the client system, we will not have a solid platform to deliver the 'content' and 'process' of help. This central focus on effective relationship building and maintenance remains the same regardless of the consultancy assignment.

This is why Weisbord (1977: 108) is so adamant that a successful contract would need to address both the task and relationship issues during the process of consultancy. He said:

> What do I mean by contract? I mean an explicit exchange of expectations, part dialogue, part written document, which clarifies for consultant and client three critical areas:
>
> What each expects to get from the relationship.
>
> How much time each will invest, when, and at what cost.
>
> The ground rules under which the parties will operate.

That is why we will always aim to have a strong contract with our clients that is social in nature, not just economic, and that covers both task and relationship issues.

Reflective question: How intentional are you in building effective relationships with those you work with? Is your relational platform strong and robust enough for you to do tough and challenging work with the system?

Focus on process just as much as task

Another practice trademark is our concern for process and not just task. What do we mean by process? It means the human and social processes through which individual, groups and organization go about doing their business. The particularly important organizational processes listed by French and Bell (1999: 164) are communications, roles and functions of group members, group problem solving and decision making, group norms and growth, leadership and authority, intergroup cooperation and competition and conflict resolution.

When clients ask us to address any task issues, we know it is our duty to ensure the task issues are resolved, but our job has to focus beyond what the task is about – we need to be intentional in how the task is being done. In practice this means we need to draw client attention to how they go about getting the work done, and whether the approaches they take are supporting their intention or derailing it. We need to help them to get rid of the myth that anything that is not a task is 'soft'. When they start thinking more on how they should approach the job and how they can carry people with them, then we know we have fulfilled one of our mandates.

In light of this, does focusing on process more than task mean that we should be technically incompetent or commercially naive? No, in fact it is important to know that most OD practitioners – as open system subscribers

– are committed to being contextually savvy and therefore we are proud of our technical expertise and industry sector knowledge. So this practice trademark is not condoning commercial naiveté, or contentment that we are without technical skills, but instead affirms that our default approach is to use well-designed processes to help a client to develop effective habits to do their own work in the long run.

Reflective question: How conscious are you in setting up various processes to help the client to learn 'how' to get things done? Do you also set up processes to pass on to the client whatever skills you use during the journey?

Process-facilitative-educator role rather than the expert-advice-giver role

The focus on process rather than just on task defines the OD practitioners' approach more as a facilitator-educator than an advice-giver, as illustrated by the following quote:

> We believe it is possible and desirable for the OD consultant to be an expert in the sense of being competent to present a range of options open to the client, but any extensive reliance on the traditional mode of consulting, that is, giving substantive advice, will tend to negate the OD consultant's effectiveness.
>
> (French and Bell, 1999: 257)

Schein has been very explicit in all his writing about why the expert role does not fit into OD (1988: 5–11). He listed the following reasons:

- **Expert role builds dependency** – to help the client system to develop its own resources, we need to support continuous internal skill development. Our expert role will not do that; instead it will help to build a level of dependency.

- **Expert role is not conducive to collaboration** – the expert role will automatically lead to a 'selling role' and a 'defending role' when we present our recommendations. This style will cut short the joint exploration process and negate a collaborative and development approach to improve organizational effectiveness.

- **Expert role can lead to an adversary position** – the expert role, particular when played out mainly among the senior leaders, will lead to us losing credibility with the people below because they know that we did not have all the data on which to base our recommendation since those who have the answers were not included in the decision-making process.

- **Expert role will induce unrealistic expectations** – if we continue giving substantive advice, it will increase the expectations from our

clients that we are able to give more and more advice – this reliance prevents us from achieving our central mission to help them to be self-sufficient in capability and resources with the change processes.

It is this facilitative, inquiring, educative role which enables multiple parties to get the task done in a sustainable way, and not acting as an expert advocating a certain position for clients to take, that makes OD practices unique.

Reflective question: What type of developmental support work have you done to enable you to free yourself from needing to be an expert with your client? What type of results do you get when you take more of the process-facilitative-inquiring-educative role?

The use of 'Big I' intervention – self as instrument

OD founders make a clear distinction between the many tools and techniques practitioners employ to support clients from the use of oneself to effect changes. One of our practice trademarks is that we will deploy our 'self' constantly to intervene in the client system. From the moment we make contact, we use our 'self' to facilitate the multi parties to agree what type of future or outcomes they want for their organization. We work with the various concerns of different groups before we can finalize the contract. We also use our intuition and judgment to guide the clients through every phase in the OD cycle and to personally model some of the ethics and values that we expound. All those processes are held together by our conscious intention to use ourselves for results and that is what Tschudy (2006) calls the 'Big I' intervention, which speaks of the 'intentional use of self to create the impact' and 'the artful interaction with the client system in which the organization moves from its current state to some desired state' (Tschudy, 2006: 166).

Reflective question: Are you currently satisfied with the way you use yourself to achieve the impact you want? If yes, name the areas where you think you are doing well. If not, think about what you need to do more to sharpen your instrumentality.

The total system approach (multiple system level of intervention)

The final key trademark of OD practice is our subscription to system theory. In practice, it means that even though we may be commissioned to carry out a specific task for a specific group, as OD practitioners we will need to focus on the multiple systems that may be impacted by the introduction of that change. In fact we need to help clients always to look out for the intricate

interdependencies of the various parts of the system. We need to spend time with clients mapping out the intended and unintended consequences of the change on the various parts of the organization. Sometimes, we do not have the mandate to touch those other areas, but it is our job to bring the system perspective to the attention of the clients, so that they can pay attention to them.

This is the question that Richard Beckhard repeatedly asked – 'Where is the O in OD?' He saw the difference between 'using OD approaches' and 'doing OD'. According to him, doing OD fulfils the following definition which he delineated: 'OD is an effort that a) is planned; b) is organization wide; c) is managed from the top; d) increases organizational effectiveness and health through e) planned interventions in the organization's "processes" using behavioural-science knowledge' (Beckhard 1969: 9). The 'O' for him is to hold on to the systemic impact of any work we have done, always aiming to build the organization as a whole. Bradford and Burke commented that most OD consultants 'use OD techniques' – and in doing so, they have minimal impact and are seen by executives as providing marginal value.

Reflective question: How systemic are you in your practice? Do you automatically think whole system? What can you do more to make your systemic thinking and therefore approach more evident?

Last word on practice trademarks

I am sure there are other practice trademarks that I have missed, but I think it is important to put this question back on the table for debate. Based on the eight practice trademarks above, I am asserting that one cannot do OD consulting just from the 'neck up', using only skills, rational mind, tools and competency. OD also involves 'neck down' work. It has often struck me how hard it is to do good OD work because the OD approach to help actually goes against our human need to be needed, recognized and esteemed for our expertise and the value we can bring into the system. As Schein said, our greatest work is to resist the seduction of being an expert demonstrating our special gifts to the clients; instead we should be acting more like a shadow consultant, staying in the background and working ourselves out of a job. This approach requires us to be firmly grounded in our self-worth. How many of us can truly say we are there?

Returning to the practice trademarks of OD, I wonder whether we can now risk stating boldly something most of us avoid defining: who is doing OD and who is not? Can we venture to name activities as only truly OD? Maybe I will try. One is doing OD if one is there to improve an organization's effectiveness in a self-renewal way by focusing on the human enterprise of the organization; paying attention to the total systemic relationship between parts; using process interventions that are based on behavioural

science theories and principles and informed by the humanistic value framework. If all the support work is done in a collaborative and developmental approach, through a trusting partnership between the OD practitioners and the client system – then it is truly OD.

Summary

I began in Chapter 1 by talking about the role of OD practitioners as a third-party change agent and self as the most important instrument in the helping relationship. In Chapter 2, I outlined the five building blocks of OD practice – tools and techniques, the navigation map of the OD consultancy cycle, theoretical grounding, value and ethics and the use of self. I looked at the importance of practitioners moving through the life journey building up the five key blocks. In Chapters 3 to 10, I hope I have managed to pull together the different aspects of the use of self in the field of OD. I hope you have understood the unique gift of being an OD practitioner and the type of developmental journey you need to embark on.

Many of us know we cannot ever achieve perfect instrumentality. However, we can begin the journey towards that ideal by undertaking a process of lifelong discovery and of owning and refining our instrumentality.

However, let's just imagine if we collectively (without a formal licensing procedure) agreed to create a bright future and make a major impact in the field of OD by the effective use of self. How would things change? I believe that organizations all over the world would be well disposed to a group of effective helpers who would become likely partners with them in the pursuit of optimal health for their organizations. Through time, we would pass on the baton to managers (our clients) and coach them to play a key role in transforming the way their organizations are run. Ultimately, a healthy organization can develop itself with its managers as the primary practitioners. In this way, more managers will come to understand the necessary balance between freedom and constraint, democracy and authority, profit and ethics in organization life and health.

Power and politics and Organization Development

In the past few decades there has been keen interest in the typologies of organization and some of the most frequently quoted models are: bureaucratic, rational, political, pluralistic, and collegial/consensus organization.

- In a **bureaucratic model**, decisions are made on the basis of rules, procedures, traditions and historical precedents.

- In a **rational model**, decisions are made on the basis of rational problem solving: goals are identified and agreed upon; situations are analyzed objectively in relation to goals; alternatives are chosen and implemented.

- In a **political model**, decisions are made on the basis of coalitions, partnership, jockeying for dominance, influence, or resource control based on preserving the interest of one's part of the organization.

- In a **collegial/consensus organization**, decisions are taken by collective interest and leaders work hard to find common ground among staff.

- In a **pluralistic organization**, the organization is made up of different interest groups, each pursuing their individual functional or specialist interest legitimately.

While some organizations may claim that they operate mainly from a specific model, most exhibit aspects of all of these models, and all of them, especially those in the Western world, are both political and pluralistic in nature – as a pluralistic organization is evidence of the working of democracy.

In pluralistic organizations *power* is an inherent feature. The following outlines the characteristics of a pluralistic organization:

- Organizations are composed of different interest groups each legitimately pursuing its own goals.

- Each division is charged to pursue their own functional agenda – power therefore becomes the intervening variable between desired outcomes and actual results.
- Conflict is, in this context, an inevitable and normal part of the way things get done.
- Bargaining and formation of coalitions is a necessary means to deliver goals.
- Sideways power is recognized as a necessary and frequently exercised component of managerial effectiveness.
- Political behaviour is part and parcel of the life of those who run organizations – it is the inevitable result when one's attempt at influence is countered by another interested party or group.

With power as an inherent feature of pluralistic organizations, those who are interested in helping the organization to work better will be ill equipped to do the job if they do not understand power.

Two OD leaders have clearly articulated this necessity:

Organization development signifies change, and for change to occur in an organization, power must be exercised. For the purpose of OD, therefore, the consultant must understand the nature of power, from both a personal and an organization perspective, and be able to determine, within an organization, who has power, how power is exercised, and where the leverages for change (exercising power) are likely to be.

(Burke, 1982: 127)

Power and politics, indisputable facts of organizational life, must be understood if one is to be effective in organization... the OD practitioner
needs both knowledge and skill in the arenas of organizational power and politics.

(French and Bell, 1999: 282)

In the past 40 years, there are many authors who wrote impressively about the crucial role of power in change agents, so it is surprising there has been so little interest in this area. There are many factors that may have led to this attitude; the meaning being assigned to the word power, people's perception that power is incompatible with OD values, the cumulative negative experience of seeing how power is abused. My hunch is that the key factor remains the lack of distinction between the positive and the negative use of power which McClelland (1970) wrote about.

In this chapter, I will cover the following:

1 What is power and politics? Why is it relevant for OD practitioners?
2 The two faces of power – the work of McClelland.
3 How power dynamics work within the organization – four theorists.

4 The application of the use of power in three key OD activities:

a diagnosis;

b change programmes;

c building a healthy organization.

5 Using personal power more effectively to achieve greater impact.

What do we mean by power and politics? Why are they relevant for OD practitioners?

Here are some of the definitions of power by OD writers:

- 'Power is the potential for influence... the potential must be acted upon' (Burke, 1982: 149).

- 'Power is the intentional influence over the beliefs, emotions, and behaviours of people. Potential power is the capacity to do so, but kinetic power is the act of doing so. One person exerts power over another to the degree that he is able to exact compliance as desired' (Siu, 1979: 31).

- 'Power is the ability of those who possess power to bring about the outcomes they desire' (Salancik and Pfeffer, 1977: 3).

- 'Power is defined simply as the capacity to effect (or affect) organizational outcomes. The French word "pouvoir" stands for both the noun "power" and the verb "to be able to". To have power is to be able to get desired things done, to effect outcomes – actions and the decisions that precede them' (Mintzberg, 1983: 4).

Analysing these definitions, the following properties of power emerge:

- **First,** power is about creating the outcome one wants or what the situation requires – whether this is about influencing and shifting behaviour, or changing the course of events, or managing resistance or getting people to do things that they would not otherwise do.

- **Second,** the exercise of power happens within the social arena, between two or more parties. The word 'potential' signifies that without being in a relational arena power cannot be exercised. The only exception to this is in the extreme form of power use, eg dictatorial and terrorist situations.

- **Third,** the effectiveness of power use is dependent on how one channels what one has (power base) through the choice of appropriate activities and behaviours (power strategies). The exercise of power comes through the behaviour of individuals and the activities they undertake.

This last point defines the word 'politic'. Politics is the processes, actions, and the behaviour you use to achieve the influence you desire, as French and Bell (1999: 286) put it:

> Organizational politics is power-in-action in organization; it is engaging in activities to get one's way.
>
> (French and Bell, 1999: 286)

Both power and politics are often used interchangeably with other terms like powerful, impactful, and influential and they all point to the same outcome – getting things done that otherwise would not have been.

Why use of power is relevant to OD practitioners

Back in 1988, two of the most significant researchers on power summed up the relevance of power to OD in this succinct way:

> The effective combination of OD and power represents, for us, taking the high road to organization improvement. It begins by adhering to the valuable roots of OD where an educational process is used to encourage people to collaborate in making decisions that affect their own destiny. But as we will attempt to show in this book, OD goes on to incorporate modern approaches to power by (1) building its own power base so that it has access to those in power, (2) utilizing power strategies that are open and above board for influencing key power holders to address critical substantive issues that prove more creative and efficient than political bargaining, (3) assisting the power structure to confront and transform itself so that change can be more lasting, and (4) upholding the concerns and interests of those with less power who are affected by these changes.
>
> The low road represents vested political interest groups, who, if left only to power and deception without OD, can destroy organizations by failing to tap human potential. Ironically, the low road also includes not only traditional champions of power who think that manipulation and political games are essence of success, but those OD chameleons who sell out to power.
>
> (Greiner and Schein, 1988b: 7)

What is so challenging from their words is that not only do OD practitioners need to engage in the high road of power – being skilful in our power use – but we should also use OD values and methods to show the power users better ways to wield power for the good of the entire organization to prevent them going down the 'low road'. The rest of the chapter is to further explore why the use of power is such a critical aspect of OD practitioners' work.

Two faces of power – the work of McClelland

According to McClelland, there are two faces of power, which operate very differently, and they must not be confused as the same. They are the negative face of power and the positive face of power.

Negative face of power

The negative face is the most dominant view of power. This is the 'unsocialized' way of using power, ie to dominate and control others often to benefit a single party (the power user). This use of power is characterized by extreme pursuit of self-interest, an unsocialized need to dominate others, and a tendency to see power plays in win–lose terms. Negative power tactics often revolve around secrecy, deception, hidden agendas, withholding information and, worst of all, dishonesty. The sad thing is, these aspects of the negative power play are real and continue to operate in organizations in overt ways, perpetuating the view that power is negative and corrupt. This should be the target that any OD programme should aim at – to help the organization members to move away from this type of power play towards more positive use of power.

Positive face of power

The positive face of power is characterized by a socialized use of power, where the user tends to have an empowering impact. Such people are conscious that when they use power and influence, not only will they reach their goals but in the process of doing that they can also facilitate others to reach their goals. Therefore the positive face of power is characterized by a balanced pursuit of self-interest and the interests of others, as the users tend to view situations in win–win terms as much as possible; engaging in open problem solving followed by action and influencing. Their tactics are different as they tend to promote collaboration, building alliances, doing joint working instead of using power coercion.

While proponents of the positive approach detest the negative use of power, they are however pragmatic enough to accept that all organizations have negative power users; therefore if they want to be effective and to get things done, they have to engage with the power dynamics in the organization – except they aim to do it constructively.

McClelland's work should encourage the OD practitioner to work with power in an organization because the positive use of power fits very well with OD core values, especially in the areas of *power equalization, humane use of power, the importance of empowerment* and *helping organization members to deploy an alternative way of using power.*

First, **power equalization** – this is a key characteristic of the positive power use and is one of the core values of OD. Emphasis on power equalization stems from two OD beliefs: problem solving is usually superior to coercion as a means to finding solutions to problematic situations, and power equalization increases the amount of power available to organization members, and by so doing adds power to the organization.

Second, the founders of OD were motivated to help organizations to be **more humane in their power use**. As Greiner and Schein (1988b) argue, OD values of trust, cooperation and collaboration can not only coexist within the 'pluralistic/political' model of organization, but can also make those organizations more humane and effective.

Third, one of the features of a healthy organization is an **empowered organization**; hence it is crucial that all practitioners think about how to help members build multiple positive power bases in the organization (more power to everyone) by promoting OD values such as *trust, openness, collaboration, individual dignity*, and *promoting individual and organizational competence*, which are consistent with the positive face of power. The goal of OD work is to ensure individuals within any large system do not lose their individuality and their sense of power and dignity to make choices. Without engaging in the realm of power and actively promoting the use of positive power, our talk about empowerment will be rendered worthless.

Fourth, since power use is a critical aspect of the organization, OD practitioners not only need to learn about the various positive aspects of power and politics, the positive strategy and tactics of influence, adopting the characteristics and behaviours of positive power users, but also to help your clients to learn as they watch you model them. By upholding an **alternative way of using power**, you can show others that negative political bargaining and dysfunctional politics is not the only way.

How power dynamics work within the organization – four theorists

In this section, I will review briefly the work of four theorists whose work gives us a fundamental understanding of how power plays out in social relationships within the organization context.

Emerson's power dependence theory (1962)

This theory states that power is inherent in any social relationship as long as one person is dependent on another person to satisfy his/her needs and wants. Emerson actually has a formula to express this:

The dependence of A upon B is (1) directly proportional to A's motivational investment in the goals mediated by B, and (2) inversely proportional to the availability of those goals to A outside of the A–B relation.

(Emerson, 1962: 32)

In other words, Emerson believes that if person B has something person A wants badly, then person B has power over person A. This is because person B has the 'desired commodity'. What Emerson tells us is that in any social relationship, if someone has something that another person desires and the probability is that that person cannot get that something outside of this relationship, then that is how power can be exercised. The key to the power dynamic is in the 'desired commodity'.

What is a 'desired commodity'? It all depends on who is doing the desiring, but in a work situation there tends to be two types of desired commodity. Some are very tangible and concrete, eg a pay rise, promotion, interesting projects, expertise, knowledge that can support the programme, key information, access to decision makers and so on. But there are also less tangible desirables that may often be even more powerful than the tangible ones. For example, public praise, consistently fair standards, social approval, affirmation, warmth, helpfulness and empathy can be more desirable, especially in a soulless corporation.

This view of power has its origin in the social exchange theory, which believes that in social situations there are a lot of things that humans need and want; therefore our instinct is to engage in exchange activities with others in order to be able to give and take different things we value from each other.

How does this apply to OD practitioners and our understanding of organizations?

In a pluralistic organization, there is such a complex web of knowledge that no one person will be able to achieve all the key results they are responsible for through sheer talent and hard work alone. In that context, everyone is mutually dependent to achieve their key results – staff, partners, sideways colleagues. Therefore, social exchange of resources, support, knowledge and expertise are all part and parcel of the pluralistic organization. Once you understand that, you will accept that not participating in power play is not an option if you are to be effective in your delivery of work.

If you are an internal change agent, do pay attention to the complex web of social exchange opportunities that you have. The earlier you learn to identify a) who has the 'desired commodities' you need to get your job done, and b) what type of 'desired commodities' you can offer to others, the sooner you will be able to build a balanced power relationship. Also remember, finding opportunities to create favour for others by helping them to achieve the work goal is actually good organization citizenship behaviour that will lead to the building up of an attractive reputation.

Emerson's theory will also help you to assess the current ways the organization plays this social exchange game. If the assessment shows that the social exchange is done in a dysfunctional way, eg bullying, then as an internal OD practitioner you will need to formulate strategies to help the organization to move away from the negative power play to a healthy and above-board approach to trade favours and do the necessary social exchange.

Salancik and Pfeffer's strategic-contingency model of power (1977)

Salancik and Pfeffer see organizational power as a good thing and believe that power in organizations tends to be situated in those sub-units (individuals, units or departments) that are most important for solving the organization's most critical problems. Since the organization often faces critical problems, they actually mean the continuous uncertainties posed by the environment. Therefore, power, in the hands of the critical problem solvers, will actually help the organization cope with the various realities it faces.

The strategic-contingency framework is a strategic model of power that gives those on whom the organization depends most for survival power over those who do not have that role. This has its origin in the rational machine model about how power should be used. In the words of Mintzberg, those in core functions will have more power residing in them than those who are in support functions.

How does this apply to OD practitioners and our understanding of organizations?

First, accept that power differentials within an organization will always exist between those who carry the organization's critical activities and who hold core roles and those who do not.

Second, these core people, if they are not challenged and supported, will ultimately build up a lopsided view of themselves and ride roughshod over those who are not in those positions. For example, in a university it will be the academics versus administration staff; in a medical organization it will be doctors versus the nursing or administrative staff. Therefore, in order to equalize the power dynamics, OD programmes need to be designed to mix the powerful core groups with other units in the organization to promote mutual understanding and to appreciate the level of interdependence they have with each other. In that way, a more holistic perspective of itself will develop in the organization. Any initiative that helps the system to respect expertise without diminishing the roles of others will be a good intervention.

Third, in a change programme, if any of these core groups are not engaged and are not given key roles to lead the change, the change programme will

have only a limited chance to succeed. Therefore, it is important to single out key opinion formers from these core groups and give them key roles to support the change programme. It is also our job to ensure, especially in the diagnostic phase, that all voices from the whole system can be heard instead of just the powerful core group.

French and Raven's 'bases of social power' (1959)

French and Raven (1959) believe that power is used by those who, in Emerson's terms, have control of desired commodities by accumulating various bases of power, and then using it to get things done. They go further to delineate five forms of power:

- **Reward power** – power based on the ability of the power holder to give something valued by another. These can be tangible or intangible things. In this over-capacitated environment, just giving people time or sitting down to listen to their struggle, or showing empathy will often be deemed by some to be a reward.

- **Coercive power** – power based on the ability of the power holder to punish another. This type of power base often does not need to be exercised; just the potential is enough to create impact. A good example is the power that comes with regulatory bodies.

- **Legitimate power** – power based on the belief that the power holder is someone who has the legitimate right to exert influence, and that those around him/her have a legitimate obligation to comply. This legitimacy is often the most common basis of power within an organization. However, seldom does it operate alone to create sustainable effect.

- **Expert power** – power based on the power holder possessing expert knowledge or information or important facts that are needed by another. This will be especially important if the type of information and expertise is regarded by the organization as important.

- **Personal referent power** – this is the highest form of power base: because of being who the person is, they attract people to them. People around them 'refer to' or 'identify' with them. Hence by being themselves, they pull and attract others, and others are willing to be influenced by them.

The key theme from French and Raven is that whoever has these power bases will be able to get things done in the organization. I think regardless of how one feels about the different forms of power, it is important to own what you have because sometimes just having them will be sufficient to create the impact you need.

How does this apply to OD practitioners and our understanding of organizations?

As an OD practitioner you need to intentionally develop, accumulate and expand as many power bases as you can, so that by having an adequate power base, you can create the impact you need in your relationship with your colleagues and clients.

First, seek purposefully to increase your personal referent power so that by being who you are, people are drawn to you – and give you the platform to help.

Second, it is important to be able to analyse the various power bases that exist among the stakeholders so that you can navigate through the power terrain of the client system.

Third, you can encourage clients to cultivate their own and their staff power base, so that they can individually and collectively deliver successful outcomes at work.

Fourth, in managing change, you need to understand who has a power base that can help to facilitate or block the change progress. You also need to know whether the change team you put together has sufficient power base to move the change on within the current hierarchical structure.

Mintzberg's theory of power (1982)

Mintzberg's theory of power is built on the premise that organizational behaviour is a power game in which various players, called *influencers*, seek to control the organization decisions and actions. He specified that there are three basic conditions for the exercise of power:

- possession of some source or basis of power (desired commodity);
- coupled with a purpose to expend energy (intentional activities);
- in a politically skilful way.

He believes that not only must the influencer be in possession of a commodity desired by others, but they also need to have the 'will' and the 'skill' to use it within the organization context. Will and skill means the influencer has to want to enter into this power game within the organization, and also have sufficient skills to play it well for results.

The five bases of power Mintzberg pinpointed are: control of resources, control of a technical skill, control of a body of knowledge (all of these three must be critical to the organization), legal prerogatives – being given exclusive rights to impose choices – and access to those who have power based on the first four categories.

How does this apply to OD practitioners and our understanding of organizations?

First, you need to understand organization politics and what resources clients have. You need to be alert to whether your client has a sufficient

power base but also whether they are willing and skilful enough to engage in activities to get things done. If not, you will need to coach them.

Second, political skill is something you can teach, by designing a programme showing people how to be more savvy in their power use, eg within a temporary change team you put together. By educating them about the skills of power use, they may become more willing.

Third, you will need to deliberately demonstrate to your client your own willingness to engage in power and politics and to show that power play is not only legitimate but also necessary, especially in times of change. You need to ask yourself, 'Do I have the will and skill to engage in power and politics in a positive framework and to role model how power and politics can be used in an ethical way?'

What can we learn from the work of these four theorists?

First, their work shows us how power dynamics work within an organization. They all believe that power stems from possession or mediation of desired resources. The definition of resources is very broad – it can include the ability to reward and punish, having critical skills, knowledge or information, ability to solve critical problems or exigencies for the organization, empathy, time to listen, collaboration – anything that people can trade off to support the organizational work they are in charge of.

Second, in modern organizations, everyone is dependent on others to achieve their key results. Hence possessing desired commodities would enable you to engage in mutual trade-off, doing favours, exchanging knowledge and information within the organization.

Third, power differential does exist in organizations, with power located mainly among those individuals/units that are most important for solving the organization's core problems. These power differentials need to be adjusted through OD programmes to ensure all those who are outside those core roles will have a voice, especially during change.

Finally, power bases can be cultivated as there are different forms available to individuals and once you have a power base, you need to increase your 'will' and 'skill' to engage in the use of power for the effect of organization results.

The application of the use of power in three key OD activities

Having clarified the two faces of power, and how power dynamics work, I hope you are now convinced of the relevance of power to OD work. In this next section, I will look at three specific areas: (a) diagnosis, (b) change,

(c) building a healthy organization, where the understanding of power use can enhance the impact and result of our work.

Diagnosis

Since power is a key aspect of organization life, it is an important datum that you will need to investigate during the diagnostic phase. If you do not understand how power works in the form of how decisions are made, how resources are allocated, how people in the back room trade off and bargain, how projects are stopped, how conflicts get started and get resolved, how to obtain sponsorship, etc, you will be like a guide trying to lead your clients through a dense jungle without a map. Without knowing what the power terrain is like, it will be difficult for you to help the organization get the gist of how things are currently done and therefore how to get things undone and changed.

In Chapter 4, I wrote about the importance of gathering a 'power map' of the stakeholder groups during the diagnostic phase as well as the importance of using that power data to guide us in building a coalition, enlarging the engagement of those critical power users and using them to carry out the diagnosis. In this chapter I will not repeat those areas, but instead will focus on what other power data you should look for when entering an organization.

How power is distributed in the organization is an important area OD practitioners should pay attention to in diagnosis work. Burke (1982) pointed out that OD practitioners should ask:

- What proportion of the workforce appears to be out of the mainstream and feel alienated because they have no access to sources of power?
- What proportion of the workforce appears to have authority by virtue of their position but in reality they are not linked either informally or politically to the power centres of the organization?

Burke believes the greater the proportion of the workforce that has no access to power, the more likely feelings of powerlessness will pervade the organization. If that is the case, organizational morale will be lower than normal or necessary, and the efficiency and overall productivity of the workforce is likely to fall short of potential. Effective change will be hard to manage in that context unless there is permission to use the change approach to shift the condition.

Along similar lines, Kanter (1977) warned of the danger when a majority of people within the organization feel powerless. To be powerless in an organization is to have responsibility without system power. In her words:

> People held accountable for the results produced by others, whose formal role gives them the right to command but who lack informal political influences,

access to resources, outside status, sponsorship, or mobility prospects, are rendered powerless in the organization... they lack control over their own fate and are dependent on others above them.

(Kanter, 1977: 186)

When a majority of the people are in this state of powerlessness, they shut down their emotions and attempt to:

- control others as part of defensiveness and self-protection – manifesting in bossy and critical behaviour;
- develop rule-mindedness – as controlling rules may represent one of the few avenues for exercising power;
- exert territoriality or turfmanship – protecting one's domain can provide a sense of power.

In that state, powerlessness is a corrupting factor in an organization.

Both Burke and Kanter believe that when people are showing symptoms like the above, the organization will never excel in its performance, which in the long run will impact on its future viability. Therefore, once diagnosed, it is important that you aim to help the organization to create conditions whereby people can be shifted out from the state of powerlessness towards exercising authority on their own or in groups – and therefore a normative direction for OD practitioners.

So in diagnosing, you will need to look at the various ways that power is played out and the impact of that on organization performance. Possible questions are:

- Who are the primary decision makers?
- Where are they located in the managerial hierarchy?
- How are their decisions typically made?
- What sources of power does a client manager appear to have?
- How does the informal network operate and how effective is it in getting things done?
- What types of alliances currently exist and what are their views towards the change area?
- Who are the informal power leaders other than those who hold the formal titles in each division?

Change programmes

The second area that makes power highly relevant for OD is change. Within every political system, there are different interest groups, informal cliques, and multiple coalition formations. During periods of change, an upsurge of political activity will happen as people try to find a strategy to resist the change. Those who have power worry about losing it and work to tighten

their control; those with less power see new openings and begin manoeuvring for a bigger share of the pie. As Nadler pointed out (1998: 5), 'change always involves power and politics. Change brings instability, upheaval, and uncertainty... change means new patterns of power, influence, and control – and consequently, high-stakes office politics'. Therefore, change agents need to be extra-sensitive to how power plays out between people during change and use methods and processes to minimize the negative use of power and turn covert trading to overt negotiation.

Power means energy. During change a paramount energy source is required to run the human side of the organization. For change to be planned and channelled properly, energy (power) must be located and used, eg through committed senior change leadership, who are key leverages of power in the organization. On top of that, you also want to look for evidence of powerlessness – for where powerlessness exists, you will find problems in the change progress. Change processes need to be designed to give individuals affected by the change an appropriate level of distributed leadership so that they can direct their personal energy source to be used behaviourally to support the change. Using change processes to spread the power use, you will be tackling a prime facet of the organization's culture.

Whenever change is instituted, there will be an opening power play in the form of selling, persuading, pushing, particularly during the transition state – that period after the change programme has begun when people know what is going on but are uncertain about what are the required new roles, new competencies and new behaviours. During this period of high instability, uncertainty and tension, three key problems – power, anxiety and control – will surface. Those who are in charge of change will need to find various ways to help people to manage these three areas. For example, proposing more distributed decision-making processes will give power and control back to people. Choosing a leader who has credibility and impact to lead the change and front the communication process will help to contain people's anxiety. Finally, by choosing people who have various power bases to form the temporary change structure, you would also increase the influencing power of the team and hence control.

Building a healthy organization

The third area that makes power highly relevant to OD is in the concept of the 'healthy organization'. One of the mandates of OD practitioners is to help leaders to build sustainable organization health – but what is a healthy organization? Different types of organization operating in different contexts may have different answers to this question. However, among the number of OD writers who wrote about the subject, there are a good proportion of characteristics that focus on the use of power.

Here, I have chosen only to review the work of Beckhard (1969), who has devised the most comprehensive list. Of his 10-point characteristics of

a healthy organization, five are related to positive power relationships. They are:

- Decisions are made by and near the sources of information regardless of where these sources are located in the organization.
- Communication laterally and vertically is relatively undistorted. People are generally open and confronting. They share all the relevant facts including feelings.
- There is a minimum amount of inappropriate win/lose activities between individuals and groups.
- There is high conflict (clash of ideas) about tasks and projects and relatively little energy spent in clashing over interpersonal difficulties because they have been generally worked through.
- There is a shared value and management strategy to support it, trying to help each person (or unit) in the organization maintain their integrity and uniqueness in an interdependent environment.

Besides outlining the characteristics of a healthy organization, Beckhard asks OD practitioners to consider undertaking five key OD efforts to pursue healthy organization. Of the five key OD efforts he listed, three of them are related to helping an organization to build healthy power relationships. They are:

- Move towards high collaboration and low competition between interdependent units so that lower amounts of dysfunctional energy will be spent in inappropriate competition and hence make energy more available for the accomplishment of tasks.
- Create conditions where conflict is brought out and managed so that less energy is wasted by trying to work around, or avoid or cover up conflicts. The goal is to move the organization towards seeing conflict brought out and dealt with in an open way.
- Help the organization to reach a point where decisions are made on the basis of information source rather than organizational role within the hierarchy. This means the need to move towards a norm of the authority of knowledge as well as the authority of roles.

To sum up, Beckhard recognized that if any organization wants to move towards health, it must tackle the inappropriate and negative use of power that exists within the system. Therefore, a key part of your OD efforts is to help the organization to develop healthy habits relating to each other, working within a 'power equalization' context, and building a humane working environment within the hierarchical and power structure they create. Your task in working with leadership is to get them – the power elite – interested in transforming the organization in ways that are beneficial for all concerned. To take these areas of work seriously, you will need to have a balanced view about power and be willing to enter into the power zone,

roll up your sleeves to 'muck in' with what you may deem unpalatable in order to help an organization to increase the positive face of power and decrease the negative face of power.

By choosing to 'take the high road' of power intentionally (Greiner and Schein, 1988b), you will build a power base, influence key power holders to accept the OD programme, and then utilize a facilitative OD process to resolve conflict. By helping those who are in the power structure to realize that collaborative power is preferable to manipulation and deception, you will help to protect the interest of all concerned, even those with little power.

From its inception, OD addressed issues of power and politics by proposing that collaboration, cooperation, and joint problem solving are better ways to get things done in an organization than relying solely on bargaining and politics. OD programmes like the following are 'power interventions' you can consider doing more:

- promote joint problem solving, not negative politics, as a preferred way to get things accomplished;
- increase the system's ability to collaborate, work across boundaries, and effectively pursue goals while decreasing reliance on the negative faces of power and politics;
- encourage the organization to create slack resources that people can bid for through collaborative effort;
- encourage more positive coupling of interdependent relationships;
- use methodology to help multiple parties to gain agreement on goals and means;
- help clients to build a distributive leadership culture in decision making;
- help the leadership team to look at different models to gain compliance;
- generally help leaders to be interested in building empowered culture on the ground.

This way you can help to modify the political climate. In the process of supporting organizations to build up and maintain their health, OD practitioners must not deny the reality of power use or attempt to abolish the reality of power in organizations; rather, we need to be skilful in enhancing the positive face of power, thereby making the negative face of power less prevalent or necessary.

Using personal power more effectively to achieve greater impact

So being savvy in power and politics is a key characteristic of an effective OD practitioner. You will therefore need to take an interest in these two

questions: 'What are my power bases? Or what is in my "goodies bag" that entitles me to use power?' and 'What power strategies do I need to deploy in order to channel my power base for results?'

Power bases

Power bases are composed of unique resources over which you have control. The type of power base you have will determine your available power strategies for influencing others. Power bases are dynamic, which means they can be developed, expanded or eroded depending on your circumstances and what action you do or do not take.

According to French and Bell (1999), OD practitioners operate from a range of potentially strong power bases that we can use to our advantage. These include:

- **Legitimate power** – the OD programme is authorized by the organization's decision makers and the appointment of OD practitioners is backed up by organization leaders.

- **Expert power** – the practitioner possesses expert knowledge in those areas that most leaders do not have.

- **Informational power** – the practitioner has a wealth of information about the organization as well as specialist knowledge on groups and organization functioning.

- **Referent power** – people will identify with and be attracted to the presence of the OD practitioner, who is non-reactive, non-judgemental, tolerant and supportive.

Another writer, Michael Beer (1980), has identified a similar set of power base by which an OD practitioner can gain and wield power in organizations:

- **Competence** – demonstrating competence in delivering the jobs that you are commissioned to carry out by leaders.

- **Political access and sensitivity** – cultivating and nurturing multiple sources of support by offering your services to people and being personally supportive to their organizational agenda.

- **Sponsorship** – having multiple senior leaders giving sponsorship, speaking publicly about the value OD functions offer to the organization because they have witnessed the work you have achieved.

- **Stature and credibility** – having early success on any OD initiatives will lead to the building of credibility and stature. When your OD programme demonstrates usefulness to key managers, then their level of satisfaction will help to promote the OD reputation. Power will accrue to you because you have been successful and effective.

- **Resource management** – power accrues to those who control resources – in this case, the resources of OD expertise and ability to help organizational sub-units solve their pressing problems will strengthen your power base.

- **Group support** – if the OD group is strong internally, it will be strong externally. If the OD group is cohesive and free of internal dissention, it will gain more power. This is a key point for the internal OD function to remember.

All these sources of power base will help you and the OD function to be impactful. By accumulating a variety of power bases, you and your colleagues are in a position to help leaders to deliver sustainable changes time and time again. Once the OD function builds up its reputation, then the likelihood of success for OD programmes will go up.

So it is important to start each project by taking time out to review what you have and what you will need to build up to ensure you will be effective in your support to senior leaders.

Power strategies

Power strategies are what power holders use (action, activities) to achieve work-related objectives. There are many types of power strategies; the main ones include forming alliances and coalitions, surrounding oneself with competent colleagues, trading favours, focusing on needs of the target groups, working around 'road blocks', using data to convince others, presenting a persuasive viewpoint and being persistent. The list can be endless depending on who you are, what type of power bases you have, and the context in which you operate. The cultural context will also give signals as to what type of activities are deemed as legitimate and constructive. Remember, when OD practitioners use power, you are there to promote the use of positive power and role model an alternative set of power behaviour.

The work of Kanter (1977) helps to identify two main power strategies in organizations: *activities* and *alliances*.

There are three types of **activities** that are key to power. They are:

- **Extraordinary activities** – for example: being the first in some new endeavour, supporting certain organization changes in an innovative way, or helping the organization to take some risks in order to achieve bigger gain.

- **Visible activities** – for example: showing people how to make things happen so that they learn how to support themselves, using them to spread the impact of your work. Backing up visible leaders and supporting their initiatives with results will help to make you visible, attracting attention to what you are doing or are about to do.

- **Relevant activities** – for example, focus on delivering activities that are specifically addressing the pressing organizational problems.

According to Kanter, the first two types provide opportunities for one to have impact, and the third type assures access to key information and to important connections, which she calls alliances.

For me, these three *power activities* are what OD practitioners are supposed to do anyway – taking our clients to new places by focusing on their sustainable development, which will produce results in relevant areas in the business. So, if you do your job well, you will be halfway there to building your reputation and credibility.

What would **alliances** achieve for OD practitioners? According to Kanter, alliances provide power through or from others.

First, OD practitioners need to *seek alliances with senior sponsors and mentors*, as they give us access to decision makers and that provides power in the form of someone to (1) fight for you; (2) help you by-pass the hierarchy at critical times; (3) show that you have 'reflected power'.

Second, OD practitioners need to build *alliances with peers*. If more senior allies are very important sources of power, so are peers. In fact, peers are often the most valuable source of information and backing in any organization. Peer acceptance is necessary to any organizational power base. For OD practitioners, alliances with strategy, finance and HR colleagues, and all the key functional heads will be important, or at least something you should aim for.

Third, there is an often unseen edge of power – its 'democratic' side. Power grows through empowering others, through *allying with subordinates*, and sharing power with them so that they also have the capacity to accomplish. Some of you may have subordinates and some of you do not. For those who have, developing your staff and gaining their loyalty will give you a solid base from which to operate. For those of you who do not have staff, you can always find opportunities to support the young emerging leaders of your senior clients, hence leaving people clearly able to take over what you started. By cultivating the staff of your senior client, you are doing multiple favours for multiple people. You will help your senior clients to secure sufficient internal resources to deliver their agenda, and you will groom younger leaders to be able to add real value to their division and therefore make them visible. You will ensure the OD initiatives started will have a chance to be successful. All these gains will add to your credibility and stature.

Finally, the importance of alliance is illustrated by this quote:

One of the most important ways of gaining power in an organization is by establishing a broad network of task and interpersonal relationships... networks are critical to effective performance for one compelling reason: except for routine jobs, no one has the necessary information and resources to accomplish what's expected of them. Indeed, one investigation of the determinants of effective management performance concluded that a key factor distinguishing high and low performances was the ability to establish informal relationships via networks.

(Whetton and Cameron, 1991)

On top of the above, I think the following strategies are what OD practitioners need to adopt and use:

1 **Become a 'desired commodity', both as a person and as a professional.** Being the type of person that others want to relate to and spend time with means that by being who you are, you attract. This is what French and Raven called 'personal referent power' – the highest form of power. The development of this power base will involve your intentional use of self as an instrument, cultivating your ability to be a good listener, good communicator, good developer, coach, counsellor, and knowing how to show appreciation for the strengths of others. On top of this, being trustworthy will also help people see you as reliable, dependable, and honest in your dealings with others and will also help you greatly. These skills and traits are highly valued in social exchanges. The people whom you deal with are infinitely qualified to judge your honesty, authenticity, trust and level of concern. They notice when the practitioner has little energy, exhibits symptoms of stress, gossips or cannot handle feedback. Practitioners diminish their personal power when they fail to 'walk the talk' especially when clients expect to see you act as models of OD values, and will begin to tune out when your behaviour does not match the values being expressed. Personal referent power enables consultants to influence others by their mere presence.

 Professionally, a desired commodity means you have competence, stature and credibility in dealing with the range of relevant organization issues, and are not just stuck in your own sense of mastery. Good OD practitioners are expert on people, organization and change and such expertise is a rare and valuable commodity among the leadership community. Hence when you work hard to perfect your craft on people, groups, organizations and get results, while simultaneously increasing the capability of your client in the process, you will become a very sought-after commodity, I guarantee you.

2 **Make your OD initiative itself a desired commodity for multiple strata of people.** Make the OD programme a valued commodity for multiple powerful people in the organization. When the OD programme serves the needs of top executives, it gains an aura of respect and protection that sets it above most political entanglements. So a useful rule of thumb is to make sure you pay special attention to the needs of top executives. Then you also need to make sure that OD programmes should be made accessible to people from all levels. That way, you spread the programme to multiple groups rather than a single one, securing increasing support and reducing the likelihood that the programme will become the target of political activities. Not only will you have intervened with the whole system, you will also have robust data from all strata of the organization to feed back

to leaders, hence helping them to make discerning decisions. The power holders may then turn to you to seek further guidance as to how to secure greater support from those strata. After that, decision makers will commission more work from you and listen more to your advice.

3 **Get involved in strategic management issues**. If you are an internal OD practitioner, make it one of your top priorities to get involved in the strategic management issues. OD is a twin to strategy. As strategists focus on the external adaptation issues, you focus on the internal integration issues – constantly asking what needs to be modified, adjusted, abolished or introduced in order to ensure the internal capability is able to support the strategic ambition of the organization. When OD initiatives are tied to the organization's strategic priorities, you then can demonstrate the value OD can add to the organization's success. Knowing the organization's strategic content, getting involved in the strategic processes is a key power tactic. In the 1980s, Greiner and Schein stated this point clearly:

> We argue that a 'new OD' must emerge to help the power structure change not only itself but the strategic alignment of the firm with its environment. OD can, if properly devised, provide a more effective process than political bargaining for assisting the dominant coalition to address pressing strategic issues. In essence, OD must enter the arena that has long been sacred ground to the power elite – the strategy of the company, its structure for delivering on it, the positions that key leaders will hold in the structure, and the manner in which they will lead.
>
> (Greiner and Schein, 1988a: 60)

4 **Create win–win solutions**. The nature of organizations and nature of OD suggest this rule. Organizations are social systems in which members have both a history and a future of interacting, and effective conflict management techniques are required to enhance stable, constructive social relationships. Many OD interventions promote win–win solutions for conflict situations. OD professionals who are skilled in conflict management techniques and OD programmes that encompass conflict resolution activities become valued commodities.

Summary

There are three key points that emerge from this chapter. First, power exists in all organizations; to ignore it is to your peril.

Second, there is a normative direction of work for OD practitioners – to help organization to shift from negative power use to positive power use. Your job is to help your client to look for ways to build a healthy system

that is marked by a positive use of power, by first teaching them how to engage in power play with an ethical twist.

Third, OD practitioners have to be politically savvy, first by cumulating sufficient power base, second by learning a variety of power strategies. The minimum power base OD practitioners should start with is:

1 knowledge from behavioural sciences and organizational theory;
2 ability to know how and when to apply such knowledge;
3 interpersonal competence.

Fourth, OD practitioners need to pay attention to how their own need for power is played out with clients. Burke (1982: 149) told us that there is evidence that people in the helping professions, including OD practitioners, are likely to have a higher need for power than that of the general population. McClelland and Burnham (1976) also documented empirically that more successful managers have a stronger need for power than less-successful managers do. This potentially can create 'competitive needs' in the relationship between client and OD practitioners.

In addition to being sensitive to the client's need for power and to one's own need to influence, you must also be prepared to take a position regarding how power is exercised in the organization, especially in the planning intervention phase, as that will guide you towards what kind of activities, and at whom to target them.

Finally remember, the most effective source of power in the OD world is your personal referent power; aim to become the type of person that your client will want to 'refer' to.

Postscript

As mentioned in our introduction, since the first edition of our book four years ago, a lot has changed in the global, regional and national environment which impacts significantly the way work is being done in organizations. Organizations from all sectors face an increasingly unpredictable and turbulent environment which places ruthless demands on them, with shrinking resources, while still driving to maintain the same level of productivity. Many organizations instinctively become even more competitive and more aggressive in cost cutting; people are asked to work at breakneck speed while having to carry even more responsibilities. The seams of organization seem to be at bursting point in all dimensions. People's capacity is deployed in a 'max-out' fashion. These environmental challenges have left no one untouched, and often one hears the cry from all levels of the organization – 'Can we go on like this? If so, for how long?'

At the same time, there have also been many exciting developments that are encouraging to witness. As more people are searching for meaning, new business models of operating are emerging from the attempt to manage the value-driven and financial-driven polarity. Younger and younger entrepreneurs are joining the power elite in the corporate world, questioning some of the key assumptions about how businesses should be run and how organizations should operate, often pushing ahead with experimenting with new ways of linking work to wider social and environmental issues. There is a growing group of leaders from the business community looking for innovative ways to build a sustainable, socially responsible form of capitalism who have found alliance with those who work in the Third Sector and together they are calling for ethical and transparent methods of conducting business. On top of that, the younger generation either choose to stay at the fringe of the work world, or demand a different type of work-life balance when they choose to enter – not due to the requirements of family, but due to their desire to have a life outside of work to express their values and/or other personal interests. All of these factors pose direct challenges to the old way of running and operating organizations, and throw organizations from all corners of the earth into an unforeseen scenario which is simultaneously exciting and scary. Agility, engagement, changeability, leveraging the discretionary commitment of knowledge workers, and facilitating behaviour/culture change continue to be key areas of interest both for leaders and practitioners.

In this context, the role of OD practitioners needs to evolve in order to keep faith with the overarching purpose of our mandate – to ensure organizations are in a condition that will enable people to achieve optimal performance while building and maintaining a sustainable, healthy organization – they remain as OD premium objectives.

Consequently, the field of OD has also been adapting, going through a creative, innovative journey in order to keep ourselves useful and impactful to organizations we support. A special challenge faced by OD practitioners is how we can help leaders to realize they must **not** just think about pushing the organization to greater heights of performance without paying simultaneous attention to building organization health at multiple levels. We particularly need to create processes that help leaders to give attention to systemic alignment and encourage self-initiated efforts among members of the system to help build attractive conditions of success for its members to achieve optimal work output as well as satisfaction.

Since the last edition, new OD theories, tools, methodologies, and innovative processes have been evolving, all for the purpose of supporting organizations to be smarter in working with change, stretching them to combine profit and humane practices. Sticking to the fundamental values of OD, while adapting and updating some of our classic theories keeps us on solid ground. This work continues to contribute to the maturity of the field and helps practitioners to do more in integrating theories and practice and, through time, develop new theories. We have also been working hard to demonstrate the importance of joining up with other functions to collaboratively find ways to take care of the human assets within the system.

In times like this, it becomes even more important for practitioners to continue to hold onto the following:

- Stay confident that OD is **the** principal discipline that deals specifically with organization health, effectiveness, change and transformation.

- OD practitioners have more applied behavioural science research and literature at our disposal to equip us to help client organizations to improve, develop and undergo people-centric transformation.

- We are committed to building strategic alliances with other functions which together will enable us to touch the life of the organization from multiple channels with impact in every dimension.

As for practitioners, our challenge is how we can maintain our place in supporting organizations and their leaders, and how we can discharge our role with dignity, greater impact and credibility. To sum up, the following essentials will aid us and ground us in our work in a complex context:

- Become **a trusted adviser and helper to leaders.** We need to forever expand our ability to build constructive relationships with people and trust with members of the wider system. Support the leaders

rather than judge them, use all covert ways to help them to pay attention to both task and people issues.

- **Keep our passion for building healthy and effective organizations alive** and do our best not to become cynical about people and organizations, no matter how challenging work situations become. Once cynical attitudes creep in, we soon lose our credibility to help.

- **Keep alive our transformational learning attitude** with each client and self. Each work situation teaches us something about ourselves – through affirmation or discovery or mistakes. The stronger our emotional reaction is to challenging situations, the more critical it is for us to embrace those areas of work on self. As we do OD work, we need to continue to do our **life** work.

- **Keep to the core of OD** – our values and our theoretical roots. From decades of research, the trademarks for a sustainable, high-performing organization are still: high trust, strong community, honouring human nature (Weisbord's definition – dignity, meaning and community) and value alignment between organization and staff. We are there to convey such values through our interface with clients, and the work we design to do with them. Sticking to those core principles of OD is crucial.

- Increase our impact in our service to our client by **becoming a 'highly desirable commodity' to our client system** by ensuring the work we do supports people at all levels to be effective and successful, so that they will equate our support as something they value – not to build up dependence, but to increase our influencing power with them.

- **Treat relationships as our top work** – because we will need to earn our right to **help.** We are there to demonstrate what is missing in the organization, especially when most of those organizations are broken and fractured – hence we will need, through our relationship with the client group, to demonstrate how to build collaboration and assume good will.

- **Build a community and contribute.** In Sibbet's words (2003), nature's way of seeding, mitosis, producing goods, etc. can be adopted to secure the future of OD. We need to share knowledge, publish, create and share tools, take on apprentices, hold seminars, donate time and engage in reverse learning with colleagues around the world. Contribute to education, teach, support the growth of networks, etc.

- **Build strategic alliance with other functions**: we will continue to grow our network and partners to give more integrated support to the client system. For example, we will need to work with HR and strategic planning functions, building a tripartite approach to support the organization. Partnership with those who audit and evaluate organizations is also important as we need their help to

build organization effectiveness and health indexes into that auditing process. Other partners include those who have external-facing functions eg on customers and clients, not to mention other enabling functions like IT, finance, procurement, health and safety, quality, etc.

- **Believe that we have the power to make a difference.** To share Margaret Mead's sentiment – never doubt that a small group of thoughtful, committed people can change the world® (used with permission). Indeed, that is what we had in history. What we need is to keep our vision for our clients, and hone our skills to collectively make a difference.

- Do not forget the importance of working with the **middle** (Weisbord, 2004:470).

As I end Part One of this second edition, may I remind ourselves that all of us need to be futurewise. The future of OD is in our hands as we learn to take care of the present. As Weisbord wisely shared, *'The future never comes – today is the future you imagined yesterday. It is slipping into the past by the second.'* Therefore I believe that, as a community of practitioners, the only way we can predict the future of OD is to build it on what still excites us, our values, and what the world is calling us to do on a day-by-day basis. We must continue to take a proactive strategy to do just that.

Someone once sent me the following text (adapted from Jim Rohn) which has managed to keep me going for a long time, no matter how tough the work environment, how challenging the consultancy project, and how difficult the clients. May I share this to end this part of the second edition by encouraging all of us to keep the bigger agenda of OD highly conscious, to refuel and inspire ourselves to do even greater work in the coming years?

> Let others lead small lives, but not you;
> Let others argue over small things, but not you;
> Let others cry over small hurts, but not you.
> Be future wise; take hold of what you want to
> see happen – and make it happen.

PART TWO
HR in relation to OD: practice examples

HR in relation to OD

In the first part of this book Mee-Yan has eloquently spelled out the essence of OD, and provided rich insights into OD practice. One of the clear themes coming through is that while OD is a specific body of expertise, and that there are specialist OD roles, OD itself needs to be a shared effort between OD experts, as helpers, and other key players such as executives, line managers and HR. Therefore, whether you are an OD practitioner, executive, line manager, HR or Learning and Development (L&D) professional, these messages will have something relevant to say to you.

In this part of the book the focus shifts to what OD means in practice to those who are not OD specialists. As HR and L&D professionals will be only too aware, they are increasingly expected to take a lead or at least play an active part in organizational change initiatives. How well equipped they may feel to do this is another matter. And it is how HR professionals can either integrate OD as part of their work, or recognize when they need to contract for OD work that these next few chapters address.

I shall therefore be focusing on some of the change themes on which senior HR professionals are increasingly expected to take a lead – such as organization design, organizational transformation and culture change, building organizational agility and resilience, employee engagement, and leadership. I shall illustrate some of these themes with examples of what HR professionals are actually doing to help their organizations successfully navigate across today's choppy waters. So whether you are an HR generalist or specialist, such as a learning and development practitioner, or a line manager/executive who wants to know how to build a sustainable successful organization, the chapters which follow should show how HR and OD can together produce some of the key outcomes that matter – ie resilient, flexible, agile and high-performing organizations full of motivated, innovative and high-performing employees and other workers.

In this chapter I shall look at:

1 Why is it important that HR 'gets' OD?
2 How well equipped is HR to be change agent?
3 A strategic agenda.
4 How to get the 'licence to play'.
5 How HR and OD can work together.

Why is it important that HR 'gets' OD?

A challenging context

In recent years the business landscape has had a radical shake-up as a result of the banking crisis and subsequent economic challenges. New 'rules of the game' are only just emerging.

Some things are already clear however. Irrespective of today's economic and geo-political turbulence, this is a period of global hyper-competition with disruptive innovation changing markets and consumer behaviour overnight and new competitors, ideas and categories of products emerging at a rapid pace. Throughout much of the developed world, knowledge and service work is now a major driver of economic growth; thus people are the primary source of production. Technology and globalization are transforming the ways in which businesses operate, with the emergence of multiple and more fluid forms of organization, more diverse workforces and ways of working. Change processes that are driven by connectivity are allowing people to interact with immediacy and ease. The ways organizations relate to their customers are changing. In fact, in most organizations today the only constant is change.

Traditional approaches to running business are being challenged and hierarchical management structures and styles are eroding. There are growing demands for stronger regulation, better governance, greater transparency and fairness over executive pay, new forms of leadership and greater accountability. The challenge will be to balance risk management with a climate supportive of innovation. And many of the practices related to these demands fall directly or indirectly within HR's remit.

The HR challenge

So HR has the challenge of both improving current organizational practice and building the foundations for future business success. How well HR is able to do this will depend to a large extent on the capability of the function, how it is viewed by organizational members, and especially how senior stakeholders conceive of HR's role.

HR as a discipline emerged in the 1980s at another time of fast change following a period of significant industrial unrest in the UK and United States. In these countries many traditional industries had become uncompetitive as new competitor nations undercut their relatively high cost of production. New approaches to management were called for and legislation was introduced to limit the power of trade unions to hold employers to ransom over changes they wanted to make. HR sprang from the ribs of new managerialism to represent the employers' interests in managing the increasingly individualized employment relationship with employees. As free-market globalization accelerated, new knowledge-based industries such as financial services were encouraged and aided by progressive deregulation. These environments

were largely not unionized and in many sectors the collective employee voice disappeared altogether.

HR is based on unitarist assumptions ie that employers hold the power in the employment relationship and that what is good for the business is good for the people and vice versa. While these assumptions largely held true in times of economic growth, their validity is more questionable in periods of rapid and seemingly unpredictable change. With the prospect of an ever more competitive landscape, economic recovery, and public sector cuts the danger is that organizations will embark on a wave of macho downsizings and restructurings that will rip the guts out of organizations. If this were to happen, the hidden costs could become enormous: the human and business costs of stress would need to be managed; the opportunity costs of loss of employee motivation, innovation and customer focus would be incalculable; and the contribution of business to the creation of a fairer society would be questionable.

Top management increasingly recognizes the importance of people and organizational issues. CEOs, finance directors and other business leaders know that things will have to change, but are often at a loss as to how to go about making the changes. That's why they are crying out for HR, the professional function with overall responsibility for people management within organizations, to make a more effective contribution to managing change. In particular they want senior HR professionals' advice, expertise and practical help in change management, culture change, organization (re) design and employee engagement, all of which require at least an understanding, if not deep expertise, of OD.

The need for 'change-ability'

We know that if organizations are to survive and thrive they will need to be agile. Agility is about adapting quickly and effectively to the changing context, its challenges and opportunities. Agile organizations are 'change-able'; they can change continuously and effortlessly while improving performance and achieving breakthroughs because they have flexibility built into their organizational DNA. Change-able organizations have forward-looking management teams, swift and competent decision-making processes and a happy blend of innovation and risk management. They are also resilient, able to bounce back from failure having learned what to do differently next time. They can reinvent parts of the organization, scale back others, develop new products and services to meet ever-changing customer needs.

In my view this change-ability or adaptive capacity is a central component of organizational effectiveness and developing it represents a vast OD challenge for organizations in every sector. Organizations need the 'right' people 'engaged' in the 'right' ways to deliver the 'right' products and services. But who are the 'right' people? While many low-skill jobs are increasingly being replaced by technology, in high-skill jobs talent is often a scarce resource and talent shortages in industries as diverse as civil engineering and pharmaceuticals risk undermining growth potential.

Yet as companies vie with each other to attract and retain the talent they need to drive business forward, they are finding that today's highly skilled knowledge workers are no passive 'resource'. People have learned that organizations will not provide them with a career for life – nor do younger generations want this. They have absorbed the idea that with longer working lives in prospect they can anticipate a number of career moves, and even changes of career direction, during their working lifetime. So they want to take charge of their own career destinies and increasingly expect organizations to collaborate with them in pursuing their interests. They are certainly not likely to commit to an organization unless the 'deal' is right. Employers may therefore not be in the driving seat when it comes to being able to attract and retain key talent.

The challenges of managing change

Organizations must also manage continuous change. As we know from innumerable research projects, managing change can be difficult and as many as 70 per cent of conventional business-driven change efforts are reported to fail to achieve their intended outcomes.

Why is it that defeat so often seems to be seized from the jaws of success?

The main causes of change failure are typically found in how the change process itself is managed and its human consequences. Deep organizational changes have a profound impact on people within organizations and company reputations are most at risk around 'people issues' arising from change. More often than not, top-down business change processes can drain the very lifeblood from organizations ie the commitment, discretionary effort and wellbeing of employees, on which sustainable performance depends. The 'survivors' of change are usually beset by the complexities of working life today – the fast pace of change, heavy workloads, ambiguities over resources and accountabilities, the common mismatch of employee and organizational needs – which prevent the positive change outcomes from becoming embedded. Even when the initial goals of change have been achieved, the opportunity to build on that success is usually missed as management attention moves elsewhere. In current circumstances, such wasteful change outcomes are intolerable.

Worse still, failed change efforts undermine change-ability. They leave behind scar tissue in the form of resentful, cynical and disengaged 'survivor' employees who no longer trust the organization or its leaders and are unlikely to give of their best to the organization in future. The pursuit of the holy grail of 'employee engagement' by many HR teams in recent years is perhaps symptomatic of a misaligned employment relationship and employee alienation resulting from one-sided change experiences. Perhaps for these reasons, it seems genuinely difficult for many organizations to get onto the 'front foot' and proactively shape the context they are operating in.

This vicious cycle – the need for change, destructive change processes, loss of employee morale and performance leading to the need for more

change – must be broken. Given the context, people are desperately needed who can change organizations to make them more effective and provide participants with a higher quality of experience. HR should be uniquely well placed to equip organizations and people for change. After all, HR has many tools to effect culture change, not least recruiting the 'right' people, developing managers, designing reward systems etc. So this is a make or break period for the HR function – to genuinely add value, build future capabilities, or other alternatives that exist.

How well equipped is HR to be change agent?

But how well equipped is HR for this role in practice? Here's the rub; for years HR has been criticized for being too reactive and internally focused. It is especially in the areas of agility, change management, culture change and organization design that HR's value is most put to the test since many senior HR practitioners struggle due to:

- lack of HR capability;
- ineffective technology;
- managing the 'push' from the leadership team and the 'pull' from line managers;
- lack of ability to manage change within the HR function.

Ulrich and Brockbank (2005) found that the change management competency more than any other determines how credible HR practitioners are in other people's eyes, and that in general HR avoids this role. This is not surprising given that HR's role is evolving rapidly and practitioners' previous career experience and professional development may not have equipped them for the task of leading change and building capability. Many of the real challenges of culture are to be found in the informal system, for instance in the nature of organizational politics, the way leaders operate and how power is used – not issues usually addressed in professional development.

And in certain organizational contexts, it must be recognized that managers really want a basic personnel service – anything else would be a hard sell. Many stakeholders still expect HR to concentrate only on operational effectiveness and continuous improvement – both in terms of providing the organization with key processes such as performance management systems, dealing with conflict, addressing issues of underperformance and also in terms of providing a competent and cost-effective HR operation.

Conventional wisdom suggests that all forms of management are concerned with three things: *keeping things going, putting things right* and *doing new things*. It might be argued that HR's role has classically focused on the first two but not so much the latter. Many successful HR leaders have built

their credibility and reputations on being known for running a tight ship, being 'a safe pair of hands', ensuring that people are employed in line with legal and business requirements. Their confidence and ability to influence may be linked more to *putting things right*/sorting out problems for powerful players rather than challenging or breaking the mould, which may feel less legitimate and riskier. Yet if HR focuses only on operational effectiveness, the function then usually attracts criticism for being detached from the 'real world', for not doing enough to aid line managers with the daily challenge of people management, for being the function that says 'no', or puts bureaucratic hurdles in the way of the organization's ability to do new things. Breaking out of this vicious circle of perceptions can be a challenge.

The *'do new things'* HR contribution has tended to be restricted to experiments at local business partner level or to introducing a new policy, developing a new performance management framework or innovating within functional disciplines such as L&D where technology and new thinking are being applied to learning processes. In recent times HR has also focused its *'do new things'* energy on restructuring HR for greater effectiveness, often along the lines of the 'three-legged stool' structural model usually attributed to Ulrich, consisting of shared services, centres of excellence and business partnering united by a corporate centre. The intention is usually to ensure that HR's traditional 'levers' – such as management development, reward, performance management, career development and employee relations – can be used to help organizations achieve competitive advantage through people, at least in the short term.

Yet today's economic climate demands an even more strategic contribution from HR. So great are the organizational challenges and opportunities that the *do new things* focus becomes more important and must be integrated into business practice to be effective. This contribution must of course be built on foundations of reliable, high-quality HR operations. HR professional bodies such as the UK's Chartered Institute of Personnel and Development (CIPD) and Strategic HRM Society (SHRM) in the United States are keen for HR to be seen to step up to the mark and make a positive difference to the future of their organizations. Interestingly a similar shift in emphasis is becoming apparent in the Internal Communications (IC) community where the value of business partnering is increasingly being questioned. The argument is that business partnering focuses practitioner effort on local and often short-term projects instead of furthering the organization's bigger goals, so in some contexts a remodelling of business partner services appears to be underway to offer more limited business partner support and focus resource instead on key business priorities.

Ram Charan, a management and leadership writer, goes further arguing that in the next stage of HR functional evolution the role of Chief People Officer should be eliminated. He proposes that the HR function should be split – into administration (HR-A) and leadership and organization (HR-LO). The former should report to the chief finance officer (who should see compensation and benefits as a talent magnet, not just a major cost) and the latter should report to the CEO and focus on improving people capability

in the business. Charan argues that HR-LO should be led by high-potential talent from the line where 'one way or another, it will have to gain the business acumen needed to help organizations perform at their best' (Charan, 2014). There could be some merit in this argument, particularly in certain sectors, organization types and leadership context. Certainly the potential HR-LO contribution is what we are advocating here.

So what does *'doing new things'* look like for HR?

A strategic agenda

Organizations that can thrive in today's fast-changing environment need the 'right' people, working in the 'right' ways, effectively and ethically managed and led. They will require people who can adapt, learn and perform in new ways and at speed, so recruitment and development are key processes. But even 'the right people' working in a toxic organizational culture are unlikely to succeed. So HR increasingly needs to use its levers to create cultures conducive to high performance and employee engagement, to unblock barriers, shape new behaviours and reward desired practices such as knowledge creation and sharing. These strategic contributions require an OD mindset and the ability to proactively use HR's own 'tools' – such as developing employer brands, performance and reward systems, leadership development – to stimulate and systemically reinforce the desired direction of travel. In short, organizations need HR practitioners to be change agents, able to initiate and bring about the shifts their organizations need to make.

Current trends suggest that HR's role is expanding rapidly to address these challenges. As the practitioner case studies over the next few chapters illustrate, HR practitioners can play many valuable parts to advance their organizations' interests. They can be effective organizational prospectors who scan and interpret this changing business landscape, anticipate future workforce needs, influence stakeholders and create employee value propositions which attract and retain skilled employees. HR practitioners can be organizational architects: able to design agile structures, taking the lead in 'future-proofing' their organizations by developing flexible, self-renewing organization cultures, using HR levers to shift behaviours. HR can develop individual, team and organizational capability by designing processes to grow people's skills, supporting line managers to create conditions which stimulate people to release their discretionary effort. HR can facilitate collaboration and knowledge sharing, developing processes through which ideas can be translated into knowledge capital.

A more strategic contribution still is made when these levers are used to fulfil HR's purpose, which is to build sustainable high performance through people. 'Sustainable' implies longer-term, ethical and self-renewing; self-renewing involves holding the needs of business and of employees in balance. CIPD defines this as 'better work and working lives'. This means that HR has to make a shift – away from seeing itself as only a vehicle for

pursuing business interests to ensuring that business success can also produce success for people.

This twin focus may produce tensions and difficult-to-resolve dilemmas for some practitioners. For instance business-led change can trigger a threat response in employees; forcing people to re-apply for their jobs can make them feel anxious. Arguably a more humane and ultimately more effective approach is to gradually change work processes but stabilize people and roles. So should HR and management be challenging the need for top-down change and instead set the expectation of iteration, or continuous improvement, avoiding chronic reorganization wherever possible? At the end of the day HR professionals must know where they stand on such issues in their situation and be prepared to go for what they think is right.

This more complex HR agenda derives from the fast-changing context, of which just some of the implications are summarized below.

CONTEXT DRIVER	WORKPLACE IMPLICATIONS	HR IMPLICATIONS
Turbulence and complexity	Need for 'new' leadership	Developing leadership and leader mindsets, new forms of succession planning
Ongoing change	Need for change-ability (agility and resilience)	Proactive, OD response to influencing culture
Globalization and technology	Flexibility of operations and workforce	Strategic workforce planning; design for agility; stress management; development; facilitating cross-boundary working
Global workforce and talent shortages	Global sourcing, diversity, multi-generational, motivation and engagement	i-deals and EVPs; raise standard of people management, careers etc
Hyper-connected: rising expectations – speed of response	Consumerization; internal communications, social media	Mobile HR; two-way communications, meaningful employer brand(s)
Knowledge as competitive edge	Need effective processes to support innovation and knowledge sharing	HR as innovation hub, sustainable engagement; jobs offering job security, challenge and autonomy; team working

And in today's volatile economic context, this purposeful agenda becomes ever more urgent. As a CIPD strategy adviser put it, 'At its best, HR today is building agility, addressing the post-credit crunch crisis of leadership in business, and shaping organizations for future success' (Eccleston, 2010).

In summary, HR needs to exercise leadership, stepping up to the plate to:

- create a people and organizational mission for the business, not an HR agenda;
- ensure the organization has the right talent in the right place at the right time;
- transform the business to ensure it meets its full potential;
- build cultures conducive to employee engagement and sustainable high performance.

HR has many ways in which it can deliver this agenda and here are some of the **how's**

Fit for purpose HR

These various HR contributions must build on strong foundations of operational effectiveness, achieved by:

- upgrading the quality of HR team performance;
- developing a simple and effective customer-driven service;
- enabling line managers eg by providing technology-based self-service for line managers, developing mobile HR;
- continually ensuring employment practice is compliant with legal requirements;
- balancing efficiency with effectiveness;
- ensuring compliance and enabling innovation.

Enabling performance:

- improving the quality of line management, developing line managers as coach;
- co-designing with managers and employees roles that are interesting, stretching and fulfilling which have role autonomy and line of sight to organizational purpose;
- co-designing simple and fit-for-purpose performance management processes where feedback is continuous and helpful and people themselves work together to set and reach ever-higher standards;
- encouraging, enabling and developing teams and team working.

Workforce planning and talent management:

- strategic workforce planning;
- building a compelling Employer Brand to attract, develop and retain talent, making the brand real through;

- workforce development and career opportunities;
- enhancing employee wellbeing and morale;
- developing effective people managers.

The 'right' kinds of management and leadership:

- acting as coach/counsel to senior management;
- securing and developing forward-looking future top talent;
- sourcing and developing global leaders;
- developing distributed leadership;
- improving the capability and practice of leaders; challenging poor leadership practice.

The 'right' organization design:

- co-designing new organizational architectures, structures, decision-making processes, accountabilities, use of space, pay systems, communications processes which enable speed, flexibility, customer focus etc;
- aligning reward and other systems.

Managing transformational and culture change:

- being at the heart of organizational change initiatives, managing downsizings, relocations;
- managing integrations; capitalizing on cultural differences in acquisitions;
- equipping leaders and line managers for their role in managing change;
- changing the quality of conversations and interactions;
- improving communications;
- transparent decision making;
- constructive employee/industrial relations;
- developing future leaders and communities of leaders at all levels.

Which of these activities require an OD frame?

It is tempting to say 'all'. Certainly the threads running through all these activities include change management, alignment, the development of organizational capability and cultures conducive to high performance – all of which require an OD orientation ie a proactive, systemic, longer-term perspective. They all require that the needs of business and those of people be held in balance – and HR is better placed than most to know what these are at any point in time.

So it is important to carry out the HR 'day job' within an OD frame of understanding though HR practitioners do not have to be the real change experts. The danger of working on HR projects is isolation from the bigger picture is that they can wither on the vine. For instance one L&D professional was asked to design a new performance management process. He carried out a competency analysis, created a new appraisal form with input from line managers, but failed to follow through to see how the process was working and what difference it was making. In practice the new scheme was poorly received, perceived as unhelpful and patchily used. It was only when he took an OD approach, working with senior management and other stakeholders (including employees) to identify what the scheme really needed to achieve, diagnosed some of the pressure points in the system and how these could be relieved, simplified the process and deliberately built in support and feedback loops, that the whole organization started to realize the intended benefits of positive learning, individual and team recognition and performance improvement.

What is evident in truly change-able organizations is that there is usually a powerful and effective partnership at work. This consists of strong line leadership (the real OD practitioners who influence the work context on a daily basis), OD and HR experts working together to achieve both the short-term requirements for aligning people and resources with business goals while also working towards the longer-term goal of building future organizational capability. In more complex change scenarios, HR should contract with OD specialists to manage the change process and work jointly to deliver the change outcomes. In all cases HR needs to work with senior management to help them become effective commissioners of OD, ensuring that business leaders also retain a strong commitment to the change effort once it is under way. Increasingly too it is important for HR and OD to develop close collaboration and integrated team working with other functional specialists – such as finance, internal communications, property management, IT – to enable grounded solution generation and achieve change faster.

Why is this partnership so effective? While conventional approaches to change are often unsuccessful, because they typically neglect the people aspects of change, an OD approach typically succeeds precisely because it takes employees' needs and personal reactions into account. And while HR practitioners may not be change experts their policies and practices are a key factor in building 'great places to work' which are both affordable to the business and attractive to the 'right' employees. HR's systems are a means of embedding new behaviours. HR and OD working together offers the prospect of a more impactful and mutually beneficial means of developing the organization, since both organizations and employees will gain from change. This mutuality of interest is at the root of sustainable high performance, HR's strategic mission.

That's why it is crucial that HR 'gets' OD, and why collaboration is needed between OD, the change specialists and HR, the expert function on the people aspects of organizations, to prepare organizations to survive

and thrive through challenging times and come into the sunlit uplands well equipped for future growth.

How can HR and OD work together?

In theory working together should be easy. For a start HR and OD have a number of things in common. In systems thinking terms, HR and OD working together can complement the work of the CEO – whose focus is typically on the system input ie the changing market demands and other external environmental factors, and the output, or results. HR and OD work on the throughput – what happens within the organizational system; their focus is on how this can be improved to make sure that the output matches the input.

HR and OD are after similar ends and have different means of getting there. The disciplines of HRM, HRD and OD are all underpinned by a belief in the self-renewal ability of individuals and organizations. They are concerned with ensuring that the people side of the organization works, value life-long learning, are engaged in performance improvement, and aim to stimulate mindset shifts which enable cultural change. While OD is 'a long-range effort to improve an organization's problem-solving processes' (French and Bell, 1999), HRD's focus is on bringing about the possibility of individual and team performance improvement and/or personal growth. HRM's focus tends to be aligning HR practices and people processes to the requirements of the short-term business agenda.

But there are real differences between the disciplines which can produce tensions and misunderstandings.

Values

OD in particular has strong humanistic, democratic values and participative methodologies which ensure that people have a voice in the way change is handled. Change is not something done 'to' people but done 'with' people. What OD does is provide 'a process (and its associated technology) directed at organizational improvement' (Margulies and Raia, 1984). In contrast, in the past the personnel function was often seen as 'the people champion', but somewhere along the HR functional transformation journey, HR's focus on people's well-being and employee relations took a back seat. Indeed in times of industrial strife or when downsizings are planned, HR is more firmly identified with business interests. Yet in today's more challenging employee relations environment, and with key talent shortages to address, HR needs to strike a better balance and regain its identity as 'people champion' alongside that of 'organizational champion'.

Moreover HR's traditional responsibility for ensuring that people are employed in legally compliant ways is even more important in today's increasingly complex regulatory and legislative environment. Rather than running the risk of being seen as the 'business preventer' function which says 'no', HR must be seen as a 'business enabler,' aiding organizational

agility and innovation by both keeping the organization legal and also ensuring that it can achieve what it needs to do legally.

Content versus process

The disciplines of OD and HR have followed somewhat different development paths. OD's specialist expertise is in process and the role of the OD specialist is that of change agent and catalyst, process expert and helper, applying their skills real-time to group or business level issues. The art of the OD specialist (what Mee-Yan calls 'magic') is the skill of using the right process to help clients to solve their own problems.

HR in contrast relies more on content expertise, often playing an advisory role, giving direct guidance on employee cases. HR gets credit for being directive – giving people the line to follow if they are to 'stay out of jail'. They are called upon to act as 'fixers' – to solve the difficult employee case such as disciplinary and redundancy situations and to avoid damage to the company's reputation. They also act as advocates, for instance using feedback and other data to make the business case for new processes or to argue in favour of better practice. HR's functional development to date has favoured content expertise over process or behaviours, though new HR professional qualifications should address this gap. Consequently while some HR specialists may have considerable experience in change management, on the whole the function is often described as 'reactive' and poor at managing change. It is only over the last decade as some HR responsibility (and content) has been devolved back to line managers that the ability to handle the process of change has come to be seen as a key element of HR's more strategic contribution.

Stereotypically L&D professionals are between these two approaches – with a body of content or particular methodologies, and also 'up-front', catalysing and leading learning and training processes with individuals and groups. A growing minority of L&D professionals now act as OD experts in many aspects of systemic change and are able to facilitate for instance large-scale employee involvement in strategic conversations.

Where OD sits though is perhaps a red herring – the key to success is the ability of these two complementary functions to be able to collaborate over things that matter. Unless HR and OD are working closely together there is scope for suspicion and resentment. If HR and OD are working closely together, surfacing and resolving tensions, there is a strong possibility of mutual learning and the real embedding of positive change.

How to get the 'licence to play'?

Of course, the role of change agent is not easy and many HR practitioners may say that the sort of approach we are advocating here will not work in their organizations – and they may of course be right. If yours is a context of entrenched power structures, low trust, rigid thinking at executive level

and weak people management capability among line managers, then carrying on with 'business as usual' may be the wisest course. Similarly, if yours is a simple, slow-moving business with a successful track record, it may require nothing more than a good personnel service to 'keep things going'. On the other hand, if your organization needs to compete vigorously, if your product is the result of knowledge or service work, if you have talent shortages and if your business model is under pressure, then a more proactive and strategic HR approach may be needed to build your organization's capacity to survive and thrive.

So it's important to take stock of your organization's readiness for a new approach:

- Why does your organization exist?
- Who are its customers?
- What are the key environmental factors that are likely to affect your organization in the medium and long term?
- What are the key drivers for change coming from within the business and organization?
- How open are senior management to change?
- What are the key decisions that your organization faces currently?
- What culture do you need to accomplish your strategic goals?
- What aspects of organization and culture need to change?
- What do key stakeholders want from HR?
- How ready are they for a different kind of HR offering?

Then it is important to work out what you are ready for. Many HR professionals have built their credibility by being skilled at operational HR over the years. They may feel they lack the confidence to take on a change agent role or the know-how for instance to proactively build the case for change by using workforce analytics. If this is the case, as the old adage says: 'If you think you'll lose you're lost'. Kanter argues that people's perceptions of powerlessness can be more damaging in its effects on their behaviour than power since it drives defensiveness and closes down learning. She argues that staff professionals, who may find themselves easily replaced by outside experts, may resort to turf protection and information control, becoming conservative and resistant to change. Similarly, top executives, who may lack information about lower levels of organization or experience challenges to their legitimacy, may focus on short-term results, taking a top-down 'punishing' approach and surrounding themselves with like-minded subordinates.

Conversely, as Dan Ariely (2013) points out, the challenge of achieving something that is difficult can make us feel good. If you want to try and break through to a different level or type of contribution you may need to be prepared to rethink and redesign your own contribution to some extent. This may require adopting a different focus and building a new basis for credibility linked to your emerging role.

So it's important to ask yourself:

- What do you do that is valuable?
- What could you do that is more valuable?
- What's stopping you from achieving your potential?

When I was researching the nature of HR leadership a few years back (Holbeche 2009) I interviewed a number of extremely effective leaders of HR functions, all of whom acted as leaders in the broadest sense and shared the following common characteristics:

- Sense of purpose – this underpinned all their actions and was clearly reflected in their language and priorities.
- Business focus – they all understood how their business worked and its context drivers. They were able to contribute to board and management meetings on all aspects of business, not just HR matters. They did not wait to be invited to participate.
- Able to construct effective functions – they all recognized that their own function had to be an exemplar of good practice, efficiency, excellent advice etc since their own credibility depended on it. Consequently they recruited high potentials and high-performing staff into HR and spent a lot of time and effort training and developing their teams.
- Self-knowledge and emotional intelligence – they were able to use these forms of awareness to tune into their own and other people's motivations and know when and how to land key messages.
- Credible – they were respected not only for their 'business as usual' but also for the business-enhancing changes they had proactively initiated and delivered. They were good at anticipating, strategising and making things happen – swiftly and well.
- Ability to influence – they had selective networks and used their influence to greatest effect with key stakeholders. Membership of the 'golden circle' ie a privileged and private network of the CEO, Chief People Officer and Chief Finance Officer allowed the most senior HR professionals to be involved in key business decision-making and to advise, coach and challenge other key business leaders on their practice.
- Performance drivers – they saw HR as a means of enabling high-performance working practices across the organization – and modelled these in HR itself.
- Courageous – they had a strong perspective on what needed to be done to improve their organizations, took judicious risks and usually had the evidence to back up their judgement.
- Resilient – they had often taken on major daunting new tasks with little chance for preparation but had learned from both mistakes and successes.

- 'Nosy' – they were inveterately curious about people and organizations, had amassed a raft of insights into what makes them tick but were always open to new thinking.

While none of these HR leaders would claim to be a paragon of virtue, there are perhaps some broader messages here for people on a personal or functional transformation journey.

So if you wish to adopt new approaches, it is useful to take stock of your own values and practices to determine the strengths you can build on and what might need to shift:

- What will need to become key priorities?
- How well equipped do you feel?
- What do you want to achieve?
- What are you currently known for? How will your reputation help or hinder you move in the direction you are aiming for?
- What will you need to be good at?

In taking stock it's important to know what to preserve that is part of your core identity and what can be given up; and what you are willing to acquire that will help you to achieve critical priorities.

Actively learn

Learning agility is a key enabler of new forms of contribution (Miller, 2014). To increase your learning agility, borrow learning from personal-change programmes and act your way into a new way of thinking. Look and work beyond your own current boundaries.

- Examine your own assumptions about how things should work in organizations. Test whether your assumptions match those operating in your organization by entering into the organization's or groups' cultural lenses, learning to see the world through those lenses instead of imposing your own.
- 'Know your stuff'. When you don't know, ask for answers or further data. Questioning itself is part of the change intervention. Think carefully about which parts of your toolkit to bring to the party – in terms of change models, practices and know-how. Identify how the given end state could best be reached by various means. Be discerning in your analysis; constantly question yourself and your various clients about their analysis of the situation, culture, behaviours and change outcomes. Again, this is all part of the overall OD intervention.
- Develop your ability to work effectively with complexity. In HR you will have coached others to develop their confidence in handling,

if not thriving in, ambiguity. Now apply that learning to yourself: building your own confidence is crucial to articulating and developing your personal strategic positioning. To improve your 'sense-making' skills, use scenarios to scan and build hypotheses and models about what is happening. Get your team to read broadly and explore new ideas together. Create and sustain an openness to change. Think about areas of greatest risk and exposure and develop plans to proactively manage each of them – focus on the higher-risk, under-managed relationships:

- learn from reviewing what went well... and what didn't go so well;
- allow time and space for learning and change to percolate and stick;
- play the long game*.

* Incorporates some of Julia Tybura's advice to HR practitioners from the first edition.

Building credibility

To build credibility as an internal change agent HR must maintain operational effectiveness while earning a new reputation based on doing new things well. HR professionals should model the way forward by preparing for change, keeping up to date, transforming their own delivery and developing their own capacity while continuing to deliver results which count. To be credible they must understand the business and its key drivers as well as the motivations of business partners. So HR must build commercial acumen, be numerate, avoid HR jargon, speak the language of business and be insight-ful about how to improve the effectiveness of business, culture and people. HR needs to demonstrate both a strategic and process orientation and apply new skills and approaches such as workforce planning and analytics, organization design and development, internal communications – with impact and agility. So it's important to not only get HR processes right – such as designing a good performance management system – but also to pull out meaningful organizational messages and insight from the data so that these can be acted upon.

However it is structured, HR should act as a high-calibre cohesive team, role modelling good practice, getting the basics right, focusing on the short term with an eye to the long term, building a track record of high-quality delivery. An effective HR leader cross-trains and frequently moves people around to broaden their skill/knowledge base. If, like many HR functions, your team is overwhelmed by endless projects, acknowledge your responsi-bility to move things forward, be selective and focus on the big ticket items where you want to make most difference. Recognize that some initiatives are for later; prioritize, communicate and manage expectations. Be clear about what you can stop doing, what you need to start doing and what can be simply maintained.

Build your personal power and influence

In Chapter 11 Mee-Yan examined the nature and power of politics in organizations. As an HR practitioner it's important to strategically personally position yourself and support others in doing the same. Skills are only part of the picture. If your role involves trying to work constructively with people over whom you do not have formal authority, access to power can be vital. Mintzberg (1983) describes the prime bases of power as being in control of (1) a resource (2) a technical skill (3) a body of knowledge, all of which must be critical to the organization, concentrated, irreplaceable and in short supply. In addition to formal power, another key source of power is personal, where credible individuals are granted access to power often through trading favours. This is about using and sharing your networks, ideas and practice, coaching individuals to 'see' their organization through different frames or lenses so they can work out how to position themselves effectively and positively in challenging times. In that sense, power is reciprocal and increases with being shared.

Greiner and Schein's pluralistic/political model assumes that all expressions of power – downward, upward and lateral are necessary to getting work done. Conversely Mintzberg argues that power alone is not enough to get things done; individuals must become active influencers who pick and choose their issues, concentrating their energy on those most important to them. They also need the support of powerful stakeholders whose tacit support they can bring to their work unit. Building political alliances through which power can be exercised therefore becomes crucial to getting the 'day job' done effectively.

To be really influential therefore an individual needs also to be able to deploy political skill to use their bases of power effectively; so increasingly political acumen (PQ) is considered a critical leadership requirement (Reffo and Wark, 2014). Political skills can be baffling to those who still think of organizations as well-oiled machines, when in practice they're really a series of conversations between clever people. It is important to focus intently on things you want to change and find ways to have different conversations.

So as an HR practitioner it's important to have confidence in yourself and fortify yourself by remembering that you have a number of forms of power and influence – not just your position power and role of trusted adviser but also your own personal power, your relationships and networks, specific forms of expertise and access to resources. Be bold, don't compromise on quality – take on challenges, use your judgement to take decisions quickly that align with the value set and help the business achieve.

Win support for change

In building any case for change it is useful to engage in strategic (enterprise-wide) risk assessment to determine the basis of your argument. Map the political terrain to determine:

- Who are your stakeholders and influencers? Who are the key influencers? How do they perceive you? How do they perceive these issues?
- Who are they connected with? How can your allies prepare the ground with decision makers?
- Different attitudes to change manifested in the leadership team and assess their likely appetite for organizational transformation. Use one of the change resistance analysis models in your toolkit; think about who might be for, against or persuadable to support your recommendations.
- How to handle those likely to resist or pay lip service.
- What will be their greatest concerns/motivations and how your proposal can help allay/match these.

In making the case for change:

- Be clear what the key problem is, what you are trying to achieve and how to make it sustainable over time. Some people will want data so put it in front of them – such as the business risks or opportunities the organization faces and the workforce costs and benefits of what you propose; use data analytics to help people see the issue for themselves.
- Others will want to know that the CEO is committed to change. With leaders use examples, stories, highlight quick wins, get them to focus on what needs to change, on their role in implementing the change and their own feelings about that – use your focus to get them to be very focused.

When I looked into the nature of constructive political skills (Holbeche, 2005) I interviewed many company directors and other managerial and professional staff who were deemed to be effective influencers. This study highlighted the importance of laying strong foundations of relationships, networks and alliances to build support rather than simply relying on powerful arguments to make the case for change. So it is important to keep your own networks and stakeholder relationships in good shape.

Implementing change

Assuming you get backing for change, where to start? It is often easiest to gain access to parts of the organization where a business leader is already 'up' for change. Pushing at an open door allows you to experiment and review pilot projects, adopting the kinds of agile approaches described in Chapter 15 where change is implemented in short iterations that can adapt to changing needs. Unlike conventional change approaches, client participation and review are continuous throughout so there are no nasty surprises at the end of a lengthy project if the client's needs have moved on the meantime.

Once change is underway HR must be able to quickly deploy and then redeploy resources, talent and skills as needed. So it's important to keep actively involved: find out what's happening and communicate with others. If you are a team leader, involve others in decisions at least about the 'how' if not the 'what' and the 'why' of change. To ensure flexibility of response learn to hedge bets and avoid over-commitment from the outset; form fast-response teams around key issues.

As you co-construct and deliver successfully you will effectively be building your referent power – creating what Kanter describes as 'cheerleaders' who will act as your advocates with other influential stakeholders even when you are not present. Working as part of an integrated team with clients and other specialists is the best way to ensure that change delivers the desired outcomes and more besides.

Performing under pressure

Bringing about change can be hard work so remember what happens to your personality and to others' when under stress (use psychometric tests, coaches, etc); think about what support you need and ask clearly for it. Manage your own energy levels and help others do the same. Observe how others are doing and be prepared to flex your style to provide what others need.

The volume of activity generated by change can make decision making very difficult. Keep control over your own destiny: take decisions faster – avoid procrastination by going for the 60:40 rule rather than 80:20. If delayed or distracted get back on track as soon as possible. Build resilience by learning how to deal with the consequences of failed plans – 'take the hit' and react appropriately. Minimize losses by avoiding escalation and learn from the process how to anticipate it better the next time. Measure, evaluate and embed positive practice. Reflect on, and celebrate, the progress and learning that you and others have made.

Above all, remember to use yourself as instrument. Envision and role model the changes you want to see; build your repertoire of power and influence to create positive reverberations throughout the system. Act as a conduit for innovation by linking up people to others who are doing new things; provoke debate, change the conversation. Get a critical mass of carriers to adopt the new values. Become the positive virus – after all, viruses are essentially self-renewing and self-sustaining and through their essence change the nature of their 'host'.

Conclusion

This is why HR and OD need to work together. Neither discipline working independently is likely to produce optimal outcomes. OD's change purpose

is to improve organizational effectiveness, to stimulate organizational renewal, to enhance organizational health for the long term. OD achieves this by working towards the longer term, seeing the organization as part of an open and ever-changing system, getting people directly involved in the process of change and helping people to help themselves. OD is about improving the system's ability to deliver its outcomes by focusing on the WHOLE SYSTEM.

As HR takes on an increasingly transformational role, the adoption of an OD perspective to HR work will enable HR professionals to:

- create and support strategies for organizational transformation, including the design and delivery of HR interventions in support of these;
- take a lead role in shaping organization design;
- support clients in major change and organization design projects;
- analyse and improve the overall health and wellbeing of individuals and the organization as a whole;
- use the 'HR levers' to address short-term business requirements and build capability for the future.

This practice shift will require HR practitioners to look closely at their own learning and practice – at how they deal with organizational and professional issues and also at their individual preferences and habits, including their level of comfort at dealing with ambiguity. For some people developing an OD mindset will be easy; for others this may be a bridge too far. The key then is for HR as a whole to take an OD approach, working with or alongside a specialist OD team.

In later chapters we shall look in more detail at what is involved in organization transformation and culture change, organizational agility and resilience, employee engagement and developing effective leadership. Above all we shall look at the importance of building a more mutual employment relationship with employees in Chapter 16. In the next chapter we shall look at what is involved in designing organizations.

Organization Design

<div style="text-align:right">13</div>

Organization Design capability – knowing how to flexibly use design features to achieve desired outcomes – constitutes a significant competitive advantage in today's global business environment, according to Lawler and Mohrman (2003). Organizations are essentially collections of parts with endless points of discontinuity. Good designs build organizational capabilities, for instance to manage innovation, which equip organizations to compete successfully. Capabilities are the product of a combination of knowledge, routines and behaviour that are enabled by well-designed work processes, structures and lateral processes, management practices and systems, and rewards and people practices.

As organizations struggle to adapt to changes in the technological, economic, political and sociological environment, their strategies are often experimental, and they must continuously reconfigure their resources and flexibly alter their designs. As a result organization models are increasingly built around projects and networks. This messy organizational reality reflects the fact that change is the constant and that organizations must be smart, fast and flexible to win or sustain success. In other words they must be 'built to change' (Lawler and Worley, 2006)) or 'change-able' (Holbeche, 2005b). Moreover, according to Whittington and Mayer (CIPD, 2005); 'in a fast-changing world, *organizing capabilities* are a more enduring source of advantage than the characteristics of any particular organization structure.'

Increasingly senior HR professionals are expected to be advisers on organizational redesigns and restructuring, even if they may not themselves be experts in ODS processes. ODS has traditionally been the domain of executives working closely with external consultants. Consequently HR and many line managers may have only a fragmented view of what is involved in designing and building change-able organizations. Today's challenging environment is forcing executive teams to think more systemically about external and internal structuring, relationships and linkages which both hold the organization together and connect it to necessary stakeholders.

Since the processes of change and re-organizing are likely to be ongoing, there will be real benefits in growing internal organizational design and development capability. Even the most talented employees are unlikely to thrive in a context in which structures, processes and management processes

are dysfunctional, therefore HR practitioners really need to understand the implications of design for producing the best environments for people and for work. At the very least HR professionals (and executives who commission organizational redesigns) need to have a working understanding of the principles of ODS to ensure that there is a better chance that what they want to see happen, can happen. OD practitioners too will need to master both organization design and organizational development disciplines: to become architects as well as developers. After all, problems in group dynamics often arise because of design failures which manifest themselves in poor interpersonal relations.

In this chapter consider:

1 What is Organization Design?
2 Challenges for the business and for HR.
3 The changing field of ODS.
4 The Star model.
5 An HR/OD approach to designing organizations.

What is Organization Design (ODS)?

Designing organizations is 'the process of purposefully configuring elements of an organization to effectively and efficiently achieve its strategy and deliver intended business, customer and employee outcomes. The resulting configuration is the organization's design' (Mohrman, 2003).

The aim of (re)design efforts is to build the firm's value proposition and achieve the best organization of a company's people to deliver this. As a result, good organization design is assumed to be closely linked to the ability to create high profits per employee. It does this by enabling and optimizing the development and deployment of the organization's special capabilities to produce relevant responses to today's unstable, ambiguous environment. ODS focuses on the internal capabilities – the organization structures, talents, business models, management styles and other intangibles which are essential for delivering a business strategy. Capabilities are composite bundles of competences, skills and technologies rather than single discrete skills or particular jobs. They are 'the know-how that enables the organization to achieve its intended outcomes and implement its strategy' (what Lawler describes as a 'core competence').

What is the difference between Organization Development (ODV) and Organization Design (ODS)?

ODS and ODV are entirely complementary and increasingly recognized as core capabilities required for the design and delivery of a really strategic organizational agenda. These two traditions are historically distinct but

are strongly related. Organization Design is conventionally associated with the 'technical' top-down aspects of organizational structure and system change. Its fundamental premises are about economic rationalization. It involves designing structures, networks, processes and roles to align the organization around strategy and business imperatives. Typically ODS drives structural change and will impact on cultural change. The success factor of ODS is the extent to which organization-wide alignment is achieved.

As previously discussed Organization Development is about building healthy and effective organizations. It does this by improving the ways people work together and uses techniques based on behavioural science and process facilitation. ODV takes forward the design by delivering the internal changes required by the strategy. A holistic ODV approach is to define and enable the culture, capabilities and performance needed to execute strategy. The success factor for ODV is the extent to which organizational effectiveness is achieved and sustained.

Galbraith (2005) distinguished between ODS and ODV as follows:

> Any change in strategy – from global expansion to one-to-one marketing, a shift in how the business will compete, restructuring or an M&A – will require design interventions. But organizations initiating culture change do not need organizational design – that's an organizational development job.

The right blend of ODV, with its focus on group dynamics, and ODS, with its focus on congruence and alignment enables the deliberate building of high-performance environments and practices as a source of sustainable competitive advantage.

Challenges for the business

Redesigning organizations can be fraught with difficulty. Organization design tends to be seen as a top-down, strategy-driven process that focuses on alignment for business performance and control. Consequently the human implications of a new design are rarely thought through or not seen as a priority. ODS itself has also become tainted in recent years by its association with expensive consultancy offerings and management fads such as business process reengineering which have proved difficult to implement. Typical redesign emphases are on structures, processes and pay, all of which can be sensitive issues for the people involved and affect people's employment relationship. 'Lean' approaches have become synonymous with 'mean'.

The theoretical ideal of alignment can be hard to achieve in practice. In many organizations strategy lacks focus and outdated structures inhibit progress; resources are misaligned with strategy and priorities; co-ordination and customer interfaces are inefficient or ineffective; processes contradict how outputs need to be achieved while people and functions often work at cross-purposes. Conversely some organizations have pursued the holy grail of complete alignment to such an extent that they become too rigid

to respond if conditions change. Rather than equipping organizations for change, many organization designs equip them for stability!

Challenges executives are grappling with as business conditions and strategy change typically include:

- devolve and customize control to the frontline;
- improve cross-business unit governance;
- how to leverage knowledge;
- make better use of networks;
- to achieve centralized control of key processes in a global organization;
- redesign performance management and financial control measures.

Structure change in particular is often done in patchwork, leading to inconsistencies and duplication. A redesign may be driven by an incoming executive who feels the need to make his or her mark by changing the organization chart, when lower-level changes might have produced a better outcome. And poorly implemented designs can create chaos. Given that on average 50–60 per cent of costs in any organization are staff costs, this represents a significant waste of potential. As Gaius Petronius (1st Century AD) said, designing organizations is 'a wonderful method for creating the illusion of progress'.

In many cases, rather than redesigning organizations it is possible to make existing designs work better by improving group dynamics or information flows. In practice, many problems in alignment are being identified and worked on informally most of the time as teams address co-ordination issues, discover and implement better work practices, or find new and improved ways of organizing their resources.

Challenges for HR

Sometimes an organization redesign is necessary, because no matter how well meaning people are, the organizational design gets in the way of good working arrangements such as when manager/direct report relations are sub-optimal because of poor design features:

- too many or not enough layers to add value;
- inability to have quality time and attention from managers;
- work assignments are unclear;
- too many priorities and slow decision making leading to problems escalating;
- base pay is inappropriate;
- excessive costs relative to competitors;
- loss of competitive advantage.

Many HR practitioners are involved in ODS to some extent at least, for instance when proactively redesigning a reward scheme to fit changing requirements. Some have been involved in design activities involving relocation and the use of physical space. However HR usually only gets involved in large-scale restructuring once the decision has been taken at board level. Consequently a relatively small population of senior HR practitioners has been fully exposed to the process of redesigning an organization from decision-making to implementation. With the growing expectation that HR will work alongside executives acting as adviser or enabler of the process of generating new designs, it makes perfect sense for HR to partner with Organization Design consultants and OD specialists.

Looking ahead, I believe that it's vital HR practitioners develop some organizational design understanding and/or capability if they are to help organizations achieve flexibility and sustainable high performance. While some aspects of organizational design are technical and require specific forms of expertise, HR has many of the specialist design levers, such as reward, to produce new behaviours. Using these levers to achieve flexible alignment is the way to go. HR needs to support management teams in creating a change structure. They can provide content and process knowledge on change and learning. They can work on systemic alignment, and help the system balance learning and performing.

The changing field of ODS

The antecedents of contemporary Organization Design theory can trace their roots back to scientific management, the time and motion studies and classical hierarchy studies of the 1920s and '30s. These ways of thinking about organizations reflected assumptions that organizations should operate as rationally designed and well-maintained 'machines' and tended to favour the technical aspects and largely ignore the human element of organization. ODS came to the fore as a field in its own right in the 1960s and '70s when a number of publications on design and structure started to appear. Key thinkers on ODS include Lewin, Bennis and Daft with some of the best-known works including Galbraith's *Designing Complex rganizations* (1973) and his work on the 'Star model' (see below), and *Matrix* by Davis and Lawrence (1977).

Organization development (ODV) has influenced ODS through the concept of the socio-technical system, ie the interweaving of social and technical work system elements to produce a 'top-down' design of effective organization. ODV practitioners who have written about organization design, such as Nadler and Gerstein (1992), have also emphasized the crucial importance of systemic alignment between structure, people, work, technology and information. By the 1980s various analytical frameworks were developed – such as the 7-S framework by Pascale and Athos, Galbraith's Star model,

Weisbord's Six Box model, the Nadler and Tushman Congruence model and the Burke-Litwin model – which bridged the gap between ODS and ODV. All of these frameworks emphasize the importance of 'fit' or alignment between the environment and the organization as a human system. In other words, the successful organization design must both align structures with business models and their related systems and also take into account the human dynamics and cultural aspects of organization.

By the 1990s, as Marsh *et al* (2009) point out, a shift occurred away from traditional hierarchical structures and control cultures to more flexible, commitment-oriented organizations. Weisbord (1993) for instance goes beyond alignment to consider the democratic value that drives restructuring – focusing on the autonomous work design process that is critical to producing a high-performance work unit. This has led to a range of new approaches not traditionally associated with ODV becoming the focus of attention – such as total quality management, employee empowerment and involvement, 'whole task' job divisions, network structures, the need to acquire and retain talent and to create a 'learning organization'.

In recent years the ODS field has come to be dominated by consultants who assist CEOs and HRDs with complex reorganizations, for instance during mergers and acquisitions, and with structure-related processes such as job evaluation. As a result HR professionals may lack detailed knowhow about the process of organizational redesign.

Moreover, HR, along with other support functions, has itself been subject to significant redesign in recent years in order to improve value and reduce cost. Transactional HR processes for instance are increasingly delivered through technology-enabled self-service, or through outsourced arrangements. The process of HR transformation has in some cases proved all-consuming and it illustrates the importance of interweaving ODS and ODV to produce good outcomes. As many HR teams have found, even with the best self-service IT-enabled tools available to help them, many line managers do not wish take on devolved HR activities unless they have been involved, or given practical support to help them take ownership of the new arrangements.

The Star model

Jay Galbraith's 'Star model' remains perhaps the best-known and most influential organization design framework. The Star highlights the interconnections between strategy, structure, processes, people and the way people are rewarded. For example, in order to make a matrix work, good relations between departments are needed, planning processes are necessary to get aligned goals, the aligned goals must go into the reward system, and people who are matrix-savvy must be selected and developed. The design process, itself, is an organizational change process and must be managed as such (Galbraith and Kates, 2007).

a) Uses

Galbraith uses the Star model for five main purposes:

1 to provide a total design view of the organization;
2 to clarify how its elements are viewed – strategy, structure, processes, people and reward;
3 to identify both the positives and negatives of the current design;
4 to assess the state of current alignment towards strategic focus;
5 to help managers sell the idea of strategic change and manage its implementation.

The 'Star' model guides the diagnosis and design activities. It consists of a series of design policies that enable redesign of organizational technologies, processes and structures to meet changing strategic needs. These design policies are underpinned by the following assumptions:

- Form follows function – to fulfil an organization's strategic goals, structure and all elements of organization must support the strategy.
- Design for the nature of complexity – provides the rationale for layering and grouping work.
- Match and clarify accountabilities and authority – be thoughtful and explicit – delegate down to lowest level.
- Plan the manager-direct report relationship – define and communicate it.
- Span of control – should be determined by work outputs and management requirements.

Lawler has added the dimension of organizational capabilities or 'core organizational competencies' and emphasizes that these elements collectively comprise an organization's distinctive identity. These develop over time and cannot be separated from other points of the Star – they are an integral part of the socio-technical system. Since change must be ongoing, growth and agility will require flexibility in all elements of the Star.

b) Design criteria

The real work is to answer the question: what are we trying to achieve with our design, driven by our strategy, to be successful in our environment?

- *What* areas will we need to keep, to consolidate and expand, in light of the environmental challenges?
- *What* areas need development?
- *What* will we need to lose?
- *What* data will confirm our own observation?
- *What* are the required areas of intervention?

However, rushing to answer such questions without asking: *what's important to us, what do we need to know, what criteria are we using?* is a mistake. In other words it is vital to specify the criteria before beginning the design process as these will guide both the questions and the answers/solutions. Criteria relate to the potential performance improvement areas most strategically and tactically relevant to the organization's current state and business strategy. Examples of design criteria include:

- facilitate fast reaction to market changes;
- speed the creation of new products;
- enable alliances with other organizations;
- facilitate cost efficiencies;
- foster web service delivery;
- measurement – should guide and assess design.

Design features can then be selected to deliver against the criteria required for success. Design criteria can also be used to manage the trade-offs necessary when there are conflicting demands, or to assess the current design's effectiveness in comparison with other proposals.

c) Key elements of the Star model

Galbraith (2005) suggests that once the strategic focus is clear you should first get the structure right, then work on roles, responsibilities and decisions in operations and functions. Work systems design (in contrast to organizational design), is a second order focus 'from within' (the Star model), and addresses how the activities of the organization can be configured to most effectively carry out the work processes required to deliver value to the customer.

Strategy

Strategy is the framework for all design decisions and a good design should ensure that 'person hours' are used for the maximum benefit for the organization. Different strategies lead to different structures. The Center for Effective Organizations argues that a robust strategy requires both a long-term identity (the relatively enduring metaphor that conveys *how* an organization will achieve its goals) and elements of strategic intent. These include:

- *Logic:* the business model that drives the organization or the method for generating profits.
- *Breadth:* the complexity of the strategy in terms of its range of products and services offered, markets served, or technologies pursued now and in the future.
- *Aggressiveness:* the goals of the organization indicating the urgency of operations with regard to its competitors, customers, suppliers.
- *Differentiation:* the salient features of products and services.

Treacy and Wiersama (1997) and Porter (1980) identify four broad areas of strategic focus and their related design elements as follows:

- *Operational-centric*:
 - deliver most value at least cost;
 - strong marketplace competition;
 - process focus and improvement teams;
 - systems excellence;
 - culture of efficiency and numbers.
- *Product-centric*:
 - deliver best product portfolio to customer;
 - cutting-edge product design, features and applications;
 - product centres and teams;
 - product development excellence;
 - new product culture/innovation.
- *Customer-centric*:
 - deliver best solutions for customer;
 - strong customization/personalization;
 - customer segmentation and teams;
 - customer relationship management deployed;
 - customer-focused/solutions culture.
- *Knowledge-centric – example: professional service firms*:
 - deliver 'unique' intellectual services;
 - strong internal/external knowledge networks;
 - multi-disciplinary expert teams;
 - one-to-one marketing/offering;
 - virtual, knowledge-sharing culture.

Strategy is a nested concept with strategies at different levels (corporate, business unit and functions) constraining one another. For example, the strategy may be right, the people may have the right competencies but without the right information those competencies can be frittered away. If the design is basically sound, organizational development (for instance in the form of executive development, capability-building and talent management) is required to shift the focus.

Strategies at all levels must account for their environmental context. Every organization needs to be able to change quickly as its business changes. Dynamic capabilities theory focuses on the skills, processes and organizational structures that create, use and protect intangible and difficult-to-replicate assets, such as knowledge and innovation. This approach to strategy reflects the continual dynamism of technology, markets, and organizations when information is constrained and circumstances unpredictable. The capacity

to sense threats and realize opportunities is the key to competitive advantage. Any major recharge of the strategy will touch all aspects of the organization design to some extent:

- What changes and capabilities are required?
- What new value will be delivered to customers?
- What work processes/capabilities are critical to strategy?
- How does this fit with current strengths/weaknesses? What is the gap?

Galbraith argues that when a company lacks sustainable competitive product advantage, the winners will be those who create a series of short-term temporary advantages. As he points out: *'Under this scenario, leaders will be future-oriented and will continuously create capabilities that lead to customer value'*.

As guidelines for identifying what kind organization redesign may be required, the Corporate Research Forum (2004) suggests:

- Focus on what you are 'excellent' at strategically, what you can deliver and what you can improve. Be realistic.
- If you need a different strategy, re-focus on a 'centric' option (see above).
- Decide on whether change requires ODS, ODV or both to make the shift.
- Decide on the model or approach to be used, including internal sources of expertise.
- Any new focus, and therefore design, must be reflected in strategy, structure, processes and people.

Structure

To be agile the organization and its structures need to be 'reconfigurable'. The majority of organizations even today are structured hierarchically, usually in functional organization forms. Hierarchies have many advantages, not least:

- clear command and control;
- easy to understand who does what;
- efficient;
- familiar, can be comfortable and most career paths still follow hierarchical paths.

On the other hand they tend to:

- be difficult to work across;
- make the development of general management capability a challenge;
- build lots of functional specialist activity that potentially adds little value to the enterprise as a whole;
- can be slow to change and monolithic.

Lateral integrating mechanisms

Today's challenging environment is causing a different organizing logic to emerge as organizations struggle to meet more complex demands through vertical functional hierarchies, since finding solutions to complex problems rarely resides entirely within a single vertical 'silo'. Lateral integration mechanisms are required to provide greater flexibility. Such mechanisms include specific *people* and range from informal cross-functional teams at one extreme to formal integrator teams and roles at the other end of the scale. The HR function is one example of a functional integrator. Other conventional integrating mechanisms include *processes* such as:

- the planning process itself, including setting up metrics and making sure goals are aligned;
- standard processes – these allow handoffs to be clear so that duplication and wastage are avoided and 'person hours' are used well.

However, when things become more complex still, other ways of 'gluing' the organization together are required. Multi-divisional organizations such as GE are so structured in order to help them achieve product and functional excellence, as well as reach new market segments and geographies. However, the larger an organization becomes, the greater the challenges of integration. 3M deliberately keeps its divisions small (no more than 300 people in any business unit) to enhance market-facing responsiveness, while centralized functions provide the 'glue' and make strategic decisions about which divisions to invest in or break apart. What goes at the centre of such structures – such as talent management – is a critical business decision, since this should allow the organization to achieve maximum leverage and speed and use its resources more cost-effectively. For instance a common purchasing and procurement system should allow the organization to secure better value from suppliers. Similarly, a common IT platform across divisions should reduce cost and inefficiencies.

The 'reconfigurable' organization

How organizations and work are designed impacts both on organizational performance and the use and development of the organization's talent. For greater agility, Galbraith (1994) argues that organizations need to be 'reconfigurable' as characterized by:

- teams and networks across organizational departments;
- the organization uses internal prices, markets and market-like devices to coordinate the complexity of teams;
- the organization forms partnerships to secure capabilities that it does not have. These partnerships require external networking capability.

In summary, structure assessment questions include:

- What core units are needed to achieve focus on strategic deliverables?
- What lateral structures?
- Where is the gap?

Management processes

For Galbraith, the reconfigurable organization needs accounting systems, data structures and planning processes which allow it to operate as miniature business units. Information and goal-setting processes need special attention and common processes are required for new product development, order fulfilment and strategic planning. Above all, a flexible reconfigurable organization needs a strong management team who are skilled at making frequent priority decisions, allocating resources, communicating effectively and the timely resolution of conflicts. Ensuring that the management team is able to perform in this way should be the number one focus of the HR Leader. Key assessment questions include:

- What are management strengths and weaknesses?
- How do the management processes need to change to achieve focus on strategy?

People

The HR function and its policies must be aligned to create policies and mindsets that support the development of a change-able culture. For instance recruitment should be geared to attracting people who fit the organization not just the job; who are able to work well in teams, have the desire and potential to grow and learn new skills. Career management and assignments will also be cross-functional to enable people to not only build important product and functional knowledge but also new skills and relationships. Training will be continuous and targeted, for instance, to helping new cross-functional teams become established and training events are also used for the purposes of building social capital. HR professionals need to be cross-functionally skilled, with good internal and external networks.

Key questions include:

- What are our talent gaps?
- What are the strengths and weaknesses of our talent management/ knowledge management models?

Rewards

Reward systems are usually the biggest barrier to change since reward is a sensitive subject for many people. The reward system needs to enable

flexibility and will typically have fewer bands than old-style reward systems. Individuals will be rewarded for their skills and performance, rather than being based on job descriptions. The appraisal process is also moving towards team-based and feedback-based models. Flexible reward systems typically have more variable elements, have simpler pay scales and grades.

Key questions include:

- What is currently rewarded and how?
- What are the gaps, given our new strategy and capability requirements?

An HR/OD approach to designing organizations

I am grateful to Becky Spears, leader of the Global OD Consulting Practice in the Organization Talent & Development Group at Oracle Corporation for this description of the organizational design process she developed and used at Sun Microsystems where she was Senior Human Resources Director responsible for the Organization Consulting (OC) group. Becky originally joined Sun in 1999 as an HR Business Partner supporting the Sun Chief Information Officer and her organization design work in Sun Microsystems began when she was still an HR Business Partner. Oracle Corporation acquired Sun Microsystems in 2010.

a) Organization Design at Sun Microsystems

As HR business partner Becky worked with clients who would carry out a restructure every year, with varying degrees of success. As Becky wanted to improve the chances of design succeeding she proposed a different approach with one client. Becky suggested running a two-day off-site for a design team and key stakeholders to produce the macro design so that the organization itself could then implement the design down to the micro levels. Initially the client was sceptical about the need to spend so much time on this, but in practice he found the two days a valuable investment.

The resulting engagement far exceeded expectations and began Becky's serious practice in Organization Design. Indeed the process became so successful that Becky was sought out by other HR Business Partners and internal clients, and eventually became responsible for the OD consulting group within Sun. Details of the workshop content and process can be found on Becky's website blog: (changinglikeariver.blogspot.com/ 2009/08/whos-on-first.html). Becky went on to partner with senior executives to develop the global IT leadership team, align practices to Sun business requirements, plan workforce development, develop reward and recognition strategies, analyse and then lead action planning in response to employee and leadership feedback systems.

Although this is the process Becky often uses with her clients, OD consulting engagements vary significantly based on scope, business issues and organization complexity. Organization Design is the brains of the work and depending on the scope it may take months, during which time many brains are better than a few and benefit from coordination and facilitation. Implementation (and associated change management) is the heart of the work. This step can also last for months, often begins with the assessment and ideally includes measurement.

b) A self-design process

Becky's Organization Design Practice model is based on the Self-Design strategy devised by the Center for Effective Organizations at the University of Southern California's Marshall School of Business. The 'self-design strategy' assumes there is no single design template that will work well in every context. A good design is what makes sense in a given organizational setting. The self-design process is a way of involving relevant stakeholders and achieving shared ownership and commitment to making the new organization design work. Moreover since organizational redesign is ongoing the self-design process is iterative and involves a continuous cycle of designing, testing, learning, redesigning and confronting new challenges.

- The self-design process involves understanding the business context and strategic focus, contracting with key stakeholders, developing the design concept, aligning design elements to the design criteria, the strategy and to each other. Galbraith refers to what is involved as 'The Four D's' – ie dialogue, decisions, design and development.
- It is an iterative process involving:
 - preparation;
 - contracting;
 - assessment;
 - planned Learning;
 - organization Design success criteria;
 - organization Design;
 - change implementation.
- Implementation begins by involving others in the design process which can typically take several months. Then implementation is measured and leads to learning and renewal as changing circumstances drive new strategy.

c) Design team

Becky recommends designing with a team, especially when starting a new company or division, responding to significant change in scope (growth or

shrinkage) or when the organization is under-performing. Working with a design team is also important when there are changes in leadership, strategy, internal or external environment.

The design team will consist of relevant stakeholders, including senior managers, leaders, HR business partners, OD and technical specialists and external resource if needed. The team reports to the senior sponsor, or main client of the redesign. For large organization design engagements, there are frequently two (or more) teams of people directly involved in the design process – the Executive team and one or more design teams. Often one member of the Exec team is also an active member and 'champion' of the core design team. Involving senior managers in design has many benefits. It tends to enable business performance, create the best design, strengthen the leadership team, prepare the leadership team to manage change, build and align the leadership team, develop future leaders and signal the importance of change. As an activity therefore designing organizations can be hugely developmental for both the individuals involved and for the organization.

d) The stages

1. Preparation, research and planning

Preparation and then contracting with the client are vital first steps. At the start of an organizational design engagement, Becky typically works closely with the HR Business Partner and others who understand the business issues to prepare for a first meeting with the client, who may be any leader within the organization, but is typically a member of the top executive team and responsible for a significant part of the Sun business. She then discusses the situation with the executive and if the outcome is an organization (re)design Becky sets up a partnership between herself, the executive and the HR Business Partner.

As Becky points out, as an organization design practitioner (ODP) you need a lot of information from the leader to make sure you are planning a design process that will meet the business needs. Prior to meeting with the leader, it is important to learn about the organization and its known challenges, collecting background information for example by talking with people familiar with the business and people in the business, looking at website information, understanding the scope, size, charter (if available), known challenges and strategy.

It is important to plan the contracting session, for example how to handle the client session and potential areas to probe; if attending with a partner, decide on roles. Think through the potential benefits of a design team workshop approach. Be prepared to discuss the relevant benefits of a team-based approach. However, if the leader already knows what s/he wants to achieve, and key design decisions have already been taken, it is not effective to take a team through a frustrating process of trying to come up with the answer the leader wants, or being overruled. For instance, one executive had a particular structure in mind and was not prepared to budge. It was only when

Becky asked, 'so *who* is going to do this (implement the structure)?' that the executive began to relinquish control and the organization design process with a team could begin in earnest.

2. Contracting (with the leader)

Contracting and consulting is the beginning and continues throughout the engagement. Contracting properly with the leader establishes a relationship of trust and partnership between the ODP and the leader. This involves agreeing what both the leader and ODP can expect of each other (and others) during the process since success will depend on clarity around mutual dependencies and commitments.

It is vital to listen and show understanding of the leader's viewpoint:

- their business challenges and issues;
- organization performance;
- strategy, plans, key objectives;
- the business readiness for change;
- the dynamics within the leadership group.

As Becky points out, 'they are the leader of the business, they are responsible for the business performance, and they know more than you do about what is needed; it is critical to meet their needs'. Becky suggests that the right balance of dialogue 'air time' should be roughly the leader talking 80 per cent of the time and the ODP 20 per cent, mainly at the end of the conversation. It is important for the ODP to learn from the leader, and only by first learning can the ODP offer the right solution. If the relationship between the leader and ODP is awkward the design process is in jeopardy.

Agreeing desired outcomes

As part of the contracting process it is important for the leader and ODP to agree on desired outcomes for the design engagement. These then become the performance guide for the ODP in managing the design process. Desired outcomes typically fall into three 'buckets' – those the ODP is confidant can be achieved, those where there is a good possibility of achieving them, but an external problem might derail them and prevent them from being achieved, and those that are more ancillary to the process – they might be achieved and may require other OD work to resolve them. It is in the latter two categories that problems tend to occur. The leader and ODP have to decide how to manage risks. The leader in particular has to be actively engaged rather than passive in agreeing with the ODP about what is achievable versus what is ambitious.

Agreeing engagement specifics – design team(s)

At the start of the contracting process, the composition of the design team needs to be determined. This will depend on the scope of activity (what is

included, excluded, focus of work). It is important to agree time commitment and schedules (relates directly to desired outcomes) and respective roles (their expectations of me, my expectations of them, roles of any others). HR Business Partners, for instance, may be involved as assistants to the ODP (often in the assessment process or facilitating team breakout sessions) but sometimes instead they are a member of the design team itself. Deciding who will be involved and how these teams will work together can head off many issues and enable sound criteria and designs.

There must be good communication between the teams and regular report-outs that include the opportunity to discuss concepts and options. Problems can occur if the Executive team is not intimately involved in these areas. Becky recalls how things once went badly wrong when it became clear that the Exec team member assigned to work with the design team actually was not empowered to make design decisions on behalf of his colleagues. Consequently the design team proposals were turned down by the Executives because what had been proposed cut across the power bases of several Exec team members. On that occasion, by clarifying the reasons for the objection, Becky gained insight into what really mattered and used this insight to help the design team create a more politically acceptable design which also still delivered the key performance elements vital to the business strategy.

3. Assessments

These are vital for providing insight into issues and opportunities and then aligning the team as some commonality emerges. The assessment process defines the issues that could interfere or are interfering with the business strategy. It essentially involves identifying the current state, including things that are going well and may include suggestions regarding what is needed. The Star model provides a template for checking the interview questions to make sure they cover all the topics.

Becky adapted the 'Star' elements to work within the Sun culture. For instance the 'rewards' part of the Star model was culturally challenging in Sun since many managers struggled with the lack of control over monetary rewards. By re-labelling the 'reward' Star point as 'norms and behaviours' and placing the emphasis on recognition instead of financial rewards, Becky found that the Star model could more readily apply to the Sun culture and encourage the performance needed to meet the organization's unmet or changing needs.

Agreeing criteria

Agreeing Organization Design success criteria is the most critical step. This strategic activity provides the direction that differentiates organization design from simply making a change (such as restructuring, or changing leaders or modifying charters). Strategy is the key place to start in the assessment process since logically the criteria define what the organization must do to achieve the strategy.

Sometimes organizations do not have a written strategy – particularly in a fast-paced and competitive business sector focused on continual technological change. In these cases, strategy work may need to precede organization design. Where clients are resistant to this, although not optimal, the process of identifying design criteria can act as a proxy for strategy. Sometimes the business strategy is not changing but the issue is that people are not aligned to it and/or are not performing well. In Sun's case, the decision to be acquired by Oracle Corporation in Spring 2009, led to a protracted period of uncertainty for employees. The challenge then was to keep smart people aligned to the existing strategy before a new strategy became clear.

Interviews/data gathering

Typical diagnostic questions help guide the assessment. Many of these are chosen based on their relevance to the current business strategy:

- Based on your reading about (eg the new technology area) what are the emerging opportunities and challenges facing our group?
- What are the implications for our organization due to current company challenges?
- What is your view of how well our work processes support execution of our strategy?
- What are the most critical performance gaps in our organization today?
- How well do our current competencies align with our future needs?
- What is the most critical challenge we face as an organization?
- Are there key problems that you believe we should focus on during this process?
- How well does our management team manage this business?

Other regular topics:

- Inquire about change readiness – starts to set the stage for organization design also needing change management.

- Collect advice and feedback for the leader – influences leader behaviours particularly during the engagement.

- Check to make sure the question set covers all elements of the star model; if it doesn't, include some specific questions about the missing elements.

Becky also enhances the discussion by asking interviewees to review and comment on high-performance characteristics (drawn from Galbraith, Mohrman, Worley and others) as a lead-in to asking them about current realities.

High-performance characteristics

- Responsibility for a whole work process that provides value to the customer or client

- Capability to achieve this value without daily management control

- Efficiently and effectively accomplish objectives

- Clear responsibilities and decision-making authority

- Leaders who direct and develop the organization's capability

- Flat/lean management structure

- Strong lateral linkages:
 - Groups are held accountable for integration with other units
 - Effective and efficient lateral teams

- Measurements and accountability for results

- Mechanisms enable organization to learn and improve performance:
 - Benchmarks
 - Shared learning

- Members share in the success of the business, and know how their work contributed

Becky does not ask them to compare their current organization with these:

- *Analyze thematically, not by question, and produce a report.*
 Themes might include – lack of alignment between groups – need to determine global versus local – decision making – need to increase speed – need one face to the customer etc.
- *Review the report with the leader* well before the first team session, but don't share it with the team yet.

4. Learning

For Becky learning is not a specific or separate step in the process since learning and change are happening throughout. However, it is an important factor that needs to be planned into the design process. The planning needs to consider the organization design awareness and knowledge in the design group prior to the engagement. For instance some teams may already be

familiar with the Star model and a design process – for others the very concept of design criteria may be new. The ODP needs to determine the right mix of theory and tools for the design team and the business situation. In some cases the design team may need specific information related to their function or technology. This also then becomes part of their learning curve, and needs to be planned.

Organization Design learning areas to choose from include:

- the Star model itself – to provide perspective and the scope of design needs;
- data from the assessment – to create shared awareness, performance focus;
- organization models – function, product, matrix, customer etc – to create understanding of design implications, trade-offs etc (see Appendix for examples);
- organization design criteria – to define what is meant by criteria;
- lateral capability and other design needs (typically used in design);
- change management – design process starts this work, particularly via involvement, alignment, champion building, exploration of change readiness, implementation planning.

5. Change implementation

Often change management is embedded throughout the design process ie change management began with the assessment and is furthered by the design process. The leadership team has the advantage of executing a designed change:

- communications build on the criteria thinking;
- leveraged involvement creates champions and people who understand the direction;
- teams are often created to complete design work – broadening the base of those who understand the change and have had a hand in the design;
- champions are often assigned to new key focus areas;
- check-up and adjustment processes ensure completion of the change.

Summary: what works

- Focus on more than structure. Use frameworks such as the Star model, lateral design, decision matrices or Responsibility Assignment Matrix (RAM), also known as RACI matrix. Using the Star model provides a good backbone for assessment both before and after the change. In the real world, a complex interplay of many factors influences the design, and an aligned design is more likely to achieve business outcomes. Designs should aim to be sufficient, yet simplified.

- Involve teams in the design – begins the change management process, and builds good teamwork and champions. It also results in better designs since there is more knowledge, awareness and insight to draw on. The ideal team is a group that is familiar with some of the concepts and where there is clarity about business strategy and completeness.

- Identifying well-developed and prioritized criteria before the design is vital as is developing multiple design options for review against the criteria.

Becky recommends that design teams start with realism about the commitment and outcomes required of them. Further, she believes that the ODP should allow the group to follow their passion about priorities, despite the assessment, since they own the business and the outcomes. Then use re-assessment to drive completion of the remaining work – graceful persistence pays off!

6. Where ODS thinking is moving to: designing flexible, high-performing organizations

Increasingly Organization Design thinkers are taking into account the external context within which an organization attempts to deliver its strategy. According to Lawler (2010) what will be needed are 'maximum surface area structures' which focus attention and resources on the competencies and capabilities required to create and deliver value. These will support ongoing change by enabling a strong external focus. Hierarchies will be flatter and organizations will be structured around *customers*. Drivers include:

- globalization of the customer;
- customers require customized solutions;
- they want partnership arrangements;
- relationships are fewer but closer, longer and more profitable;
- e-commerce developments;
- buyer power in transactions.

There will be heavy use of teams and small, wholly-contained business units. The organization will be integrated through management processes, with decision making pushed down the organization, alignment to create transparent information systems, job descriptions and budgets eliminated.

The most recent development in Galbraith's thinking too is that ODS should focus on how organizations are structured and arranged around *customers* rather than products. Organizations such as Cisco Systems, Sony and Nokia Networks have adopted more lateral forms of organization design to enable customer focus and responsiveness. True customer-centric organizations design in lateral organizational forms, processes and arrangements which enable them to be 'smart, fast and flexible'. In practice all organizations need some kind of customer dimension which will be

defined in different ways according to their strategic focus, ambitions and circumstances.

For Galbraith the most developed lateral forms are interpersonal networks which tend to enable strong matrix working. Organizations adopting this 'network-centric' or 'enterprise model' can rapidly add on new ventures, assimilate acquisitions and change effectively. However, as Galbraith himself points out (2005), *'the paradox here is that good ODS will simplify and grease the skids of customer-facing processes, but will also make the organization more complex by introducing the customer-focused groups, networks and relationships underpinning social capital. This is the future of organizational design'.*

What Worley and Lawler (2010) call 'Built to Change' organizations use integrated design and development and are high-involvement organizations. There are clear implications here for HR. Key to effectiveness is a policy of hiring people who are skilled but are willing to change and develop along with the business. They are supported by change-enabling processes such as enriched work designs, participative decision-making structures, community, shared leadership, commitment to the development of people and pay for skills.

The best way to learn is by doing. Therefore collaborate with organizational design and development specialists to ensure a complementary blend of skills and input. After all, developing the organization design is only the start of the process of implementation. Organizational Development (ODV) and change management provide the 'how' of design ie how to mobilize the key people to journey in the same direction; how to generate and sustain both energy and commitment during the change. In the next chapter we shall consider how change management and culture change can deliver healthy and effective organizations and sustainable business outcomes.

Transformation and culture change

A turbulent backdrop

In today's challenging competitive environment, organizations everywhere are in flux and change is the constant. While this situation may seem unprecedented, even back in 1994 D'Aveni was describing as 'hyper-competition' the frenetic context and resulting volume of organizational change initiatives as organizations struggled to grow or maintain their competitive advantage. Before the economic crisis began in 2008 the think-tank Demos (Miller and Skidmore, 2004) termed as 'hyper-organization' the frenzy of restructuring and change initiative overload taking place in organizations – becoming lean, stripping out positions and people, outsourcing non-core activity to improve the bottom line. All this while keeping up performance, producing innovations and increasing market share!

No wonder many organizations never seem able to achieve their change goals before yet another change is introduced. It can even seem as if change itself has become the goal, rather than the goal being the goal and change being the means to achieve it!

Transforming organizations is perhaps the greatest challenge facing OD specialists, executives, line managers and HR professionals. In this chapter we shall look at how HR can support transformational change, using the example of mergers to illustrate HR's potential contribution to integration success. Strategic change requires not only profound change within existing business models, but also business model innovation itself. Moreover, the challenge many leaders face is that it is NOT enough to change strategies, structures and systems unless the thinking that produced them also changes. This will require significant shifts of mindset, focus and capability – not only amongst senior management but across the workforce.

As we look ahead, we can conclude that the pace of change will continue to accelerate; therefore successful organizations – from the largest corporations to the smallest entity – need the ability to change in their cultural DNA. No longer is change management just about managing a specific

change initiative; it is really about building organizations' capacity for ongoing change ie their 'change-ability', as we shall explore further in the next chapter.

In earlier chapters Mee-Yan described processes for understanding and influencing the patterns and rules which underpin culture, or the 'way we do things around here'. In this chapter we shall consider if and how a change-able, high-performance culture can be 'built', and the role HR can play in this. We shall cover:

1 the challenges of profound change;
2 culture;
3 planned change approaches;
4 HR-led integration;
5 culture change approaches;
6 HR's role in changing culture.

The challenges of profound change

In profound, transformative change – such as massive downsizings, acquisitions or 'corporate reinventions' – strategy and culture are twins, with leadership the vital conduit between the two. Many change efforts are still introduced 'top down' yet top-down change processes are increasingly regarded as ineffective and most major change efforts are reported to fail (the usual figure quoted is 70 per cent). With respect to acquisitions McKinsey research found that 60 per cent fail to deliver returns exceeding the cost of capital (Rivlin, 2004). The high failure rate of mergers used to be ascribed to the content of change – the weak rationale and lack of strategic fit. Nowadays there is much wider recognition that the main causes of failure lie in the process of change and how it unfolds and especially in the consequences of change for people and culture. OD is concerned with all three categories but in particular the process and people aspects of change.

The content of change

In the case of mergers and acquisitions (M&A), more energy is typically put into finding a target company to acquire, or fleshing out the acquisition plan, than into figuring out how to capitalize on the new organization's combined capability. Without this bigger vision in view the organization's design, use of talent and access to key resources can be sub-optimized and limit the organization's ability to enact the ultimate strategy. Using a mathematical analogy, most mergers are handled in such a way that $1+1=1$ rather than 3, 4 or 5.

The process aspects of change

With mergers the way the integration process is handled impacts on the emerging organizational culture.

About culture

Culture is 'the pattern of shared beliefs and values that reflect "the way people think about things around here"' (Louis, 1983) that 'give members of an institution meaning, and provide them with the rules for behaviour in their organization' (Davis, 1984). What is perceived, and the way it is perceived, becomes reality for the individual or group and is reflected in shared memory – people's history and experience, what people feel and think about the organization. These perceptions drive shared patterns of behaviour – strategic, operational, decision making, information flow, managerial and leadership – that tend to stabilize and sink below the level of consciousness over time, becoming so taken for granted they are largely invisible to organizational members (Holbeche, 2005). As the Chinese proverb says 'the fish in the pond does not see water'.

Conversely, in merger scenarios employees often become hyper-conscious of their own culture. If the process of bringing together two or more companies with very different ways of doing things is badly handled, it can result in culture clashes that persist unproductively for years. Similarly, poor people management can result in involuntary turnover of skilled staff, loss of goodwill, organizational knowledge and intellectual capital.

It is very easy for the integration process to be handled as a purely transactional exercise. Indeed many acquirers pride themselves on their 'hundred day' plans and smash together the different financial, IT, human resource and customer handling systems in the shortest time possible. This is understandable since business as usual must be maintained and customers kept happy while the mechanics of integration are under way. Yet if speed results in confusion, dissatisfied customers or undermines the employment relationship, the benefits of pace may be short-lived. Since organizations can be viewed as complex adaptive systems, what happens to parts of the organization during a process of change can have profound knock-on effects on the emerging organization's culture. And as one HR Director involved in the acquisition of a DIY chain commented 'you can't paint the culture on afterwards'.

Another cultural issue relates to the *depth of integration* required when one company acquires another. Often the acquirer's modus operandi is imposed on the other party wholesale and in a heavy-handed way. Leaving cultural differences and misunderstandings unaddressed can lead to tensions, culture clashes and 'them and us' attitudes. People being assimilated in this way, even if their jobs are 'safe,' may feel that their previous company's brand and good practice have been swept away without consideration. In one pharmaceutical company, the effect on scientists developing new products was dramatic; work slowed down until people could see how things would work out – and whether they would like the future company. This phenomenon became known as 'burying our babies' – people hoarded their best ideas in case they wanted to jump ship.

Common process pitfalls include poor communications – not using the channels available, breakdowns/blockages and mixed messages being conveyed at the top. Weak transitioning and badly managed exits result in reduced employee commitment and motivation and loss of critical talent (and knowledge). Slow decision making, mandating impossible timelines, unforeseen costs incurred, insufficient budgets, failing to track results are all recipes for failure. Lack of senior leadership unity compounds the problems.

The people aspects of change

The largest category of failure factors relates to ignoring, neglecting or mishandling the people aspects of change. Since in today's knowledge- and service-based economy business success crucially depends on people's skills and willingness to deploy their discretionary effort to the benefit of business, what employees want and need should be taken into account. But how often are their voices heard in today's challenging environment despite employee engagement having become the HR 'holy grail' in recent years?

Some of the main people risks include people's emotional reactions and behaviour; their degree of engagement, acceptance and commitment to the change. When change is imposed top-down it is usually much harder for people to 'buy in' or engage with it. Moreover people tend to resist or subvert change that is imposed. The deep changes – in how people think, what they believe, how they see the world – are difficult, if not impossible, to achieve through compliance.

While change may benefit some employees, it can also undermine employee wellbeing if people end up with increased workloads, redesigned roles and responsibilities, 'compulsory' redeployment or demotion and changing work standards/practices. Staff may suffer anxiety, stress, job insecurity, loss of confidence and faith in the organization. These can impact on employee engagement and lead to less discretionary effort, lower productivity, work disruption, change fatigue, human error and strained employee relations. This in turn may result in the loss of the best people, ideas, capability, experience and knowledge – either because cuts have been too deep or people seek more stable prospects elsewhere. This in turn impacts on business effectiveness: customer service, relations with suppliers and the company's reputation may suffer.

Ironically, in the case of mergers, when people may be expecting and ready for something different, the typical lack of information, delays and uncertainty of the merger process may cause people to assume the worst about the potentially negative impact the merger will have on them. 'Brownie points' amassed in the past are swept away; career paths become cluttered with unknown new rivals; new ways of doing things are imposed; head-hunters start circling and key people leave.

If the human side of change is so important, why is it generally so badly handled?

Many organizational change efforts are handled in Newtonian, mechanistic ways which ignore the importance of human dynamics and cultural fit. As we discussed in the last chapter, when organizations change their design, the huge operational effort involved can easily distract leaders from paying enough attention to the psychological and emotional impact on the workforce. Managers in particular are often attempting to balance time spent on restructuring with pursuing their business objectives. They may lack commitment to the restructuring rationale or have little experience of restructuring. They may be unprepared to deal with difficult situations, such as having to let people go, especially if those colleagues are loyal and valued. They may be facing redundancy themselves and must deal with their own apprehension while also managing staff reactions described above – at team and organization levels. And even though they may be suffering personal issues arising from restructuring, such as change fatigue and stress, they are expected to remain positive and engaged with others since they are in the front line of trying to re-engage staff. These responses are typical of much of the theory about how human beings react to change.

Human reactions to change

There is a raft of research and theory about the emotional implications of change for individuals which I have covered elsewhere (Holbeche 2005). Of the many models to explain the psychological shifts many employees experience as they are affected by change, Elizabeth Kübler-Ross's Bereavement Curve (1973) and William Bridges' Transitions model (2004)

are amongst the best known in management circles. These suggest that people typically experience different emotions at different stages of a change cycle. In the early stages people are likely to experience heightened responses, anxiety and uncertainty; in the latter stages people let go of the past, learn new things, feel relief and achievement or else hang on to the past and gradually disengage. Employees who become emotionally disengaged are likely to become critical of the organization and its management, their perform-ance may suffer and they usually want to leave at the first opportunity. The HR/OD and leadership challenge is to anticipate these various phases and to put actions and communications in place to help people navigate the transitions with as much ease as possible.

Unless employees engage with the new reality and change their expect-ations and behaviour, the restructure will not succeed. Therefore the less certain the environment and the less agreement there is about what needs to be done, the more employee engagement in change is desirable.

In Chapter 8 Mee-Yan has discussed ways of approaching behavioural change and addressing the issue of 'resistance'. Lewin (1948) recognized the need to provide a process to engage employees and help them change their behaviour. He developed action research and his famous three-step model of change – of unfreezing, moving and refreezing. He argued that crises can be leveraged for initiating culture change (unfreezing) since the system is more open, permeable and vulnerable at such times. Normal rules are suspended, including the covert norms of the entrenched culture. Hence mergers can be a powerful spur to something new and better if the opportunity they present is used as such.

Bridges's Transitions Model – with a similar structure to Lewin's – puts much greater emphasis on the emotional change journey, seeing this as a series of transitions through the various phases of change with features such as anxiety, reduced performance, polarization, and conflict that should be anticipated and planned for. The key change lesson is to involve people in change since as Senge (1999) points out, real change is about '*activating the self-energizing commitment and energy of people around changes they deeply care about*'. Hence the importance of embracing dialogic, involving approaches to change, even when managing a conven-tional top-down change programme.

Planned change philosophies and approaches

Given the pace of change, the notion of linear 'change management' is becom-ing questionable. So we need to rethink how organizations can be trans-formed in such a way that change 'sticks' – for a while at least. Mee-Yan earlier drew on the work of Marshak, Eoyang and others to describe the differences between conventional change management and OD approaches.

Building on this, we are seeing blends of 'old' and 'new' approaches being applied to managing complex change.

'Change management'

Planned, top-down change is in keeping with the metaphor of organization as machine and assumes that change can be efficiently engineered to achieve predictable outcomes. The right mix of **plans, assets** and **culture** is supposed to lead to superior performance. It also requires people to adjust their **beliefs, values,** and **assumptions** to ensure appropriate patterns of behaviour to implement strategy.

Such change is usually treated as a project with a defined start and finish that requires a formal change model and an orchestrated approach to address both the mechanics of the change process and the human aspects of change. The change process is often supported by project management tools such as Gantt charts, 'go live' dates etc. For instance, the well-known '8 Steps' change framework of John Kotter (2006) is widely used and reflected in Prince 2 project software:

1 Establish a sense of urgency – examine market and competitive realities for potential crises and untapped opportunities and convince at least 75 per cent of managers that the status quo is unsustainable.

2 Form a powerful guiding coalition – encourage a group with shared commitment to work as a team outside the usual hierarchy.

3 Create a vision to direct the change effort and develop strategies for realizing the vision.

4 Communicate the vision – using every possible vehicle and teaching new behaviours by the example of the guiding coalition.

5 Empower others to act on the vision by removing systems or structures that undermine the vision.

6 Plan for, and create short-term wins – engineer visible performance improvements and reward those who contribute to these.

7 Consolidate improvements and produce more change – build further change on the back of enhanced credibility as a result of improvements already achieved.

8 Institutionalize new approaches – for instance create leadership succession plans consistent with the new approach.

Critics of such approaches argue that change should not be seen as a single linear 'waterfall' process since it may be necessary to revisit strategy for instance if changes in legislation or company policy mean that the strategy is no longer relevant. So change management entails constantly monitoring the need to loop back to earlier phases and get them right before moving on, even though a 'burning platform' or urgent need no longer exists. Axelrod

argues that such approaches work on four old change beliefs (Axelrod 2010:19) namely:

- the few decide for the many;
- solutions first and people second;
- fear builds urgency;
- inequality is the norm and life is not fair.

These four beliefs create major engagement gaps since what the process communicates to people is that their voice does not count. Consequently individuals end up isolated from other people; people trust neither the institution nor its leaders; self-interest breeds self-defences.

Systemic change

From the 1980s onwards there was wider recognition that organizations are living systems that can be deliberately developed and renewed. The metaphor most commonly associated with classic OD is that of 'organism' or 'eco-system'. The OD process model has its sequential steps, interventions and underlying ideals. It involves identifying the key stake-holders; listening to and including their ideas in the solution; working towards alignment of views, intent and implementation. This approach has merit for incremental and process change or to support formal change models. Thus classic OD approaches still have elements in common with the mechanistic view. For example, the systems theory search for general systems concepts and processes clearly reflects the classical search for cause and effect relationships.

There are differences however. Whereas the role of the manager in planned change is to deliver the plan, in systemic change the focus is on human dynamics. The leader articulates a vision, employees are engaged in 'pull mode', patterns are recognized and feedback loops reinforced. The assumption is that diversity must be surfaced during change and common ground sought; that multiple gains are possible and engagement is critical to maintaining change momentum.

More recent OD approaches are built on social constructivist principles. They emphasize the dialogic, with conversation between people and co-creation being the primary means of effecting change. They include models such as appreciative inquiry, world cafe, solution-focused dialogue and reflexive inquiry. Bushe and Marshak's (2008) general dialogic approach (creating generative images, hosting generative conversations and sponsoring emergent change) is increasingly being embraced not only as a suite of tools and techniques but more importantly as a way of being.

Therefore OD as a discipline is responsible for 'democratizing' the change process – putting greater emphasis on:

- Living system paradigm – honouring the nature of human dynamics, autonomy, freedom, sense of agency, need to contribute and so on.

- Everyone counts – regardless of rank, individual voices are to be captured.
- Working from the end game up – involving key groups in the implementation from the beginning of the process.
- Helping people to personalize, influence and co-construct the change case and process.
- Setting the problem and letting people work out the solution, always using large group methodology to close down the power differentials. We do believe that wisdom exists in groups.

Axelrod (2010) argues that the leader's task is to widen the circle of involvement, connect people to each other, create communities for action and promote fairness. The leader's challenge is to align thinking, manage the tensions and get people to work out for themselves how best to achieve alignment in a way that responds to the needs of the stakeholder group. In the final analysis, OD believes that 'people support what they help to construct' (Weisbord, 1978).

Therefore, whichever change model or approach your organization is considering, the likely impact on people should be assessed:

- Does it make sense for your organization to have a single approach to change?
- Will it help your organization manage more change, faster and better?
- Does the model's assumed range, scale and speed of change suit your organization's circumstances?
- Will the model mobilize the people/behavioural/cultural dimensions of change to match your organization's ambitions and capabilities?

Of course the majority of organizations are still operating in the prevailing Newtonian paradigm. As Mee-Yan points out, it may be sensible for the HR/OD practitioner to glean useful approaches and techniques from the traditional way of effecting change, and then blend these with the OD systemic and complexity understanding – which should remain as the dominant base. As a result, HR/OD can help clients learn how to do change differently.

HR and transformational change

Especially in the case of radical complex change – such as M&As – there is a good case for adopting a formal change (project) management approach and adapting to it to embrace classic and more dialogical OD approaches. Given the importance of 'getting the people bit' right, Roffey Park research (Devine *et al*, 1998) argued that HR should be directly involved in planning from the outset. There are distinct phases of M&A activity – the run-up

period to the deal being closed, the transition period when the two organizations come together and the longer-term integration when the two companies effectively become one. Each phase is marked by a different level of activity with many groups having roles to play. HR should ideally be involved in all three but is frequently limited to providing data to transition teams in the run-up period.

Roffey Park found that mergers that were strongly HR-led anticipated and resolved many of the people issues during the merger, leading to real integration and synergy. That's because the merger experience shapes the emerging culture and climate of the new organization and determines people's commitment to the new business. With intellectual capital being a major driver behind many acquisitions, failure to retain key talent can become an own goal for acquirers!

In working together on change projects HR and OD need to agree who is doing what. Managing the overall change process and working closely with the CEO and top team to design the change methodology is likely to be the task of the OD specialist while HR must work closely with senior management throughout to advise on the people issues and make sure that leaders are aware that their values and behaviour will have a profound influence on others.

Designing the new organization for high performance

As we discussed in the last chapter, transformational change offers the chance to refocus the organization's design on value creation, enabling the new organization to move to higher levels of performance and embark on new strategic opportunities. HR can play a key role in helping redesign organizations so:

- Remind yourself what the change is trying to achieve then go for the full potential, enabling the new organization to move to higher levels of performance and embark on new strategic opportunities.
- Design the structures, work processes, employee roles and value proposition to reflect the kind of business you are aspiring to be, the business model(s) you are working towards and the kinds of people you need to attract and retain to make the model work.
- What roles, knowledge and skills will create value for the business? What staff numbers will be required?
- What will help bring about high-performance climates?

It is important to be proactive and decisive about what you intend to do. See that you have a robust yet flexible process in place – the shorter/quicker, the better. Keep it as tight as possible and get the right people to manage it.

The change process needs to be designed and implemented in a disciplined way, using project management disciplines and continuous tracking of key indicators to ensure that the transition and employee morale are in good

shape. Handovers need to be clarified between those who are managing the transition as a project and line managers who must keep business going as usual in the midst of upheaval and also implement the plan.

A disciplined approach

It is important to adopt a phased and professional approach to HR issues, identifying sensitive matters as early as possible. Establish the process by which the new structure will be agreed and the timescale for changes.

A rigorous, disciplined approach is needed to:

- prepare a due diligence database and algorithms for all benefit costs in different countries;
- work out the guiding principles for appointments, relocation and exits – and communicate these;
- carry out a risk analysis on key jobs and talent;
- handle redundancies with care both for the outgoing people and the survivors;
- think about how to support hard-pressed line managers, individuals and teams;
- work out what resources will be needed to support high-quality implementation of job change.

Pay particular attention to the technical and practical aspects of restructuring. To make a really effective contribution, HR needs to be able to access key information in a hurry so make sure that your information systems are working properly. Settle the HR structure quickly so that people are not distracted by uncertainty about their own position. Support communication activity and set up help desks. Use external expertise where appropriate. For instance employees being redeployed or whose jobs are redundant may value having an impartial external view as well as support from internal experts such as HR.

Be aware that leadership and senior management problems may well occur, including their level of commitment to executing restructuring. HR may need to challenge specific restructuring decisions and particularly how individual employees are selected for termination. For a whole host of reasons, not least avoiding damage to the employer brand, HR should encourage the line to consider alternatives to redundancy such as internal redeployment, reduced hours/pay, external placements, shared jobs and working, leave of absence and education/learning schemes.

HR must lead on the following:

- retaining key talent;
- handling redundancies and other exits;
- supporting line managers;

- supporting individuals and teams;
- ensuring effective communications;
- re-engaging the 'survivors';
- combining action and learning.

Retaining key talent

Change disturbs people, even those not at risk of redundancy. If you want to retain key talent for the future, identify them as early as possible in the change process and let them know. CIPD (2010) research suggests that people often leave organizations to seek better career opportunities so it is important to persevere with talent management and development during times of major change when key talent is often 'poached' by competitors. Look for opportunities to stretch your key employees by giving them new responsibilities or secondment onto a change project team. Giving key employees the chance to lead some aspect of the change process will keep them involved, interested and learning.

Retention incentives may be needed but 'golden handcuffs' are not always the best option. HR should also encourage line managers to help retain talent by showing understanding for employee concerns, being honest and open and recognizing excellent performance. Managers should find judicious ways to recognize and reward exceptional performance and stay true to the organization's values. Be discreet. If you make too much fuss of key employees, others may feel their own prospects look bleak.

Handling redundancies and other exits

If redundancies are deemed necessary HR must consult openly and transparently with employees and/or their representatives from the beginning of the process. Good pre-planning should help to minimize or offset difficulties in exiting people. HR must work through the planning, logistics, administration and pitfalls of redundancy, the termination process and how it needs to be managed/supported with help from other managers and HR staff, interim managers, legal experts, external agencies and outplacement providers. HR is likely to be involved in redundancy selection panels, the integration project team, new resourcing forums, project working parties and outplacement projects. It may be necessary to pull in extra management and HR resources to cope with work overloads and pressure points – particularly if there are large numbers of leavers.

The way exits are handled will affect not only the people who are leaving (who may become future customers) but also those who stay – the 'survivors'. Both managers and leaders need detailed guidance on how to manage this process sensitively and still maintain 'business as usual' during a period of redundancy consultation. HR should provide training for managers in handling difficult conversations and workshops for leavers

via internal/external outplacement providers. In all matters HR must show empathy with people however they may be affected, treat them fairly, give reassurance and support.

Supporting line managers

HR must prepare managers to manage change by ensuring they understand restructuring, have specific restructuring roles and accountabilities and are measured/evaluated against these. Managers must keep people focused on 'business as usual' (ie on the customer) even while things are changing. They must make it easier for people to do difficult jobs and reduce stress at a time of uncertainty. So HR can help by:

- Giving managers tools and techniques to manage through change and to handle difficult situations. These include: restructuring, change and transitions workshops/off-site meetings usually facilitated by HR; full briefings from HR and other experts on the technical/legal aspects of restructuring, delivered either before the process or during it; process plans, guides, documentation, Frequently Asked Questions (FAQs), desktop support, scripted interviews etc.

- Providing line managers with support to manage their own stress levels so that they can better support their teams.

Supporting individuals and teams

Of course people have different degrees of resilience to change; however, if people feel well-equipped for change and are involved in decision making they are more likely to recognize change as opportunity than as threat. So it's important to:

- Avoid becoming drowned in a spate of project work which prevents you from supporting others. Use consultants and others to spread the load.

- Keep your finger on the pulse of employee morale and watch out for vulnerable individuals. Provide access to practical support and counselling. Arrange open-access change awareness workshops for employees; provide team building for new or transitioning teams.

- Encourage top teams to be visible, build trust, show respect and help people to say farewell to the past.

Ensuring effective communications

A key principle of change communications is that you cannot over-communicate. Communication must be consistent and also meaningful to recipients. As we have discussed, people typically experience various

emotions as a major change process unfolds and some of these phases can be anticipated and planned for.

First people must understand why change is needed. When initiating change executives must set the context by communicating to all staff what the organization is trying to accomplish and how it must change. They must spell out the link between the change programme and the long-term strategy, making clear the goals/objectives and key milestones (Mohrman, 2007). However, recognizing that in major change there will be many overlapping change initiatives and continual adjustments occurring, leaders must remain in active communication with employees throughout, the more 'two-way' the better.

Coach leaders and managers in effective communications

Working closely with communications experts, HR can help coach senior managers in how to communicate effectively, especially face to face, during a potentially challenging period. 'Engaging leaders' provide a strong strategic narrative and vision that glues together the organization and aligns individual, workgroup and company goals (Macleod and Clarke, 2009). The vision derives from the organization's higher purpose and should be an idea so simple, so powerful, so compelling and so insightful that it unifies the organization and drives everything they do. Fundamentally it answers the question 'Why?' Why should I care? Why does it matter?

A variety of forums and channels, (especially face to face as in town hall meetings and roadshows) can be used. People typically want to know why the change is happening and, most particularly, how the change will impact them and if they will still have a job. If so, they will want to know what their role will be and whether they are winning or losing with respect to career prospects and terms and conditions. They will want to know how they can succeed in the new organization, how performance will be managed and what training and development will be available. So communicate the timetable by which answers to such questions will be known – then stick to it.

To create a climate for change real dialogue is needed. So an effective communications strategy will gradually incorporate two-way communications so that people can start to gain a sense of ownership.

Target specific communications at different groups

Employees will be affected by change at different times. HR should ensure that external and internal communications are professional, well-targeted and timely, and work with managers to localize messages. Front-line staff need early briefings about what is going on so that they can deal with customer queries in a way that sends the right messages.

As the change process unfolds HR needs to keep closely tuned in to how people are feeling, checking that people understand what is happening, how the change will affect them and what the way ahead looks like. Major change can help employees to 'pull together' but people need to

believe that change was the right thing to do. Since the benefits of change may not yet be obvious, the reason for the change may need to be reiterated often. When tough decisions must be taken, people need to feel confident that the right decisions have been made and that all concerned have been treated fairly.

HR is a vital conduit between employees, their representatives and management and employees must have opportunities to raise their concerns. HR must make senior management aware of key people risks so that these can be addressed. It is important to maintain employee surveys, pull out key areas for improvement and act on feedback. During one major acquisition the HR manager set up an integration website where employees could feed back thoughts, feelings and questions to which HR would respond. The annual employee survey reflected an improvement in engagement levels.

Re-engaging the 'survivors'

Organizations must make special efforts to re-engage employees who remain, including acknowledging the losses people might be feeling (especially about colleagues who have departed and their own changes of role). So it's crucial that managers do not adopt 'bunker mentality' during times of crisis, letting communication and team work lapse. They must make the first move to reassure anxious employees whose confidence in the company's direction may have waned. They must be honest, forthright and communicate with employees with greater frequency, give regular updates on business performance and the financial position, where possible sharing recent successes, as well as reaffirming values and communicating the organization's new strategy and business plans, priorities and targets. Concentrating on the positives achieved during the first wave of change influences and motivates people for the next wave of change. New structures, roles and ways of working can be confirmed and a return to the new 'business as usual' can be heralded.

This should not be just top-down communication (which can actually hinder engagement) but honest and genuine dialogue which builds trust. HR can also help people see the bigger picture by connecting the dots between the multiple initiatives that typically accompany strategic change; from their vantage point they are better able to see the pieces. By so doing they reduce uncertainty and help people cope better with change. In many organizations HR has helped the CEO to communicate directly with employees by becoming a regular 'blogger'; HR is also often instrumental in setting up 'innovation teams', organizing visioning/team-building workshops and away days which point to new beginnings.

Accelerating change

More generally HR can accelerate change through the following change leadership activities:

- Define the new employment relationship. Bring people together to discuss what the new organization is expecting from them in terms of the new design/job/performance requirements and the new behaviours required. This is about defining what success will look like and how it will be rewarded.

- Help people succeed. Work with line managers to design stretching roles which provide development opportunities and real business value. Ensure that employees can integrate well into new teams and are clear about the way ahead. Help people develop the skills and competencies they really need, integrating business-relevant learning and role design. Create opportunities for individuals, teams and units to learn and develop eg through mentoring, online learning, team development sessions, training programmes, visiting other organizations, sharing examples and ideas. This is about giving people time and other resources to learn without fear of punishment if they make a mistake as they experiment with new approaches.

- Keep talent management in focus. Recruit the right people. Good-quality appointments matter – they are hard to undo. Populate the integrated organization with high performers, especially in line management roles, even though this might not appear equitable at first.

- Ensure that existing staff have the chance for learning and growth. Many employees will wish to reassess their personal and career development needs as a result of change. It's important that HR restores people's faith in the employer brand by providing support, guidance and coaching and developing fluid career tracks so that people can still progress their careers even in challenging times. It's about giving people a chance to change roles/re-energize themselves and the organization.

- Build a performance culture. Train line managers how to coach and develop their teams, how to clarify goals and priorities and hold people to account.

- Encourage the establishment of cross-functional and cross-organizational teams to work on major new initiatives. Work with an OD consultant to assist in this process.

- Keep performance management and other people processes simple. Encourage managers to set clear short-term objectives.

- Help people feel valued. Use non-financial benefits eg forms of recognition that matter most to people. Provide a sense of purpose and progress. Honour the past and celebrate success in the new era. Stabilize and share the benefits.

To sum up, there is a hard business case for taking the people aspects of change seriously. HR needs to develop a credible, fast-moving response to both the short- and longer-term implications of transformational change.

Through skilled HR planning, organization design and development interventions HR can make a substantial contribution to sustainable business success.

HR's role in changing cultures

When it comes to successfully implementing strategy, culture or 'the way we do things around here' probably has more impact than anything else. It is no good having a strategy which calls for intensive customer focus if the organization's norms, standards, working practices and values focus people's energies and behaviours in another direction. As Peter Drucker said, 'culture eats strategy for breakfast.'

About culture change

Culture change essentially involves people changing their behaviour. It can be triggered by many factors, such as a new CEO, or a business crisis, or a merger, or when an organizational culture has become 'toxic' and low-trust – that's when 'silos' and internal politics cause the organization to become inwardly focused and slow to respond. Symptoms are evident in 'blame cultures' and departments being unwilling to share resources.

Many cultural issues are to do with power – people's use of, or lack of it. The examples set by top leadership can breed sub-optimal behaviour in others. Dysfunctional leadership teams are often poor at decision making. In strong, successful and arrogant cultures a controlling and punitive leader will tend to become surrounded by 'yes people', executives may become complacent about their brand and miss clues about how the marketplace is changing.

Another category of cultural challenge concerns the degree of mismatch between the preferred (espoused) cultures – reflected in organizational value statements – and actual practice (cultures-in-use). For instance if a company advocates teamwork and ethical conduct but promotes individuals who act exclusively in their own interests, people know what really counts. When managers in particular fail to 'walk the talk' on values and when there is also a legacy of failed change efforts, employee cynicism soon grows and makes managing change more difficult. New recruits who were attracted to the organization by a strong 'employer brand' may find the reality very different. Even the 'right' people cannot thrive in the 'wrong' environment.

However, since organizations are complex adaptive systems, deliberate management-driven culture change is rarely effective. Moreover Lewin (1948) maintained that it is fruitless to concentrate on changing the behaviour of individuals because in isolation individuals are constrained by group

pressures to conform or else be rejected entirely. The focus of change should be on changing the context to alter the habits and routines, creating 'disequilibrium' in factors such as group norms, roles, interactions and socialization processes. Consequently, culture change is essentially about working with group dynamics and managing meaning through information and relationship networks. CEOs therefore need to demonstrate some understanding of group dynamics and, by creating new groups, alter the quality of 'between-ness' of people, groups and organization.

Principles of culture change

For cultural shifts to be sustainable, the following principles apply:

- Root culture in performance and the job to be done – thereby ensuring relevance. Otherwise people (including leaders) are likely to revert to operating in their old ways, thus limiting the organization's ability to implement its new business strategy and design effectively.
- Leaders must demonstrate obvious commitment to change, set and model the climate for individuals, teams and business units to change.
- It's about practising new behaviours, not changing attitudes.
- Cultural change takes time, is not linear or 'programmable'; uncertainty, ambiguity, risk and setback are inherent.
- Involves recognizing and working with intellect and emotions.
- It creates experiences and opportunities for people to behave in new ways.
- It is implemented in a way which reinforces the new ways of working.

Leaders and culture change

Leaders at all levels have a profound effect on the culture of organizations. According to Schein (2004) the dynamic processes of culture creation and management are the essence of leadership; leadership and culture are two sides of the same coin: *'I believe that cultures begin with leaders who impose their own values and assumptions on a group. If that group is successful and the assumptions come to be taken for granted, we then have a culture that will define for later generations of members what kinds of leadership are acceptable. The culture now defines leadership.'*

Thus culture emanates from leaders' **beliefs** about 'success' which are translated from **core values** – 'what's important' and come to be represented by **norms and behaviours**.

Leaders transmit and embed culture through what Schein calls *primary embedding mechanisms*:

1 what leaders pay attention to, measure and control;
2 leader reactions to critical incidents and organization crises;

3 deliberate role modelling, teaching and coaching by leaders;

4 criteria for allocation of rewards and status;

5 criteria for recruitment, selection, promotion, retirement and excommunication.

And through *secondary articulation and reinforcement mechanisms*:

1 organizational design and structure;

2 organizational systems and procedures;

3 design of physical space, facades and buildings;

4 stories, legends, myths and parables about important events and people;

5 formal statements of organizational philosophy creeds and charters.

Many failures occur when CEOs try to transfer what works in one organization to another without referring to the new situation. Such top-down approaches can breed a sceptical workforce.

Peter Senge (1999) argues that the interplay between three groups of leaders is crucial in sustaining change initiatives. These are:

- *Local Line Leaders:* People who are accountable for results and have sufficient authority to undertake changes in the way that work is organized at local level.

- *Internal Networkers – 'Network Leaders':* People who have an enabling role and are natural 'seed carriers' of ideas, support and stories throughout the organization.

- *Key Executive (Senior) Leaders:* These have overall accountability for organization performance and create the conditions for others involved directly in value-producing activities to be successful by:
 - setting the tone and 'walking the talk';
 - leading the change movement, championing its reasons and benefits;
 - putting support into the change process;
 - positioning it as a top priority;
 - giving clear messages;
 - measuring change outcomes, holding staff accountable.

It is on the acceptance and agreement of these 'key groups', and their competence in implementing change, that the success of culture change critically depends. They need to be able to implement culture-change strategies and to align organizational elements, accepting that this takes time. If not culture change gets displaced by other organizational priorities. HR and OD specialists must ensure that all groups of leaders understand their role in culture change, provide feedback and challenge if leaders' behaviour is inconsistent with values.

Help people become aware

In contrast to top-down leadership approaches, emergence methods are based on the belief that distributed leadership will sustain change; therefore that those who will be most affected need to be directly involved. '*Change the patterns of participation, and you change the organization. At the core of the 21st-century company is the question of participation. At the heart of participation is the mind and spirit of the knowledge worker...*' (Seely Brown and Gray, 1995).

Unless there are obvious reasons for changing the culture, and strongly shared principles and values to validate the need for change, culture change will be seen as going through the motions. Therefore people must become aware of how the culture really operates and identify what degree of change is both possible and desirable. Leaders can raise people's awareness of the need for change by exposing them to contexts and experiences where real change may be occurring outside the current remit of the organization. System members need to audit 'our way of doing things' in every key dimension of the company – shared assumptions, beliefs, values, norms, especially the covert ones – and the institution-limiting patterns of behaviour they generate. Ideally such audits should essentially be conversations. Recognizing that the group is the basic unit for stimulating and sustaining change it is important to find out what the group identify with and help them determine what keeps these patterns of behaviour in place – for instance in strategy, operations, structure, role design, human resource management or leadership.

Leaders must be able to engage and enthuse people in shaping the change, tap into their knowledge, experience and build their ownership of the future state. Employees need to know that their ideas and potential solutions are needed. Dialogic, discursive or conversational approaches assume that organizations are co-constructed realities; energy is as important as the logic of change; that people need to participate in planning change from the beginning to 'personalize' the change. This is the kind of dialogue which helps employees understand the purpose of change and have the opportunity to redesign how they work in order to deliver value to the customer. Therefore co-construction – not consultation – is key to releasing energy. As Margaret Wheatley (1998) points out: '*Participation is not a choice... people only support what they help to create. Life insists on freedom to participate and can never be sold on or bossed into accepting someone else's plans*'.

Change can be accelerated through inquiry, generative inter-connections, changing conversations, building and drawing on existing and new networks. These methods focus less on diagnosing the current system than on developing narratives or 'stories' that will help establish a more effective way of organizing. So rather than polishing up their communication plans leaders 'need to focus equally on starting the conversations that enable the development of new *shared meanings* of the logic of the changes and *new agreements* about how people will work together to accomplish something new' (Mohrman, 2007). Within this context people can figure out

how they can contribute in ways which make sense to them. Having a formal process where people can try things out and learn from success and failure is important.

Peter Block (2008) also argues that the most important thing leaders can do is to create the opportunity and process for people to discuss/debate both what is happening and how to make change go a bit faster. In essence culture change is about generating a social movement ie 'a voluntary collective of individuals committed to promoting or resisting change through coordinated activity, to produce a lasting and self-generating effect, and creating as they do a sense of shared identity' (NHS Institute for Innovation and Improvement, UK). Such networks not only carry out learning reviews; they can also provide feedback and 'feed forward'. With a focus on learning as a personal and group activity, and as a means of influencing others, the change process should not only result in a more successful business but also help employees grow and prosper.

To mobilize a critical mass to move in the same direction use large-scale engagement methods, rather than 'cascade and tell' methods with one group at a time. Encourage people to co-create the future that matters to them – as people support what they help to create. Use the human network to spread the positive virus. IBM for instance runs a 'Values Jam' with worldwide participation online. People have the chance to talk about and make sense of what is happening; the process creates energy and momentum to create significant change. The conversations people have are less about 'when will change be over?' and more about 'what's the next change?'

Of course in power-based cultures these newer forms of OD may seem threatening to leaders and to people who think leaders should provide all the answers to the organization's problems. It is vital that there is genuine support from top management for such practices, so the management team must model openness and be prepared to take ideas on board.

To 'change', 'strengthen' or 'balance' culture?

Another way of thinking about developing culture derives from the work of Stokes and Harrison (1992). They argue that it is better to think more in terms of 'strengthening' and 'balancing' an organization's culture than of *'changing'* it. *Strengthening* a culture involves intensifying the culture's expression, especially its higher aspects, and doing the same things, only better. *Balancing* a culture is the approach to use if you want to preserve the culture's benefits, add countervailing elements or encourage cultural differentiation. It is only when some aspect of culture is a real impediment to success that talk of *change* is relevant. Even then, '... often change need not be cajoled or coerced. Instead it can be unleashed' (Kelman, 2005). It's therefore important to identify which aspects of the organization's culture to strengthen or adapt so that change is sustained and take action (eg aligning structures, performance management, reward, behaviours or skills) to address these changes.

Appreciative Inquiry (Cooperrider and Srivastva, 1987) is perhaps the best known of the strengths-based approaches. Appreciative Inquiry (AI)

assumes no inherently real form of social organizing to be discovered; instead AI seeks to provoke new constructive ideas that will produce self-organizing change. For example, two UK NHS hospital Trusts were in the early stages of merger. Forty people from each Trust were trained in AI and began a process of inquiry into each others' organization to understand what happens when the best patient care is being delivered. As people pooled the intelligence arising from this exercise, they realized that aspects of both Trusts' practices would be helpful in delivering good patient care but that something new would be needed to allow previous standards to be exceeded. Starting from a strengths-based approach allowed new ideas to be discussed without defensiveness.

By seeking to use inclusive approaches from the outset and progressively engaging the whole organization, leaders have a better chance of succeeding in their aims since staff will feel a sense of ownership of improvements and will better understand how change plays into the organization's journey. Change will then become second nature and part of everyone's job.

Training as an enabler of cultural integration

The following case study outlines how training can be used to effect cultural integration in a way that meets both business and employee needs.

CASE STUDY Ashfield Meetings and Events

Ashfield Meetings & Events is the product of a merger of two leading event management companies – Universal Procon and WorldEvents. From the outset, aware that merging two companies with different cultures could cause disruption, Ashfield management set out to understand the potential negative impact on the business and develop strategic plans to counter these issues.

In order to better understand the thoughts and feelings of staff in the combined company the company undertook the Denison Culture Survey in 2012. This survey measures an organization's progress toward achieving a high-performance culture. From the survey it was clear there were some weaknesses, especially surrounding the company mission and consistency across the newly merged company. It was clear that employees needed to be informed about the company's future. Senior management accordingly asked employees to work with them to help develop and clarify the company's mission and values.

Similarly the capability development and learning segments of the Denison model showed scope for improvement. As the company had grown it was essential

that everyone continued to meet Ashfield's minimum standards and knew exactly what steps to take to get there. It was imperative that all staff operated at a high standard in terms of legal compliance and were familiar with the latest legislation that governs how they do their day-to-day jobs, and also with advances in technology, changes to preferred suppliers and Ashfield's internal standard operating procedures and best practice.

The 'Bitesize' programme

Ashfield employed a dedicated Training & Development Manager to identify and help prioritize requirements. The events industry is fast paced and time demanding. Therefore taking employees out of work for sessions to make changes to the company culture was not practical. The 'Bitesize' training programme was conceived, developed and introduced in 2013 and is now an ongoing programme. The aim was to provide training that was up to date, accessible and relevant to each individual and of such value that employees wanted (and felt they had time) to attend.

As the name implies, Bitesize sessions are short (usually just an hour long), interactive and informative and available in a range of formats including face to face. The project was implemented in agile fashion on a quarterly basis to overcome any obstacles and ensure the courses are aligned to the company culture. So while some sessions are compulsory, the nature of the programme is fluid, ever-evolving. To ensure that training is relevant to employees' day-to-day tasks, employees are invited to put forward suggestions of what subjects they would like to see scheduled for the future. In 2013–14, 74 Bitesize courses covering 33 topics were run or made available in seven countries. On average each employee attended six courses in the calendar year.

Along with 'Capability Development', 'Empowerment' also scored low on the Denison survey, so management also wanted to give employees a platform to feel empowered and take control of their own development. Many courses are aligned to soft skills to develop employees' personal skills and attributes. Employees are provided with the information and tools to develop their career. They are empowered to sign themselves up to Bitesize sessions; these are scheduled six months in advance to enable employees to plan ahead. Training attendance is reviewed regularly with their line managers during one-to-ones and guidance is provided on which courses are suitable for each individual's development. The training also ensures employees have opportunities to network, learn relevant skills and share best practice across a broad range of subjects.

Bitesize is harnessing the plethora of expertise that exists across the company and anyone from Senior Project Executives to Business Directors can run Bitesize sessions. Management believe that exposing employees' knowledge and sharing best practice incentivizes individuals whilst also raising their profile within the

company. There is a strong correlation between attendance at Bitesize courses and internal promotions. Indeed 70 per cent of promotions in 2013–14 went to people who had run Bitesize courses for their colleagues.

Benefits

To date Bitesize is proving an effective way of communicating with employees and rolling out new processes and procedures. The Bitesize training forms a key part of new starters' induction programmes, allowing them to fit into their new roles quickly and with all the tools they need. It also forms a key part of each employee's staff development plan, which is monitored regularly through appraisals. Also, Ashfield partners with preferred suppliers to deliver specific Bitesize training sessions in-house which allows for a higher level of interaction – as well as higher uptake levels – than standard supplier visits. As well as training staff this allows Ashfield to foster meaningful relationships with key suppliers.

The Bitesize courses help to motivate employees, keeping them up to date on matters that allow them to perform to the best of their ability and enhancing relationships across the business by sharing best practice. By delivering process change in this format Ashfield has seen a more efficient transformation and fostered a more collaborative workforce. Ashfield regularly receives feedback from clients praising employees for their knowledge and professionalism.

A year on from the start of the Bitesize course Ashfield Meetings & Events undertook the Denison Culture Survey again. In just twelve months the initiatives introduced saw Ashfield's percentile leap from 41 per cent to 90 per cent. It was clear from the results that the Bitesize courses were having the desired effect within the company, improving the scores surrounding the company mission and consistency. All employees now have a much clearer understanding of the overall purpose and direction for the company moving forward. This improvement is clearly felt within the business as a whole and has indicated the need for the Bitesize course to continue. In the same period Ashfield has registered double digit EBIT growth during a challenging period for the industry.

As this case study suggests, giving people voice, helping them develop the skills to do their jobs well, and giving them responsibility for managing their own development, can lead to greater agility and resilience. Empowerment is a common thread running through individual performance and the empowerment principle needs to be embedded as the new 'way we do things around here'. So after aligning on a common purpose, an organization needs to make purpose concrete through a set of quality standards: priorities that guide front-line staff in delivering the desired customer experience. When people are trusted to do their job and given clear expectations rather than

an instruction manual, they feel more valued and empowered – qualities that can't help but show in the customer experience they provide.

HR stimulating culture change

- Grapple with the culture as it really is; work with the power brokers to expose the reality. Ask 'naive' and even 'impertinent' questions. 'Why are we doing that this way?' 'What purpose does this serve?'
- Discover in particular the culture of the leadership team. Use 360-degree feedback and survey results to get through to senior managers if they are difficult to reach. What is their attitude towards the culture change? Where are the individual and collective gaps in terms of readiness and capability?
 - Are all change leaders clear about their roles and objectives?
 - Are they actively and positively engaged?
 - Do leaders and managers demonstrate desired cultural attributes? Is there effective role modelling?
- Craft a leadership strategy, focusing both on leadership bench strength and future top talent. Such a strategy should also focus on developing the collective capability of individual leaders and a shared leadership culture. What type of ownership management/transition management processes should be put in place?
- Transform the executive team. Coach senior leaders (both individually and as a group) to develop their readiness for leading culture change.
- Link culture change to every key project, programme or change effort. Encourage employees to care intensely about executing strategic objectives. This makes sense since many change efforts fail because they do not take account of cultural realities.
- Establish action teams made up of high potential and other leaders who work across boundaries to develop new and better ways for the organization to operate.
- Support provocateurs and mavericks.
- Focus and magnify. In one organization there was sustained criticism by employees about the poor management communications. Instead of attacking dysfunctional attitudes and norms, the HR team flooded the place with action strategies for improving communication. The formal campaign lasted a year. By that time there were enough converts to this new mode of thinking, and enough champions promoting it that the new culture drove out the old.
- Actively promote the new values. If you want a different culture, mount training programmes that promote it. Develop a supportive infrastructure. Shape group norms through incentives.

- Use symbolic acts to mark the transition from the old culture to the new. Relax or remove 'old' rules and controls. While in themselves they do not change anything, they send powerful messages.

- Build trust: this is a vital cornerstone of a change-able culture – not 'blind' trust which is doomed to disappointment, but trust based on reciprocation and people doing what they say they will do. This applies to (top) leadership in particular (who stereotypically in times of change become less trusted by employees) and also to HR. Act on some aspect of the employee survey findings to show people that management has listened and also intends to make people's lives a bit easier. Trust has to be earned.

- Celebrate milestones in fighting outmoded values and norms.

- Align talent processes and recruit people with flexible and collaborative mindsets.

- Give people tools to be self-managing. Ensure that people have a clear line of sight to the purpose, mission and goals of the organization through their day job and have the chance to develop and grow in roles which have some 'stretch'. Work with line managers to create positive work environments so that people can feel part of a winning team. Ensure that people can gain appropriate reward and recognition, even if much of this is non-financial. Employees then become the vocal advocates of the new culture.

Conclusion

Today's challenging business context makes understanding organizational culture and how to bring about change more relevant than ever. Since we can confidently predict that the context will keep on changing, organizations will need to reconfigure themselves many times in pursuit of greater agility. As we have discussed, transforming organizations and changing cultures is not easy. The key to success for all types of change is to engage key staff in the changes sufficiently that they help shape sustainable change outcomes. Agile organizations need a 'change-able' culture exemplified by rich learning; good employee relations; open, honest and involving styles of management; and empowered and accountable employees at all levels.

HR has many traditional 'levers' to help build healthy and 'change-able' cultures – such as recruitment, induction, promotion, training and development. Insights from organization development can help us understand how to use these levers in a systemic way to reinforce desired aspects of culture and to create the new 'way we do things around here'. For OD and HR practitioners this will mean ongoing learning and becoming skilled at the kind of culture change approaches that work for your organization. This is a theme we return to in more detail in the next chapter where the focus is on organizational agility and resilience.

Building organizational agility and resilience

After a decade of unprecedented global economic and geopolitical uncertainty many companies and institutions face extreme competitive conditions and operating pressures with squeezed budgets and margins. As growth returns, significant changes in customer and employee demographics suggest that there will be no return to 'business as usual'.

Many market changes are driven and enabled by technological advances as new information technologies – including high-speed internet, low-cost devices and intuitive social media platforms – create new social ways of linking up, enable new communications channels and shift consumer patterns. These advances are leading to continuous disruptive innovation whose pace is ever accelerating. For instance the invention of the iphone has destabilized the already saturated market for mobile phones and within a short space of time has opened up whole new categories of wearable devices such as smart watches.

Is it any wonder then that organizational agility now sits high on executive and board agendas in every sector? An overwhelming majority (88 per cent) of executives in a substantial 2009 study by the Economist Intelligence Unit (EIU) cited agility as key to global success. Agile organizations use agility in a strategic sense to drive competitive advantage. And the benefits of doing so are considerable. Not only do agile companies grow 37 per cent faster than their non-agile peers — they also boast profit margins that are 30 per cent higher (EIU, 2009).

Since we can confidently predict that the challenging business context is going to keep on changing, organizations must be 'change-able', ie agile, flexible, innovative, capable of operating with speed and intense customer focus if they are not to become obsolete. This represents a massive OD challenge and makes understanding organizational culture and how to bring about culture change more relevant than ever.

In this chapter we shall consider how agility and resilience – that together represent an organization's 'change-ability' or adaptive capacity – can be built and what this means for people and culture. Getting the balance right is crucial; one without the other does not work. Focusing on agility alone – especially through cost cutting – can become a zero sum game if vital trust and employee engagement are undermined; focusing exclusively on resilience can result in risk-averse, slow to act cultures.

In particular we shall look at how people management practitioners can contribute to building a change-able culture based on a shared sense of purpose, values and trust. We shall consider some of the 'tools' at HR's disposal for shifting organizational structures and cultures – such as workforce planning, change management, organizational design, talent acquisition and development and performance management (Gartside *et al*, 2013). Finally we shall consider how the HR function itself can become more agile and resilient.

1 What is organizational agility and why is it needed?
2 Why are agility and resilience so elusive?
3 Unpacking organizational agility and resilience
4 How can HR help develop organizational agility and resilience?
5 HR modelling agility.

What is organizational agility?

Originally linked with lean manufacturing, just-in-time supply chains and process improvement in the 1990s and since informed by software development and complexity science, agility is now more broadly defined as an organization's capability to respond and adapt quickly and effectively to the changing environment (McCann *et al*, 2009).

The top characteristics of the 'agile' business include a high-performance culture, flexibility of management practices and resources, and organizational structures that support collaboration, rapid decision making and execution (EIU, 2009). A range of capabilities are required. In today's hyper-competitive phase of globalization speed is of the essence as technological advances pressure costs and prices ever faster through increasingly connected supply chains, squeezing margins ever tighter and making the very notion of *sustainable* competitive advantage questionable – as firms like Microsoft, Nokia and Blackberry bear witness. Indeed Rita Gunther-McGrath (2013) argues that rather than pursuing sustainable competitive advantage, organizations should aim instead for multiple transient advantages (TA).

Organizations that can't move fast enough to meet customer needs, or fail to seize opportunities, innovate, trim costs and avoid major errors, soon go out of business. Just look at the UK's retail sector where a combination of tough trading conditions, reduced consumer spending and fierce competition from online retailers has led to the closures of big-name high street

firms like Woolworths and Comet in recent years. In contrast, agile organizations react swiftly and decisively to sudden shifts in overall market conditions, to the emergence of new competitors and the development of new industry-changing technologies. They make good decisions fast, execute strategy nimbly and develop a range of innovative products which satisfy a range of customers.

For organizations whose products and services are becoming obsolete, the strategic choices are stark. They must find new and non-traditional avenues to apply strengths if they are to remain competitive and responsive. They may need to implement not just one business model, but several. Keeping ahead requires innovation and fresh thinking around strategy. Take the case of Kodak, a company founded in 1892 and which made photography available to the masses, but had failed to adapt its business model to the development of digital photography. Kodak filed for Chapter 11 bankruptcy protection in January 2012. In contrast, Fujifilm, a firm whose roots are in photographic film, an industry that declined with the advent of digital photography, took a different course, choosing to reflect on how it might apply its expertise to new markets. In September 2007 the firm launched a line of skincare products called Astalift based on technology it had developed for film (EIU, 2009).

Resilience

Agility alone will not secure sustainable success. In a future defined by ambiguity, unpredictability, complexity, multiple stakeholders and rapid change, organizations also need to be resilient, capable of responding rapidly to unforeseen and problematic change, and of bouncing back from setbacks with speed and determination (Marcos and Macauley, 2008).

Resilient organizations anticipate and address pivotal events that affect their business by being alert to both internal and environmental changes – opportunities as well as threats – and responding to those changes using available resources in a timely, flexible, affordable and relevant manner. Such organizations carry out continuous wide-deep scanning of the changing context at all levels, spotting trends. Collective intelligence is captured and acted on. For a notable retailing success story look at the John Lewis Partnership, a company founded in 1864 which became the largest multichannel retailer in the UK in 2014 through its shrewd anticipation of changing customer preferences and the timely development of its online business.

The theory is fine; in practice, despite most executives in the EIU study viewing organizational agility as a competitive necessity, many admit their companies are not sufficiently flexible to compete successfully. And while the good news is that Kodak has re-emerged from bankruptcy protection slimmer and with a new business plan – focused on packaging, graphic communications and functional printing – company leaders will need to lead cultural change and find fresh ways of making business faster, easier and less expensive for its customers if the firm is to thrive in this highly competitive market.

Why are agility and resilience so elusive?

Many barriers to change-ability can be found in the 'tangible' aspects of organization. Many organizations have evolved their current operating models over a period of time and have arrived at a way of organizing that is often highly complex, with fragmented legacy systems, duplicated business processes and sub-optimal use of IT. Thus they may struggle to make sense of the volumes of information at their disposal and poor data management is a common problem. Evidence of misaligned systems is everywhere. Conflicting departmental priorities and goals, complex decision-making processes and silo-based information can slow down the organization's ability to pursue market opportunities, reduce its ability to mobilize resources and increase operating costs.

For instance, the largest ever study into the culture and behaviour in the UK National Health Service (Universities of Lancaster and Aberdeen, September, 2013) researchers found that unclear goals, excessive box ticking, regulation and poor organizational and information systems can cause staff to waste valuable time hunting for information, struggling to deliver care effectively, disempowered from initiating improvement and lacking valid insights into the quality of the care they provide.

However, the main barriers to agility are directly linked to people management practices and the 'intangible' aspects of organization – in people's mindsets, behaviours and culture, and also in the nature and state of the employment relationship between employers and workforces. HR practitioners ought therefore to play a major role in unblocking these people and culture challenges to equip their organizations to survive and thrive in fast-changing times.

Leadership approaches

In particular, the style of leadership and its alignment with strategy, the degree to which leadership is trusted, the robustness and speed of decision making, and the clarity of communication significantly influence how agile and resilient organizations can be. Given the level of business complexity, together with the need to respond quickly to change, the effectiveness of conventional top-down leadership approaches is increasingly being called into question. Many large organizations are caught in a vicious bind. Often headed by very risk-averse CEOs they typically work to very short-term time horizons, referred to as 'quarterly capitalism'. In contexts of increased regulation and scrutiny many organizations develop risk-averse cultures, making them reactive rather than proactive. Fear of unintended consequences can lead to stagnation and stifle innovation.

Ironically, previously market-leading businesses often prove to be the least resilient under pressure since if executives come to believe their own successful brand rhetoric they may ignore what lies round the corner,

under estimate the strength of new competition or the potential of new technology applications to change consumer tastes. Similarly, even with a clear strategy, there is often a large gap between an organization's strategic intent and its implementation. All of this is putting pressure on leaders and boards to find new ways of running business in contexts where there are no easy answers and where recipes of success from the past may not be helpful.

Consequences of agility for people

To be resilient organizations must be able to harness employees' ability and willingness to adapt and do what is necessary to help the organization survive and thrive. Yet the common pursuit of organizational agility through cutting core operating costs and embracing flexible workforce models often undermines employee engagement and leads to increased workloads, outsourcing, redundancy, short-term contracts and reduced protection for employees. Thus staff end up bearing the brunt of agility in terms of lost jobs, security and satisfaction. Moreover the typically wide disparities between executive rewards and those of the remaining workforce undermine a sense of common purpose and make a mockery of the message 'we're all in this together'.

When the employment relationship between an employer and its workforce becomes heavily unbalanced in terms of relative risk and return, it tends to become more transactional and low trust in character. And even when jobs are not at risk, demands for ongoing change may cause some staff to progressively disengage and to passively resist anything which challenges their work world. In such circumstances, speed, innovation and willingness to 'go the extra mile' become empty aspirations.

Yet demands for a new relationship approach are increasing. Talent shortages, changing workforce demographics and the need to respond to employee expectations will increase calls for new ways of managing and leading. In such circumstances attempting to increase agility simply by tinkering with the more instrumental aspects of organization – while ignoring their potential impact on people and culture – is like rearranging the deckchairs on the Titanic.

Unpacking organizational agility and resilience

Before looking at how organizational agility can be built, let us look at what agility involves in a little more detail. Rather like debates around whether an organization *is* a culture or *has* a culture, viewing through the lens of complex adaptive systems I would argue that agility and resilience are both part of an organization's DNA and can also be increased by adopting certain practices, routines and behaviours which unblock rigidity and release

energy. In this section I will summarize aspects of agility and resilience reflected in my Resiliently Agile model (Holbeche, 2015). These fall into the broad categories of strategizing, implementing, linking, people and culture.

Strategizing

Agile organizations focus on their core, where they are the most differentiated, and remain strongly in touch with constantly changing customer needs. Focusing on the core and a customer-centric approach provides parameters for innovation, helps create value and ensures flexibility. Strategizing may require mindset shifts away from relying on conventional linear thinking about strategy towards developing greater ease working with paradox and trusting to trust instinct. The focus should be on bringing the outside in, using scenarios to look beyond the organization or even industry to instil processes of strategic anticipation and promote the identification, testing and exploitation of emerging opportunities.

Having decision making exclusively concentrated at the centre makes little sense in today's fast-moving times. In strategizing the 'implementation gap' is narrowed because devising and executing the best strategy it is the responsibility of empowered, cross-functional teams. Shifting to a strategizing approach requires top team commitment to agility. So rather than viewing strategy making as an annual business-planning ritual, leaders need to involve others in strategy, turning it into the ongoing process of strategizing. It's important to bring together the right parties from the outset, including experts from around the business, communicating strategic intent and encouraging internal dialogue. Generation Y in particular expect to be involved. They have grown up in an era of high connectivity and interchange across networks. They want to be informed and to have voice.

Implementing

Implementing involves translating strategic intent into practice through a target operating model and making the changes necessary for the organization to succeed. In agile organizations the corporate structure, channels, processes, systems, organization and data are simplified, standardized and aligned to deliver the strategy and enable the organization to respond quickly, efficiently and effectively to market changes.

The ability to access the right information at the right time is crucial. The effective integration and automation of fundamental knowledge-sharing processes should help people improve their use of critical data to problem solve, make good decisions, convert information into insight and produce superior innovation. The leaders' role is sense making, arming decision makers and employees with the tools to find, filter and focus the information they need. Top management must allocate resources and strike an effective balance between risk taking and risk containment to ensure ongoing innovation, but in the context of prudent risk minimization.

Leading organizations have flatter management structures with cross-functional and self-organizing teams, and clear delegated decision-making authority at all levels. Such teams bring together people with different forms of functional or subject matter expertise, each contributing their expertise as needed to deliver shared goals for which they are, as a group, accountable. Unlike in more traditional, hierarchical organization structures leadership of a project shifts according to requirement and skill. For functional specialists in HR, IT or Internal Commus this means that interactions with business partners at local level must be tightly managed and limited since the larger corporate goal counts for more.

Agile organization structures feature adaptable supply chains, strong and robust operations and processes, with process improvement and team working as embedded norms. Lean tools and Agile methodologies such as agile project management are embraced. These treat the high-level objective as constant while allowing strategy and execution to evolve as needs shift. In contrast to conventional project management that follows a rigid waterfall-like design and production process towards a pre-defined goal, an agile workflow is a flexible process that breaks projects into manageable chunks or 'sprints' which add up to 'iterations'. Throughout there is review and client feedback allowing for adaptation, refinement, and learning to achieve desired outcomes.

All organizations have to manage costs. The challenge is to also remain focused on product innovation and quality improvement. In agile organizations working practices are geared to both short-term excellence and medium-term innovation so routines of experimentation, testing, refining and learning are the norm. High-performance work practices are embraced – roles offer a high degree of autonomy, there is a philosophy of empowerment and outcome-based indicators of achievement.

Most people want to do a good job and HR can build simple and effective performance processes which reflect this belief. HR should work with line managers to create high-performance work climates and manageable workloads. Role design can have an important mitigating effect against heavy work demands if roles and accountabilities are stretching and well crafted, have clear line of sight to organizational purpose and create room for discretion and autonomy. Let staff figure out the 'how' of objectives; involve people in improving the day job – ask all staff about how the organization can innovate and improve customer relations.

Linking

As never before, business success requires a global presence. That means organizations must communicate across cultures, continents and time zones to meet the demands of global customers who want just-in-time delivery and 24-hour customer service. Thanks to a vast and sophisticated communication network, business, projects, tasks and jobs are being transferred to where knowledge is to be found in different locations. Globally distributed development, production, sales, logistics and management functions are now commonplace. The global workforce must be able to operate as a single,

seamless team to service customers and maximize revenue streams. So managers and HR must source, connect with and coordinate a multi-cultural global workforce, often virtually.

In an era of open source and collaborative networks, agile organizations are dynamically connected via partner relationships including outsourced suppliers which can act as sensors for relevant emergent changes in the environment and potentially as co-builders of new markets. Collaborating across organizational boundaries can be challenging for staff and rife with ambiguity. HR can play an important role in equipping people with the teaming skills and approaches they need to be effective. HR can also help spread the learning from alliance working by mainstreaming these more sophisticated relationship skills within development programmes for the wider organization.

Flexible work location and hours and a flexible work environment are conditions that support collaboration and high-trust working relation-ships (CIPD, 2008). Alongside developing flexible working options, HR may need to train managers and teams who work virtually in outcome-based management, effective communication and other remote working protocols. For people working in global teams, team building and cultural awareness training may be useful.

People

Agile, resilient organizations need flexible, multi-skilled and competent staff who are engaged and productive, willing and able to adapt to con-tinuous change. People processes must therefore be agile too. In the face of growing talent shortages in key areas and the fast-evolving nature of organizational forms, strategic workforce planning is needed to allow busi-nesses to establish an optimal workforce and provide the benefits of a greater match between the people, the demand for services and increased productivity. The workforce mix may need to change over time and change-ability can be accelerated by bringing in, motivating and developing employees with the skills, attitudes and behaviours required to operate effectively in a highly uncertain, unstructured environment. Some people may need support in adjusting effectively to new circumstances; all should continue to develop their skills.

There must therefore be a systematic strategy for people selection, develop-ment and support to improve talent attraction and retention. This strategy will need to take account of changing workforce expectations, for instance individuals increasingly preferring to hold multiple jobs over the course of a career, some of which are lateral rather than upwards promotions. This means that strategies for talent management and succession planning must be co-created with people to ensure that both employer and employee needs are met.

And of course even with the 'right' workforce an organization cannot be agile if its employees are not 'engaged'. We shall consider in the next chapter how contexts can be built that are conducive to employee engagement.

A change-able, innovative culture

Viewing organizations as complex adaptive systems, the notion of a change-able innovative culture describes the enabling conditions for creative adaptability. As in learning organizations, these include collaborative ways of working and a broad-based, systematic approach to continually generating and sharing insights and new ideas, including using internal and external networks. In what Kevin Kelly (1999) calls 'chunking' the interdependent parts of organization share control and act locally in parallel since in a distributed network a central command structure slows things down.

Generative relationships are crucial, leadership is not just top down but dispersed; there is a genuine sense of community, with many people at all levels taking personal responsibility for proactively driving things forward. Networks of empowered and connected employees typically self-organize into communities of practice for learning and mentoring. Instead of planning, then acting, here people act-learn-plan. They lead and organize teams, experiment, commit to action and do what needs to be done. It's about building on what emerges and grows.

To create such a culture, leadership in innovation is needed which is about fostering a superior customer experience and turning knowledge into value. Senior leaders need to actively champion the direction of travel, provide focus and inject pace, setting priorities and targets that cannot be reached through 'business as usual'. The idea here is that employees feel challenged to innovate, drive change and to be accountable for outcomes, not just outputs. Roles should allow scope for initiative and achievement so that individuals can experience meaning, value their work, feel recognized and valued for what they contribute. The leader's task becomes one of sense making, improvising, learning, noticing emergent direction and building on what works.

Trust and purpose

These organizational cultures are underpinned by a strong vision and values and a purpose focused on customers and society tends to drive improvements. People have roles in which they can grow and have clear line of sight to how their job delivers the purpose. As a result, short-term actions are informed by what is needed longer term. For instance an NHS study advocates that organizations should 'put the patient at the centre of all they do, get smart intelligence, focus on improving organizational systems, and nurture caring cultures by ensuring that staff feel valued, respected, engaged and supported' (Point of Care Foundation). It's about leaders 'unblocking' the organization, removing the bureaucracy and other barriers which clutter the sight line to purpose.

And while consistent 'no surprises' execution is theoretically ideal, it is how the organization deals with the consequences of past decisions that

will determine whether or not people are willing to risk experimenting (and potentially failing). So a blame culture kills innovation while a learning culture enables it. Of course innovation can emerge, but it can also be designed in. Google's famous rules encourage employees to spend 20 per cent of their time on innovation projects, whether or not these are aligned to Google's current business plan. Innovation can be part of everyone's work routine if they incorporate it into accomplishing their team's goals.

Values-based leadership

As discussed in the last chapter, what leaders pay attention to has a major impact on culture. Therefore leadership becomes part of the problem, or part of the solution. If people don't trust their leaders they are unlikely to be willing to transform their own behaviours and work practices or to go the extra mile for the organization. Leaders who are best able to build trust embrace the notion of values-based leadership ie ensuring that management behaviour is consistent with the organization's core values.

Value-based leaders rebuild trust and create a more resilient employment relationship with employees by ensuring that every aspect of organization, especially their own behaviour, is sending staff messages that are consistent with the values. Any gaps between rhetoric and reality must be closed – such as saying 'we are customer focused' yet in reality incentivizing sales and paying less attention to service, care or quality or ensuring that their own compensation package is generous while keeping rewards for the workforce under tight restraint.

Leaders also need to gain an understanding (from organization development and design) of how they influence cultures. As culture builders leaders need to develop self-awareness, reflection and effective communication skills for promoting constructive dialogue. They need to be willing to share power and involve employees in decision making, so communications must be two way with consistent messaging and genuine involvement of staff and of customers in co-creating the 'how' if not the 'what' and 'why' of strategy. Indeed, many of the skills associated with agility have long been identified with psychological and change-management studies.

What sets outstanding leaders apart, according to the Work Foundation (Tamkin *et al*, 2010), is that they think systemically and act long term, bring meaning to life, apply the spirit not the letter of the law, grow people through performance, are self-aware and authentic to leadership first, put their own needs second. They understand that talk is work; they give time and space to others and put 'we' before 'me'. When there is authentic leadership, a genuine belief in the value of helping people to help themselves and great partnering between executives, customers, staff and OD/HR to deliver the big vision, any organization can become more agile.

How can HR help build agility and resilience?

HR has many ways to help develop organizational agility and resilience. Here are some of key contributions HR should be well placed to make:

Accelerate the pace of strategic renewal

Workforce planning can help organizations get to grips with the people implications of their changing business contexts and models. The aim is not to create an exact picture of the future workforce but instead to enable the organization to build its capability and capacity for improvement, innovation, leadership, spread, scale-up and sustainability over time. Technology is vital for getting to grips with the data you gather, and already have, in order to better understand your current, and likely future talent needs and recruitment, retention and deployment challenges.

CASE STUDY The Branch of the Future at Nationwide

I am grateful to Craig Pocock, Head of HR, Group Retail at Nationwide for the following case study.

About Nationwide

Nationwide – the world's largest mutual financial institution – enjoys a strong position as the UK's most trusted High Street financial services provider. It has been ranked number one for customer service satisfaction amongst its high street peers for three consecutive years and offers a range of market-leading products The financial services sector is highly regulated, and, like its competitors, Nationwide must account to regulators for how it treats its customers and employees; it has a strong and positive track record in both respects. Unlike some of the clearing banks Nationwide has emerged from the financial crisis and recession with its reputation relatively unscathed and indeed, enhanced.

As a mutual, Nationwide is owned by its members (customers) rather than shareholders so safeguarding members' financial interests is at its heart. The vision is to become the first-choice financial services provider. It serves a diverse demographic member base with a range of financial products designed to meet the needs of members of different ages and circumstances. Financial transactions

are traditionally carried out face to face in branches, of which there are 700 throughout the UK.

Drivers for change

The retail banking environment is changing fast in a way that threatens to disrupt this mode of operating. The UK's low interest rate of recent years means smaller margins and there is increased competition from the big banks who, forced by the Regulator to separate their investment from their retail banking arms, now want to take nationwide's space in the market.

Moreover, many customers are changing the way they choose to bank, with more people opting to interact digitally using devices such as smartphones. Anticipating how these trends might pan out, Nationwide recognized that it should grow its digital share of the market. Nevertheless Nationwide remains committed to providing face-to-face services at branches across the UK.

Nationwide carried out research to understand changing customer behaviours and the changing landscape for physical distribution including the importance of maintaining a high street presence. The research concluded that although many people may no longer need to go to branches in person, nevertheless customers still wanted to see Nationwide on the high street. This confirms a somewhat counter-intuitive trend – even Amazon is apparently contemplating having a high street presence. The research also confirmed what members wanted from their branches; carrying out the basic financial transactions with staff sitting behind counters was not one of these requirements.

The Branch of the Future concept

So the 'Branch of the Future' project was born, which represents a strategic reinvigoration of the Nationwide brand. The idea is to maintain a branch presence throughout the UK but to concentrate the provision of the complete service into branches large enough to provide it and gradually and sensitively move more of the sales and servicing to digital over the next five years. As financial transactions are increasingly automated, counters will be eliminated. Several branches throughout the UK are trialling the new approach.

The project also addresses the issue of how to recreate Nationwide's renowned customer service in a digital way. Within branches, staff will maintain the face-to-face connection by offering members a 'help or advice' service and access to specialist services will be extended via digital. For instance in smaller branches mortgage advisers are often only available on certain days, so members have previously had to fit in with staff availability. Nationwide NOW is a branch-based service using high definition video to connect customers in participating branches

across the country to UK-based mortgage, banking and financial planning consultants for expert advice.

Learning from these trials has crystallized into a robust plan of action that is supported by the Board and Executive Committee. The Nationwide Board wants to make sure that the people response is right so the plan addresses the capabilities, culture, talent, resourcing, reward and recognition and leadership needed to take the organization forward. There is strong governance around the emerging organization design to ensure that investments in people (as with technology) are done in the right way. HR is playing a significant role in shaping and implementing the plan and skilled HR project managers are helping drive the change implementation forward.

HR's contribution

For HR it is critical that the change journey works as well for staff as for members since staff are the face of Nationwide. This has meant painting the journey ahead, creating and communicating an authentic vision in an inspiring way. It has also meant consulting and negotiating with the trade union, taking time setting out plans so that staff know what's happening and can buy in to the changes.

Adjusting to these new ways of working may prove challenging for some staff. Nowadays customers expect to receive service 24/7 so staff who are used to working 'nine to five' may need to work different hours. The challenge is to get the service right for a given area and its different demographics without disenfranchising employees. Although some staff may be unable to make the skills transition required of them, there is a real commitment to retraining staff and in the trial branches there have been hardly any redundancies. HR has invested in developing front-line leaders so that they can continue to lead change and raise performance.

Modelling the way ahead

Craig Pocock recognizes that HR must model the way ahead so 'HR has a duty to become digital as well'. HR policies are being reviewed and simplified to keep up with the changing demands of customers and are now available to read on the internet. More HR services have been automated and are now available digitally, by telephone and face to face.

Strategic manpower planning has been crucial to knowing the steps to take towards the desired end state so that the transition can be smooth with the minimum of redundancies. This has involved looking into the future, identifying future capabilities, where employees may come from and what they may be looking for. While many existing employees have long service, today's employment

patterns look different. So Nationwide is committed to supporting current employees while also transforming the employment proposition into something that will help it stand out from the competition.

Nationwide models mutuality in its employment practices with employees. It has an honourable record of continuing to invest in its people during the recession. Ironically this makes Nationwide staff prime targets for 'poaching' by competitors so Nationwide has a robust resourcing strategy in place. With respect to recruitment there are fair and transparent assessment processes so that the 'right' people are employed in the first place, as we shall discuss later in this chapter. 'Geo-fences' are used to target recruitment opportunities to certain people. Nationwide's employee value proposition offers clear career paths and development opportunities and a dedicated redeployment team helps people have the opportunity to experience other roles within the organization.

As this case study illustrates HR can play a key role in helping people make transitions, preparing them through training for new roles. They can work with line managers on role design to ensure that people have interesting, stretching and fulfilling roles.

With its proactive and strategic response to changes in the business landscape, and by developing new member propositions in a timely way, Nationwide should be well placed to maintain and grow sustainable business streams in years ahead. By being fair to employees and demonstrating that a win-win approach is possible even in today's fast-moving and somewhat ruthless times, Nationwide deserves to stand out from its competition. Thus Nationwide's members, employees and society at large should reap the benefits.

Attract, engage and retain talent

We know that in today's more knowledge- or service-based economies *people* are the source of production. It's not enough to have flexible business models, structures and processes. People – their skills, behaviours and mindsets – must be agile too. There are global shortfalls of available specialist talent in industries as diverse as oil and gas, construction, pharmaceuticals, defence and high technology, with even greater shortages predicted thanks to the growing impact of demographic trends. In such industries the need to source scarce talent is high up amongst board priorities and the links between talent management, employee engagement, leadership, good governance and business success are inextricable. Thanks to these global talent shortages a new 'War for Talent' is underway.

Attracting rare talent has therefore become a key priority for many HR teams who will increasingly also be required to help source and nurture agile teams as well as develop agile managers/team leaders. Employees increasingly want the same kind of individualized attention that customers receive and skilled workers can and do exercise their options if they are not happy with their lot. Highly skilled employees may increasingly be able to negotiate what Denise Rousseau (2005) calls '*i*-deals', or idiosyncratic deals which are tailored to them.

'Employer branding' approaches are commonly used to attract the kinds of recruits the organization needs. As with other forms of branding, such messaging implies a promise – about the values of the company, the kinds of opportunities an employee might have and about what it feels like to work for the company. If the lived reality of the brand is different from the promise, the customer-employee goes elsewhere. HR therefore needs to ensure that what is promised gets delivered. Since leaders and managers deliver the daily reality of the employer brand, developing engaging managers and leaders becomes a key priority for HR.

These days growing numbers of employers are using big data analytics and other new methods to target potential recruits and help make the fraught process of sourcing and hiring talent more scientific. Yet the 2014 Employer Perspectives Survey by government skills experts the UK Commission for Employment and Skills (UKCES) shows that, despite the meteoric rise of social media, just 7 per cent of employers say they have used it to recruit new staff.

CASE STUDY Recruitment at Nationwide

Nationwide is a pioneer in this respect. Until recently its recruitment practices were fairly traditional and involved advertising on its careers site, posting vacancies on job boards or using recruitment agencies. The bank has fair and transparent assessment processes so aims to ensure that the 'right' people are employed in the first place. However in today's more connected age, the resourcing team increasingly recognized that Nationwide was little known to its target skill populations in the digital generation and traditional practices were no longer reaching them. So a new cost-effective and innovative approach was needed.

This began with research, listening closely to a wide range of people with different backgrounds, skills and capabilities, looking at emerging trends with respect to people's behaviour and perspectives on Nationwide's brand. Clearly candidates' expectations were starting to shift; lifestyle and balance appeared more important than salary. It was also clear that social media was a key means by which potential candidates now interact. Digital tools would therefore be part

of the solution and IT support was needed to help the recruitment team develop the career site to advantage and use social tools to get more candidates through the door.

Now there is an ongoing focus on ensuring the brand is enhanced via social media and other channels in imaginative ways that grab the attention of potential recruits. As potential candidates swipe barcodes on recruitment material relevant videos spring to life on their smart phones. Proactive approaches to increase the candidate pool include 'Geo-fences' that are used to target locations where the 'right' candidates might be and make them aware of possible recruitment opportunities. The resourcing strategy feeds into the people strategy which in turn feeds into the corporate plan. While Nationwide may not be able to compete with the wealthy big banks by offering inflated pay and rations it aims to be fair, in keeping with its mutual ethos. And it puts resource behind its employee value proposition by offering clear career paths and development opportunities and a dedicated redeployment team to help people move around the organization.

Build line manager capability

In a business environment where the only constant is change, successful organizations are likely to require new capabilities, not least change-ability. The real work of change rests squarely on the shoulders of managers, irrespective of level, because they manage both people and the business assets. So today's managers need to be sufficiently experienced and resilient to be able to withstand pressures – and also able to manage change fairly, judiciously and effectively.

As structures become more agile and teams become more self-managing, there will inevitably be a transition in the nature of line management roles and the skills required to do them. HR can accelerate this capability building by recruiting and developing new kinds of line manager, with relevant change management ability. These will be managers who can cope with ambiguity, are mentally tough and have good communication, engagement, trust-building and listening skills. They will make good use of data to be objective and to guide selection and other decisions. They will be able to understand and cope with the 'stress environment' they and employees have to work in, becoming 'more strategic' managers rather than just being 'technical/professional' managers.

Improve the quality of leadership

As discussed earlier, there must be strong commitment to organizational agility at the top with cohesive and coherent management teams modelling the way forward. Yet today's context shifts make great demands of top leaders

who must now be able to lead in complexity, build relationships and networks, develop culture, manage change, nurture talent and enable shared leadership. Shifting to a distributed leadership model requires senior leaders to be willing to make fundamental changes within their organizations. For many leaders this may mean stepping out of their comfort zones, developing new skills, opening their minds to new approaches to leadership and learning new techniques.

To develop agile leadership HR should adopt a systemic and integrated approach that takes account of what else needs to shift apart from leader attitudes. Long-standing practices may need to be revisited and the current values of leaders and managers put under the spotlight. For instance, what is rewarded within the organization? How are leaders selected? How can senior leaders get to grips with what it will take to align the whole system? System alignment work takes broad inclusion to get it right. What consequences are there for leaders who don't live up to the desired values? This journey will not be an easy one, and there will be many forces that will fight the change.

Particularly with respect to future leaders HR can help recruit and develop people who recognize the need for a new leadership model and have learning agility. Leadership development interventions should be designed to stimulate people's curiosity and confidence to start experimenting. Learning approaches should focus outside-in – exposing people to new thinking, experiences and insights. They should also be inside-out – with leaders finding sources of advice they can trust such as coaches, learning groups and mentors to encourage self-awareness and reflection.

Succession planning is adapting to meet these changing needs. Many organizations are moving towards integrating succession planning with broader talent management approaches. And although succession planning remains primarily focused on senior leadership and management roles it is increasingly used for selected 'critical' roles at a range of levels where the organization is vulnerable. There should be a mix and match approach to filling vacancies, blending the open job market with managed career moves, identifying and using external as well as internal successors as appropriate. In particular agile succession planning involves individuals in planning and delivering their own skill and career development.

Develop people

In the long run, when talent is scarce, developing people will prove much less costly than recruitment. Training employees and making them more effective and productive helps build organizational flexibility and resilience – which have a direct impact on the company's success and profitability. This is about taking a long-term view, helping people and organizations develop the capacity to improve and adapt to the changing needs of the business. Development may need to be about more than information transfer, or even skills or competency development – instead it probably

needs to be about shifting mental models and creating knowledge in a way that is team, partner or community-centred. Increasingly training and development aims to grow people's self-awareness and ability to thrive in more fluid work environments. The popular focus in recent years on emotional intelligence is being complemented by insights from neuroscience.

While holders of business-critical roles will still be given extra development support, the shift taking place is towards nurturing a broader spectrum of talent, finding talent in unexpected places, with exclusive and inclusive talent approaches existing side-by-side. So by offering real-time development for everyone, for instance via peer coaching and team learning, and investing in employees at junior levels, such as via apprenticeships or the chance to study for employer-based qualifications, employers send strong positive signals to employees about the company's priorities and about how it values them.

By forging creative collaborations with learning providers or other organizations keen to create shared learning opportunities for their workforce, HR can contain costs and increase the value of learning. In many organizations, course participants are selected based on their motivation to learn and managers' support in applying the learning. Policies to enable mobility, developing line managers as coach, providing tools for self-assessment, holistic succession planning and innovative career management are just some of the HR tools in the new 'War for Talent'.

Enable flexibility and knowledge sharing

In line with the changing career expectations, the norm of when and where people work is also changing. CIPD research (Zheltoukhova, 2014) suggests that people increasingly want the flexibility to change the start/finish time of the working day, decrease the number of hours worked, change the number of days worked and be able to vary their working patterns day to day. HR must ensure that flexibility benefits both the organization and its employees and that the careers of flexible workers do not stall.

In a context of disruptive innovation, organizational climates conducive to experimentation and learning are key to flexibility, yet many larger conventional hierarchies appear to reinforce the status quo and stifle innovation. HR can support the development of collaborative working by encouraging or facilitating knowledge networks and communities of practice that aid knowledge sharing and co-creation.

Working with OD, HR can help to resolve conflicts and improve human dynamics, facilitate cross-boundary team working, expose people to new ideas and opportunities both inside and outside the organization, help them capture, share and capitalize on their knowledge in ways which create a win-win for the organization and its employees. HR can make it easier for people to do difficult jobs by simplifying processes, reducing bureaucracy; enabling both compliance and innovation. HR can devise recognition and reward systems that reinforce innovation, teamwork and knowledge sharing.

HR modelling agility

As the global marketplace becomes ever complex, the HR function must change to meet it and become an active role model of agility. So HR may need to adopt a different stance and mindset – from service function to strategic cultural enabler – that will in turn lead to a different type of HR contribution.

The role of change agent may require HR to broaden its focus to become multi-skilled specialists or generalists who can collaborate with other internal experts and change when the need arises. To act as change agent HR should fully understand how the business operates and be aware of external and internal drivers for change that may impact on the business. Rather than waiting to be invited to participate in change initiatives, HR should adopt a proactive, anticipatory approach, using analytics to pinpoint issues and driving the business case for change and investment.

The role of change agent may also require a shift in the locus of HR's attention. Arguably since its inception the notion of business partnering has produced many 'local' business benefits since HR business partners have been able to identify and respond to executives' needs and wants effectively, even if these needs may not advance the organization as a whole. The challenge now is to use HR resources to greatest effect for the benefit of the business overall, focusing instead on delivering major corporate goals that ultimately benefit the end customer.

Simplify and standardize

A key area where HR can increase organizational agility is by removing complexity from the HR service itself. This means applying agile principles – such as customer-focused, simple and effective feedback, review and learning – and agile work practices like lean and agile project management disciplines to HR delivery.

So it's important to take a process view to understand how the HR service is currently delivered across the organization. HR should gather data from service users about how the processes are currently performed and generate baseline. Then current practice should be evaluated against leading-edge customer-focused practice to truly understand and challenge the cost of delivery, identifying where processes are duplicated or fragmented. This is about addressing key 'implementation gaps' – identifying underpinning issues, removing barriers using agile problem analysis and team working.

PWC (2012) advocates that functions such as HR should adopt the three 'S's: *simplify* – overly complex processes; *standardize* – processes that can reduce cost and improve the customer experience; *share* – spread new effective practice to benefit the whole organization. Simplifying processes such as performance management can produce real benefits. Adobe for instance has replaced formal performance appraisals with a more discursive

model that provides people with meaningful feedback and has freed up time and energy for business development. Developing a standard process model that everyone understands provides a framework for generating ideas and opportunities for improvement.

Delivering the desired benefits may mean changing the ways that customers interact with HR by, for example, introducing customer self service. HR services should be designed back from the needs of the end user and available 24/7. Given the trend towards mobile, HR must embrace technology as a means of speeding up response times, personalizing and improving the consistency of service quality. Improving HR processes may mean changing the way work moves between business units by, for example, introducing transactional shared services or business support models. It is important to understand the interdependencies across the transformation programme since these changes can impact the management structures, information systems and data that are needed to support the business.

Apply agile methodology

An effective implementation plan can be designed to ensure that the benefits are realized as early as possible. However, instead of linear planning approaches which assume change happens in a predictable way, it's important to adopt iterative planning to be more adaptable; flexing and learning as change takes place at any point during the change process. For instance, with respect to improving employee engagement, in a fluid context engagement levels may fluctuate so to make the greatest progress it is important to work on matters in which employees invest a high amount of emotional energy at a given time. It's a question of identifying quick wins and strategic business opportunities that can be prioritized to create a portfolio of improvements that can deliver in the short term and also provide medium- and long-term benefits.

Transformation is thus delivered as a series of change iterations rather than a single major change programme. Reaching milestones towards the vision allows progress to be celebrated, and also aspirations to expand. This provides the rationale for ongoing change which employees too can initiate and is the spur to innovation. Employees are up for the next challenge – after all, delivering an engaging purpose is a journey, not a destination.

Similarly, agile project disciplines – such as having retrospectives at the end of 'sprints' – can be applied to problems such as a bad hire so that real learning takes place and practice can be changed for next time. By involving leaders, managers and employees in these retrospectives HR is modelling openness to learning and creating a 'safe' environment for others to experiment without repercussions in order to create new ways forward.

Conclusion

An agile, resilient organization is becoming the template for organizational competitiveness and survival in the 21st century. Resilient organizations recognize that, since in an unpredictable context nothing is guaranteed, failing to anticipate will increase the chances of failure. With a change-able culture an organization becomes much better at spotting opportunities and speedily implementing strategy. As a result the organization becomes better able to innovate, serve market needs and capture opportunities faster, at less cost, with less stress and chaos. In addition, rather than dreading change, a change-able workforce will welcome change, seek it out, be prepared for it and find ways of adjusting themselves, contributing to the overall success of the organization. Employees are more likely to believe that the organization's leadership really knows what it is doing in leading the organization's change strategy.

HR's crucial contribution to building such change-able cultures requires an OD mindset to discover how to use HR levers systemically to build healthy and self-renewing cultures. HR's own transformation must be accelerated and line managers up-skilled so that you can focus on new responsibilities. Managers must be action oriented, focused on achieving results and also good at getting the best out of others. HR must help build line management capability – for people management, change management, stress management and conflict management. HR has a vital role to play in building effective leadership for the future, as well as providing challenge (and coaching) to today's senior managers if their behaviours fall out of step with company values. Employees too must be willing to use their initiative and make efforts to further the interests of the organization.

By taking the long-term view and focusing on the customer, on the workforce and on the culture, leaders can build adaptable, innovative organizations where people want to give of their best. In terms of results, what works for the business also works for its key stakeholders – customers and staff – and directly benefits the community. With assets like these, truly agile organizations will be able to pull ahead of their competitors, generate increased market share and sustainable advantage. In an unpredictable environment, this seems a pretty reasonable bet!

In the next chapter we shall look at an essential ingredient of a resiliently agile culture – employee engagement. We shall consider how a context for engagement can be built and the importance of developing the more mutual employment relationship that I believe underpins sustainable employee engagement.

Building the context for employee engagement

With the prospect of economic recovery in view, interest in employee engagement is on the increase. This suggests that engagement is increasingly recognized as key to business prosperity and sustainable change. In today's knowledge- and service-intensive economies, people are the main source of innovation, production and service excellence. High-performance theory places employee engagement, or 'the intellectual and emotional attachment that an employee has for his or her work' (Heger, 2007) at the heart of performance, especially among knowledge workers.

Of course every organization wants committed and enthusiastic people working for it and employee engagement is **not** a management fad. Considerable evidence has been amassed showing that companies with engaged employees outperform their peers in terms of growth and profitability. Yet various surveys suggest there is a serious shortfall in levels of motivation in UK workplaces with typically only a minority of workers positively engaged at work at a given time. Lack of engagement could be seen as putting a brake on productivity costing the UK economy by as much as £25.8bn (US$42.6bn) per year (engageforsuccess, 2015). Previous estimates for the US economy have produced correspondingly higher figures.

As we have discussed, organizations need to become 'change-able' ie agile, flexible, capable of sustainable effectiveness in scenarios of ongoing change. Ironically the drive for agility, together with dwindling resources and cuts, can undermine both employee resilience and engagement since today's 'more for less' environment puts employees under ongoing pressure, potentially resulting in burnout and sagging morale. So employee engagement is at significant risk.

So concerned was the UK Government in 2009 that it backed a taskforce created to examine the assumed links between employee engagement,

performance and productivity. The resulting report – *Engaging for Success*, otherwise referred to as the 'Macleod Report' (MacLeod and Clarke, 2009) – concluded that the business case for employee engagement is overwhelming and subsequent research continues to confirm this to be the case.

How then can organizations both increase organizational agility and also maintain positive relations with their workforces? How can organizations get the best out of their people? These questions are not new, but today many employers are seeking to find answers by building organizational contexts conducive to employee engagement. This is what we shall address in this chapter:

1 What is employee engagement?

2 Engagement and the employment relationship.

3 The business case for employee engagement.

4 Whose job is it to manage employee engagement?

5 What motivates people to want to do a good job?

6 What should employers do to create the context for engagement?

7 Maintaining engagement in times of change.

In particular we shall look at how HR can help build a positive and mutually responsible employment relationship between employers and employees.

What is employee engagement?

Engagement is more than simply satisfaction, or even commitment. Producing a satisfied and committed workforce is a worthy aim but on its own it is not enough. Satisfied employees may be happy but make little contribution to the organization; committed employees may be focusing on the wrong objectives. While definitions vary, most agree that employee engagement is a vital driver of improvement and higher performance as this definition by the Institute of Employment Studies (IES) suggests:

> (Engagement is)... A positive attitude held by the employee toward the organization and its values. An engaged employee is aware of business context, and works with colleagues to improve performance within the job for the benefit of the organization (Robinson *et al*, 2004).

The state of employee engagement is generally characterized by what Csikszentmihalyi (1990) describes as 'flow' – where people are so pleasurably immersed in their work that they freely release their 'discretionary effort'. This feeling of commitment, passion and energy translates into high levels of persistence with even the most difficult tasks, leading people to exceed expectations and take the initiative. Surveys also show that engaged employees see their work as more meaningful and fulfilling. Engaged employees are more productive, more service-oriented, less wasteful, more

inclined to come up with good ideas, take the initiative and generally do more to help organizations achieve their goals than people who are disengaged. Moreover research shows that engaged employees tend to be more resilient too.

However at the other end of the engagement spectrum is burnout (Maslach *et al*, 2001). Some employees may be so engaged (and also perhaps driven, ambitious, or insecure) that they overwork for extended periods and end up damaging their health. Employers have a duty of care to prevent this from happening and employee wellbeing is a critical element of any engagement strategy. So employee engagement is *not* a synonym for work intensity: on the contrary, high engagement levels are found to be associated with flexible working patterns.

Engagement and the employment relationship

The organization provides the context for employee engagement. Levels of engagement tend to reflect the state of the employment relationship between individuals and employers at a point in time. IES argues that a healthy 'psychological contract' (ie the unwritten, mutual expectations between the employee and employer that are underpinned by trust) must exist before engagement is possible. Perceptions of fairness are the basis of trust. If what employees and employers expect from each other is matched by what they offer each other, a positive psychological contract is thought to exist, in the minds of employees at least! When this occurs, employees are likely to be actively engaged with the organization and '... evidence suggests that organizations that treat their employees with fairness, integrity and sensitivity are more likely to find that those employees respond with increased commitment and productivity' (CIPD, 2013).

The notion of employee engagement also comes nearer than any other contemporary management philosophy to the concept of 'pluralism' which underpinned much academic thinking about industrial relations. In other words, employee engagement focuses on the employment relationship as being at the heart of sustainable high performance, and recognizes that both employer *and employee* must make a genuine contribution. That level of performance cannot be achieved by a top-down (or 'unitarist') style of management (Emmott, 2009).

For HR the challenge is to improve the quality of the employment relationship and 'work to develop and nurture engagement, which requires a two-way relationship between employer and employee' (Robinson *et al*, 2004) by '... creating opportunities for employees to connect with their colleagues, managers and wider organization. It is also about creating an environment where employees are motivated to want to connect with their work and really care about doing a good job... It is a concept that places flexibility, change and continuous improvement at the heart of what it means to be an employee and an employer in a twenty-first-century workplace' (Gatenby *et al*, 2009).

The business case for employee engagement

CIPD research (Alfes *et al*, 2010) shows that engaged employees perform better than others, are more likely to recommend their organization to others, take less sick leave and are less likely to quit. They also experience increased job satisfaction and more positive attitudes and emotions towards their work. This suggests that enhanced levels of engagement benefit both individuals and employers. Businesses as diverse as Campbell's Soup, Unilever, Marriott Hotels, AstraZeneca and HSBC have found that employee engagement has a significantly positive impact on their business results.

Evidence for the impact of employee engagement on business performance also comes from many consultancy studies. For example:

- Research by the Corporate Leadership Council (2004) found that engagement accounts for 40 per cent of observed performance improvements, while highly committed employees try 57 per cent harder, perform 80 per cent better and are 87 per cent less likely to leave than their disengaged colleagues.

- A survey conducted by Towers Watson (2008) of over 85,000 employees working for large and midsize organizations in 16 different countries found that companies with high employee engagement levels also experienced a higher operating margin (up to 19 per cent), net profit margin, revenue growth and earnings per share (up to 28 per cent) than companies with low employee engagement.

- A Watson Wyatt study of 115 companies asserts that a company with highly engaged employees typically achieves a financial performance four times greater than a company with poor employee attitudes.

The main drivers of employee engagement

With respect to engagement, there are two types of employee commitment – emotional and rational commitment – with emotional commitment being four times more powerful than rational commitment in driving employee effort. Employees stay with their organizations when they believe it is in their self-interest to do so (rational commitment). But they exert discretionary effort when they believe in the value of their job, their team and their organization (emotional commitment).

Some of the common elements of the many surveys of employee engagement fall into the following categories:

- Social – is this an organization where I feel involved, part of a good team; is my organization serving the community?
- Intellectual – am I able to grow; is my job stretching and interesting; do I know what's happening; do my opinions count?
- Emotional – do I care about the organization and feel I belong; am I valued? (Khan, 1990)

Underpinning these elements are the key principles of voice (am I listened to, am I told what is going on?) and equity (am I treated fairly?) The right kind of leadership and followership are needed to create an adult-adult reciprocal relationship based on mutual needs and benefits.

The MacLeod report found that 'engaging managers' and 'engaging leadership' are pivotal to creating contexts conducive to engagement, yet in his 2009 report about the state of employee engagement in the UK David MacLeod found strong evidence of an 'engagement deficit' amongst many UK senior executives. An earlier large survey by DDI (Pomeroy, 2006) found that only 61 per cent of global business leaders feel they have the skills to 'bring out the best in people'. This may be because some leaders and managers are not aware of employee engagement or its importance. Some leaders may be concerned that addressing people-related issues risks being too complex, or that the results may take too long to materialize. In other cases leaders understand its importance but appear ill-equipped to implement engagement strategies: 'The issue seems to lie in their unwillingness to talk the talk and truly relinquish command and control styles of leadership in favour of a relationship based on mutuality' (Accor, 2009 in MacLeod Report).

The declining levels of employee engagement appear to reflect a weakening of trust, an essential precondition to engagement. Now people are inclined to distrust first rather than trust and consequently are less willing to give their discretionary effort.

Just some of the many barriers to engagement and trust include (CIPD, 2009):

- reactive decision making that does not pick up problems before it is too late;
- inconsistent management style based on the attitudes of individual managers that leads to perceptions of unfairness;
- lack of fluidity in communications and knowledge sharing due to rigid communication channels or cultural norms;
- poor work-life balance due to a 'long hours' culture;
- negative perceptions about lack of senior management visibility and poor-quality downward communication.

If the employment relationship feels one sided to employees, in these days of talent shortages and self-managed portable careers, employers with

poor engagement records risk losing key players and face a protracted battle to attract and retain new talent. Similarly staff who remain may become disengaged and unwilling to invest the best of themselves on behalf of the organization, which could be the worst of all worlds.

Whose job is it to manage employee engagement?

HR departments are usually expected to take a lead on getting to grips with employee engagement but improving it is a shared endeavour. Employee engagement is very much an outcome of good people management. Top management must take a lead in creating the right culture and the influence of line managers on people's perceptions of their work is profound. It is often remarked that people join organizations but leave individual managers. Line managers must ensure that people have opportunities to learn and grow. HR professionals can help raise engagement levels by supporting line managers to raise their game.

Strategies aimed at developing an engaged workforce should build on good people management and development policies and be aligned with those of the wider business. These policies need the active support of line managers and it should go without saying that, for any major organizational initiative to succeed, top management buy-in is crucial. When engagement is used by organizations as an integral part of their business strategy, it becomes much more of a two-way process in which employees themselves are active agents. Engaged employees are more likely than their disengaged colleagues to act as organizational advocates and can play a powerful role in promoting their organization as an employer of choice.

There are many ways in which HR departments can help build a context of engagement but tackling engagement issues effectively requires teamwork across functional boundaries. In organizations with a strategic perspective on engagement HR functions are learning how to manage and market engagement better. Increasingly internal/employee communications practitioners are taking the lead on employee engagement, working closely with HR, as I have observed and Balain and Sparrow (2009) note. Research into the psychological contract that underlines the importance of employees feeling they can trust the employer, that they are treated fairly and have voice, has fed into current thinking about the 'employer brand', which is where the marketing, internal communications and HR functions meet.

So in developing the employer brand HR needs to learn from existing research on consumer behaviour and communication (eg how to engage external customers with your brand, develop corporate values, or product and service value proposition) and translate the focus towards knowing how to engage the employee as an internal consumer by creating enticing employee value propositions (EVP) that form the employer brand. These EVPs may need to be tailored to different workforce segments. Robust and authentic EVPs shape positive psychological contract between employer and employees and help to recruit and retain employees.

Organizations should review their communications and particularly their arrangements for listening to employee opinions. These will generally include designing and carrying out employee surveys to measure attitudes, testing the findings with focus groups, establishing areas requiring attention and advising senior managers on their significance. There is widespread agreement that surveys should measure a number of factors including employee commitment, organizational citizenship, satisfaction, attitudes to management, work-life balance and intention to leave. But surveys need to be followed up by effective action to address issues identified or they will have a negative impact on attitudes, as well as on the rate of response to subsequent surveys.

What motivates people to want to do a good job?

While surveys can help managers gain some insight into what motivates their employees, it is clear that with changing workforce demographics and dynamics, a more educated workforce and different motivators by generational group, there is no 'one size fits all' when it comes to attracting, engaging and retaining people.

The key question is what exactly is it you need your workforce to engage with? And what do employees want in return? In researching for our book *Engaged: Unleashing your organization's potential through employee engagement* (Holbeche and Matthews, 2012) my co-author Geoffrey Matthews and I examined a wide variety of studies concerning what employees appear to want and need from work. While acknowledging the risk of generalization, we categorized these as desires for *connection, support, voice* and *scope*:

- **Connection**
 Most employees want job security, strong workplace relationships and to work for organizations whose purposes they can embrace – we found this to be closely associated with motivation, commitment and ultimately the energy and effort workers are prepared to put in. IES too found that engaged employees identify with their organization and its values, believe in its products and services, show a commitment to the organization and a desire for business appreciation ie embrace what the organization stands for and also understand the context in which the organization operates.

- **Support**
 Employees want to be valued for their contribution and to be dealt with in a fair and consistent manner. While pay remains important, other forms of recognition and reward – such as flexibility – are also important.

- **Voice**
 Employees want to be able to influence matters which affect their working lives and therefore need to be informed and able to participate in the direction of the organization.

- **Scope**
 They also want opportunities for growth and high-quality work that offers the chance for meaning, stretch, control and task discretion.

What does this look like in practice?

We looked at management practice in organizations where employee engagement levels are high despite the challenging context. Here are some examples of the useful practice we found.

1. Creating connection

Leadership behaviour is pivotal to people feeling connected. Engaging leaders are strategic, look beyond the current challenges, anticipate the big business issues and plot a way through to growth taking short-term decisions with the longer term in mind. They reshape the work environment and culture to enhance performance and match their unique basis of competitive advantage.

Engaging leaders are also people focused. They actively lead culture change, working to create shared purpose and a positive sense of the future: something to aim for that people can connect with. MacLeod points out that engaging leaders provide a clear strategic narrative about where the organization is going and why, in a way that gives employees information and insight for their own job. They set a clear direction and priorities so that employees know what is required and feel empowered to deliver the right outputs without the need for micro-management.

MacLeod also proposes that a key driver of engagement is *'Organization lives the values'* – 'a belief among employees that the organization lives the values, and that espoused behavioural norms are adhered to, resulting in trust and a sense of integrity'. In organizations that do this well values and behaviours are aligned; any gap between these creates distrust and cynicism. Vision and values that are truly lived provide parameters for people's actions so engaging leaders strive to role model the values, communicate consistently and demonstrate personal authenticity. They use and act on 360-degree and other feedback to show commitment. They nurture leadership at every level. In such work environments there is a strong, positive sense of community and teamwork. People generally enjoy a degree of job security since the organization's stance is to value people for what they contribute rather than 'hire and fire'.

2. Supporting people

Line managers in particular shoulder the day-to-day challenge of supporting people and maintaining or boosting employee morale, even though they

may themselves be under pressure from every angle, juggling both business as usual and managing change. In engaging work contexts line managers feel supported by top management and are developed as leaders, giving them access to new tools, techniques and ideas.

Engaging managers get to know people as individuals, care for employees, create an open and positive work environment and build teams. They execute tasks in an enabling way, aiming to keep staff motivated and developing people's performance potential. In the current context, old-fashioned stick and carrot incentives to stimulate performance are unlikely to be effective. Engaging line managers support people best by designing interesting and worthwhile jobs and ensuring employees have the skills, authority and resources they need to deliver results that matter. Role design principles supportive of 'flow' (Csikzentmihalyi, 1990) and high performance include:

- *clear goals*;
- *concentration* on a limited field of attention;
- *absence of self-consciousness*;
- direct and immediate *feedback*;
- *balance between ability level and challenge*;
- *a sense of personal control over the situation or activity*.

Engaging managers set clear objectives so that people know what is required but allow staff to work out how to deliver them. They 'de-clutter' jobs of unnecessary bureaucracy so that people have a clear line of sight through their day job to the purpose, mission and goals of the organization.

Engaging managers strive to deliver on the employer brand promise and ensure employees get a fair deal. While no organization can guarantee job security, engaging managers can help employees cope with stress and anxiety. Providing meaningful support not only shows employees that they are valued, even though their job may be at risk, but it can also help survivor employees (those whose jobs remain after downsizing) remain productively focused on their work. Engaging managers are versatile, able to judge when to involve employees and when to direct them. HR can help managers understand how to involve staff in implementing change and to develop more of a coaching style. When making change becomes part of every employee's job, it can become the spur to innovation and improvement.

HR can also provide wellbeing policies which enable staff to tap into helpful resources as the JUICE case study later in the chapter illustrates.

3. Voice

CIPD research (2006) suggests that key drivers of employee engagement are:

- employees having opportunities to feed views upwards;
- feeling well informed about what is happening in the organization; and
- believing that their manager is committed to the organization.

These findings reinforce the importance of two-way communications and the need for a shift towards a more consultative and participative management style. That requires managers who are willing to listen to people and are not afraid of relinquishing control. In companies that do this well there is a constant free flow of ideas up and down and across the organization, joint sharing of problems and challenges and a commitment to arrive at joint solutions. Managerial fairness in dealing with problems, valuing diversity and treating employees with respect also has an important influence on outcomes.

Especially in tough times, frequent and honest communication is vital for (re)building employee trust, resilience and engagement. Engaging leaders and managers are visible, accessible and approachable; they communicate authentically and consistently about the bigger picture, strategy and direction. They are also willing to listen and act on what they hear. Whether dealing with business problems or building for growth, engaging leaders take a joint approach to developing new ideas, involving dialogue and consensus building between different groups and individuals within the business. Signs of progress are important so engaging managers mark milestones, celebrate successes, stabilize and share the benefits of change.

4. Scope

For all its challenges, change can also open up opportunities for development, more autonomy/task discretion, better work-life balance and growth as people gain new skills, new networks and new responsibilities. Engaging managers work at improving the skills and competencies people really need, focusing in particular on people in new roles. They spot opportunities for employee development and actively coach their teams, involving them in working on real business issues, providing job shadowing and mentoring. They deliberately encourage people to change roles/re-energize themselves by moving between domestic and international divisions or from one country to another. This allows them to gain new experience and helps develop different parts of the business – and is also a great motivator. After all, when people feel valued and have opportunities to grow, they are likely to perform well and assume responsibility for their actions.

How can employers create the context for engagement?

If organizations are looking to achieve sustainable high performance, engagement should be recognized as a strategic issue that cannot simply be left to manage itself. The employee engagement agenda is a joint priority for line managers and HR. As should be clear from the previous section, there are many ways that HR professionals can help improve engagement levels, in particular HR by:

- coaching line managers;
- implementing effective policies for work-life balance, wellbeing and diversity;
- developing inclusive employee voice mechanisms;
- helping line managers to manage workloads and design roles and work to ensure that people can grow and have line of sight to the organization's purpose and goals.

In addition HR must:

- act on employee engagement survey findings.

Organizations that have adopted employee engagement strategies for some years do not necessarily attempt to raise engagement levels across the board but focus in on specific groups. HR brings a method and structure to the system-level data from engagement surveys and other sources such as exit interviews but the challenge is to individualize this so as not to take a 'one size fits all' approach. So, cut the data based on different groups who share the same (but different from others) values and needs. Make sure that employees know that managers take their views seriously, and act on at least the most critical pieces of feedback. This builds trust and shows employees that their views are heard and taken seriously.

Building trust and involvement

Rather than attempting to force engagement, it is healthier to encourage it by managing change with a human touch. In particular engagement strategies should offer a framework for identifying and addressing issues that can undermine positive employment relations and address the core issues of trust, respect and involvement that are central to high performance and commitment. Trust can be strengthened through:

A shared purpose

The beating heart of organization needs something more than great processes, strategies and technologies to make it tick. People want to work for organizations that do good and are respected; to belong to something they value. A clear organizational purpose and strong values are critical to gaining effective employee commitment. The most effective leaders recognize and nurture that sense of an inclusive community serving a worthwhile purpose. Such a purpose engages and inspires people, provides parameters within which they can be creative and empowered in serving the needs of their customers. The most uplifting forms of purpose identify the ultimate beneficiaries of organizational efforts whether these are patients, the environment or society as a whole. For instance employers such as Marks and

Spencer adopt policies to protect the environment ('because there is no plan B') as much to engage their workforce and appeal to customers as much as to do the right thing. The organization becomes a community in its own right, where people look to find their place, grow their skills, develop their careers and be successful at what they do.

HR can help leaders at all levels create a strong unifying organizational purpose which people can be proud of. Ensuring that people have line of sight to the purpose in their jobs means that employees' energies will not be directed towards irrelevant or low-priority targets but to meeting business priorities. When the chips are down values are key. They must be meaningful – not just on paper but embedded throughout the organization in priorities and behaviours. HR should focus on closing gaps between the 'walk' and the 'talk' on values, incorporating values into appraisals, stimulating diversity, encouraging genuinely open, honest and ethical behaviour at all levels; stamping out blame cultures.

A fair deal

Feeling fairly treated is the basis of trust as the foundation of a healthy psychological contract. While pay may not be a prime motivator for most people it is the acid test of whether people feel treated fairly or not and dissatisfaction with pay is often cited as the reason why people quit. However the real issue is often more about whether pay or promotion decisions are transparent and appear fair to the individual. For many people, the content of the job and the quality of management appear more important motivators than pay and conditions. So while a sound pay policy, including benchmarking surveys, is important for the retention of top performers, HR can help managers create meaningful work for everyone, giving careful thought to how jobs are structured and improving the working environment.

Enabling wellbeing

In today's demanding workplaces stress and mental health problems like anxiety and depression are likely to become a growing challenge for individuals and employers. Research shows that the longer someone is off sick the less likely they are to make a successful return to work. So the HR challenge is to enable people to have positive working lives and to maintain a healthy workplace climate, providing for instance access to counselling support to those who need it and developing effective work-life balance, wellbeing or diversity policies. More generally though, rather than providing well-intended generic services that may be of limited use, HR should seek to develop simple and innovative policies that people actually want.

I am grateful to Andrew Dodman, Director of Human Resources at the University of Sheffield (UK) for the following illustration of such an approach.

CASE EXAMPLE 'JUICE' at the University of Sheffield

The UK's University of Sheffield is a large 'Russell Group' (ie research-intensive) university with over 7,000 staff. In most organizations the business drivers for ensuring a fair deal for employees usually revolve around the needs of the employer – for instance to increase productivity or reduce sickness absence. HR Director Andrew Dodman turned that paradigm on its head in 2012 when he launched JUICE – a health and wellbeing initiative which actively seeks to inspire and engage employees to take responsibility for their own health, wellbeing and happiness, making the individual the start point of programme design. This is about valuing people and giving them opportunities to help themselves.

Andrew was aware that the University's various sporting and other health and wellbeing opportunities had scant take-up. He undertook research with staff to find out what people would really value and the resulting JUICE initiative redirects the resource and brings together a range of free activities, information and advice for staff under one banner. It takes a holistic approach to health and wellbeing – physical, social, mental – that is informed but informal, with a vibrant, fun and fresh website. There is fast-growing staff awareness of JUICE and there are vast numbers of website visits. Sign up to JUICE activities is very social media dependent.

In its first year of operation alone JUICE has offered on average two activities daily which can range from painting to sports to choirs to Tai Chi to ballroom dancing. A quarter of staff have taken part in at least one activity at one of 120 locations.

Unlike conventional 'top-down' occupational health initiatives, JUICE is open access so there is a growing sense of staff ownership and high levels of participation. Staff members themselves suggest what they would like to do and bring others together under the JUICE banner. The single administrator assigned to the programme helps organize rooms. 'JUICE-vocates' (staff members) act as a steering group and gather input and feedback via the University's Google and LinkedIn websites. The vast majority of reviewers who have taken part in an activity give it 5 star ratings.

The effects of JUICE are starting to work through in terms of improved staff engagement levels, with 94 per cent of staff saying they are proud to work for the University and sickness absence levels having dropped significantly.

	2012	2013
I would recommend the university as an excellent place to work	75 per cent	87 per cent
I feel valued	55 per cent	65 per cent

As the programme grows organically it is becoming a flexible and integrated health and wellbeing offering, encompassing occupational health and collaboration with the sports department. This adult-adult approach is distinctly different from more paternalistic policy approaches and its impact on staff wellbeing is already evident. Not surprisingly the idea is now spreading to other universities who are also interested in providing practical support to help their staff members lead healthy and enjoyable working lives.

Upskilling line management

The key to engaging employees is line management effectiveness. Those employees with positive views about their managers and senior managers are most engaged with their work, perform better and are less likely to quit. However, evidence from many surveys shows that people are generally unhappy with the way they are managed: employees see their line managers as being weak at many of the fundamentals that are needed to support positive attitudes – like giving people feedback on how they are performing and making them feel their work counts.

So, where necessary, HR must coach line managers in managing their teams effectively. They should also ensure that line managers are recognized for their efforts in engaging employees. Several major employers, including retailer B & Q, incorporate the findings of employee surveys into performance management processes and use team engagement scores to distinguish good and weak performance by line managers. Where engagement scores feed into the appraisal process for managers, low scores in individual units can provide as much useful information as higher scores. This is less about penalizing individuals with low engagement scores and more about using department or team results to identify managers who need help, so as to offer them appropriate coaching and development.

Similarly, conflict, bullying or lack of respect can undermine employee engagement. So while HR can develop simple and effective policies for instance on diversity and conflict management, HR must be alert to where problem issues are occurring and intervene. This may involve giving managers feedback, encouraging line managers to spot problems at an early stage

and take action to resolve them, training or coaching managers for instance in mediation skills. Moreover if managers are allowing certain individuals to consistently underperform, perhaps because they feel ill equipped to tackle the issue, HR can coach managers in how to handle 'difficult conversations.' Such interventions will be a valuable investment in developing a positive organizational culture. HR may need to directly intervene when there is dysfunctional behaviour between departments, teams or individuals that is damaging staff morale and performance and should seek to bring a swift resolution to potentially chronic problems. This will not only reduce the time and energy spent in dealing with conflict, it will help employees feel valued and improve relationships across the organization.

Maintaining engagement in times of change

Being true to purpose and values is all the more important in times of significant change when the employment relationship is most at risk of being undermined. Research shows that changing employment conditions, particularly where jobs are lost, is very damaging to the psychological contract. As we discussed in Chapter 14 anxieties about job security can distract employees and undermine their enthusiasm, especially if redundancies take place. This applies also to those 'survivor' employees whose jobs are not made redundant but who may feel anxious, guilty or overloaded as their colleagues depart and suffer from stress as a result.

Tackling 'survivor' syndrome is crucial to protecting the organization's ability to bounce back. Leaders at all levels, especially HR, must keep faith with employees during change, ensuring that the right levels of employee connection, voice, support and scope are maintained both individually and also collectively. Honouring commitments is important. During the recession JCB and the John Lewis Partnership both continued to pay employees the bonuses they were due despite challenging economic conditions and widespread pay cuts elsewhere.

Since some of the human reactions to change can be anticipated, HR should help managers take actions to minimize the negative impact of change on people. Employee assistance programmes can help and simply giving people opportunities to talk – in one to ones and in groups – can be enough. Basic elements of a strategy to maintain motivation in difficult times include:

- keeping employees in the picture even when there is no concrete news;
- using all available media to beat the rumour mill;
- briefing line managers in full on developments so they can talk to their teams – face-to-face communications are best;
- thinking about creative, non-financial ways of motivating employees such as recognition schemes and team-building days.

If it becomes necessary to reduce labour costs, adopting alternatives to compulsory redundancy such as the following can help to maintain employees' commitment:

- taking advantage of natural wastage and/or offering voluntary redundancy terms;
- cutting back recruitment and review use of temporary staff;
- retraining employees whose skills are no longer in demand and redeploying them to other parts of the organization where possible;
- reducing or eliminating overtime working;
- considering short-time working or temporary lay-offs or sabbaticals.

Consultation

Given the importance of two-way dialogue in driving employee engagement, genuine consultation can help maintain levels of engagement during periods of change. In unionized workplaces that have formal 'employee voice' mechanisms, where the relationship between management and trade unions is one of partnership, union support for engagement strategies may be valuable in raising their profile.

I am grateful to Roshan Israni, Director of People Management & Organizational Development (OD) at Northumbria Probation Trust for the following public sector case study which describes how a major organization change was successfully implemented building on the foundations of strong employee relations, employee engagement and trust.

CASE STUDY Maintaining engagement during change at Northumbria Probation Trust

Award-winning Northumbria Probation Trust (NPT) is one of only two probation trusts in the North East and is responsible for all services delivered to offenders under probation supervision. This includes offenders subject to community orders and released from prison on licence. NPT supervises an average of 7,000 offenders at any one time and employs approximately 580 staff. There are 20 community supervision teams across Northumbria, where offenders are supervised on a day-to-day basis. NPT's responsibilities cover the county of Northumberland and the metropolitan districts of Newcastle, North Tyneside, South Tyneside, Gateshead and Sunderland. NPT is recognized for excellence by EFQM and is an Investor in People Champion – a rare accolade. Yet, things were not always this way.

Back in 2005–6 when Nick Hall, NPT's current CEO joined the organization – initially as Director of People Management – NPT was a very hierarchical organization which could best be described as somewhat insular and traditional. Benchmarking took place but only against other probation services. There was a general lack of trust between staff and management. The HR function too was inward looking and reactive. Key policies – for instance around flexibility, age regulations and retirement – had not kept pace with changing times and procedures such as for disciplinaries were archaic. Yet, rather than upgrade policies locally, the HR team preferred to wait for national agreements to change. When Roshan Israni, Director of People Management & Organizational Development (OD), joined the organization in 2006 from local government, her vision from the outset was for HR to move towards becoming a truly OD function.

Developing positive employee relations

Back in 2005–6 management relations with trade unions (TUs) were generally poor. Union representatives tended to have a fixed view of management and negotiations between trade unions and management were generally about 'cutting deals'. Even though TU representatives were mostly highly qualified, intelligent and articulate, their TU skills were not up to speed and their knowledge of TU legislation tended to come from the heart, rather than being based on real knowledge.

Roshan was determined to build a new working relationship with the unions and to actively engage them in creating a performance culture. Roshan's approach was to be open and honest with TUs so that they could be empowered with greater knowledge. Between 2006–7 HR started working with trades unions in a non-confrontational way on developing HR policies. This policy development work took 18 months and, though progress was made in small steps, this collaborative approach resulted in a third of policy changes being achieved through consultation rather than negotiation.

2010 was a breakthrough year. Changes at national level meant that what had previously been the Northumbria Probation Service became an Independent Trust. Management were determined that this would involve more than simply a name change and undertook to lead a constructive culture change towards a culture characterized by openness, honesty and high levels of staff engagement and trust. Nine aspirational cultural characteristics were identified.

Employee engagement programme

One of the early tests of this new approach was the decision to carry out a staff survey – the first since 2005. The way this was handled modelled the way forward.

In a clear commitment to honesty, the HR team were candid about the (limited) extent of follow-through from the 2005 survey. A series of HR communications reviewed what had been acted on in a number of 'You said... we did' statements. There were also items labelled 'You said... we did not'. As Roshan points out, this initially shocked the board but '... staff realized we were being honest'. In addition, some issues that staff found irritating, such as problems with the national IT system, were outside the control of local management. To an audience of social workers and probation workers who were tired of national targets, it was important to be clear about what was within and outside management control. So a further column talked about 'You said... we could not'. This went down really well with staff and set the tone for more detailed discussions with staff and unions about some of the changes which the organization needed to make.

Capita were chosen to carry out the 2010 survey since they could provide a wealth of external benchmarks against which the Trust could compare itself. Roshan and her team organized roadshows and staff briefings to launch the employee engagement programme, whose brand title of 'Progress Through People' was also chosen by staff. Indeed, Roshan and senior management deliberately encouraged Capita to meet with staff without management being present. As a result the survey was kept 'live' for longer than usual since staff holidays mostly fell during the survey period. Staff focus groups also helped to design the survey items so that what was most important to employees was included. Various 'gimmicks' – such as prize draws – were used to encourage staff to fill in the survey. Ironically, such was the initial level of scepticism among employees that some asked how they could possibly win the prize draw if they had completed the survey anonymously. Persistence paid off and the response rate was 74 per cent. Staff slowly started to trust management.

Following the survey, managers from the top down took on the task of debriefing staff at different levels and of developing action plans. As a result of the way management shared the feedback, staff knew that managers would be open to scrutiny. Translating the feedback into action required real commitment from senior management. Leaders were trained in appreciative inquiry techniques to help take things forward. A number of key work streams were identified to address the key issues identified and there were many workshops and focus groups to develop implementable action plans. This appreciative approach set the tone – it was about learning from what was working well rather than simply complaining about what needed to change.

Upskilling managers

However the employee engagement programme was not limited to surveys alone. Before the Probation Service achieved its Trust status in 2009–10, the

weakest organizational link was the middle management population. At the time middle managers tended to associate themselves more with the staff and trade unions, rather than seeing themselves as managers. They had never had any management training and, while Roshan believes that training is only one facet of OD, she considers it an important one. As she points out, 'We believe the chain can break if they're not on board. That's the group we need to invest in.' She therefore worked with a local university to create a management development programme which was attended by three cohorts of managers. Managers commented that they had never seen anything like it before. The combination of self-awareness using psychometrics and ongoing middle management skill workshops proved highly effective. Indeed, so pivotal was the development programme in unlocking skills that 15 managers are now studying for an advanced diploma in coaching.

In 2013 the Trust launched its latest survey. And it could be said that the work on engagement has provided a firm foundation for yet more change to come under the Government's privatization agenda for the probation service. In particular, staff value managers' openness and informal feedback and, as one person comments, 'We are adults – let's hear it when you hear it'. True to form, NPT are carrying out intensive staff briefings. Roshan and her team are also launching a health and wellbeing initiative, including 'My Choice' health checks.

Benefits

There have been many other benefits from the employee engagement programme. Post the 2010 survey, NPT came in the top 10 of Capita's benchmark group of top 42 Public Sector Employers of Choice. Another measure of success is reflected in the Trust's Investors in People (IIP) status. In 2011 when the Trust started working on IIP reassessment (from 2005 and 2008), management took the bold step of opting for reassessment against the full standard, hoping that the organization might achieve silver standard. Trades union reps, the chief executive and 65 staff members were interviewed. To everyone's delight, the organization achieved gold standard and was invited to become an IIP champion to spread the word about the importance of employee engagement. This has led to many visits to local companies and hosting groups of professionals who want to learn how the Trust achieved the gold standard. Perhaps most significantly, the views of staff reflect the positive changes that have taken place to create the new culture of engagement. When asked if and how the organization had improved, staff overwhelmingly responded 'yes' – on all nine cultural characteristics.

As this case study suggests, times of change do not have to put employee engagement strategies on the back burner. Here staff and trade unions worked as partners with management to achieve a new way forward for the organization.

Shared purpose and values are the glue that holds the organization together during times of change. Trust is the basis of positive employee relations. Employers must maintain the confidence of their workforce by treating them fairly and ensuring that line managers give them consistent messages about the future. It is crucial that leaders at all levels are authentic – they do what they say they will do – and open – they don't hide the truth from employees; instead they invite employees to participate in the change journey, making the outcomes as win-win as possible. It's important that line managers are upskilled for the task and that everyone has opportunities to learn and develop in order to play their part in the new culture.

In summary, to build a context for employee engagement:

1 *Make engagement a priority at all levels of the organization.* If your company's actions are not being echoed in each workplace, the efforts will not take effect. Conversely, it's not enough to leave engagement to frontline supervisors; business leaders must be seen to 'walk the talk' as well.

2 *Take time to diagnose and actively address the root causes of employee disengagement.* The aim should be to make employee engagement a daily focus for managers rather than simply an annual survey process. Each organization has its own particular issues, different groups of employees are influenced by different combinations of factors, and there is no standard template for deciding which specific policies and practices will have most impact on engagement. So organizations need to consider carefully what is most important to their own staff, using pulse surveys to take the temperature and involving staff in focus groups to isolate the key factors that can make a positive difference. Staff should also be involved in taking the actions required to address the issues identified, supported with relevant resources and authority.

3 *Check everyone understands the direction you're heading in.* In times of change, business strategies may need to be sharply revised. Communication and explanation are vital so that employees know where the business is heading, can reconnect with the business's new agenda and know how they can contribute.

4 *Rethink the topic of workplace wellness.* Effective wellbeing strategies can help people make the transition through change and cope with the demands made of them. Good support here can help foster resilience in the long run.

5 *When cutting costs, cut work too.* Simply cutting staff and expecting those remaining to cope with the same workload risks raising pressure and

reducing the quality of delivery. Managers can help by coaching their staff and refocusing workloads onto priority areas.

6 *Keep your key talents in focus.* As career opportunities may be even more limited in tough times, make sure you bear your best performers in mind when filling jobs. Recruitment firms are aware of wide-scale pent-up career frustration and as labour markets ease high turnover of key talent can be anticipated in years to come. Risk management and retention plans should be applied to people and jobs where key knowledge and skills are in short supply. And even if job advancement isn't possible, how about cross-training, strategic project assignments or job enrichment? Nationwide for instance demonstrates its mutual philosophy in its employment practices. It has an honourable record of continuing to invest in its people during the recession.

7 *Measure what gets done.* Put key engagement targets into the balanced scorecard. Tracking the actions that have been put in place to improve employee engagement keeps people focused and gives something to celebrate when success is achieved.

8 *Play fair by staff.* The Global Risks report by the World Economic Forum pointed to growing income disparity as the biggest risk factor facing businesses today. The danger is that business success benefits a privileged few – such as through equity based rewards – but not all. Playing fair by staff, sharing the benefits of success at all levels and recognizing the common efforts being made is the best way to build employee engagement and commitment.

Conclusion: building a more mutual employment relationship

As we have seen from these cases, employee engagement is the key to sustainable employee performance, organizational agility and great business results. In an engaging, inspiring working environment, agility and resilience will flourish – along with increased staff morale, commitment and productivity, an improved ability to attract quality staff and an enhanced reputation with stakeholders (eg community, regulators, clients).

Today's work-intensive and insecure workplaces tend to routinely destroy meaning for people. Research into what people find meaningful at work (Holbeche and Springett, 2005) suggests that most people want opportunities to develop, to deliver to their full potential, provide useful service to others, to be part of a good community doing worthwhile things. They want

to be valued as humans, not seen as mere 'resources'. For leaders, managers and especially HR the challenge is to unblock some of the common barriers to meaning, to help people to grow, build communities working towards a shared purpose and celebrate achievements. Being fair and transparent with employees is not an optional extra. When people feel well treated by their employer and part of an organization doing worthwhile work they are happier, have less stress, more of a sense of accomplishment and contribution to society – and they are also more productive.

So if organizations and their workforces are to thrive in changing times there must be a better balance between corporate and individual needs. Employers should aim to develop employment relationships based on fair and adult-adult, rather than paternalistic and ultimately instrumental parent-child, assumptions. Employers who are forward looking, who sustain their investment in people and continue to develop the abilities of their workforce are likely to maintain their competitiveness and be well positioned for growth since they will motivate and retain valued employees. After all, employees will welcome change if, as a result, they work in a positive environment, are part of a winning team, are more capable and empowered, have learned from their experiences and have the tools to be self-managing. Ensuring mutual benefits (as well as risks) for both organizations and employees is potentially a more sustainable and honest basis for an employment relationship that is better suited to the demands of today's volatile global economy.

The engagement-performance potential is there – delivering the results is a shared effort involving leaders, managers, HR/OD, internal communications and employees themselves since employee engagement flows up, down and across the organization. There is no short cut to building and maintaining employee engagement, but the time, effort and resource investment required will be amply repaid by the performance, health and reputational benefits that should endure over time. With an uplifting and energizing purpose, employee engagement at the heart of its culture, effective leadership, management and followership, any organization and its employees can become change-able and achieve the win-win outcomes they deserve.

In the next chapter we shall consider how to develop the kinds of leadership fit for the 21st century.

Developing effective leadership

The impact of globalization and technology has to a large extent reframed the environment in which organizations create value. The 21st century is bringing rapid changes and an operating context characterized by uncertainty, ambiguity, discontinuity and intense rivalry between firms. As a result organizational change and the search for innovation are increasingly the norm.

Against this challenging backdrop the leadership task is becoming ever more complex. To deliver results leaders must build new business opportunities, protect and enhance brand, develop new markets, product and service offerings and widen their customer base. To develop the organizational agility required for sustainable performance, leaders need to actively operate as change agents. They must be able to shift organizational cultures to become more flexible and agile, secure future talent and engage employees in ways which produce discretionary effort through periods of uncertainty.

So great are these challenges that Gary Hamel and Bill Breen (2007) suggest that many of today's managers are ill-equipped to deal with them. That's because the evolution of management thinking and practice has 'slowed to a crawl' and remains stuck at being good at static efficiencies (operations, exploitation) rather than dynamic ones (innovation, exploration); this at the very time when new dynamics of competition and technological change make management as usual untenable! These authors argue convincingly that 'what ultimately constrains the performance of your organization is not its operating model, not its business model, but its management model' and that 'management as currently practised, is a drag on success'. In fact they declare: 'Management is out of date'.

I agree with these authors and believe that the 'right' kinds of leadership will be central to organizations' ability to maintain and improve performance through what are likely to be ongoing economic challenges. Yet given changing demographics and employee expectations, the definition of the 'right' form of leadership in any given context today may be different from in the past.

Why is leadership so key? Like it or not, many surveys report leadership, or lack of it, as the primary reason why people either choose to stay with their employers and give of their best, or leave; or worse still, stay but become cynical and find work meaningless. Leaders and managers are the real OD practitioners. The health of an organization is often directly linked to the attitudes, behaviours and priorities of leaders at all levels. Through their words and deeds they create and shift organizational cultures.

HR has a key role to play in improving the quality of leadership practice, and in identifying and developing future leaders. In this chapter we look at how HR practitioners working within an OD frame can foster the kinds of leadership needed for success in the 21st century.

In this chapter we shall consider:

1 changing definitions of leadership;

2 HR's role in developing leaders;

3 equipping leaders for the task;

4 HR exercising stewardship;

5 crafting a leadership development strategy.

Defining leadership

Of course there is no shortage whatever of leadership theory – a quick internet search will yield hundreds of articles which address some aspect or other of leadership. But I'm afraid that I have to agree with Augier and Teece (2005) when they say 'As a scientific concept, leadership is a mess'. Quite what is required to successfully lead in today's organizations is less than clear. A meta-analysis of some of the trends emerging from a review of leadership literature (2003–2010) helps identify some of the shifts taking place in both the nature of what is required of leaders, and in how definitions of 'effective' leadership are changing.

Leadership is increasingly defined not as what the leader is or does but rather as a *process* that engenders and is the result of relationships – relationships that focus on the *interactions* of both leaders and collaborators instead of focusing on only the competencies of the leaders. Increasingly individuals rely less on organizational authority as represented by the boss; instead they rely more on internalized images of their own authority. There is a growing challenge to the 'one size fits all' normative approaches to leadership against which leaders can be developed and measured. Emphasis is shifting away from 'heroic' leaders towards the leadership system which makes it possible for people at all levels to exercise leadership.

There is also a special focus on the demands facing leaders and a growing recognition that something different is needed. For instance in the wake of the banking crisis what is the role of leadership in legitimizing dissent

and experimentation? To build companies fit for the future do we need not only new management practices, but also a new statement of principles? How should leaders be held to account? To answer these questions there is a growing consensus within the leadership literature that new or evolved forms of management and leadership are needed that are more values based and better suited to the demands of a complex, fast-changing knowledge-based economy.

From 'I' to 'we' – distributed leadership

Another key theme emerging from the literature is that of shared or distributed leadership. The focus is on creating leadership at all levels ie empowered, proactive workforces and also on building healthy leadership systems. According to Spears (2004), 'We are seeing traditional and hierarchical modes of leadership yielding to a different way of working – one based on *teamwork and community*, one that seeks to involve others in decision making, one strongly based in ethical and caring behaviours'. Leadership is variously described as '*shared*', '*we*', or '*distributed*'.

In knowledge- and service-intensive work environments in particular, employees want and expect to be treated as thinking, capable adults. Raelin (2005) argues that in 'leaderful' organizations leadership is seen as concurrent, collective, collaborative and compassionate, in contrast to more traditional leadership which tends to be thought of as serial, individual, controlling and dispassionate. How does shared leadership come about? It seems to emerge 'naturally' in situations where there is a strong emphasis on employee development and on managers creating the environment to allow staff to release potential, as in the Oxleas case later in this chapter.

HR's role in developing leaders

Developing new kinds of leadership thinking and practice can be one of the most challenging aspects of the HR role. Ulrich *et al* (2008) argue that HR needs to lead the talent agenda and embrace a blend of leadership roles – organizational strategist, organizational executor, talent manager, human capital developer – underpinned by high levels of personal proficiency. Yet HR professionals often find themselves in a dilemma. While their organizations are asking them to become leaders and partners in running the business, they are frequently asked to implement initiatives and programmes over which they have no formal authority or with which they disagree. Migrating to different leadership patterns can be unsettling; leaders may be reluctant to share power and people may still look to leaders for idealized leadership. HR has to take care of people's anxieties (including their own) when moving into uncharted territory.

On the other hand HR has many opportunities to impact on what happens. Not surprisingly in this post-banking crisis age, given the general discrediting of many top managers over the issue of executive bonuses, short-term orientations and accusations of self-interest, a very strong and growing theme in the leadership literature concerns ethics and a leader's authenticity. Individual business leaders are required to demonstrate strong values and to exercise moral leadership. HR needs to ensure that the company values are reflected in the standards set, and that these apply to everyone, including the executive team and the board. HR must have the courage of its convictions in tackling poor standards, especially where there are clear gaps between rhetoric and practice on values.

Essentially this is about HR exercising stewardship, improving the quality of leadership through shifting mindsets and leadership practice. Since HR leaders may be directly or indirectly involved in senior-level appointments, they have the chance to influence thinking about the kind of leadership an organization needs. Before appointment HR must assess potential areas for concern which may lead to executive derailment. Once the CEO or executive is in post HR should use this data to further build the relationship and to develop and maintain the 'right' behaviours.

Within management teams HR can provide an independent voice by holding up a mirror to the CEO and executives. It's about finding an appropriate balance between supporting and challenging the organization's leadership. In the absence of other opinions the HR leader and/or ODP needs to solicit them, all this in the spirit of constructive conflict or what Peter Drucker (2007) described as 'organized disagreement'. In his seminal article 'Teaching Smart People How to Learn' (1997) Chris Argyris points out how defensive thinking is commonplace amongst knowledge workers. What Argyris calls 'single loop' learning often serves to suppress doubt and ambivalence. However, doubt, debate and reflexivity (or 'double-loop' learning) are vital to promoting real learning and enhancing the collective pool of knowledge. This is particularly the case with knowledge workers, including leaders. It is important that leaders listen and ask questions. Often, they may hear what they do not want to hear, an opposing point of view for instance.

Opening up such conversations might seem a career-limiting experience for an internal consultant and is a real test of an effective HR/OD practitioner's mettle, since many leadership groups have a vested interest in maintaining the status quo. This isn't about reckless challenge or falling on swords but it is about learning how to influence better, knowing which battles to fight and how to build alliances. Clearly to influence effectively at this level HR needs to be credible – with real business understanding and a real, deep appreciation of the drivers and motives of the CEO. Influencing with integrity requires high levels of self-knowledge, a strong set of values, good judgment and personal courage (and negotiation skills training can be useful too!). The HR professional must find a way to become a true partner with the CEO. The issue is how to become a partner with a leader, yet retain leadership behaviours yourself.

Equipping leaders for the task

Ulrich argues that the leadership skills and behaviours required should not be deduced from some ideal competency template but from the actual results leaders will have to achieve. A 'leadership brand' should therefore connect leadership development to business, organizational and individual performance. What are the kinds of challenges faced by leadership and management, and the kinds of development needed to help leaders cope with these challenges? Of course there is no overall blueprint, but some of the trends emerging from the literature and my own consultancy practice are as follows:

a) Leadership challenge: forging new business directions

Conventionally leadership from the top is associated with direction setting. Effective leaders work hard to innovate within the current business model and therefore maximize its potential. They scan the environment, consult and involve stakeholders. Of course these can be challenging enough tasks in 'normal' times but in an ambiguous, changing context leaders may increasingly be required to innovate the business model itself, potentially running with several business models simultaneously. This requires an anticipatory and proactive mindset; the ability to weigh up risks and reward and make wise choices – quickly. Leaders' priorities may also need to shift towards building capabilities to enhance their organization's potential for future success rather than just achieving cost efficiencies in the here and now. This kind of thinking may not come naturally to leaders who have reached the top of organizations by innovating within a given business model.

Providing clear direction is not just a case of issuing business imperatives and strategic plans. Organizations as human systems are subject to the ebb and flow of a wide range of emotions, aspirations, frustrations, anxieties and power play. As Marshak (2006) points out, covert processes at work can both undermine individuals and also enable things to happen. In times of change employees look for encouragement as well as direction and focus. In this context leadership becomes less about top-down direction and more about managing human dynamics and sense making. Leaders need to provide vision and support, eliminate obstacles, invest in people and build communities aligned to a common shared purpose.

HR response: We will need to develop leaders who can cope with ambiguity, manage change, deal effectively with paradox, be guided by their moral compass and help create a sense of direction and purpose through which employees become and remain engaged with the organization in ways which lead to sustainable high performance. The literature suggests that effective leaders handle uncertainty by reflective conversations, that they must find sources of advice they can trust and that the first step of any leadership development journey requires leaders to look at themselves intensely and critically ie leaders have self-insight and grapple with their shadow sides. Leaders need moral codes that are as complex, varied and subtle as the situations in which they find themselves.

HR can help by providing leaders with access to networks, action research groups and executive coaches where they can share dilemmas in a trusting environment, have the opportunity to be reflexive and make sense of the complexity of the challenges they are dealing with, not least their own confusion.

b) Leadership challenge: managing change and organizational culture

Schein (2004) argues that creating culture is what ultimately distinguishes leadership from management: '*If one wishes to distinguish leadership from management or administration, one can argue that leadership creates and changes cultures, while management and administration act within a culture.*' Schein goes on to say that '*The only thing of real importance that leaders do is to create and manage culture; that the unique talent of leaders is their ability to understand and work with culture; and that it is an ultimate act of leadership to destroy culture when it is viewed as dysfunctional*'.

The 'right' kinds of leaders fully embrace their role as organizational leaders and focus on building a sustainable organizational culture using symbols and dialogue to create moral solidarity and enriching the culture by telling stories. Such leaders use their 'self as instrument' as would an OD specialist or HR acting 'with attitude' as Ulrich put it. For Tubbs and Shultz (2006) the leaders' values strongly shape behaviours of people around them. Above all leaders must act as role models, 'walking the talk' with respect to values: 'perhaps the most important task is to build an organization with a set of values and an identity that is sufficiently compelling for talented people to buy into' (Devine, 1999).

Given the context of almost constant change, various authors argue that leaders must be versatile, able to be both strategic and operational, forceful

and enabling. They may need exposure to new ways of thinking, *'Because leading transformational change is so radically different from managing or leading a stable organization, leaders cannot simply lay their old way of thinking, behaving, and operating on this new world and expect success'* (Anderson, 2001). Leaders may need new skills, knowledge and approaches to equip them for their roles as change agents: *'Leaders must continue to lead, and consultants must continue to consult. Yet to be effective in transformation, leaders must develop people and process skills previously reserved for, or shunted to their consulting counterparts, and consultants must become more grounded in core business skills and strategies previously reserved for leaders'.*

HR response: By and large senior managers are not trained to see themselves as developers of culture. Even when they are, they may not know how to go about it. HR and OD specialists can support and develop leaders to play their role in culture change and managing change. In developing change leaders the emphasis is on authenticity and emotional intelligence as much as on intellect, and the ability to translate this self-awareness into behaviour. Effective leadership behaviours include understanding the bigger picture, demonstrating a compelling and achievable vision, inspiring others, active listening, reframing, encouraging others to be creative, creating transformational change, developing a team-oriented culture.

I am grateful to Bob Montgomery for the following short case study. Bob is Organization Development Center of Excellence leader at Lockheed Martin Corporation. Bob is responsible for performance management, leadership and organization development.

EXAMPLE Developing engaging managers in Lockheed Martin Corporation

Lockheed Martin moves product in times of crisis – the company is the world's No. 1 military contractor and is firmly on the US defence/government side of the aerospace industry; in fact the US government accounts for about 85 per cent of sales. This reliance on the US government is a double-edged sword: Lockheed can avoid turbulence in the commercial aerospace sector, but the company is

vulnerable to military spending cuts. As a Government contractor, the firm cannot carry heavy overheads. Given the current economic situation facing world governments, the challenge will be to continue to deliver product and operational excellence within an increasingly cost-constrained environment.

Talent shortages

In common with other organizations in similar industries, Lockheed Martin is facing potential talent shortages in years to come. Lockheed Martin employs a mix of military and civilian staff and its main professional group are engineers, many of whom are 'Baby Boomers' who have amassed considerable experience and valuable expertise in the company.

Over the next few years many employees are due to retire and there are worldwide shortages of engineering talent now and predicted for years to come. Consequently Human Resources in Lockheed Martin are very focused on both retention and on building the talent and leadership pipeline. What helps is that Lockheed Martin is known to be a good employer. The company has received accolades of being one of the top places to work for women, engineers and minorities. It also is viewed as one of the top 25 companies worldwide in developing leaders.

Leadership as a culture change lever

The organization's culture has always been results driven with a conventional mix of military and civilian values and hierarchical management styles. Stereotypically engineers in management positions are most interested in the technical aspects of the job, rather than the people management aspects. As the organization gears up to deal with today's more challenging economic conditions, there is growing recognition within the company that the organization's culture and the nature of management and leadership need to change to equip Lockheed Martin to be more nimble and cost effective while retaining its focus on quality, customer and innovation.

Bob considers that a shift is needed away from command and control management styles to leadership styles which are more focused on getting results through people. Employee surveys and straw polls indicate this as well. With more limited resources attempting to carry out the company imperatives without a change of management style is likely to be problematic. As Bob says: 'We should be using the intelligence of many, not just the few. We need to create a highly engaged work environment and build the competence of our managers to create that work environment'.

To start this culture shift, Bob Stevens, the CEO of Lockheed Martin, introduced in 2006 a comprehensive leadership process around recruitment, talent

management and development, known as 'Full Spectrum Leadership'. Bob Montgomery argues that attempting to tackle a major shift through just one sub-system, such as training and development, is unlikely to deliver the results needed. What is needed is a whole system approach (which this one intends to be), in which potentially conflicting sub-systems can be aligned with the strategy.

People are recruited and developed against key leadership competency areas:

- shape the future;

- build effective relationships;

- energize the team;

- deliver reality;

- model personal excellence.

There is a 360-degree feedback process which operates from the top management down to first line supervisors. New recruits are introduced to leadership development from the outset and given a strong orientation in the new approach. As behaviours start to change in the desired direction, Bob considers the next stage is to build in stronger accountability for delivery to ensure that managers and leaders 'walk the talk' – with goals and objectives which can be measured, monitored and evaluated.

As Bob argues, it is dangerous to come in with a set solution. Real success will depend on achieving both congruence with the environment and alignment of the subsystems with these strategic demands. Above all it will depend on 'your ability to adapt and change'.

What I find interesting about this case is the systemic approach to shifting towards a more agile culture by developing different kinds of leaders. Various HR and other levers are used in a synchronized way, and review is built in. At top management level change leadership is about creating new capabilities and sustaining them through time. The context has to be created so that people can become effective in the 'new'. In this case the process is driven from the top as a business imperative since there are clear environmental drivers to do so.

c) Leadership challenge: growing tomorrow's leaders

Many executives and HR teams struggle to find the kinds of future leaders their organizations need; therefore building a strong talent pipeline and also improving the quality and capability of current leadership and line management are key priorities. Succession planning is now considered

a key element of talent management, with ownership of the process widely recognized as belonging to business leaders, and responsibility for designing the process and the quality of its outcomes resting with HR.

A typical 'leadership brand' (Ulrich and Smallwood, 2007) succession planning process involves first anticipating changes in markets over the coming five to ten year period, then envisioning where the organization wants to be in those markets. By looking ahead at the kinds of results that will typically be required of managers in future it is possible to predict that managers will be required to manage more diverse workforces, including age diverse, and to manage at a distance, across different time zones and cultures.

From that, it should be possible to envisage what potential leaders will need to deliver in five years time and start to identify and develop leaders with the qualities and abilities to operate in the ways which will deliver success. These will be leaders who can develop flexible structures and roles with a line of sight to the customer, who coach and develop their teams, create a shared sense of direction in the face of ambiguity, are credible and demonstrate their values through their actions and behaviours. Then it's about growing a broad talent pool and keeping high-potential employees longer in development posts so that they can deliver meaningful performance before progressing to the next experience.

CASE STUDY Preparing managers to lead change at
 Oxleas NHS Trust

I am grateful to Simon Hart, HR Director at Oxleas NHS Trust for the following short case.

The business strategy of Oxleas NHS Trust will require significant amounts of organizational change over the coming three years, so a key element of the organizational strategy is preparing management and HR for their role in managing change.

The CEO wants the organization to be the best that it can be – he has high expectations of himself and others and is very visible throughout the organization. These high aspirations permeate the organization and set the standard for how senior managers should act. The CEO is widely respected throughout the organization. His personal style is very open and approachable and this encourages a high level of communication between staff and management that is solution focused. The proactive and visible approach of the CEO is mirrored by the executive team, for example the Director of Nursing spends at least one afternoon every week in clinical areas listening to users, carers and staff.

Holistic leadership development process

In this Foundation Trust there are high expectations that managers will be able to manage performance. Effective managers will be those who can not only actively manage performance but are also aware of their own strengths and weaknesses. HR Director Simon Hart recognizes that managers will find the business of leading change challenging, and that this is also likely to take its toll on directors. He is developing a senior manager leadership programme to support the Trust's quality agenda. The demands of the Trust's quality agenda and service development strategy are such that it is crucial that all senior managers, not simply those who are deemed to be future directors, are equipped and supported to be able to meet these demands.

A key plank of the organizational strategy focuses on strategic talent and succession planning and building a talent pool up to director level. Building consistently good leadership is a priority and of particular concern is the perceived lack of internal applicants for director-level roles. Consequently improving the quality of management below director level is important. Competencies have been developed as criteria for recruitment, management development and training and performance management. Career tracks and connections are being developed for middle managers (such as current and aspiring ward managers) and these are forming part of an integrated training, development and succession planning process.

This shift towards building communities of leaders at every level who can proactively shape some of the context around them, and deliver successful implementation through high-performing, highly motivated and committed teams presents particular challenges for HR. If leadership is distributed, what has happened to the balance of power? How prepared are leaders to share power? If people are demonstrating distributed leadership what has made this possible? What are the benefits? HR has a particular interest in answering these questions since they lie at the heart of employee engagement.

d) *Leadership challenge: managing the employment relationship*

As we discussed in the last chapter, getting the 'right' people focused on the 'right' things and *engaged* in the collective effort has never been more important to business success. And during challenging times engagement may be at risk with potentially serious consequences for people, organizations and the economy.

Engaged employees – who are aligned with organizational goals, willing to 'go the extra mile' and act as advocates of their organization – are effectively offering their voluntary effort, going beyond the minimum required to earn their pay. There is growing evidence that the criteria used by younger workers in particular to select their future employer – even more than the pay on offer – include the chance for learning and growth, respect for them as individuals, company ethics and values.

'Old' management and leadership styles, based on a convention of low trust/high control sit uneasily against a paradigm of 'volunteer' knowledge workers, who are expected to be accountable and empowered, willing and able to create shared learning and intellectual capital. To respond to the engagement challenge leadership styles need to evolve beyond command and control, heroic or charismatic models towards more collaborative leadership styles that act as the basis of mutual trust and respect. 'Engaging leaders' are accessible, show genuine concern and build a shared vision. They act with integrity, are honest and consistent. In short, they are authentic: they are who they say they are and do what they say they will.

In this new era the employment relationship needs to be based on adult-adult rather than parent-child relationships. There need to be mutual benefits (as well as risks) in becoming more flexible and sustaining high performance, for both organizations and employees.

HR response: developing engaging managers and leaders

As we discussed in the last chapter, HR has a key role to play in supporting current leadership to make the shifts required and helping select and develop the next generation of leadership who 'get' the importance of engaging employees. Current leadership development trends include the use of concepts from neuroscience to help increase leaders' self-awareness. Increasingly too vulnerability is being recognized as a leadership strength rather than weakness. From this vantage point leaders start to see the aspirations of the business through the eyes of the people they lead. As a result their leadership demeanour, focus and interactions change. Everyone benefits. So HR should consider the maturity of the leadership team. Are they able to be vulnerable, authentic, do they trust one another to speak and act as one when they walk out of the room? Sometimes work like this is a leadership team effectiveness intervention in itself. One company that has adopted such thinking in its leadership development with the help of Ashridge Business School is FrieslandCampina, the world's second largest producer of milk products. Now that a sizeable cohort of managers has experienced this approach, the positive effects of building an empowered organizational culture are being felt internationally.

e) Leadership challenge: leading a diverse workforce

Perhaps one of the generically most difficult cultural challenges is to produce a real shift in people's mindsets and behaviours with respect to equal opportunities and genuine diversity. By subtly raising awareness about diversity HR can help can produce attitude and behavioural shifts towards more inclusive practices. I am grateful to Fleur Bothwick, Director of Diversity and Inclusion for Europe, Middle East, India and Africa at Ernst & Young for the following example of one approach to shifting manager mindsets and practice with respect to better practice on diversity and inclusion.

CASE STUDY Developing an inclusive culture at Ernst & Young

In recent times the professional services firm Ernst &Young has become a global organization and has restructured accordingly, grouping the 87 countries in which the firm operates into 12 Sub-Areas (SAs). In this global and increasingly multicultural environment, employees will increasingly need to be able to work effectively across boundaries, build partnerships and consensus. With a mix of over 12 cross-national stakeholders working virtually, communicating by phone and e-mail, people need to be able to build rapport and teamwork remotely – in other words they must be able to thrive on diversity and inclusion.

Fleur Bothwick points out that there is a strong business case for building a culture conducive to diversity and inclusion. Ernst and Young's own research into other global companies found that most global companies fall short on the diversity of thought and culture needed to handle global business – boards of directors seldom reflect the global reach of their businesses. Almost half of the companies operating in 25 or more countries admitted that they had at most only a couple of foreign national on their boards, yet they cited having globally experienced staff as the leading cultural factor in successfully conducting business around the world. As they point out, a lack of diversity of thinking and experience at the senior management level could leave firms behind as they race to compete.

As might be expected, Ernst & Young has policies in place to encourage good practice and at senior levels the importance of achieving a diverse and inclusive culture is recognized. Yet despite attracting plenty of women recruits at entry level, Ernst & Young has relatively small numbers of women or people from minority ethnic groups in senior management. It seems to be at the middle management (so-called 'permafrost') layer that the reality of enacting the policies is different from the intent. For instance while the firm has policies with respect to flexible

working, in a more cost-constrained environment it can be difficult in practice for managers to obtain temporary cover when someone is on maternity leave.

Thanks to demographic shifts managing for diversity is becoming a business necessity. There will simply not be enough 'conventional' recruits coming through to fuel growth in some regions, therefore managers will have to think differently about how to source a talent pool which will inevitably broaden. Developing an employer brand which is attractive to a broader talent pool will require active policies which are supportive of a genuinely diverse culture. Similarly, potential new clients increasingly want to know what Ernst and Young's own diversity and inclusion policies are before entering into a business relationship with them.

One initiative which is starting to shift mindsets is a web-based learning tool based on work by Kandola and others which looks at the 'unconscious bias' in processes which undermines diversity. The tool helps managers to consider the issues without defensiveness because the message is that bias is natural and that people are largely unaware of their own prejudices. It allows learners to understand the benefits of shifting mindset to embrace diversity and inclusion. The tool has already been used with large numbers of managers and is now incorporated into the induction process. 'Unconscious bias' is now becoming a frame of reference as people start to use the terminology. Fleur sees this as only one of a range of initiatives which will slowly create a 'tipping point' of attitudes which will then reflect the new 'way we do things around here'.

There is evidence again here of how one firm's culture shift is getting underway without the need for great fanfare by creating dialogue across the firm with the use of a simple tool and gradually embedding new practices through other HR-managed processes such as induction. Here diversity is not seen to be a 'nice to have' but a business necessity.

Sometimes awareness-raising is not enough to shift embedded social attitudes and behaviours and more vigorous stimulating of debate and role modelling of good practice are needed. The following case describes how Brian Wisdom, formerly Chief Executive at People First (PF), the sector skills agency for the UK travel, tourism and hospitality industries, has set out to improve diversity practice across these industries. These industries are set to become leading generators of future GDP for the UK. Brian here describes his attempts to stimulate a social movement across this complex sector to produce a more representative pool of talent for future senior management roles in the sector.

CASE STUDY Breaking down barriers to equality in the travel, tourism and hospitality industries

At People First (PF) our remit is to close the skills gaps our industry suffers from by ensuring that the provision of training and qualifications for the industry is driven by demand rather than supply (which is often the case with management training too, especially in the Public Sector). In my early days at PF we researched something like 5,000 businesses in the hospitality sector to bring out what the industry needs actually were – and some really defining themes emerged about the common gap issues:

- First, *retention* – it's an industry that has very poor retention of people.
 It attracts young people but since the demographics are changing there'll
 be fewer young people so it's a high-cost – high-threat issue for the industry

- Second, the industry suffers *skills deficits*, particularly in management skills,
 alongside customer service skills and some technical skills – for instance
 chefs in particular are in short supply.

We then went into a lot more depth about where the issues might lie. The issue we struggled with most was the management and leadership one because with technical skills, it was easier to see where the issue lay – for instance a decent set of qualifications is needed, but with management and leadership it was more difficult.

More recently we've been conducting a second wave of research about the labour market. We suddenly started to see a trend around our failure to retain women in the industry. At entry level about 72 per cent of entrants are women – (it's a very attractive industry to women at entry level for all sorts of reasons), but when you get to middle management level this has dropped to 40 per cent; when you get to senior management level it drops to 20 per cent and when you get to board level it's only 6 per cent which is just under half the national average for all industries.

So effectively about 70 per cent of the talent available to the industry is being lost – and this is an industry which is well known to be one where you can work your way up through the ranks to the top. And if you think about the skills women typically bring – particularly interpersonal skills – and our challenges around retention you start to think 'well maybe it's not around retention. Maybe it's just that we're not helping women feed into management positions and the reason we've not got enough of the right management and leadership is because of that failure.

That's where we got to in a classic diagnosis way. But I guess also alongside that I've known for some time that there are other countries where there is more

systematic support available – particularly in the United States where they have something called 'Women into Service' where they have training systems for women in business.

So a few years ago I sent a high-potential manager called Sharon Glancy who's Director of our Business Solutions Division to attend their Dallas convention and she came back inspired. She said, 'Look, we could do this'. So really from that inspiration Sharon went out and talked to a lot of our government contacts and managed to get £100,000 of seed funding. And we set out then on a journey to try and create the right sort of support mechanisms for women in our industry that will get it up the agenda in all kinds of businesses and help create the environment for confronting that journey where they tend to get wiped out.

The 'Women First' programme

We've kicked off this 'Women First' (WF) programme – it's in very early stages. It's about culture and how organizations organize themselves. We're setting up for example regional networks of women managers which have been very successful. I got Cherie Blair to launch the programme. Of course this made it a very high-profile launch – the place was absolutely packed out.

We're setting up the regional networks on the one hand and we're also trying to create case studies of good examples of where women have broken through. We're finding it hard to find good case studies. We're going to have to look at what lies behind success stories in other industries with similar challenges. We want to understand better how construction for instance which has fewer women entrants has proportionately more women getting through to senior positions, despite the operational roles being equally hard.

Further research and case studies

What we're trying to do through WF is to give women the confidence and the skills to navigate their way through and also to raise the awareness and support levels from companies. One issue is the broader culture within the hospitality sector – it's definitely a 'clubby culture' I think. At the moment we've gone out looking for case studies in our own industry that we can publicise in the trade media and national press. There are one or two companies who have been pursuing this agenda and it's not surprising therefore that they feature in the Top Fifty Places that Women Want to Work.

Clearly we have specific challenges for the industry such as peculiar working hours. One of the problems is that a lot of the career routes are through operations – the working hours are just too hard for those who are having children or have family commitments. Unless the industry does something positive about that environment they will continue to struggle. I always remember in a previous

company I had two area managers who were a job share. It had quite a bit of extra cost for us but those working patterns can work well.

We're working with a training company owned by the University of Hertfordshire to provide a cradle to grave training structure for women in this industry and showing what training and development routes are available. They also do quite a bit of employment work supporting women at work and in other places as well. We're aiming to put in some support infrastructure.

We're doing a number of things to raise awareness. For instance we're looking to publish case studies and we're sponsoring an award to raise the profile of high-performing women in the industry. Ultimately we're trying to build a head of steam where we get together a group of people and companies who want to make a difference and are prepared to talk with their colleagues in the industry about breaking down a culture that's not helpful.

This case illustrates the power of good diagnosis and insight derived from evidence. It also highlights the importance of ongoing dialogue and of building momentum for change by putting shape around what is happening so that new initiatives can emerge in a helpful way and feed into work in progress. As Brian comments, 'It's interesting that the journey is partly inspiration and insight; partly it's a gradual revelation of your concerns and partly it's about how that then turns into change, whether for instance you introduce new standards in recruitment practice'. This case illustrates how strong partnership between HR and executives and between HR professionals across a sector can reinforce the positive shifts and embed new approaches in other HR practices such as via development and promotion guidance.

In a very real way Brian has been the driving force behind this cultural change initiative but he is also a commissioner of OD, in this case delivered by another senior manager and through sectoral networks. Once again, this change agenda is driven both to meet business needs and because this leader believes this is the right thing to do. Tackling such long-standing cultural and systemic issues may perhaps be beyond the capacity of any one organization to achieve but for Brian it is a personal leadership quest: 'Either way, you've got to be in it for the long haul and do what it takes to make a difference.'

HR exercising stewardship

To help build healthy organizations, HR needs to exercise a strong stewardship role, ensuring that their organization's practices are ethical and contributing to society. As Cooperrider and Srivastva (1998) point out:

'Contemporary society is not only profoundly shaped by organizations but also can be shaped for the better by them... Organizations are increasingly stepping forward to wrestle with complex issues that affect not only their shareholders, employees, and customers but also the quality of life in the world's communities and cities, the world's ecosystems, and countries around the globe'.

Another stewardship issue involves grasping the nettle of adjusting reward systems to clearly show the connection between output (specific and measurable value-add to the owners of the business) and input (behaviour of the person). The performance management process must ensure that these links are transparent and obvious. Clearly articulating business outcomes, balancing these in a scorecard and ensuring rigorous assessment and feedback are core elements of any reward system. Similarly HR must be prepared to challenge promotion and other practices which favour exclusively financial results and ignore the means by which these were achieved.

A key issue highlighted by the near-collapse of the banking system was the poor performance of non-executive directors (NEDs). HR now needs to step into this space and set out the requirements for success. This means defining the capabilities required (linked to your organizational values) and rigorously assessing these both prior to director appointments and also as part of the appraisal of board effectiveness. Insist on independent profiling of executives and NEDs as part of this process.

But HR and OD are not alone in aiming to develop healthy and ethical practice. Line managers are the real change practitioners. Through their daily actions, what they pay attention to, sanction or reward they are teaching people what is acceptable, good or not acceptable. At senior levels managers can have significant impact on their organization's system. At executive levels they can also impact on the broader external system, acting as ambassadors, contributing to policy, building influential external relationships and networks. When change leaders act with positive intent to promote healthy practice they can have a powerful effect.

Crafting a leadership development strategy

By developing more engaging management and leadership HR will make their organizations a talent magnet for skilled employees. Crafting a leadership development strategy involves making choices about where to focus:

- In making our talent management decisions how much should we put the business needs first above the individual context/requirement?
- How do we spot talent (given that people do not come wearing badges); should we grow our own?

- Should we favour internal versus external talent?
- Should we be aiming for the cadre development of the many versus the special high-potential few?
- What do we need to emphasize more – long-term/strategic thinking versus short-term operational excellence?
- And how do we ensure that we are operating to high standards with respect to equality and diversity when identifying and developing our leaders?

An effective management and leadership development strategy will focus not just on developing individual leaders but also on building shared leadership at all levels. The strategy will encompass HR teams developing the skills to coach managers and support them in creating genuine development opportunities. Using a blend of development methods is likely to ensure that learning is relevant and closes the 'knowing–doing gap' identified by Pfeffer and Sutton (1999). And while a DDI/CIPD study (2007) found that training is still the most common form of management development, leaders actually find special projects, mentors and personal coaches more effective. Other useful methods include action learning, job shadowing and secondments, as well as off-the-job development such as networks and visits. Developing communities of leaders can be accelerated by the use of large-scale methodologies such as Future Search and scenario planning to enable strategic conversations and the creation of cross-organizational networks united by a common purpose.

It is important to assess impact after development to ensure that leaders are putting their learning into practice and are operating more effectively as a result. Increasingly HR Directors advocate the setting of outcome targets which reflect what should be expected of managers as a result of development, such as developing their own staff to their full potential, and rewarding leadership excellence.

Conclusion

Developing leadership capability and improving leadership practice can be fraught with difficulty, but is fundamentally worthwhile. The real trick is to build leadership systems that make it possible for leaders at all levels to give of their best and influence their colleagues in positive directions. Line managers are the primary practitioners of organizational development. Leaders hold the custodian role, safeguarding and improving organizational health and performance. HR needs to work closely with senior leaders, turning them into commissioners of OD who understand their role in improving the organization, are able to diagnose organizational health and who appreciate that an organization is a human system, not just a technical system.

HR needs to help leaders tackle the challenges of achieving sustainable success in today's challenging environment. To make sure their organizations stay relevant to their key stakeholders, leaders need to be able to interpret the data on the horizon, to form effective strategies and delineate organization performance outcomes. They also need to focus internally to make sure that the vision, mission and culture of the organization are aligned. And they need sufficient understanding of human dynamics to be able to inspire people to come along with them. In other words, leaders need to ensure that the organization's internal capability matches the strategic ambition. So HR must continuously push back the boundaries of development, and expose leaders at all levels to new ways of thinking and behaving which increase their versatility.

Above all, HR can help build healthy and effective organizations by developing current and future leaders who take employee engagement seriously and who embrace approaches that are transformational, not just transactional. Real employee engagement will be based on mutual commitment, responsibility, obligations, needs, risks and benefits between organizations and employees, so HR must support leaders, managers and employees along the journey towards more agile, democratic and involving forms of leadership.

To be seen as credible suppliers of excellent leaders, HR leaders must exercise leadership. HR functions must understand the business; operate as cohesive teams; deliver in impactful ways which create value and capability; look beyond their own boundaries and actively share learning. In particular they must demonstrate customer focus, resilience and the ability to change. HR leaders must act as role models for the changes they want to see. As the case examples in this chapter illustrate, when HR practitioners work within a systemic frame, demonstrate leadership and focus on developing the kinds of leadership capability required for tomorrow's success as well as today's, they can bring their organizations real and lasting benefits.

Postscript – Towards a better tomorrow

In the few years since Mee-Yan and I wrote the first edition of this book a lot has changed, not least in the business environment. When we first wrote the book, the digital era was taking off in earnest. Now, thanks to globalization and advances in digitization even 'digital' is being replaced by 'mobile' as consumer tastes change.

Since organizations are open systems, global megatrends set the context for organizational success. Within the HR community there is a broader recognition today that organizations must learn to adapt quickly, so it is important to bring an OD mindset to HR practice. We have noticed that many L&D practitioners in particular have developed their OD capability; for instance many are holding stakeholder interviews, facilitating large-scale events, enabling strategic conversations at all levels. Increasingly learning interventions are being designed to help people gain self-awareness and new insights – for instance using actors, technology and other means of producing the mindset and skillset shifts required if organizations and their members are to thrive in fast-changing contexts. Leadership and personal development is increasingly borrowing concepts from varied sources such as mindfulness, neuroscience and so on.

With respect to talent, changing workforce demographics and global shortages are forcing the agenda and new approaches to attracting talent are being rapidly developed. Data analytics are increasingly being used to predict future workforce trends and even pinpoint where potential recruits may be found. In many organizations HR and Marketing are collaborating on the development of enticing employer brands and 'employee value propositions' in order to attract key talent. Social media are being used to target candidates and bring them 'on-board' before they have officially joined to the organization.

Focus on people and...

What defines a great place to work will also be in constant flux as the nature of work, workers and demand continues to evolve. This is HR's traditional heartland and today's dynamic context presents an unprecedented opportunity for HR to make a difference to their organization's health and sustainable success. Ironically in recent years HR's increasing focus on business has perhaps come at the expense of sufficient focus on employees. A CEO of a software company addressing an audience of HR professionals asked, 'Which of you believes that HR should be focused on ROI?' Almost the entire audience put their hands up. The CEO then said, 'That's a pity, because I need HR to focus on caring about people, firing all the "ass-holes", making my business the place where the best people want to be'. While his expression may be a bit extreme, he makes a good point. So perhaps we need to revisit what we believe our role to be about and gear our efforts accordingly.

The changing workforce mix, and in particular expectations of the 'connected' generations for immediacy of response, shared information and opportunities to contribute are driving a greater emphasis on employee voice. Social media is becoming a great leveller. In today's workplaces with their essentially 'volunteer' workforces, hierarchy is no longer a sufficient mechanism to drive transformational change. As labour markets become more fluid, people will only stay and give of their best if they feel that they are key stakeholders, are informed and involved in what is happening in their organizations.

Consequently HR must make efforts to understand what engages and disengages key parts of the workforce and put in place actions to improve engagement and commitment. Creating emotional commitment goes beyond the tangible elements of the employee 'deal' or psychological contract. While there is no 'one size fits all', people generally will want meaningful work, a shared purpose, flexibility over working arrangements; to feel valued, empowered and to have the chance to develop. HR needs to know how to tailor the 'employee value proposition' so that it is equitable and can also meet individuals' changing needs. Managing the employment relationship in a context of ongoing change will require HR to continuously seek to strike the right balance between employee and business interests and achieve beneficial outcomes for both.

So while today's typical HR 'people' agenda items – such as talent management, training line managers to be coaches, developing effective performance management systems – will remain very important, in future such activity will need to be part of a proactive and well-integrated approach to give the organization competitive advantage in attracting, engaging and retaining the talent it needs. This is the chance for HR to demonstrate agility, to anticipate the big people issues, do some workforce planning, apply agile methodology to recruitment processes, recruit people with flexible mindsets, work closely with line managers, help them to energize and develop their teams and prepare them for new ways of working.

HR should not only lead thinking but also implement with effect, figuring out how best to produce the largest benefits. Getting the transactional work done right – by applying business acumen, embracing technology, developing more mobile (and consistently accurate) HR services, increasing efficiency and effectiveness, building capable, high-performing HR teams – is the foundation on which other contributions can be built. HR practitioners therefore need to think and act pragmatically within a systemic OD understanding that enables them to weld together initiatives to improve the organization's functioning and increase its capacity for future success. For instance, HR can aid value creation by designing reward systems to encourage innovation and team-based working. By simplifying HR processes and focusing on talent and leadership HR can reinforce the employer brand and help create better employee engagement.

In short it's important to:

- Remember why you got into HR – it's not just about ROI, it's also about the people.

- Foster a culture of employee engagement. Start from first principles – there is no one 'right' way. What does good people practice look like in your organization?

- Find out what is most meaningful to employees in the work context. How do you know what matters to people? Listen, hear and feel for the answers. Do cuts of employee data by age etc to really understand what motivates people. Exit interviews are another useful – if belated – source of such insight.

- Make sure that what you are doing is right for your culture.

- Focus on key priority problem areas such as how to tackle employee turnover, or how to improve productivity, or cut down sickness absence. Look at what promotes disengagement. Get managers on board. Be clear what you are trying to achieve.

- In making the case for investment in people, understand what key stakeholders need to know before they will support you. For instance, to gain support for investing in improving employee engagement it may be worth estimating the cost of uncontrolled turnover, or to improve recruitment practices calculate the cost of a single bad recruitment (this usually works out at approximately 30 per cent of first year salary). What is the investment of time and money you need to make?

- Manage expectations down when developing your employer brand, so that new recruits will be pleasantly surprised when they join. Similarly current employees will not feel short changed.

- Get the basics right. The 'keep it simple' (KISS) principle applies. Develop simple policies eg on home working; reduce unnecessary bureaucracy; improve poor meeting practices or weak communications.

- Add value to basic processes. For instance, don't just design a good performance management process but also pull out the real organizational data and insight that can be acted on by executives.

Culture and climate

Looking ahead, I believe that, alongside HR's traditional focus on the people aspects of enterprise HR must also focus on improving organizational culture and climate and enabling cross-boundary linkages and knowledge sharing. After all, many workplaces have become dehumanizing and pressurized environments. If people are to thrive and do their best work, they need healthy and effective organizational cultures in which they and their contribution are valued.

Organizational culture and people management practice are key reputational risks with poor practice soon exposed to the public gaze via social media with damaging implications for business. With tighter regulation in some sectors and increased scrutiny in all sectors, transparency, authenticity and accountability must become basic tenets of company practice. So although HR's primary role is not to act as 'company police officer,' HR has a responsibility to ensure that the company's employment (and business) practice is both legal and ethical, and that employees are treated fairly. HR can learn from OD about how to challenge potentially problematic practice and how to work with the informal sides of organization, stimulate constructive politics and build momentum for better ways of working.

Similarly, the need for business agility, speed and innovation is driving new forms of organization, governance, skill requirements and high performance work practice. HR and OD can build the foundational elements of organizational agility and resilience on the base of the following principles:

- accelerate the pace of strategic renewal;
- focus intensely on the customer;
- innovate across boundaries;
- demonstrate values-based leadership;
- build a culture of purpose, empowerment, trust, meaning and accountability;
- select, motivate and support people who have the requisite skills to flourish in ambiguous and uncertain environments.

With culture in mind OD brings a lot to HR. With its humanistic values OD enables real transformation that is built on trust. With its systemic perspective and process methodologies OD does not treat individual elements of organization in isolation from one another but rather works on the linkages between them. For instance, there is no point in simply doing more

training if the underlying problem lies in the structure. This systemic approach helps ensure greater coherence and value from specific initiatives within and between elements.

By adopting an OD mindset HR will be able to contribute so much more than the sum of its parts; it will be capable of delivering a new form of organizational effectiveness. This means that HR practitioners must become very strategic in their thinking. They should proactively lead discussion about what needs to change, using everyday language and making skilful use of workforce and other data to pinpoint issues, developing strategy working back from the desired impact on the end user or customer. They must help design the work processes and roles which enable greater agility, employee empowerment and engagement.

HR must also collaborate effectively with other functions to deliver strategic goals with impact. In many organizations the agendas of HR and Employee Communications functions increasingly overlap – areas of shared focus include leadership behaviour, change communication, purpose, employee engagement and participation, strategic change, building communities of practice. Each specialist group brings different and complementary expertise to the party and there is obvious need for collaboration and joint effort to ensure that initiatives can be successfully implemented and embedded into the new way of operating.

In particular HR must give leaders the tools to make the 21st-century shift required of them. Top leaders need to pay attention to the bottom line, create an engaging workplace and ensure their organization interacts well with its environment and community. As the workforce becomes more empowered, the role of leaders becomes less about controlling and more about focusing on outcomes, creating the capability to seize emerging marketplace opportunities, encouraging experimentation and learning, and watching out for the long term as well as the short term. HR should support and challenge leaders, help them navigate the tensions, holding up a mirror to leaders and ensuring that their actions are aligned to values. These shifts do not occur overnight but require a concerted effort to align current practice to the new requirements and create a more integrated approach that helps people make sense of the emerging organization.

Moreover it is important to:

- Be intentional about culture – build trust by being open, transparent and grounded in the business and through everyday actions.
- Ask people how they would describe their current culture. What would they like it to be?
- Get a supportive environment in place at junior levels. Watch out for junior voices – empower them through eg upward feedback, exit interviews, appreciative inquiry.
- Release latent talent – value diversity.
- Encourage people to try things.

Building a change-able organization

Since organizations will need to keep on changing they must learn how to do so in ways which avoid destroying employee goodwill and engagement. The current context may mean that business models soon become obsolete; introducing new business models will have major implications for the way the organization operates and the kinds of people and skills it needs. HR can help develop the capabilities required for change-ability. In a change-able culture people at all levels are forward looking and proactive. They anticipate the big business trends and take short-term decisions with the longer term in mind and feedback loops work. There is speedy decision making and action; flexibility of structure and mindset; continuous improvement is the norm; risk is balanced with innovation; cost with investment. Agile organizations focus intensely on both the customer and also on employees.

In particular, people know why change is needed and are involved in designing and implementing solutions. Therefore change leaders must ensure that employee voice mechanisms work and that change initiatives are co-created and owned by those who must implement them. By being involved in the strategic conversation and the planning process employees get to understand the bigger picture, understand *why* change is needed and have the chance to share their thinking about the *how*, if not the *what* of change. As a result they will feel greater 'ownership' of the change agenda and gain greater meaning from their work. As people start to change their behaviour HR's 'levers' such as employee development and reward can help to embed new behaviours.

When well implemented, change offers the potential for positive new ways forward for all concerned. In profound change, the organization does not just do something new; it builds its capacity for doing things in a new way – indeed, it builds its capacity for ongoing change (Senge, 1999). By focusing on change, culture and leadership HR can help organizations become more agile and equip them for sustainable success in a fast-changing context. Recognizing that change is a journey – it never stops and success can take time – remember to celebrate breakthroughs as they are achieved.

Act now for a better future

I am personally very excited by the direction of travel for HR. This period presents an outstanding opportunity to help build the capabilities required for sustainable success. As change leaders OD and HR practitioners must work within a strategic frame, understand and influence the dynamics in play, develop and apply insight, skill and courage to where they can make the greatest difference. The task is to shape, influence and challenge people and context to produce 'better' practice. Both OD and HR practitioners must work on individual change initiatives with the longer term in mind, act as role models, using self as the most effective instrument of strategic

change. It's about recognizing that (to paraphrase Gandhi) you can be the change you want to see in the world.

Fuelled by the energy that derives from humanistic values, HR and OD can demonstrate that a new form of organizational effectiveness is both desirable and achievable. Working together HR and OD can build win-win employment relationships and mutually beneficial change outcomes for both the organization and its employees. Working together HR and OD can build change-able and sustainable organizations that are capable of achieving more than short-term competitive advantage alone. Because this is about redefining what organizational 'success' means, as David Cooperrider points out (1998, p4):

> *The best path to the good society is the construction of great organizations that nurture and magnify the best in human beings.*

A prize worth going for and today's organizations and their stakeholders deserve no less!

REFERENCES

Ackoff, R R (1974) *Redesigning the Future*, Wiley Interscience, New York, NY

Alfes, K, Gatenby, M, Rees, C, Soane, E C and Truss, C (2010) *Creating an Engaged Workforce*, CIPD, London

Allport, G W (1948) Foreword, in *Resolving Social Conflicts*, ed G W Lewin, Harper & Row, London

Anderson, D and Ackerman-Anderson, L (2001) *Beyond Change Management: Advanced strategies for today's transformational leaders*, John Wiley & Sons, New York, NY

Aon Hewitt [accessed 19 February 2015] Engagement 2.0: Focus on the right people, build the excitement, preserve the passion, *Aon Hewitt* [online] http://www.aon.com/attachments/engagement_2%200_oct2010.pdf

Ariely, D (2013) [accessed 18 February 2015] What makes us feel good about our work? *TED* [online] http://blog.ted.com/2013/04/10/what-motivates-us-at-work-7-fascinating-studies-that-give-insights/

Argyris, C (1957) *Personality and Organization*, HarperCollins, New York, NY

Argyris, C (1962) *Interpersonal Competence and Organizational Effectiveness*, Dorsey Press, Belmont, CA

Argyris, C (1970) *Intervention Theory and Method: A behavioral science view*, Addison-Wesley, Reading, MA

Argyris, C (1991) Teaching smart people how to learn, *Harvard Business Review*, 69 (3), pp 4–14

Armstrong, M (2009) *Handbook of Human Resource Management Practice*, 11th edn, pp 65–81, Kogan Page, London

Augier, M and Teece, D J (2005) Reflections on (Schumpeterian) leadership: A report on a seminar on leadership and management education, *California Management Review*, February 1

Axlerod, R H (2010) *Terms of Engagement: New ways of leading and changing organizations*, Berrett-Koehler, San Francisco, CA

Bak, P (1997) *How Nature Works: The science of self-organised criticality*, University Press, Oxford

Balain, S and Sparrow, P (2009) *Engaged to Perform: A new perspective on employee engagement*, White Paper dated September 4th, Centre for Evidence-Based HR at the University of Lancaster 1

Bandura, A (1997) *Self Efficacy in Changing Societies*, Cambridge University Press, Cambridge

Bargal, D and Bar, H (1992) Introduction: The heritage of Kurt Lewin, *Journal of Social Issues*, 48 (2), pp 3–13

Baron, A and Walters, M (1994) *The Culture Factor: Corporate and international perspectives*, CIPD, London

Barrett, F, Thomas, G F and Hocevar, S P (1995) The central role of discourse in large-scale change: a social construction perspective, *Journal of Applied Behavioural Science*, **31** (3), pp 352–72

Bate, P, Bevan, H and Robert, G (2002) *Towards a Million Change Agents*, NHS Modernisation Agency, London

Bates, C (1991) *Pigs Eat Wolves: Going into partnership with your dark side*, Yes International Publishers, Saint Paul, MA

Beckhard, R (1969) *Organization Development: Strategies and models*, Addison-Wesley, Reading, MA

Beckhard, R (1981) Who needs us? Some hard thoughts about a moving target – the future, *OD Practitioner*, **13** (4)

Beckhard, R (1997) *Agent of Change: My life, my practice*, Jossey-Bass, San Francisco, CA

Beckhard, R and Harris, R T (1977) *Organizational Transitions: Managing complex change*, Addison-Wesley, Reading, MA

Beer, M (1980) *Organization Change and Development: A systems view*, Goodyear Publishing Company, Santa Monica, CA

Benne, K D (1975) *The Laboratory Method of Changing and Learning: Theory and application*, ed K D Benne, Science and Behavior Books, Pal Alto, CA

Bennis, W G (1966) The coming death of bureaucracy, *Think*, Nov–Dec, pp 30–35

Bennis, W G (1967) Organizations of the future, *Personnel Administration*, Sep–Oct, pp 6–19

Bennis, W G (1969) *Organization Development: Its nature, origins, and prospects*, Addison-Wesley, Reading, MA

Bennis, W G (1970) A funny thing happened on the way to the future, *American Psychologist*, **25**, pp 595–608

Berger, P and Luckmann, T (1966) *The Social Construction of Reality*, Anchor Books, New York, NY

Bernstein, L (1968) *Management Development*, Business Books, London

Black, J A (2000) Fermenting change: capitalizing on the inherent change found in dynamic non-linear (or complex) systems, *Journal of Organizational Change Management*, **13** (6), pp 520–25

Blake, R R and Mouton, J S (1976) *Consultation*, Addison-Wesley, Reading, MA

Blake, R R and Mouton, J S (1978) *The New Managerial Grid*, Gulf, Houston, TX

Blake, R R and Mouton, J S (1985) *The Managerial Grid III: The key to leadership excellence*, Gulf Publishing Co., Houston, TX

Block, P (2008) *Community: The structure of belonging*, Berrett-Koehler Publishers, San Francisco, CA

Boudreau, J W and Ramstad, P M (2007) *Beyond HR: The new science of human capital*, Harvard Business Publishing, Boston, MA

Boury, D, Lucy, D, Sinclair, A and Jackson, C (2013) Management Agenda 2013, *Roffey Park* [online] http://www.wales.nhs.uk/sitesplus/documents/1096/The-Management-Agenda-2013-with-covers1.pdf

Boyatzis, R and McKee, A (2005) *Resonant Leadership*, Harvard Business Publishing, Boston, MA

Bradford, D L and Burke, W W (2005) *Reinventing Organization Development: New approaches to change in organizations*, ed D L Bradford, Pfeiffer, San Francisco, CA

Bridges, S W (2003) *Managing Transitions Making the Most of Change*, Da Capo Press, New York, NY

Bridges, S W (2004) *Transitions: Making Sense of Life's Changes*, Revised 25th anniversary edn, Da Capo Press, New York, NY

Brown, S L and Eisenhardt, K M (1997) The art of continuous change: Linking complexity theory and time-paced evolution in relentless shifting organisations, *Administrative Science Quarterly*, **42**, pp 1–34

Bunker, B B and Alban, B T (1996) *Large Group Interventions Engaging the whole system for rapid change*, Jossey-Bass, San Francisco, CA

Bunker, B B, Alban, B T and Lewicki, R J (2005) Ideas in currency and OD practice: has the well gone dry? in *Reinventing Organization Development*, ed D Bradford and W Burke, Pfeiffer: an Imprint of Wiley, San Francisco, CA

Burke, W (2002) *Organization Change: Theory and practice (Foundations for Organizational Science)*, SAGE, London

Burke, W (1982) *Organization Development: Principles and practice*, Little Brown, Boston, MA

Burke, W (1994) *Organization Development: A process of learning and changing*, 2nd edn, Addison-Wesley, Reading, MA

Burke, W (1997) What HR practitioners need to know for the 21st century, *Human Resource Management*, **36** (1), pp 71–79

Burke, W (2006) Where did OD come from? in *Organization Development*, ed J V Gallos, pp 13–38, Jossey-Bass, San Francisco, CA

Burke, W and Litwin, G (1992) Burke-Litwin Model of Organization Performance, *Journal of Management*, **18** (3), pp 523–45

Burke, W W and Hornstein, H A (eds) (1972) *The Social Technology of Organization Development*, University Associates, La Jolla, CA

Burnes, B (2004) Kurt Lewin and the planned approach to change: A re-appraisal, *Journal of Management Studies*, **41** (6), pp 972–1002

Bushe, G (2013) Dialogic OD: a theory of practice, *OD Practitioner*, **45** (1), pp 11–18

Bushe, G R and Marshak, R J (2008) The postmodern turn in OD, *OD Practitioner*, **40** (4), pp 9–11

Bushe, G R and Marshak, R J (2009) Revisioning organization development: diagnostic and dialogic premises and patterns of practice, *Journal of Applied Behavioral Science*, **45**, p 348

Bushe, G R and Marshak, R J (2015) *Dialogic Organization Development: The theory and practice of transformational change*, Berrett-Koehler Publishers, San Francisco, CH

Calarco, A and Gurvis, J (2006) *Adaptability: Responding effectively to change*, CCL Press, Greensboro, NC

Campbell, J (2008) *The Hero with a Thousand Faces (The Collected Works of Joseph Campbell)*, 3rd edition, New World Library, Novato, CA

Chan Allen, R (2002) *Guiding Change Journeys: A synergistic approach to organization transformation*, Pfeiffer Jossey-Bass, San Francisco, CA

Change Fusion (2014) *Our Collaborative Approach*, www.change-fusion.com/Approach.html [accessed 9 April 2015]

Charam, R (2014) [accessed 18 February 2015] It's time to split HR, *Harvard Business Review* [online] https://hbr.org/2014/07/its-time-to-split-hr

Cheung-Judge, M Y (2001) The self as an instrument: a cornerstone for the future of OD, *OD Practitioner*, **33** (3)

CIPD (2003) *Understanding the People and Performance Link: Unlocking the black box*, CIPD, London

CIPD (2004) *Employee Well-Being and the Psychological Contract*, CIPD, London

CIP (2006) *How engaged are British employees?* CIPD, London

CIPD (2008) *Smart Working: How smart is UK PLC?* Chartered Institute of Personnel and Development, London

CIPD (2009) *Employee Outlook*, Chartered Institute of Personnel and Development, London

CIPD (2014) [accessed 18 February 2015] Labour Market Outlook, *Chartered Institute of Personnel and Development* [online] http://www.cipd.co.uk/hr-resources/surveyreports/labour-market-outlooksummer-2014.aspx

CIPD and SuccessFactors (2013) Labour Market Outlook, *CIPD* [online] http://www.cipd.co.uk/hr-resources/survey-reports/labour-market-outlook-winter-2012-13.aspx

Cohen, J and Stewart, I (1995) *The Collapse of Chaos: Discovering simplicity in a complex world*, Penguin Press Science, London

Collins, J C (2001) *Good to Great: Why some companies make the leap... and others don't*, Harper Collins, London

Cooperrider, D L (1998) An invitation to organizational wisdom and executive courage, in *Organizational Wisdom and Executive Courage*, ed D L Cooperrider and S Srivastva, Lexington Books, Lanham, MD

Cooperrider, D L (2000) Positive image, positive action: the affirmative basis of organizing, in *Appreciative Inquiry*, ed D Cooperrider *et al*, pp 29–53, Stipes Publishing, Champaign, IL

Cooperrider, D L and Srivastva, S (1987) Appreciative inquiry in organizational life, *Research in Organizational Change and Development*, **1**, pp 129–69

Cooperrider, D L and Srivastva, S (eds) (1998) *Organizational Wisdom and Executive Courage*, Lexington Books, Lanham, MD

Corporate Leadership Council [accessed 19 February 2015] Driving performance and retention through employee engagement, *Corporate Executive Board* [online] http://www.usc.edu/programs/cwfl/assets/pdf/Employee%20engagement.pdf

Corporate Research Forum (2004) *Designing Effective Organisations*, CRF, London

Corporate Research Forum (2009) *Configuring HR for Tomorrow's Challenges*, CRF, London

Covey, S (1995) *First Things First*, Fireside, New York, NY

Covey, S (2004) *The 8th Habit: From effectiveness to greatness*, Free Press, New York, NY

Csikszentmihalyi, M (1992) *Flow: The psychology of optimal experience*, Harper, New York, NY

Cummings, T G and Worley, C G (2001) *Organizational Development and Change*, 7th edn, South-Western College Pub., Cincinnati, OH

Curran, K, Seashore, C and Welp, M (1995) Use of Self as an Instrument of Change, presented at *The 1995 ODN National Conference*, 17 November, Seattle, Washington

D'Aveni, R A (1994) *Hyper-competition*, Free Press, New York, NY

Davis, S M (1984) *Managing Corporate Culture*, Ballinger Publishing Company, Pensacola, FL

Davis, S M and Lawrence, P R (1977) *Matrix*, Addison-Wesley, Reading

DDI/CIPD Research Insight (2007) *Leadership Transitions: Maximising HR's contribution*, CIPD, London

Dent, E B and Goldberg, S G (1999) Challenging resistance to change, *Journal of Applied Behavioural Science*, 35 (1), pp 25–41

Devine, M (1999) *Mergers and Acquisitions Checklist*, Roffey Park, Horsham

Devine, M, Hirsh, W, Garrow, V and Holbeche, L (1998) *Mergers & Acquisitions: Getting the people bit right*, Roffey Park, Horsham

Dolan, P (2010) MINDSPACE: Influencing behaviour through public policy, *Institute for Government* [online] http://www.instituteforgovernment.org.uk/sites/default/files/publications/MINDSPACE.pdf [accessed 18 February 2015]

Drucker, P F (2007) *The Effective Executive*, Classic Drucker Collection Edition, Butterworth-Heinemann, Oxford

Eccleston, J (2010) CIPD defends 'Think HR, Think Again' campaign following backlash, *Personnel Today* [online] http://www.personneltoday.com/hr/cipd-defends-think-hr-think-again-campaign-following-backlash/

Economist Intelligence Unit (2008) *Securing the Value of Business Process Change*. A study commissioned by Logica Management Consulting, London

Economist Intelligence Unit (2009) [accessed 19 February 2015] Organisational Agility: How business can survive and thrive in turbulent times, *Economist Intelligence Unit* [online] http://www.emc.com/collateral/leadership/organisational-agility-230309.pdf

Egan, G (1988) *Change Agent Skills: Assessing and designing excellence*, Pfeiffer & Company, San Diego, CA

Emerson, R (1962) Power dependence relations, *American Sociological Review*, 27, pp 31–40

Emery, F E and Trist, E (1973) *Towards a Social Ecology*, Plenum/Rosetta, New York, NY

Emmott, M (2009) An HR Director's Guide To Employee Engagement, A discussion paper, *CIPD* [online] http://www.digitalopinion.co.uk/files/documents/An_HR_Directors_Guide_to_Employee_Engagement.pdf

Eoyang, G (1997) *Coping with Chaos: Seven simple tools*, Lagumo, WY

Eoyang, G (2010) Complexity demands simplicity, Blog relating to Systems Week, http://aea365.org/blog/systems-tig-week-glenda-eoyang-on-complexity-demands-simplicity/ [accessed 7 April 2015]

Ernst and Young (2010) *The New Global Mindset: Driving innovation through diverse perspectives*, Ernst and Young, London

Evans, C (2003) *Managing for Knowledge: HR's strategic role*, Butterworth-Heinemann, Oxford

Ferguson, C K (1968) Concerning the nature of human systems and the consultant's role, *Journal of Applied Behavioural Science*, 4, pp 179–93

French, W and Bell, C (1978) *Organization Development: Behavioral science interventions for organization improvement*, 1st edn, Prentice Hall, New Jersey, NJ

French, W and Bell, C (1999) *Organization Development: Behavioral science interventions for organization improvement*, 6th edn, Prentice Hall, New Jersey, NJ

French, J and Raven, B (1959) The bases of social power, in *Studies in Social Power*, ed D Cartwright, pp 150–67, University of Michigan, Ann Arbor, MI

Funches, D (1989) Three gifts of the Organization Development practitioner, *The Emerging Practice of Organization Development*, ed W Sikes, A Drexler and J Gant, NTL Institute, Alexandria, VA

Galbraith, J R (1973) *Designing Complex Organizations*, Addison-Wesley, Reading, MA

Galbraith, J R (1977) *Organization Design*, Addison-Wesley, Reading, MA

Galbraith, J R (1994) *Competing With Flexible Lateral Organizations*, 2nd edn, Financial Times/Prentice Hall, London

Galbraith, J R (2002) *Designing Organizations: An executive guide to strategy, structure and process*, Jossey-Bass, San Francisco, CA

Galbraith, J R (2005) *Designing the Customer-centric Organization: A guide to strategy, structure and process*, Jossey-Bass, San Francisco, CA

Galbraith, J R and Kates, A (2007) *Designing your Organization: Using the Star model to solve five critical design challenges*, John Wiley, New York, NY

Gallos, J V et al (2006) *Organization Development*, ed J V Gallos, Jossey-Bass, San Francisco, CA

Gartside, D, Gossage, W, Silverstone, Y, Tambe, H and Cantrell, S M (2013) *Trends Reshaping the Future of HR: HR drives the agile organization*, Accenture, London

Gatenby, M, Truss, C, Rees, C and Soane, E [accessed 19 February 2015] Employee Engagement in Context, *CIPD* [online] http://www.cipd.co.uk/NR/rdonlyres/6D7D52C8-6E51-4539-A189-1E2D6EBEF01F/0/employee_engagement_context.pdf

Gellermann, W, Frankel, M S and Landenson, R F (1990) *Values and Ethics in Organization and Human Systems Development*, Jossey-Bass, San Francisco, CA

Gilpin-Jackson, Y (2013) Practicing in the grey area between dialogic and diagnostic organisation development: lessons from a healthcare case study, *OD Practitioner*, 45 (1), pp 60

Goffman, E (1959) *The Presentation of Self in Everyday Society*, Doubleday, Garden City, NY

Golembiewski, R, Billingsley, K and Yeager, S (1976) Measuring change and persistence in human affairs: types of change generated by OD designs, *Journal of Applied Behavioral Science*, 12 (2), pp 133–57

Greiner, L and Schein, V E (1988) A revisionist look at power and OD, *The Industrial-Organizational Psychologist*, 25 (2), pp 59–61

Greiner, L E and Schein, V E (1988) *Power and organization development: Mobilizing power to implement change*, Addison-Wesley, Reading, MA

Guest, D *et al* (2003) Human resource management and performance, *British Journal of Industrial Relations*, **41** (2), pp 291–314

Gunther-McGrath, R (2013) *The End of Competitive Advantage: How to keep your strategy moving as fast as your business*, Harvard Business Review Press, Boston, MA

Hall, A D and Fagen, R E (1956) Definition of system, *General Systems: Yearbook of the Society for the General Systems Research*, **1**, pp 11–17

Hamel, G (with Breen, B) (2007) *The Future of Management*, Harvard Business Publishing, Boston, MA

Hanna, D P (1988) *Designing Organizations for High Performance*, Addison-Wesley, Reading, MA

Heger, B K (2007) Linking the Employee Value Proposition (EVP) to employee engagement and business outcomes, preliminary findings from a linkage research pilot study, *Organization Development Journal*, **25** (2), p 123

Holbeche, L S (1997) *Motivating People in Lean Organizations*, Butterworth-Heinemann, Oxford

Holbeche, L S (2005) *The Power of Constructive Politics*, Roffey Park, Horsham

Holbeche, L S (2005a) *The High Performance Organization*, Butterworth-Heinemann, Oxford

Holbeche, L S (2005b) *Understanding Change Theory, Implementation and Success*, Butterworth-Heinemann, Oxford

Holbeche, L S (2009) *HR Leadership*, Butterworth-Heinemann, Oxford

Holbeche, L S (2015) *The Agile Organization*, Kogan Page, London

Holbeche, L S and Matthews, G (2012) *Engaged: Unleashing your organization's potential through employee engagement*, Jossey-Bass, San Francisco, CA

Holbeche, L S and Springett, N (2004) *In Search of Meaning*, Roffey Park Institute, Horsham

Holman, P (2013) A call to engage: realizing the potential of dialogic organisation development, *OD Practitioner*, **45** (1), pp 18–24

Holman, P and Devane, T (1999) *The Change Handbook Group Methods for Shaping the Future*, Berrett Koehler, San Francisco, CH

Holman, P, Devane, T and Cady, S (2007) *The Change Handbook: The definitive resource to today's best methods for engaging whole systems*, Berrett-Koehler Publishers, Inc, San Francisco, CA

Human System Dynamics (2013) *Frequently Asked Questions about HSD Institute*, www.hsdinstitute.org/about-hsd/what-is-hsd/faq-about-the-hsd-institute.html [accessed 8 April 2015]

Huselid, M A, Becker, B E and Beatty, R W (2005) *The Workforce Scorecard: Managing human capital to execute strategy*, Harvard Business Publishing, Harvard, MA

Jenner, R A (1998) Dissipative enterprises, chaos, and the principles of lean organizations, *Omergo: International Journal of Management Science*, **26** (3), pp 397–407

Jones, B B and Brazzel, M (2006) *The NTL Handbook of Organization Development and Change: Principles, practices and perspectives*, ed B B Jones and M Brazzel, Pfeiffer: A Wiley Imprint, San Francisco, CA

Jung, C (1921, translated 1923) *Psychological Types; or, The Psychology of Individuation*, Paul, Trench, Trübner, London

Kahneman, D (2011) *Thinking, Fast and Slow*, Penguin, London

Kanter, R M (1977) *Men and Women of the Corporation*, Basic Books, New York, NY

Kanter, R M (1979) Power failure in management circuits, *Harvard Business Review*, **57** (4), pp 65–75

Kast, F E and Rosenzweig, J E (1985) *Organization and Management: A system approach*, 4th edn, McGraw-Hill, New York, NY

Katz, D and Kahn, R L (1966 and 1978) *The Social Psychology of Organizations*, 1st and 2nd edn, Wiley, New York, NY

Katz, D and Kahn, R L (1978) *The Social Psychology of Organizations*, 2nd edn, Wiley, New York, NY

Kauffman, S A (1993) *The Origins of Order: Self-organization and selection in evolution*, University Press, New York, NY

Kauffman, S A (1995) Escaping the red queen effect, *The Mckinsey Quarterly*, **1**, pp 119–29

Kelly, K (1999) *New Rules for the New Economy: 10 radical strategies for a connected world*, Penguin, London

Kelman, S (2005) *Unleashing Change: A study of organization renewal in government*, Brookings Institution Press, Washington DC

Kippenberger, T (1998a) Planned change: Kurt Lewin's legacy, *The Antidote*, **3** (4), pp 10–12

Kippenberger, T (1998b) Managed learning: elaborating on Lewin's model, *The Antidote*, **3** (4), p 13

Kotter, J (2006) Leading change: why transformation efforts fail, *Harvard Business School, Best of HBR*, www.oppapers.com/.../leading-change-why-transformation-efforts-fail-hypotheses-page4.html

Kotter, J and Cohen, D (2002) *The Heart of Change: Real life stories of how people change their organizations*, Harvard Business Press, Boston

Kotter, J and Schlesinger (1979) *Choosing Strategies for Change*, Harvard Business Publishing, Boston, MA

Kransdorff, A (1998) *Corporate Amnesia*, Butterworth-Heinemann, Oxford

Kübler-Ross, E (1973) *On Death and Dying*, Routledge, London

Lawler III, E E and Mohrman, S A (2003) HR as a strategic partner: what does it take to make it happen, *Human Resource Planning*, **26** (5), p 15

Lawler III, E E and Worley, C (2006) *Built to Change: How to achieve sustained organizational effectiveness*, Jossey-Bass, San Francisco, CA

Lewin, K (1943) Psychological ecology, in *Field Theory in Social Science*, ed D Cartwright, Social Science Paperbacks, London

Lewin, K (1946) Action research and minority problems, in *Resolving Social Conflict*, ed G W Lewin, Harper and Row, London

Lewin, K (1947) Frontiers in group dynamics I: Concept, method and reality in social sciences; social equilibria and social change, *Human Relations*, **1**, pp 5–41

Lewin, K (1947) Frontiers in group dynamics II: Channels of group life: Social planning and Action Research, *Human Relations*, **1**, pp 143–53

Lewin, K (1948) *Resolving Social Conflicts: Selected papers on group dynamics*, ed G W Lewin, Harper and Row, New York, NY

Lewin, K (1951) *Field Theory in Social Science: Selected theoretical papers*, ed D Cartwright, Harper, New York, NY

Lewin, K (1958) Group decision and social change, in *Readings in Social Psychology*, ed E E Maccoby, T M Newcomb and E L Hartley, pp 197–211, Holt, Rinehart and Winston, New York, NY

Likert, R (1961) *New Patterns of Management*, McGraw-Hill, New York, NY

Likert, R (1967) *The Human Organization: Its management and value*, McGraw-Hill, New York, NY

Lippitt, R and Lippitt, G (1975) *Consulting Process in Action: Examining the dynamics of the client–consultant working relationship*, Development Publications, Washington, DC

Lippitt, R and Lippitt, G (1978) *The Consulting Process in Action*, University Associates, La Jolla, CA

Louis, M R (1983) Organizations as culture-bearing milieu, in L R Pondy *et al* (eds) *Organizational Symbolism*, CTJAI Press, Greenwich, NY

Lynn, G T (1997) Levels of development for OD consultants: moving from self-acceptance to mastery, in *Organization Development Classics*, ed D F Van Eyde, J C Hoy and D C Van Eyde, pp 195–201, Jossey-Bass, San Francisco, CA

MacDonald, G (2012) [accessed 18 February 2015] Four keys to changing employee behaviour, *Financial Post* [online] http://business.financialpost.com/2012/12/07/four-keys-to-changing-employee-behaviour/

MacLeod, D and Clarke, N (2009) *Engaging for Success: Enhancing performance through employee engagement*, UK Department for Business (BIS), London

Mann, F (1957) Studying and creating change: a means to understanding social organization, in *Research in Industrial Human Relations*, pp 146–68, Harper, New York, NY

Marcos, J and Macaulay, S (2008) *Organisational Resilience: The key to anticipation, adaptation and recovery*, Cranfield School of Management, Bedford

Margulies, N (1978) Perspectives on the marginality of the consultant's role, *The Cutting Edge: Current theory and practice in Organization Development*, ed W W Burke, University Associates, La Jolla, CA

Margulies, N and Raia, A P (1984) The politics of Organization Development, in *The Best of Organization Development*, ed R A Hill, pp 90–93, American Society for Training & Development, Alexandria, VA

Marrow, A J (1969) *The Practical Theorist: The life and work of Kurt Lewin*, Basic Books, New York, NY

Marsh, C , Sparrow, P, Hird, M, Balain, S and Hesketh, A (2009) *Integrated Organisation Design: The new strategic priority for HR directors*, Lancaster University Management School, Lancaster

Marshak, R J (2006) *Covert Processes at Work: Managing the five hidden dimensions of organizational change*, Berrett-Koehler Publishers Inc, San Francisco, CA

Marshak, R J (1993) Managing the Metaphors of Change, *Organizational Dynamics*, **22** (1), pp 44–56

Marshak, R J (2002) Changing the Language of Change: How new contexts and concepts are challenging the ways we think and talk about organizational change, *Strategic Change*, **11** (5), pp 279–86

Marshak, R J and Grant, D (2008) Organizational discourse and new Organization Development practices, *British Journal of Management*, **19**, S7–S19

Marshak, R J and Grant, D (2011) Creating change by changing the conversation, *OD Practitioner*, **43** (3), pp 2

Maslach, C, Schaufeli, W B and Leiter, M P (2001) Job Burnout, *Annual Review of Psychology*, **52**, pp 397–422

McCann, J, Selskey, J and Lee, J (2009) Building agility, resilience and performance in turbulent environments, *HR People and Strategy* [online] www.hrps.org/resource/resmgr/p.../hrps_p_sissue32.3_mccann_et.pdf

McClelland, D (1970) Two faces of power, *Journal of International Affairs*, **24** (1), pp 29–47

McClelland, D and Burnham, D (1976) Power is the great motivator, *Harvard Business Review*, **54** (2), pp 100–10

McCormick, D and White, J (2000) Using one's self as an instrument for organizational diagnosis, *The Organizational Development Journal*, **18** (3), pp 49–61

McGregor, D (1960) *The Human Side of Enterprise*, McGraw-Hill, New York, NY

McLagan, P (1989) *Models for HRD Practice*, American Society for Training and Development, Alexandria, VA

McLean, G and Sullivan, R (1989) Essential competence of internal and external OD consultants, cited in W J Rothwell, R Sullivan and G N McLean (1995) *Practicing Organization Development: A guide for consultants*, Jossey-Bass/Pfeiffer, San Francisco, CA

McLean, G and Sullivan, R (1990) OD skills: An ongoing competency list, *OD Practitioner*, **22** (2), pp 11–12

Mead, G H (1934) *Mind, Self and Society From the Standpoint of a Social Behaviorist*, University of Chicago Press, Chicago, IL

Michelman, P [accessed 19 February 2015] Methodology: How great managers manage people, *Harvard Management Update* [online] http://blogs.hbr.org/hmu/2008/02/how-great-managers-manage-peop-1.html

Miller, L [accessed 31 October 2013] Leading Change: Nine keys to success, *Management Meditations* [online], http://www.lmmiller.com/2013/10/31/organization-design-and-process-improvement/change-management-five-keys-leading-sustainable-change/

Miller, P and Skidmore, P (2004) *Disorganisation: Why future organisations must 'loosen up'*, Demos, London

Mintzberg, H (1982) *Power and the Life Cycles of Organizations*, McGill University, Montreal

Mintzberg, H (1983) *Power In and Around Organizations*, Prentice-Hall, New Jersey

Mirvis, P (2006) Revolutions in OD: The new and the new, new things, in *Organization Development*, ed J V Gallos, Jossey-Bass, San Francisco, CA

Mohrman, S A (2003) Designing work for knowledge-based competition, in *Managing Knowledge for Sustained Competitive Advantage: Designing strategies for effective human resource management*, eds S Jackson, M Hitt and A Denisi, Jossey-Bass, San Francisco, 37–58

Morhman, S A (2007) *Leading Change: Do it with conversation*, CEO publication, Los Angeles, G 07-6 (516)

Mohrman, S and Mohrman, A Jr (1997) *Designing and Leading Team-Based Organizations: A workbook for organizational self-design*, CEO Publications, Los Angeles, CA

Morgan, G (1997) *Images of Organization*, 2nd edn, Sage, London

Nadler, D A (1977) *Feedback and Organization Development: Using data-based methods*, Addison-Wesley, Reading, MA

Nadler, D A (1998) *Champions of Change: How CEOs and their companies are mastering the skills of radical change*, Jossey-Bass, San Francisco, CA

Nadler, D A & Gerstein, M S (1992) *Designing High Performance Work Systems: Organizing people, work, technology, and information*, Jossey-Bass, San Francisco, CA

Nevis, E C (1987) *Organizational Consulting: A gestalt approach*, GIC Press, Cambridge

Nolan, J (2006) Organization Diagnosis Phase, in *The NTL Handbook of Organization Development and Change: Principles, practices and perspectives*, ed B B Jones and M Brazzel, Pfeiffer: A Wiley Imprint, San Francisco, CA

Olson, E E and Eoyang, G H (2001) *Facilitating Organization Change*, Jossey-Bass Pfeiffer, San Francisco, CA

Paauwe, J (2004) *HRM and Performance*, Oxford University Press, Oxford

Parker, L and Bevan, S (2011) *Good work and our times*, UK Commission for Employment and Skills, The Work Foundation, London

Pascale, R T (2006) Spotlight on Richard T. Pascale, *Management Decision*, **44** (7), pp 973–79

Pascale, R T, Millenmann, M and Gioja, L (2000) *Surfing the Edge of Chaos: The laws of nature and the new laws of business*, Crown Business, New York, NY

Patton, M Q (2010) *Developmental Evaluation: Applying complexity concepts to enhance innovation and use*, Guilford Press, London

Perls, F (1969) *Ego, Hunger and Aggression*, Vintage Books, New York, NY

Peters, T and Waterman, R (1982) *In Search of Excellence*, Harper Row, New York, NY

Pfeffer, J and Sutton, R I (1999) *The Knowing-doing Gap: How smart companies turn knowledge into action*, Harvard Business Publishing, Boston, MA

Phillips, J J, Stone, R D and Phillips, P P (2001) *The Human Resources Scorecard: Measuring the return on investment*, Butterworth-Heinemann, Boston, MA

Phillips, P P (2002) *The Bottom Line on ROI: Basics, benefits, and barriers to measuring training and performance improvement*, ed J J Phillips, CEP Press, Atlanta, GA

Pomeroy, A (2006) Rules can't ensure ethical behaviour, Executive Briefing, *HR Magazine*, **51** (11), p 14

Porras, J I and Berg, P O (1978) The impact of Organization Development, *The Academy of Management Review*, **3** (2), pp 249–66

Porter, M E(1980) *Competitive Strategy*, Free Press, New York, NY

Prigogine, I and Stengers, I (1984) *Order Out of Chaos: Man's new dialogue with nature*, Bantam Books, New York, NY

Purcell, J (2003) *Understanding the People and Performance Link: Unlocking the black box*, CIPD, London

Quade, K and Holladay, R (2010) *Dynamical Leadership: Building adaptive capacity for uncertain times*, CreateSpace Publishing, Charleston, SC

Raelin, J A (2005) We the leaders in order to form a leaderful organization, *Journal of Leadership and Organizational Studies*, **12** (1), pp 18–31, Fall

Rainey Tolbert, M A and Hanafin, J (2006) Use of self in OD consulting: what matters is presence, in *The NTL Handbook of Organization Development and Change: Principles, practices, and perspectives*, ed B B Jones and M Brazzel, pp 69–82, John Wiley & Sons, New York, NY

Reddy, B (1994) *Intervention Skills: Process consultation for small groups and teams*, Jossey-Bass/Pfeiffer, San Francisco, CA

Reffo, G and Wark, V (2014) *Leadership PQ*, Kogan Page, London

Rice, A (1958) *Productivity and Social Organizations: The Ahmedabad experiment*, Tavistock Institute, London

Rivlin, G (2004) *Mergers, Acquisitions and Divestitures*, McKinsey, New York

Robinson, D, Perryman, S and Hayday, S [accessed 19 February 2015] The Drivers of Employee Engagement, *Institute for Employment Studies* [online] http://www.employment-studies.co.uk/resource/drivers-employee-engagement

Rogers, C (1968) Interpersonal relationships: USA 2000, *Journal of Applied Behavioural Science*, **4** (3), pp 265–80

Rothwell, W, Sullivan, R and McLean, G (1995) *Practicing Organization Development: A guide for consultants*, ed W Rothwell, R Sullivan and G McLean, Jossey-Bass/Pfeiffer, San Francisco, CA

Rousseau, D M (2005) *I-deals: Idiosyncratic deals employees bargain for themselves*, Routledge, Oxford

Salancik, G and Pfeffer, J (1977) Who gets power and how they hold onto it: a strategic–contingency model of power, *Organizational Dynamics*, **5**, p 3

Schein, E H (1965) *Organizational Psychology*, Prentice-Hall, Englewood Cliffs, NJ

Schein, E H (1969) *Process Consultations: Its role in Organization Development*, Addison-Wesley, Reading, MA

Schein, E H (1980) *Organizational Psychology*, 3rd edn, Prentice-Hall, Englewood Cliffs, NJ

Schein, E H (1988) *Organizational Psychology*, 3rd edn, Prentice-Hall, London

Schein, E H (1988) *Process Consultation: Volume I*, 2nd edn, Addison-Wesley, Reading, MA

Schein, E H (1996) Kurt Lewin's change theory in the field and in the classroom: Notes towards a model of management learning, *Systems Practice*, **9** (1), pp 27–47

Schein, E H (2004) *Organizational Culture and Leadership*, 3rd edn, Jossey Bass, San Francisco, CA

Schein, E H (2006a) Foreword: Observations on the state of Organization Development, in *Organization Development*, ed J V Gallos, pp xv–xix, Jossey-Bass, San Francisco, CA

Schein, E H (2006b) *Organization Development*, ed J V Gallos, Jossey-Bass, San Francisco, CA

Schmuck, R A and Miles, M B (1976) *Organizational Development in Schools*, University Associates, San Diego, CA

Schroeder, M (1974) The shadow consultant, *Journal of Applied Behavioural Science*, **10** (4), pp 579–94

Sears, L (2010) *Next Generation HR Research Paper*, CIPD

Seely Brown, J and Solomon Gray, E (1995) The People are the Company, *Fast Company*, **1**

Senge, P M (1990) *The Fifth Discipline: The art and practice of the learning organization*, Doubleday, New York, NY

Senge, P (1999) *The Dance of Change: The challenges of sustaining momentum in learning organizations (with others)*, Nicholas Brearley, London

Sibbet, D (2003) *Best Practices for Facilitation*, The Grove Consultants International, San Francisco, CA

Siu, R (1979) *The Craft of Power*, John Wiley, New York, NY

Smith, M K (2001) Kurt Lewin: group, experimental learning and action research, *The Encyclopedia of Informal Education*, pp 1–15

Snowden, D (2002) Complex acts of knowing: paradox and descriptive self awareness, *The Journal of Knowledge Management*, **6** (2), pp 100–11

Sparrow, P, Wong, W, Otaye, L and Bevan, S [accessed 19 February 2015] The Changing Contours of Fairness: Can we match individual and organisational perspectives? *CIPD* [online] http://www.cipd.co.uk/binaries/the-changing-contours-of-fairness_2013-individual-organisation-perspectives.pdf

Spears, L C (2004) Practicing servant-leadership, *Leader to Leader*, Fall

Stacey, R D (1992) *Managing the Unknowable: Strategic boundaries between order and chaos in organizations*, Jossey-Bass, San Francisco, CA

Stacey, R D (1993) *Strategic Management and Organisational Dynamics*, Pitman, London

Stacey, R D (1996) *Complexity and Creativity in Organization*, Berrett-Koehler, San Francisco, CA

Stacey, R D (2003) *Strategic Management and Organisational Dynamics: The challenge of complexity*, FT/Prentice-Hall, Harlow

Stacey, R D, Giffin, D and Shaw, P (2002) *Complexity and Management: Fad or radical challenges to systems thinking?* Routledge, London

Stanovich, K E and West, R F (2000) Individual Differences in Reasoning: Implications for the rationality debate? *Behavioral and Brain Sciences*, **23** pp 645–726

Stokes, H and Harrison, R (1992) *Diagnosing Organizational Culture*, Pfeiffer, San Francisco, CA

Sujansky, J (2003) 20 keys to leadership, *Healthy, Wealthy n Wise*, Leader to Leader, 34: 7

Sullivan, R and Sullivan, K (1995) Essential competencies for internal and external OD consultants, *Practicing Organization Development: A guide for consultants*, ed W Rothwell, R Sullivan and G McLean, pp 535–49, Jossey-Bass, San Francisco, CA

Tamkin, P, Pearson, G, Hirsh, W and Constable, S (2010) *Exceeding expectation: The principles of outstanding leadership*, The Work Foundation, London

Tanser, G and Lee, P (2012) Using change to stretch talent, achieve real time leadership development and change culture, *OD Practitioner*, **44** (4), pp 42–46

Tichy, N M (1974) Agents of planned social change: congruence of values, cognitions, and actions, *Administrative Science Quarterly*, **19**, pp 164–82

Towers Watson (2008): *Closing the Engagement Gap: A roadmap for driving superior business performance*, Towers Watson, London

Treacy, M and Wiersama, F (1997) *The Discipline of Market Leaders*, Perseus, New York, NY

Trist, E (1960) *Socio-technical systems*, Tavistock Institute of Human Relations, London

Trist, E L and Bamforth, K W (1951) Some social and psychological consequences of the long wall method of coal-getting, *Human Relations*, **4**, pp 3–38

Tschudy, T (2006) An OD map: the essence of organization development, in *The NTL Handbook of Organization Development and Change: Principles, practices and perspectives*, ed B B Jones and M Brazzel, Pfeiffer: A Wiley Imprint, San Francisco, CA

Tubbs, S L and Schultz, E (2006) Exploring a taxonomy of global leadership competencies and meta-competencies, *Journal of American Academy of Business, Cambridge*, **8** (2), 29–34

Ulrich, D (1997) *Human Resource Champions: The next agenda for adding value and delivering results*, Harvard Business Publishing, Boston, MA

Ulrich, D and Brockbank, W (2005) *The HR Value Proposition*, McGraw-Hill, NY

Ulrich, D and Smallwood, N (2007) Leadership as a brand, *Leadership Excellence*, **24** (1), pp 3–4

Ulrich, D, Brockbank, W, Johnson, D, Sandholtz, K and Younger, J (2008) *HR Competencies: Mastery at the intersection of people and business*, Society for Human Resource Management, Alexandria, VA

Vaill, P B (1989) *Managing as a Performing Art*, Jossey-Bass, San Francisco, CA

Von Bertalanffy, L (1950) The theory of open systems in physics and biology, *Science*, **111**, pp 23–28

Von Bertalanffy, L (1956) General system theory, *General Systems: Yearbook of the Society for the Advancement of General Systems Theory*, **1**, pp 1–10

Walton, R E (1969) *Interpersonal Peacemaking: Confrontations and third party consultation*, Addison-Wesley, Reading, MA

Warrick, D D (2010) Valuable insight on OD from the contributors, in *Practicing Organization Development: A Guide for Leading Change*, 3rd edn, ed W J Rothwell *et al*, Pfeiffer, San Francisco, CA

Weisbord, M (1973) The Organization Development contract, *OD Practitioner*, **5** (2)

Weisbord, M (1977) How do you know it works if you don't know what it is?, *OD Practitioner*, **9** (3), pp 1–80

Weisbord, M R (1978) *Organizational Diagnosis: A workbook of theory and practice*, Basic Books, Reading, MA

Weisbord, M R (1987) *Productive Workplaces: Organizing and managing for dignity, meaning, and community*, p 402, Jossey-Bass, San Francisco, CA

Weisbord, M R (1993) *Discovering Common Ground*, Berrett-Koehler, San Francisco, CA

Weisbord, M R (2004) *Productive Workplaces Revisited: Dignity, meaning, and community in the 21st century*, Jossey-Bass, San Francisco, CA

Weisbord, M R (2006) The Organization Development contract, in *Organization Development*, ed J V Gallos, Jossey-Bass, San Francisco, CA

Wheatley, M J (1992) *Leadership and the New Science: Learning about organization from an orderly universe*, Berrett-Koehler, San Francisco, CA

Wheatley, M J and Kellner-Rogers, M (1998) *A Simpler Way*, Berrett-Koehler, San Francisco, CA

Wheatley, M J and Kellner-Rogers, M (1998) Bringing life to organizational change, *Journal for Strategic Performance Measurement*, April/May

Wheatley, M J, Griffin, P and Quade, K (2003) *Organization Development at Work*, Pfeiffer, San Francisco, CA

Whetton, D A and Cameron, K S (1991) *Developing Management Skills*, 2nd edn, HarperCollins, New York, NY

Whittington, R and Mayer, M (2005) *Organising for Success in the Twenty-first Century*, CIPD, London

Whyte, D (1994) *The Heart Aroused: Poetry and the preservation of the soul in corporate America*, Doubleday, NY

Worley, C G and Lawler, E E (2009) Building a change capability at Capital One Financial, *Organizational Dynamics*, 38 (4), pp 245–51

Worley, C G and Lawler, E E (2010) Built to change organizations and responsible progress: twin pillars of sustainable success, in *Research in Organizational Change and Development*, eds R Woodman *et al*, Volume **18**, Emerald Group Publishing Ltd, Bingley, UK

Zheltoukhova, K (2014) *Getting Smart About Agile Working*, CIPD, London

INDEX